RICHARD STRAUSS

RAYMOND HOLDEN

RICHARD STRAUSS
A MUSICAL LIFE

YALE UNIVERSITY PRESS
NEW HAVEN AND LONDON

For information about this and other Yale University Press publications please contact:
U.S. Office: sales.press@yale.edu   yalebooks.com
Europe Office: sales@yaleup.co.uk   www.yalebooks.co.uk

Set in Minion Pro by IDSUK (DataConnection) Ltd
Printed in Great Britain by TJ International Ltd, Padstow, Cornwall

Library of Congress Cataloging-in-Publication Data

Holden, Raymond.
   Richard Strauss : a musical life / Raymond Holden.
      p. cm.
   Includes bibliographical references and index.
   ISBN 978-0-300-12642-6
   1.   Strauss, Richard, 1864-1949. 2.   Conductors (Music)—Germany—Biography.
   3.   Composers—Germany—Biography.   I. Title.
   ML410.S93H65 2011
   780.92—dc22
   [B]

                                                                                    2010052151

ISBN 978-0-300-12642-6

A catalogue record for this book is available from the British Library.

10 9 8 7 6 5 4 3 2 1

For Mary
and in memory of Sir John Pritchard and Professor Cyril Ehrlich

Contents

Preface   *xi*

PART 1: EDUCATION AND YEARS OF APPRENTICESHIP

1 A Munich Childhood: 3
   Education and Early Impressions

2 A Rising Star: 15
   Meiningen (1885–1886) and First Munich Period (1886–1889)

3 *Enfant terrible*:   29
   Weimar (1889–1894) and *Don Juan*

PART 2: MATURITY AND CULTURAL LEADER

4 A Mozart Missionary: 45
   Second Munich Period (1894–1898) and Mozart Style

5 *Cause Célèbre*:   63
   Erster Königlicher Kapellmeister at Berlin (1898–1908) and *Salome*

6 At the Summit: 81
   Generalmusikdirektor at Berlin (1908–1919) and Beethoven Style

7 A Poisoned Chalice: 95
   Vienna Staatsoper (1919–1924) and the Performing
   Version of Mozart's *Idomeneo*

PART 3: A WORLD FIGURE

8 A German Abroad: Touring (1885–1914) 109

9 A Tarnished Icon? Touring and Recording (1914–1947) 135

Conclusion 161

APPENDICES

Appendix 1 Strauss's Performances as a Tenured Conductor 165
Appendix 2 Extracts from *Ueber die Neueinstudierung und
Neuinszenierung des Mozart'schen Don Giovanni (Don Juan)
auf dem kgl. Residenztheater zu München* by Ernst von Possart 213
Appendix 3 Structural Synopsis and Performance Analysis of
Strauss's Performing Version of Mozart's *Idomeneo* 221
Appendix 4 Strauss's Published Commercial and Non-commercial
Recordings (1905–1947) 229
Appendix 5 Score Examples 231

Notes 260
Bibliography 298
Index 308

Masonic Suite: Beginning

Preface

A great man who lived to a great age with a great appetite for work, Richard Strauss dominated the musical landscape for more than sixty years. Treading paths that had been pioneered by Richard Wagner and Hans von Bülow, Strauss juggled composition and performance for much of his life. Aware of the tradition that formed him, he inevitably looked to the past to inform the present to shape the future. For him, the compositional and interpretative processes were intertwined and were two sides of the same coin. Remembered today for a string of masterworks that have become core repertoire, he was also a major conductor who held positions of importance in Munich, Berlin and Vienna, and who performed regularly as a guest artist across the globe. Of course, he was keen to promote his own works, but he was equally keen to champion the compositions of Mozart, Beethoven and Wagner. A passionate advocate of new music, he had a conducting schedule often littered with novelties, many of which have since disappeared from the standard repertoire. Perhaps more important, he was a role model for many young conductors who not only willingly absorbed his practices and principles but passed them on to future generations of interpretative artists. His work on the podium inspired musicians and audiences around the world and it is no exaggeration to say that the composer of *Ein Heldenleben* truly led a hero's life.

Unlike previous histories of Richard Strauss, this book examines in detail his activities as a performing artist. As a jobbing conductor for the greater part of his life, Strauss enthusiastically filled his diary with engagement after engagement. If this book were simply a biographical overview of those performances, it would have been possible to chart his journey as a performer in a sequential and a chronological manner. But because he actively set out to create a distinctive performance aesthetic when tenured and because of the sheer number and importance of his guest engagements, it seemed better to divide the book according to those issues. Consequently, Parts 1 and 2 chronicle sequentially his activities from his earliest years to the end of his Vienna period, while Part 3 documents his activities as a guest conductor from near the beginning of his career to his last public engagement. In Chapters 3, 4 and 6, it was necessary to juxtapose narrative with analytical comment so that his performance aesthetic could be considered in detail, and in Chapter 8 it was necessary to revisit his early career so that his work as a guest conductor could be discussed as a unit. The appendices supplement much of the material found in the main body of the text and are a useful guide not only to Strauss's working practices in particular but also to the performance environment of the late nineteenth and early twentieth centuries in general.

Throughout the preparation of this book, I received enthusiastic support from the Strauss family, in particular from the composer's grandson, the late Richard Strauss, and his wife, Gabriele Strauss, who granted me unfettered access to the composer-conductor's marked scores, diaries, engagement books, letters and other performance artefacts, and from Christian Wolf and Dr. Jürgen May, who generously made available the resources of the Richard Strauss-Institut at Garmisch-Partenkirchen. My colleagues at the Royal Academy of Music have also been extremely supportive throughout the project and I would like to thank particularly its Principal, Professor Jonathan Freeman-Attwood, its Deputy Principals, Dr. Timothy Jones and Mark Racz, and its Registrar of Collections, Janet Snowman, for their help and kindness. I would also like to thank Dr. and Mrs. Kenneth Birkin, John Woollard, Daniel Snowman, Dr. David Patmore, Professor Christopher Walton, Daniel-Ben Pienaar, Jonathan Del Mar, Hannah Riddell, Maria Razumovskaya, Margaret Dziekonski, Michael Kennedy, the late Dr. Franz Trenner, the late Felix Aprahamian and Hofrat Dr. Günter Brosche for their generous help and counsel. I would like to thank particularly my friend and editor, Malcolm Gerratt of Yale University Press, and my friend and former teacher, Albert Landa, for their unswerving support, patience and advice during the preparation of this book. But my greatest debt of gratitude is to my wife, Mary, for her unfailing optimism and encouragement. She sustained me throughout this project, and without her support this book would not have been written.

Along with the above, I would like to thank Dr. Peter Hagmann (*Neue Zürcher Zeitung*), Christoph Ballmer (Head of the Music Department, Öffentliche Bibliothek der Universität Basel), Carol Jacobs (Archivist, Cleveland Orchestra), Michael Fritthum (Vienna Staatsoper), Dr. Barbara Lesak (Österreichisches Theatermuseum, Vienna), Alison Hinderliter (Archivist, Rosenthal Archives of the Chicago Symphony Orchestra), Frank Villella (Archivist, Chicago Symphony Orchestra), Prof. Dr. Hans-Joachim Hinrichsen (Universitäts Zürich), Herta Müller (Kulturstiftung Meiningen), Ute Nawroth (Staatsbibliothek zu Berlin), Dr. Clemens Hellsberg (Wiener Philharmoniker), Libby Rice (Archivist, London Symphony Orchestra), Sigrit Fleiss (Herbert von Karajan Centrum, Vienna), Bernd Gellermann (Archivist, Berliner Philharmoniker), Andrew Kemp (Head of Copyright, Boosey & Hawkes, London), Karin Scheider (Librarian, Deutschen Nationaltheater, Weimar), W. Chr. Pieterse (Archivist,

Gemeentearchief Amsterdam), Dr. Otto Biba (Archivdirektor, Gesellschaft der Musikfreunde in Wien), Anthony Pollard (*Gramophone*), Iolanda Blaya (Music Department, Gran Teatre del Liceu, Barcelona), Hans Ferwerda (Archivist, Koninklijk Concertgebouw Orkest, Amsterdam), Frau Buchholz (Archivist, Landeshauptstadt Magdeburg), Nóra Wellmann (Archivist, Magyar Állami Operahaz, Budapest), Barbara Haws (Archivist, New York Philharmonic Orchestra), Gerhard Antoniacomi (Archivist, Österreichischer Rundfunk), Brigitte Euler (Archivist, Sächsisches Staatsoper, Dresden), JoAnne E. Barry (Archivist, The Philadelphia Orchestra), J. Rigbie Turner (Archivist, The Pierpont Morgan Library, New York), Laurette Mumper (Manager, Public Relations Communications, The Pittsburgh Symphony Orchestra), Dr. Richard Bletschacher (Chefdramaturg, Wiener Staatsoper) and the archivists and librarians of Bühne der Stadt Magdeburg, the Central Westminster Music Library (London), the Cincinnati Symphony Orchestra, the Conservatoire national supérieur de musique et de danse de Paris, Das Meininger Theater, Der Bayerisches Staatsoper, the Deutsche Oper am Rhein (Düsseldorf), the Deutsche Staatsoper (Berlin), the EMI Archive, the Gürzenich Orchestra (Cologne), the Hamburg Oper, the Hamburg Staats- und Universitätsbibliothek, the Institut für Stadtgeschichte (Frankfurt am Main), the Johann Wolfgang Goethe Universität (Frankfurt am Main), the Mikrofilm Archiv, Der Deutsches Sprachung Presser (Düsseldorf), the Nationaltheater Mannheim, Oper der Stadt Köln, the Österre icher National Bibliothek, the Österreichisches Theater Museum, the Richard Strauss Gesellschaft (Munich), the Royal Albert Hall (London), the Sächsisches Landesbibliothek (Dresden), the Salzburger Festspiele, Sotheby's Auctioneers (London), the Staatsarchiv Hamburg, the Stadt- und Universitätsbibliothek (Frankfurt am Main), the Stadtarchiv Zürich, the Stiftung Weimarer Klassik, The British Library (London), the Theatermuseum der Universität zu Köln, the Tonhalle Orchester (Zurich), the Zentralbibliothek (Zurich) and the Zürich Oper.

Thanks are due to the Richard Strauss-Institut for providing photographs of the composer.

PART 1

EDUCATION AND YEARS OF APPRENTICESHIP

'ssst, winds for too loud', 'O wonderful little castle'

CHAPTER 1

A Munich Childhood

EDUCATION AND EARLY IMPRESSIONS

Munich was a hotbed of artistic intrigue in the mid 1860s. Alive with gossip about King Ludwig II and his protégé, the composer, conductor, writer and political activist, Richard Wagner, the sleepy Bavarian capital suddenly found itself at the centre of a cultural maelstrom that swept aside all who dared enter its path. Wanted by the north German authorities for his part in the uprisings of 1848 and 1849 in Dresden, the Leipzig-born composer took refuge in Zurich before moving to Venice, Lucerne, Mainz and, finally, Munich at the behest of the eighteen year old Ludwig in early 1864. As the idol of the newly-crowned king, Wagner quickly had his debts discharged by the young monarch and was awarded an annual stipend of 4000 Gulden by his royal fan. Wagner's love of luxury, his infamy as a spendthrift, his reputation as a womanizer and his already intimate relationship with Liszt's illegitimate daughter, Cosima von Bülow, the wife of his disciple, Hans von Bülow,[1] meant that Munich's often parochial residents were eager to be shocked by his every move. It is understandable, then, that many of its 150,000 inhabitants were unaware of the birth of Richard Strauss, later its most famous son, to one of the city's best-known families.

FAMILY

The third of four children of the Munich Hofkapelle's principal horn player,[2] Franz Strauss, and one of only two to survive from his two marriages,[3] Richard Georg Strauss was born in Altheimer Eck above the Pschorr Beer Hall on 11 June 1864.[4] For Franz, the birth of his third child was one of the great moments of his life. Brimming with pride, he wrote to his father-in-law the day after the delivery that 'My heart swells with a father's joy as I do myself the honour of informing you, my dear father-in-law, that yesterday (Saturday) at 6 o'clock in the morning, my dear good little wife bestowed on me the happiness of a boy, healthy, pretty and as round as a ball, and at the same time it gives me the greatest pleasure to tell you that mother and son are both very well.'[5] The birth seems to have been far from easy, however, as the new mother 'suffered all through the night, until 6 in the morning when she was freed from her travail and bore me a darling boy'.[6]

Strauss's mother, Josepha, was born in Munich on 10 April 1838 and died there on 15 April 1910. As the daughter of the Munich brewer Georg Pschorr, she was the product of a comfortable middle-class environment but was unstable emotionally and was often susceptible to periods of deep anxiety that troubled her for much of her life. Her condition might well have been exacerbated by her husband's rather unpredictable behaviour. In maturity, Strauss recalled that his father was extremely volatile, bad-tempered and tyrannical. This meant that his fragile mother often had to placate her quick-tempered husband and was cautious of him. To the end of his long life, Strauss remained troubled by his father's unpredictable behaviour towards his mother, who appears to have been long-suffering yet loving. It is obvious, however, that her often uneasy relationship with her husband contributed to her deep-rooted and long-lasting anxiety. Her defence mechanism seems to have been to spend time embroidering at her brother's villa where Richard and his cousins would meet after school on summer evenings to play skittles.[7]

Franz Strauss appears, therefore, to have been a severe taskmaster who was difficult both personally and professionally. Known for his loathing of new music in general, and the aesthetic of Richard Wagner in particular, he became a key rabble-rouser in the anti-Wagner clique that began to emerge in Munich by the 1860s. Born in Parkstein in north-east Bavaria on 26 February 1822,[8] Franz was abandoned by his father at the age of five and was raised by his three maternal uncles, Franz Michael Walter, Franz Joseph Michael Walter and Johann Georg Walter.[9] All were musicians and all made a profound impression on the young Franz. The eldest of the brothers seems to have played a particularly important role in the boy's upbringing and it was during his years as tower master at Nabburg that he introduced his nephew to music. Having dabbled with the horn, the dulcimer, the trumpet, the guitar and the violin, Franz quickly gravitated towards the French horn, the instrument that remained for him his lifelong passion. When his uncles Joseph and Johann Georg moved to Munich to join the private orchestra of Duke Max, Franz travelled with them and later joined the city's Hofkapelle in 1847.[10] His assured technique and his refined musicianship secured his place in that orchestra and it was there that he remained for the next forty-two years.

After being promoted to principal horn of the Hofkapelle, Franz acquired a formidable reputation as performer, teacher and composer, prompting the redoubtable Hans von Bülow to dub him the 'Joachim of the Waldhorn'. Conservative by nature, Franz objected greatly to Wagner's presence in Munich, both artistically and morally, and only reluctantly played in the first performances of *Das Rheingold*, *Die Walküre*, *Tristan und Isolde* and *Die Meistersinger von Nürnberg*.[11] For him, those works were monstrous creations to be shunned at all costs. In contrast, the compositions of Mozart, Haydn, Beethoven, Schubert, Spohr and Mendelssohn were to be revered above all others and were to be considered the bases for any well-rounded music education. His admiration for these composers was selective, however, and his fixed ideas meant his choice of work was often enigmatic. According to his son, the late works of Beethoven from the last movement of Symphony No. 7 onwards had little appeal for him because they 'were no longer "pure music" [as] . . . one could almost scent in them that Mephistophelean [figure] Richard Wagner'.[12] Of Schumann's piano works, again only the early compositions appealed to him. Those after the 1830s were of less interest because they reminded him of the worst elements of Mendelssohn's compositional style with 'their rhythmic monotonies and repetition of phrases' . . . which he labelled 'Leipzig music'.[13] Despite his profound reservations about much of Wagner's music, he approved of *Tannhäuser* but was less enthusiastic about *Lohengrin*, which he found too saccharine for his taste.

At odds with the late works of Wagner, Franz Strauss was, nevertheless, the consummate professional and when the operas were scheduled for performance at the Hofoper, 'no one gave as spirited a rendering of the horn solo in *Tristan* and *Die Meistersinger* as he'.[14] Even his arch-nemesis Wagner famously commented that 'Strauss is an unbearable fellow, but when he plays his horn, one cannot be cross with him'.[15] Hostility between composer and horn player was the never far away, however, and at Bayreuth in 1882, the two men fell out over lunch arrangements for the orchestra. When the Munich Hofkapelle had been dispatched by Ludwig II to play in the pit for the first performance of *Parsifal* at that year's Festival, Franz Strauss acted as the orchestra's spokesperson. In that capacity, he had arranged for its members to be fed at a communal lunch to be held at the local Bürgerverein for the reduced price of one Mark each, while Wagner had organized a similar meal for the players at the Festival Theatre's restaurant. Ever keen to scupper the Master's plans, Strauss announced that Wagner's arrangement did 'not suit the members of our orchestra [as they would] prefer to go home after the rehearsal and to eat in the town'. To which the composer replied 'Then eat your sour gherkins where you please'.[16]

As Franz's artistic and moral conservatism was a defining feature of the Strauss household, his son later claimed that he heard nothing but established masterpieces until he was sixteen.[17] This antithetical fixation with all things new soon spilled over into Richard's music education, which quite quickly became something of an obsession for his father. It is hard not to make parallels between their relationship and that of Leopold and Wolfgang Amadeus Mozart – a composer with whom Strauss would later become strongly associated – a century earlier. The American conductor and musicologist Leon Botstein argues convincingly that 'ironically, Strauss's relationship to his father, a distinguished professional musician, has an important parallel in W. A. Mozart's relationship to Leopold Mozart. In both cases the aesthetic judgment of the father was a crucial force in terms of imitation and accommodation. It also served as a psychological impetus for subsequent innovation and rebellion'.[18]

EDUCATION

Strauss began his musical studies in 1868 at the age of four with piano lessons from the harpist of the Munich Hofkapelle, August Tombo.[19] His progress was quick and he was soon able to impress visitors to the family home with his fledgling pianism. For him, music was fun and he rejoiced in his relationship with his teacher. According to his sister, Johanna, 'Richard made swift progress in playing the piano . . . [and] sight-reading presented him with no problems. His teacher played to him a great deal . . . and there was one trick that delighted Richard. His teacher played the bass part with his left hand, the top line with his right hand, and the middle part with the tip of his long nose'.[20] Violin lessons soon followed in 1872 with his father's first cousin, the leader of the Munich Hofkapelle, Benno Walter,[21] and by 1882 his progress was such that he was able to join his father's amateur orchestra, the Wilde Gung'l.[22] He never enjoyed playing the violin, however, and only practised the instrument intermittently. Even though his playing never exceeded a relatively basic level, he did learn the rudiments of string playing and was able to put that knowledge to good use in later life, as both composer and conductor.

As a pianist, Strauss's technique was also problematic, and although he later became a respected interpreter of his own songs, his left hand was never dexterous enough to handle some of the more demanding virtuoso piano literature. An attempt to improve his facility was made when Franz sent him to the distinguished pedagogue Friedrich Niest,[23] the teacher of the respected German pianist and composer Sophie Menter,[24] in October 1878.[25] Strauss's change of teacher made little impact on his playing, and in later life he recalled that he was a bad pupil who loathed practising but did enjoy sight-reading. He was soon able to play orchestral scores at the piano and was fond of showing off with his piano reductions of *Tristan und Isolde* and Liszt's *Eine Faust-Sinfonie*. He felt that this was the reason why he never developed a secure technique and why his left hand remained problematic throughout his career. His friend Ludwig Thuille[26] used to tease Strauss about his facility, claiming that he could always recognize his chum's playing by his unconventional approach to fingering.[27]

Keen to ensure that Richard should have as rounded a musical education as possible, the family took him to see Weber's *Der Freischütz* and Mozart's *Die Zauberflöte* in 1871. Although the works were relatively long for a boy of seven, they were presumably chosen by his parents for their visual appeal, their easy melodic content, their supernatural interest, their fairy-tale-like qualities and their familiarity through domestic music-making. According to Johanna, his sister,

> Richard was about seven when our parents yielded to his passionate wish to go to the Court Theatre. Mother could not leave home with him early enough, for of course it was all immensely important for him and an experience of the very greatest significance.... The opera was Weber's *Freischütz*. The tuning of the orchestra caught his attention especially, because Father was there of course ... Richard had already often played the overture as a piano duet, and he knew the arias very well too. He was almost trembling with excitement as he waited for the great moment when the curtain rose.... *Die Zauberflöte* was the second opera Richard heard ... [and] [h]e had played it all on the piano beforehand, mostly as duets: the overture, the choruses, Sarastro's great aria and the great entrance of the Queen of the Night.[28]

While Johanna was only four years old when Richard made those visits, and while her account might be coloured by nostalgia, it seems likely that her description contains more than a modicum of truth. Moreover, as the music heard by artists when very young often has a special place in their mature performance aesthetics and as these works were later central to Strauss's repertoire, her recollections are credible.

Eager for his son to be grounded in the techniques of his musical idols, Franz arranged for Richard to have harmony, counterpoint and orchestration lessons with Friedrich Wilhelm Meyer.[29] Meyer was a very experienced musician who was greatly respected by many of his colleagues. Having joined the Munich Hofoper in 1854, he was promoted quickly to Hofmusikdirektor in 1858 and was later elevated to Hofkapellmeister in 1869. At the time of his tenure, his superior was Franz Lachner,[30] a particular *bête-noire* of Wagner. Considered wrongly by Wagner to be a conductor of only average ability, Lachner was in fact a fine musician of catholic taste who had links with both Ludwig van Beethoven and Franz Schubert, and who used their works as the basis for his personal aesthetic. The artistic environment created by Lachner and Meyer, with its emphasis on classical masterpieces, was clearly attractive to Franz and it was because of their interest in the great composers of the past that Richard was sent to Meyer between 1875 and 1880. The impact that Meyer had on the young Strauss was deep and that influence remained strong for the rest of his life. As a way of repaying his debt of gratitude to Meyer, Strauss later dedicated to him the Serenade in G major, the Overture in A minor and the Serenade in E flat major. When he learned of his teacher's death in 1893, he was affected greatly by it and in a letter to his parents from Florence on 10 June that year he wrote that 'Kapellmeister Meyer's death has troubled me deeply; he was a straightforward and noble man. I will always have true and thankful memories of him. He did more for my development than perhaps he knew.'[31]

Strauss's general education was no less rigorous than his music studies. For a boy who would later become a confirmed atheist, it was somewhat ironic that he entered the Domschule (Cathedral School) in the autumn of 1870. While he was clearly a bright little boy, enjoyed school and was a quick learner, the family were careful not to leave any aspect of his education to chance. It was therefore decided to send him to the Widmann'sche Lehranstalt[32] to cram for his entry examinations for the Ludwigs-Gymnasium in the autumn of 1873. His time at the Lehranstalt seems to have paid scholastic dividends, because he was fast-tracked in the autumn of 1874 into Form 2A of the Latin School, the Gymnasium's junior department. There, he quickly made a good impression, prompting his form-teacher, Carl Welzhofer, to write at the end of Richard's first year:

> There can be few pupils in whom a sense of duty, talent and liveliness are united to the degree that they are in this boy. His enthusiasm is very great, he enjoys learning and finds it easy. He attends closely in class; nothing escapes him. And yet he is incapable of sitting still for a moment, he finds a bench a very tiresome object. Unclouded merriment and high spirits sparkle in his eyes day after day; candour and good nature are written on his face. His work is good, very good. No teacher could help but take to a boy like this, indeed it is almost difficult to conceal one's preference. Strauss is a promising musical talent.[33]

First Compositions

Strauss's 'promising musical talent' was certainly in evidence by the time of this report. Having made his first tentative steps as a composer with his 'Schneider' Polka ('Tailor's' Polka) for Piano in 1870, Richard then completed no fewer than thirty-five works by 1875. Many of these are multi-movement compositions and most are dedicated to family members. These dedications reflect the love and respect that the young Strauss had for his relatives in general and for his 'Dear Aunt Johanna [Pschorr]' in particular. Johanna was a gifted amateur singer, for whom he wrote some twenty-seven songs and one sonatina for piano. These early experiments in song writing proved useful in laying the foundations for Strauss's life-long interest in the female voice and even though the standard of them as a group is uneven, they are a useful indicator of his approach as a fledgling composer as a whole. Of course, Franz's musical fingerprints were all over many of these early works. This was particularly true of the 'Panzenburg' Polka for Piano, which Franz orchestrated and performed at a rehearsal with the amateur Harbni Orchestra on 31 May 1872. The title of the work means stack of beer barrels ('Panzenburg') in Bavarian dialect and it was the name of the Pschorrs' country house on the Theresienhöhe. At the rehearsal, Franz was keen for the players to think that the Polka was entirely the work of his son and denied all participation in its composition, including its orchestration. As a proud father, he gave the complete credit to Richard, a gesture that might have been misguided ethically but understandable paternally.

Richard Strauss began to develop an interest in the orchestra and chamber music by the middle of the 1870s. Previously, he had focused sharply on songs and piano music, which he wrote largely for personal or family use. Between 1875, when he began lessons with Meyer, and his first professional appointment a decade later, he produced a string of works that demonstrated increasing confidence as a composer. Chamber music was attempted first and after several ill-fated experiments, he composed a number of works that are still viable today. Of these, probably the most well-known are his String Quartet, his Serenade for Thirteen Wind Instruments, his Sonata for Cello and Piano, his Suite in B flat major for Thirteen Winds, and his Piano Quartet in C minor, all of which were composed between 1880 and 1885 in Munich. The first of these to be given by an important ensemble was the String Quartet, which was performed by his cousin's group, the Benno Walter Quartet, on 14 March 1881. The works that established his reputation outside his home town, however, were his compositions for wind ensembles, which were taken up by leading groups, including the Hofkapellen of Dresden and Meiningen, centres that would later be inextricably linked to Strauss, both as a performer and as a composer.[34]

When the Serenade was first performed at Dresden on 27 November 1882, the conductor was Franz Wüllner,[35] a musician who championed Strauss's works widely and who later invited him to give the first performance of his *Wandrers Sturmlied* for six-part choir and large orchestra with the Gürzenich Concerts at Cologne on 8 March 1887. Strauss's professional relationship with Wüllner flourished throughout the 1880s and the 1890s, and it comes as no surprise that the conductor's name crops up several times in the young composer's correspondence with his parents. Impressed by Wüllner's well-rounded musicianship, Strauss reported to his parents on 12 December 1883 that he had spent a day with him, heard an impressive eight-part *Stabat Mater* by Wüllner at Dresden six days later, and attended the rehearsals for the first European performance of his own Symphony No. 2 under Wüllner at Cologne on 12 January 1885.[36] This was the last major Strauss première that Wüllner conducted in the presence of the composer, because as Strauss's reputation grew, he was unable to be present at the first performances of some of his later compositions. Consequently, he could not attend the world premières of *Till Eulenspiegel* (5 November 1895) and *Don Quixote* (8 March 1898)[37] with

Wüllner and the Gürzenich Orchestra, but was pleased to learn by telegram from the conductor that the latter had been a 'fabulous performance and a great success'.[38]

The phenomenally successful tone poems that catapulted Strauss into the public consciousness during the late nineteenth century were the direct beneficiaries of his early attempts at writing for the orchestra. Blessed with a forensic mind that processed musical information discerningly and effectively, he was later able to explore existing structures and genres, and to manipulate them to suit his own compositional needs. This process was completely dependent on what he learned as a teenager and was a synthesis of the musical milieu that he experienced at first hand in Munich. The artistic life of his hometown was not simply a means to a compositional end; it was also a means by which to disseminate some of his early works. This was certainly true for his Symphony No. 1 in D minor, which was his first major orchestral work to be given in Munich. Composed between March and June 1880, it was performed at the Odeon[39] by the Hofkapelle under the city's leading conductor, Herman Levi,[40] on 30 March 1881. Clearly the work of an apprentice composer, it lacks any of the hallmarks of Strauss's mature style. The *Münchner Neueste Nachrichten* seems to have hit the nail on the head when it reported that the composer had potential but that the work showed little originality.[41] Strauss was a quick learner, however, and by the time of his Violin Concerto in D minor and the Horn Concerto No. 1 in E flat major, he had begun to develop a more distinctive style. Both works were given first with Strauss playing the orchestral part on the piano: the Violin Concerto with Benno Walter at the Bösendorfersaal in Vienna on 5 December 1882 and the Horn Concerto with Bruno Hoyer at the Munich Tonkünstlerverein in March 1883.[42] Apart from being important premières for Strauss as a composer, they were the first significant occasions at which he appeared in public as a performer. Previously, his playing was confined to domestic music-making or to school concerts, where he performed regularly as a chamber musician.[43]

Early Influences

Throughout this early period, Franz Strauss's influence can be detected strongly in Richard's responses to the music that he encountered. Of particular importance was his early introduction to the music of Mozart. Having heard *Die Zauberflöte* at his second visit to the Hofoper, Strauss became increasingly interested in the composer's works. While in later life it was his activities as a Mozart interpreter that caught the attention of listeners and musicians around the world, it was the 'knowledge and understanding of Mozart [that] came from the practices of his family and in particular his father'[44] that laid the foundation for his approach to the composer in general. From his correspondence with his boyhood friend, Ludwig Thuille,[45] the impact that Mozart made on the young Strauss is clearly apparent. His letter of 22 July 1879 is particularly rich in its praise of Mozart and it indicates clearly his already increasing forensic approach to performance:

> At the moment I'm very diligently playing the Mozart piano concertos from our Mozart edition,[46] and I can tell you it's wonderful, it's giving me enormous enjoyment. The abundance of the ideas, the harmonic richness, and yet the sense of proportion, the marvellous, lovely, tender, delightful ideas themselves, the delicate accompaniment. Yet one can't play anything like that any more! All you get now is drivel; either twittering or brash roaring and crashing or sheer musical nonsense. While Mozart, with few means, says everything a listener could desire to be refreshed and truly entertained and edified, the others use all the means at their disposal to say absolutely nothing, or hardly anything. The world is crazy! To blazes with it! But I've made a vow, when I appear at an important concert for the first time, where I shall be well and sensitively accompanied, I will play a Mozart concerto.[47]

As Mozart was the musical god whom the young Strauss worshipped above all others, it was only natural that some of the other giants from the past were viewed less favourably by him. Even Beethoven was of less importance, and although *Leonore* No. 3 Overture was 'wonderfully beautiful', it was '*never greater than the Jupiter Symphony*',[48] an opinion that he would probably have defended well into maturity. That said, Beethoven's music was high on his list of great works to be admired, and when Thuille rather foolishly compared an adagio by Schumann to one by Beethoven, Richard sneered 'A Schumann *Adagio* comparable to a Beethoven *Adagio*! ha! ha! ha! ha! ha! ha! That is terrible! What are you thinking! That is the limit! That makes one want to run and hide. Schumann may have beautiful things; but comparable to Beethoven! ha! ha! ha! ha! ha! ha!'.[49]

Unsurprisingly, the composer who raised Strauss's hackles most during his youth was Richard Wagner. Having begun to attend performances at the Hofoper and by the Hofkapelle regularly from 1878, Richard used those visits to extend his knowledge of the operatic and concert literatures and to sharpen his critical skills. After a performance of the 'imposing' *Der Freischütz* on 31 March that year,[50] he saw Wagner's *Siegfried*, Auber's *La Muette de Portici* and Boieldieu's *La Dame blanche* in May and June, and Wagner's *Die Walküre* and Marschner's *Hans Heiling* in October and November. Bowled over by the Auber and the Boieldieu, he reported to Thuille that the operas were dramatic, beautiful, orchestrated admirably, and full of memorable melodies and harmonies. *Siegfried*, on the other hand, was a completely different matter. Wholly unimpressed by the work, he was quick to criticise it as utterly boring and having few redeeming features. The opening struck him as 'so stupid' that he 'laughed right out loud' and the constant use of melodic sequences verged on the interminable. What melodies there were appeared to him to be completely incoherent and the incessant use of diminished and augmented triads and seventh chords meant that 'cats would have died and the dissonances were so horrible that even rocks would have turned to puddles'.[51]

These early impressions frequently came back to haunt Strauss in later life and he often felt embarrassed by his youthful judgements. Nevertheless, he was clearly an intellectually gifted boy who must have felt that he was on a wonderful journey of discovery during his teenage years. Experience after experience presented themselves, prompting him to communicate his impressions to all who would listen. It seems strange that he later doubted his academic ability and felt that he was less than a good student during his years at the Gymnasium. In 1945, he recalled that 'I cannot say that I was a particularly good pupil of the Ludwigsgymnasium in Munich, especially since, musically precocious, I was always fonder of composing than of studying, but nevertheless I managed to pass my matriculation examination without discredit at the age of eighteen: it was only mathematics that I failed, because I could not come to terms with algebra'.[52] As Richard was awarded his Absolutorialprüfung (matriculation certificate) in July 1882, his lack of algebraic skills was a flaw that did little to harm his academic progress, and at the awards ceremony held at the Gymnasium on 5 August he was able to impress teachers, fellow students and their parents by acting as pianist in a performance of the first and second movements from Mendelssohn's Piano Trio in D minor.

TEENAGE TRAVELS

With his final school year firmly behind him, Strauss travelled with his father to Bayreuth for the first time in August 1882, where he possibly attended an early performance of *Parsifal*. In November, Strauss then attended lectures in aesthetics, cultural history, Shakespeare, Schopenhauer and the history of philosophy at the Ludwig-Maximilians-Universtät, Munich. As he was an avid reader with an insatiable appetite for learning, it might be assumed that Strauss was in his element as a university student, but he found the whole experience dull. For him, learning was best done privately or in discussion with friends and relatives. That said, he realized that there was a world of opportunities to be explored outside of Munich, and from December 1883 he travelled in North Germany to experience the cultural life of Leipzig, Dresden and Berlin. Keen to maximize both the educational and professional benefits of the trip, he not only attended concerts and operas at Leipzig between 4 and 8 December 1883,[53] but also marketed his wares as a composer there by performing part of his Symphony in F minor on the piano for Heinrich and Elisabeth von Herzogenberg[54] and by playing the Concert Overture in C minor[55] for the composer-conductor Carl Reinecke.[56]

While his visit to Leipzig was relatively short, Strauss's stays in Dresden and Berlin were more substantial. In later years, Dresden became synonymous with Strauss the composer and it was there that the first performances of his operas *Feuersnot, Salome, Elektra, Der Rosenkavalier, Intermezzo, Die ägyptische Helena* (first version), *Arabella, Die schweigsame Frau* and *Daphne* were given between 1901 and 1938.[57] As a novice musician, however, the ten days that he spent in Dresden in December 1883[58] were important to him not only culturally but also professionally. There, he was able to see Ernst von Schuch[59] conduct for the first time, to take part in the first local performance of his Sonata for Cello and Piano with Ferdinand Böckmann,[60] a cellist from the Dresdner Hofkapelle, and to spend time with Franz Wüllner.

It was Strauss's three-month stay in Berlin, however, that proved most decisive. Between 21 December 1883 and 29 March 1884, he became a familiar face at the city's leading concert halls, theatres and salons, where he met musicians, impresarios and publishers who would later shape his future career and his mature performance style. Amongst the musical glitterati whom he either heard or met in the German capital were the violinist Joseph Joachim, the composer Johannes Brahms, the pianists Karl Klindworth and Eugen d'Albert, the impresario Hermann Wolff, the publisher Hugo Bock and the conductors Robert Radecke and Hans von Bülow. As a chamber musician, he played his Cello Sonata with the distinguished cellist and member of the Joachim Quartet, Robert Hausmann, and his Horn Concerto with the Principal Horn of the Meininger Hofkapelle, Gustav Leinhos.[61] And, as an orchestral composer, he heard Franz Mannstädt and the Meininger Hofkapelle give the Berlin première of his Serenade Op. 7 on 27 February, and Robert Radecke and the Berlin Hofkapelle give the local première of his Concert Overture in C minor on 21 March.[62] Overjoyed by the performances, he reported proudly to his parents the day after the second concert that the overture was played well and was an outstanding success.[63] With the applause still ringing in his ears, Strauss then set off for home on 29 March, stopping only briefly in Dresden to hear Wüllner perform Beethoven's Symphony No. 9 ('Choral'). Within months of his arrival in Munich, Strauss's life would change forever when he was transformed from a somewhat gangly, talented young composer into an increasingly fêted composer-conductor with one of Europe's most prestigious orchestras.

Ride of the witches. fffffffo

CHAPTER 2

A Rising Star
MEININGEN (1885–1886) AND FIRST MUNICH PERIOD (1886–1889)

'THE MASTER-CONDUCTOR HANS VON BÜLOW'[1]

With the arrival of Wagner and Bülow in Munich in the mid 1860s, the Bavarian capital quickly polarized into pro- and anti-Wagner cliques. Gossip about the composer's extra-marital relationship with his protégé's wife, Cosima,[2] swept through the city like wildfire and it was not long before Bülow was humiliated by the Munich press. Engaged initially in November 1864 by Ludwig II to assist Wagner as a copyist and as a personal pianist, Bülow had to endure duties that were often less than inspiring and that were hardly fitting for a musician who was later to become one of the nineteenth century's most respected interpretative artists. Tedium turned to excitement, however, when he was entrusted with the première of *Tristan und Isolde* on 10 June 1865,[3] the opera that changed the harmonic landscape of Western music. For Bülow, the opera was 'as beautiful as the most beautiful of dreams . . . [and] simply indescribable . . . [because of the] dreadful fascination it exerts[;] . . . an experience beyond time and place'.[4] For Franz Strauss, however, it was yet another glimpse into the artistic abyss into which Wagner had plunged music with his aesthetic reforms from *Lohengrin* onwards. It was hardly surprising, then, that when he chanced to meet Wagner shortly after its first rehearsal in the Residenztheater,[5] he dismissed the composer's comment that it 'sounded wonderful!' with 'I don't agree. In that small theatre with its rotten acoustics it sounded as if it were an old saucepan'.[6]

With the press snapping at his heels over the Wagner–Cosima affair, Bülow attempted to defuse the situation by taking his wife to Pest after the last performance of *Tristan und Isolde*[7] to attend the world première of Liszt's *Die Legende von der heiligen Elisabeth*.[8] Hoping that the public's interest in his personal life had ebbed, Bülow then returned to the Munich Hofoper as Hofkapellmeister in May 1867, where he conducted the world première of *Die Meistersinger von Nürnberg* in 1868. The affair between Cosima and Wagner continued to be a source of public humiliation, however, and by the summer of 1869 Bülow decided to separate permanently from his wife. He was devastated by the break-up and in a letter to his friend Karl Klindworth at the end of July 1869, he wrote that his 'health [was] ruined, physically and morally'[9] and that he could 'hardly pull [himself] together to carry on with [his] official duties until the holidays'.[10] His note to the piano manufacturer Carl Bechstein[11] two days later was no less depressing and in desperation he asked Bechstein to recommend a *'thoroughly enlightened* attorney' because he intended to dissolve his marriage. Keen to be free of the situation, he also mentioned to Bechstein that he had submitted his resignation for a second time and that he had been assured that 'care has been taken not to have it refused in high quarters this time'.[12] By the end of the summer, Ludwig had released him from his contract, but Bülow neither forgot nor forgave the way he was treated by the Munich public during his tenure there, and in later life the city and its inhabitants remained his *bête-noire*.

After a period as Hofkapellmeister at Hanover from 1877, Bülow took charge of the Meininger Hofkapelle from 1880. He had met the orchestra's patron, Herzog Georg II von Sachsen-Meiningen,[13] the husband of the actress Ellen Franz,[14] a former piano pupil, some seven years earlier in 1873. Georg was passionately interested in theatre and music and was keen to reform fully the performing institutions at his ducal seat, the Duchy of Meiningen. First, he overhauled the Hoftheater by mounting productions that strove for the highest possible standards of ensemble acting, that were accurate historically, that ceded artistic control to the director, and that used sets and costumes representative of the period being portrayed. His reforms quickly paid dividends and, by 1874, the standard of the company had risen so substantially that he decided to allow it to tour for the first time. The troupe was soon celebrated internationally and by 1890 it had performed 2,591 guest performances from London in the west to Moscow in the east.[15]

Next to be overhauled was the Hofkapelle. For Georg, Bülow was central to that process and was the obvious choice if the orchestra was to be transformed into a major European artistic force. But Bülow was a hard man to pin down and after initially declining Georg's offer, he was only wooed to Meiningen in March 1880 by the lure of complete artistic sovereignty. While the Duke could only offer a salary of 5,000 Marks, 1,000 Marks less than Bülow had received in Hanover,[16] the conductor would have a free hand concerning all things musical and the rank of Intendant. Bülow was also attracted by the chance to explore and to disseminate his chosen repertoire systematically and didactically, the opportunity to prepare model performances of works by Beethoven, contemporary composers and others over extended periods, and the option of performing chamber music in a series that was linked programmatically to his work with the Hofkapelle. To implement these changes, he increased the orchestra's strength from thirty-six to forty-nine players, engaged members of the orchestra as soloists and as chamber musicians at the subscription concerts, introduced the Ritter viola, the pedal tympani and the five string double bass into the orchestra, insisted that the Hofkapelle stand while performing, and trained the strings to play his arrangement of the *Grosse Fuge* from Beethoven's String Quartet Op. 133 from memory.[17]

Like the theatre troupe, the Hofkapelle toured regularly and quickly became the byword for technical and interpretative excellence. Of the many the tours that it undertook with Bülow, it was the fifteen-city tour of Germany and the Austro-Hungarian Empire between 31 October and 5 December 1884 that had a particular relevance to Strauss.[18] The repertoire performed on that thirty-three concert trip included not only works by Beethoven, Berlioz, Brahms, Chopin, Dvořák, Raff, Rheinberger, Schubert, Spohr, Wagner and Weber,[19] but also Strauss's Serenade for Winds Op. 7, a work that first appeared in the Hofkapelle's repertoire the preceding season. Its inclusion seems to have caught the young composer by surprise, however, because on 3 December 1883 he wrote to Bülow that 'To my greatest joy I received news the day before yesterday from Herr Spitzweg[20] of Your Honour's kind intention to give a performance of my Wind Serenade opus 7 at one of your concerts. I am supremely happy at the great honour thereby accorded to my small beginner's effort. – To you, revered Master, my most heartfelt and deepest thanks for this. – No matter how hard I have hitherto tried, I never as yet had the fortune when Your Honour was in Munich to be presented to you personally, and so the good news about the performance of my Serenade came as all the more of a surprise.'[21]

On 26 February 1884, Strauss finally met Bülow personally and later that year he commissioned the young composer to write the Suite for Thirteen Wind Instruments Op. 4 for the Meininger Hofkapelle. The overall form of the work – Präludium (Allegretto), Romance (Andante), Gavotte (Allegro) and Introduktion und Fuge (Andante cantabile – Allegro con brio) – appears not to be what Bülow originally had in mind, however, because Strauss was 'unable to follow [his] kind suggestion' as he 'only got [the conductor's] letter from Herr E. Spitzweg after [he] had already planned the first movement (Prelude) and the Second (Gavotte) . . .'[22] Nevertheless, Bülow liked the work and invited the young composer to perform it without rehearsal at the Meininger Hofkapelle's matinée concert at Munich's Odeon on 18 November 1884. As Strauss had never conducted an orchestra before, the invitation hit him like a bolt of lightning and he later recalled that he conducted his work as if in a 'slight coma.'[23] Bülow had remained in the artists' room throughout the performance, smoking incessantly, and when Strauss's father came in to thank him for allowing his son the opportunity of performing the work, the conductor pounced on him screaming 'You have nothing to thank me for . . . I have not forgotten what you have done to me in this damned city of Munich. What I did to-day I did because your son has talent and not for you.' Even though Strauss's moment of glory was spoiled, Bülow more than compensated him for his vitriolic outburst by arranging Strauss's appointment as Hofmusikdirektor at the Grand Duchy of Meiningen from October 1885.

Before taking up his post at Meiningen, Strauss used the period to consolidate some existing projects and to explore some new avenues. As composer, his star was in the ascendant during the first part of 1885, and along with the world première of his Symphony in F minor by the New York Philharmonic and Theodore Thomas[24] in the United States of America on 13 December 1884, his Horn Concerto was performed for the first time with orchestra by Leinhos and Bülow at Meiningen on 4 March 1885. Chamber music and song continued to occupy him during these months and he added to his output in those genres by completing his Piano Quartet in C minor on 1 January 1885 and the songs 'Die Nacht', 'Zueignung', 'Nichts', 'Die Georgine' and 'Geduld' that summer.[25] Between the composition of the Piano Quartet and the songs, Strauss continued to broaden his musical horizons by attending Bülow's piano masterclasses at the Raff Conservatorium at Frankfurt in June. The music performed, heard and discussed at the classes was drawn directly from the emerging canon of Central European masterworks and included compositions by Bach, Handel, Mozart, Beethoven, Mendelssohn, Raff and Brahms. Strauss attended at the suggestion of Bülow, who told his future assistant that if he wanted to understand his approach to conducting, then that could be achieved best by observing his method of teaching.[26]

The job vacancy that Strauss filled at Meiningen was the direct result of Franz Mannstädt's engagement as a conductor of the Berlin Philharmonic from the beginning of the 1885–1886 season.[27] As Bülow's newly appointed assistant at the Duchy, Strauss was the envy of his contemporaries, of whom two, Felix von Weingartner and Gustav Mahler, had openly coveted the position. Weingartner was deeply jealous of Strauss and in later life bitterly resented his success as a composer. Mahler, on the other hand, was on better terms with him but famously wrote to Bülow in January 1884 that

When I asked you for an interview, I did not yet know what a flame your incomparable art would kindle in my soul. . . . I am a musician who is wandering without a guiding light. . . . At the concert yesterday, when I beheld the fulfilment of my utmost intimations and hopes of beauty, it became clear to me that I had found my spiritual home and my master, and that my wanderings would come to an end now or never. . . . [I] beg you to take me along in any capacity you like – let me become your *pupil*, even if I had to pay my tuition fees with my blood. . . . I give myself to you heart and soul, and if you will accept the gift, I cannot think of anything that could make me happier. . . . I am ready for anything you have in mind.[28]

Mahler's letter did little to impress Bülow, who must have considered it the ravings of an obsessed sycophant. At any event, Bülow did not respond and passed the letter on to Mahler's seniors at the opera house in Kassel. Years later, Bülow met Mahler frequently, and although he neither liked nor understood the younger musician's compositions, he did admire him as a conductor. After they became acquainted in Hamburg, Mahler regularly attended many of Bülow's Hamburg Subscription Concerts, where there was a seat kept for him directly behind the podium. When Bülow entered the auditorium, he would hurry down the steps of the platform and offer Mahler his baton. After ceremoniously inviting him to mount the podium in his stead, which Mahler would invariably decline, Bülow would take his place on the rostrum and begin the concert.[29] While Bülow's overt gestures of respect for Mahler might have been excessive, they were meant sincerely. Mahler was deeply touched by Bülow's interest and he retained for many years a presentation wreath that was inscribed 'To the Pygmalion of the Hamburg Opera – Hans von Bülow'.

HOFMUSIKDIREKTOR AT MEININGEN (1885–1886)

When Strauss was appointed Hofmusikdirektor at Meiningen from 1 October 1885, he became the beneficiary of Bülow's sweeping artistic reforms. As Bülow's assistant, he was required to teach the piano to the Duke's daughter, Princess Marie,[30] to perform as a chamber musician,[31] to take orchestral rehearsals and to direct the local choral society. More important, Strauss was able to observe Bülow's conducting style at close quarters and to absorb his painstaking method in rehearsal, his eye for detail and his graceful baton technique. Within days of taking up his appointment, Strauss heard Bülow prepare Beethoven's Symphonies Nos. 1, 5, 6 and 7, the Overture to *Egmont* and Piano Concertos Nos. 4 and 5, and to conduct a programme that included works by Beethoven, Chopin, Hiller, Liszt and Schubert.[32] The concert proved a revelation to the fledgling conductor, who later recalled that Bülow's interpretations were compelling in their intensity, were without any trace of arbitrariness, and were the direct result of the work's form and poetic content. As Strauss's teacher, Bülow insisted that his protégé should learn to read Beethoven's scores accurately and to use that accuracy as the basis for his interpretation. The influence that Bülow exerted over the young Strauss was profound and he never forgot nor betrayed what he learned from his mentor during his short stay at Meiningen. The reverence Strauss had for Bülow was life-long and in maturity he always maintained that his mentor's influence was the 'most decisive factor' in his career.[33]

Another 'decisive factor' in Strauss's career was Alexander Ritter,[34] the Estonian-born German composer and violinist, who was a member of the first

violin section of the Meininger Hofkapelle. As the son of Richard Wagner's
financial supporter, Julie Ritter, and as the husband of the Master's niece,
Franziska Wagner, Ritter developed a close artistic affinity with *Zukunftsmusik*
and became one its greatest missionaries. Until his Meiningen appointment, Strauss had been under the total artistic influence of his father,
who dismissed the new aesthetic trends absolutely. Consequently, he had
never encountered the writings of Wagner nor the philosophic milieu of
which they were a part. In Strauss, Ritter saw a near-virgin mind which could
be moulded in his own image and who might be receptive to the philosophy
of Schopenhauer. Of Ritter, Strauss later recalled that he had introduced him
to the publications of Wagner and Schopenhauer and had converted him to
new German music.[35]

Confident of Strauss's abilities, Bülow decided to introduce him to a
Meiningen audience on 18 October 1885 by having him play the solo part in
Mozart's Piano Concerto No. 24[36] and to conduct the local première of his
Symphony in F minor.[37] Strauss later recalled that 'although I had practised
busily all summer, the idea of playing the concerto with Bülow conducting
filled me – by no means a fully-trained pianist – with fear and trembling.
When we had negotiated the first movement quite creditably, the master
encouraged me with the words, "If you weren't something better, you might
become a pianist." Although I did not think that I fully deserved this compli-
ment, my self-confidence had been increased sufficiently to enable me to play
the last two movements a little less self-consciously.'[38]

Having performed the Mozart concerto, Strauss then immediately mounted
the rostrum to conduct his Symphony in F minor. In the audience was Johannes
Brahms, at Meiningen to conduct the première of his Symphony No. 4 with the
Hofkapelle.[39] Keen to hear Brahms's opinion, Strauss approached him after the
concert and was told that his symphony was 'quite nice'[40] but was 'too full of
thematic irrelevances.'[41] Brahms also felt that the profusion of such themes was
pointless when 'only contrasted rhythmically on one triad'. His advice opened
the young Strauss's eyes to a more refined aesthetic world in which 'counterpoint [was] only justified when poetic necessity compel[led] a temporary union
of two or several themes contrasted as sharply as possible, not only rhythmically but especially harmonically'. Brahms also advised Strauss to 'take a good
look at Schubert's dances . . . and [to] try [his] luck at the invention of simple
eight-bar melodies'. Strauss acted on Brahms's suggestion and was subsequently
unafraid of 'incorporating a popular melody in [his] work'.[42] Bülow, on the
other hand, seems to have been more impressed than Brahms by his protégé's
composition and wrote to Hermann Wolff that 'Str[auss's] Symphony is <u>very
important</u>, original, mature in form . . . and [he is] a <u>born</u> conductor. He ticks
every box excellently: elastic, an eagerness to learn, rhythmic and tactful. . . .
His playing, like his conducting début, is really astonishing.'[43]

When Bülow resigned unexpectedly from the Hofkapelle in November 1885, Strauss took sole charge of the orchestra and was responsible for its rehearsals and concerts. Even though he inherited an orchestra that had been drilled by one of the world's most practised artists, he was a novice conductor with little experience of either the standard or the emerging concert repertoires. In an attempt to expand his practical knowledge and to keep the musicians occupied, Strauss had the orchestra play 'the whole of their concert repertoire' to him at their daily morning rehearsals.[44] While his remark was something of an overstatement, he certainly had the enviable chance of exploring works that were new to him with an outstanding orchestra in the relative privacy of a closed rehearsal room.

Strauss's first opportunity to stamp his authority on the Meininger Hofkapelle came on 6 December 1885, when he directed his opening concert with the Hofkapelle as Bülow's successor.[45] For that performance, he conducted Gluck's Overture to *Iphigenie en Aulide*, an aria from Handel's *Semele*, Mozart's Requiem and Brahms's *Schicksalslied*. He used Wagner's concert ending for Gluck's Overture and revised Süßmayr's completion of the Requiem.[46] Hot on the heels of that concert, Strauss then rehearsed Schubert's 'Unfinished' Symphony, Thuille's Symphony in F major (from the autograph score), two unidentified Haydn symphonies and Beethoven's Symphony No. 2 between 10 and 18 December. Curiously, only Schubert's 'Unfinished' was subsequently performed by Strauss, who included it at the Hofkapelle's Christmas Day concert at which music by Reif, Gluck, Princess Marie Elizabeth von Sachsen-Meiningen, Schumann and Brahms was also heard.[47]

On 17 January 1886, Bülow returned to Meiningen, where he shared the podium with Strauss for a concert with the Hofkapelle twelve days later. The programme was typical of Bülow for the period and included Rheinberger's Overture to *Der Widerspenstigen Zähmung*, Rubinstein's Piano Concerto No. 3, Bülow's tone poem *Nirwana*, Liszt's *Fantasie über ungarische Volkweise* and Beethoven's Symphony No. 3 ('Eroica').[48] The concert overwhelmed Strauss both musically and emotionally and in a letter to his father, his enthusiasm for his Bülow's interpretations leaps from the page:

Finally, I can write to you! The concert was outstanding and the theatre was sold out (1,017 in the audience); a colossal success! Everything went well, Bülow played beautifully [in the Rubinstein and the Liszt works] and was pleased with my conducting [of them]. He is very difficult to accompany because although he was in tempo, he was very flexible. *Nirwana* went particularly well – I played the cymbals – and as far as one can judge from one hearing of such a difficult work, it is a wonderful piece. Bülow is perhaps as great a composer as he is a pianist and conductor. The performance of the 'Eroica', without rehearsal, was the most splendid that you can imagine. Although our orchestra lacks the shine of the Munich orchestra, although our hall has a poor acoustic, although the Finale contained a small error in the violins, it was a performance that I will scarcely encounter again. In the Funeral March every note contained a spirit and a soul that I did not think possible from an orchestra, and the Finale: concerning the Finale, I can say that it was the first time that I encountered the full brilliance of Beethoven's Sun. . . . I was so moved after the last movement that I wept like a child in the artists' room. I was alone there with Bülow, who embraced me and gave me a kiss, which I will not forget for the rest of my life.[49]

After Bülow's departure, and facing the possible reduction of the orchestra to thirty-nine players, Strauss soon began to lose interest in Meiningen. Even though he was offered a salary of 2,000 Marks[50] to remain there, he sent his letter of resignation to Georg II on 31 January 1886. Nevertheless, Strauss was tenured until April that year and remained a musical force at the Duchy by leading concerts with the orchestra and the choir on 23 February, 18 March and 2 April.[51] The comings and goings at Meiningen inevitably attracted the attention of the national press, and shortly after the March concert the *Berliner Tageblatt* reported that there was 'disharmony between Hofmusikdirektor R. Strauss and members of the orchestra'.[52] Strauss seems to have remained on good professional terms with Georg II, however, because he was able to assure his father that the Duke had congratulated him on his performance of Brahms's 'Academic Festival' Overture after the February concert and that he had awarded him the 'Verdienstkreuz für Kunst und Wissenschaft von Herzog Georg II' ('Duke Georg II's Cross for Service to Art and Science') on the day of the April concert.[53]

At Meiningen, Strauss remained active as a composer and was in increasing demand as a performer of his own works.[54] Understandably, the only music that he completed during the first month of his tenure was the song 'Allerseelen', which he finished on 3 October. In November 1885, however, he could concentrate more fully on composition and was able to turn his attention to *Burleske* (for piano and orchestra) and to put the finishing touches to the songs 'Die Verschwiegenen' and 'Die Zeitlose'.[55] With Bülow's sudden departure, composition again took a back seat in December, but by 3 February *Burleske* was sufficiently advanced for Bülow to play the work through on the piano, and by 19 February *Bardengesang* was ready to be rehearsed on stage.[56] While *Burleske* was completed on 24 February and was rehearsed with the orchestra on 3 April, Strauss's hope that Bülow would give the first performance came to nothing when his mentor refused to play it because it was 'unpianistic and with too wide a stretch for him'.[57] Never one for pulling his punches, Bülow then grumbled 'a different position for the hands in every bar – do you think that I'm going to sit down for four weeks to learn a cross-grained piece like that?'[58] The world première of the work was delayed, therefore, until 21 June 1890, when Eugen d'Albert and Strauss performed it at the twenty-seventh Tonkünstlerversammlung des Allgemeine Deutschen Musik Vereins in Eisenach.

PODIUM STYLE

Unable to escape the musical clutches of his father completely during his stay at Meiningen, Strauss soon found that his stick technique was a contentious issue, and within weeks of his appointment as Hofmusikdirektor, his father tackled him over his use of gesture. Strauss's movements, being those of a novice conductor, lacked sophistication, prompting his father to write that 'it is unattractive when conductors make such snake-like movements, and particularly by such a tall person such as you. It is even unattractive in Bülow, who is small and graceful in stature.'[59] Franz also stressed that a conductor's left hand had no other function but to turn pages, that if no score was being used it should remain still, that baton control was of great importance, and that eye contact was essential. Richard quickly adopted these suggestions and modified his technique accordingly. His restrained approach soon became a feature of his podium style and he later commented famously that 'the left hand has nothing to do with conducting. Its proper place is the waistcoat pocket from which it should only emerge to restrain or to make some minor gesture for which in any case a scarcely perceptible glance would suffice. It is better to conduct with the ear instead of with the arm: the rest follows automatically.'[60]

Using a long, thin, tapered baton, Strauss believed that short movements of the arm, an emphasis on the wrist, a decisive upbeat and an 'extremely precise' downbeat ensured the players' complete attention.[61] Along with a judicious use of the eye, these techniques, wittily caricatured in his *Ten Golden Rules for the Album of a Young Conductor*, were the fundamental elements of Strauss's podium style.

Ten Golden Rules
For the Album of a Young Conductor[62]

1. Remember that you are making music not to amuse yourself but to delight your audience.

2. You should not perspire when conducting: only the audience should get warm.

3. Conduct 'Salome' and 'Elektra' as if they were by Mendelssohn: Fairy Music.

4. Never look encouragingly at the brass, except with a short glance to give an important cue.

---

5. But never let the horns and woodwind out of your sight: if you can hear them at all they are still too strong.

6. If you think that the brass is not blowing hard enough, tone it down another shade or two.

7. It is not enough that you yourself should hear every word the soloist sings you know it off by heart anyway: the audience must be able to follow without effort. If they do not understand the words they will go to sleep.

8. Always accompany a singer in such a way that he can sing without effort.

9. When you think you have reached the limits of prestissimo, double the pace.*

10. If you follow these rules carefully you will, with your fine gifts and your great accomplishments, always be the darling of your listeners.

(*ca.* 1922)

* Today (1948) I should like to amend this as follows: Go twice as slowly (addressed to the conductors of Mozart!)

In maturity, Strauss's economical method was criticised heavily and it was viewed by some as a sign of lack of interest in the music that he was performing. That was not the impression of the distinguished German conductor Wolfgang Sawallisch,[63] however, who argued 'that is certainly not true. One thing is absolutely true, that his conducting always retained a certain distance between himself and the symphonies. Some people have said that his conducting was too cold and with a certain reservation but I feel it wasn't true. He was too great a musician to make too many personal influences in the music. Perhaps for this reason and because he was an active composer that he had such respect and kept a certain distance.'[64] The influential Vienna-based conductor and teacher Hans Swarowsky[65] was also impressed by Strauss's approach and from the copious notes that he took during conversations with him, recalled that:

Strauss realized quite rightly that technically conducting consists of an uninterrupted series of upbeats. The beat should not show what has just been played but what must be mastered in the next division. 'If you show a musician what he is already doing, you are quite superfluous!' . . . Upbeat and downbeat were the backbone of conducting and the rest would take care of itself. Everything else should be shown with no more than the elements of the metric beat without any technical extras. . . . The tempo must be carefully considered before preparing the upbeat. One should sing to oneself a characteristic passage of the work that is in the main tempo and then beat the upbeat into this silent singing. . . . Above all, a conductor must 'start the orchestra playing' or, cum grano salis: 'a good conductor is superfluous after the second beat'.[66]

First Munich Period (1886–1889)

From 17 April to 24 June 1886, Strauss took an extended holiday in Italy, where he visited Bologna, Rome, Naples, Sorrento, Salerno, Capri, Florence, Milan and Como. Although impressed by the painting, sculpture, architecture, landscape and people of Italy, he was often disappointed by its music and performing institutions. On 18 April in Bologna, for example, he heard Verdi's *Aïda*, which he described both as 'execrable' ('scheusslich') and as 'Indian music' ('Indianermusik'),[67] and on 21 April in Rome, he attended a performance of Rossini's *Il barbiere di Siviglia*, which he described as 'very average!'[68] While very little composing took place on this trip, it did serve as the inspiration for his symphonic fantasy, *Aus Italien*. Written after his return to Germany between June and October 1886, the work is composed in four movements and dedicated to Hans von Bülow. It was one of Strauss's first major attempts at writing symphonic programme music and it depicts some of the sights and sounds that he experienced during his journey. Unfortunately, he incorporated *Funiculì, Funiculà* into the Finale, which he thought was an Italian folk song but which had, in fact, been composed by his contemporary, Luigi Denza.[69] Denza reacted badly to the song's inclusion in *Aus Italien* and later successfully sued Strauss for using it without permission.

On 19 December 1885, the Intendant of the Munich Royal Theatres, Baron Karl von Perfall,[70] offered Strauss the post of Musikdirektor (Third Conductor) at the Munich Hofoper with a view to his eventually succeeding Hermann Levi as the theatre's principal conductor.[71] Before accepting the post, however, Strauss sought the advice of Bülow, who predictably counselled him against taking the job. On 23 December, he wrote:

I should naturally like to advise you to stay [at Meiningen] for the time being. But it depends on what part H. H. [Georg II] is disposed to play in the future cultivation of music on the banks of the Werra:[72] a question for the highest quarters. If, for instance, the orchestra is to continue at its present strength of 49 men, then it appears to me that your baton could nowhere find a more admirable and satisfying possibility of employment. If you want to go to Munich out of patriotism or homesickness for your family – good – a private matter. But . . . in your place I should turn it down for the time being. You are one of those exceptional musicians who do not need to serve from the ranks upwards, who are of the calibre to take over one of the higher posts of command right away. . . . Put it off. For the present do not run the risk, admittedly, for your lively temperament not a particularly menacing one – of becoming a Philistine, becoming a lout, becoming a snob on the banks of the Isar.[73] Wait for H[ermann] L[evi's] valetudinarian crescendo and then – later – step into his place without previously going up the bureaucratic promotional ladder.[74]

Aware of the artistic pitfalls that Munich might present and aware of Bülow's unfortunate personal and musical experiences there, Strauss nevertheless decided to accept Perfall's offer[75] and to become Musikdirektor at the Hofoper from 1 August 1886.[76]

Apart from the pleasure of directing a first-rate orchestra that included his father, the job proved disappointing. For much of the time, and in keeping with the rank of Musikdirektor, he was obliged to conduct operas from the standard repertoire. Along with a performance of Mendelssohn's incidental music to *Ein Sommernachtstraum* (*A Midsummer Night's Dream*) on 25 January 1887, Strauss took charge of twenty performances of nine operas by eight composers during his first season.[77] Statistically, the ratio of performances were 11 French: 8 Austro-German: 1 Italian. With the exception of Mozart's *Così fan tutte*, an opera that he championed throughout his life and with which he would later be associated closely, all the operas that he performed were popular and in keeping with his junior rank. Strauss's second season at Munich bore a striking resemblance to his first, with four of the eight operas being carried over from the previous year.[78] His third season as Musikdirektor was again dominated by repeat performances and, of the nine performances of five operas by five composers that he performed during that period, only Donizetti's *La favorite* and Verdi's *Un ballo in maschera* were new to his repertoire.[79]

Having been quickly converted into a fervent Wagnerian by Ritter at Meiningen, Strauss continued to explore his new-found passion when he returned to Munich, and he accepted with some excitement responsibility for conducting the Hofoper's first production of Wagner's early opera, *Die Feen*, in June 1888.[80] Preparations for the staging began in the spring of that year and Strauss continued to superintend the production until the final rehearsals. At the eleventh hour, however, Perfall informed him that his immediate superior, Franz Fischer,[81] was to take charge of both the dress rehearsal and the first performance. Strauss was devastated. This was an early and valuable insight into the nastier machinations of operatic life and he felt nothing but contempt for his superiors at Munich: he later described Perfall as 'a disgusting cad'[82] and Fischer as 'one of the most untalented musicians I have ever met and a real criminal at the rostrum'.[83] Distraught, bewildered and insulted by the behaviour of his colleagues, Strauss inevitably turned to Bülow and on 17 June 1888 wrote:

Perfall reveals to me that he has transferred the conductorship of the 'Feen' to Fischer, as being my superior in rank (*Hofkapellmeister*) and seniority (artistic!). Just think! . . . I had set terrific hopes on the work . . . [and] now they have all gone overboard through the infamous meanness of Fischer (who quite happily let me prepare the work), and the unprincipled impudence and rascality of Perfall. . . . In the interview with Perfall, in which I behaved like a lioness defending her young, I was told, among other things, the following: he (Perfall) could not so basically discredit the 'Feen' as to give it to an assistant conductor. . . . Furthermore: talent, etc. does not come into consideration at all here; it goes here, as everywhere, by seniority. Then above all he cannot stand my Bülovian conducting, now came the usual abuse of you, whose school must be extirpated once and for all. Then he expatiated on my arrogance, to be already at my age making such claims, etc. You will understand that I cannot put up with all of this. I have gradually come to realize that this is not the soil in which a happy musical life can thrive. I could not by myself pull the cart out of the mud in which I find everything stuck here. A dreary bog, a beer bog everywhere. But you know that better than I.[84]

Bülow's urge to say 'I told you so' must have been overwhelming, but instead he remained supportive of Strauss, whose best interests he always protected. The distress caused by the débâcle over *Die Feen* never fully left Strauss and it inevitably diminished his effectiveness as a junior member of the music staff. In maturity, he recalled that he lacked the necessary routine that was required for such a post and that he had yet to develop the skills needed to deal with the repertory system. For a young artist with strong interpretative views, this lack of routine often proved disastrous, and conflicts with singers and orchestral musicians inevitably ensued. Throughout his tenure,[85] he remained in close contact with Bülow and it was to his mentor that he again turned for advice and practical help as his sense of disillusionment grew.

Determined to escape Munich at any cost, Strauss applied for a post in Hanover. Bülow refused to support the application, commenting laconically 'Why exchange the Hanoverians of the South for the Bavarians of the North?'[86] Nevertheless, he was sympathetic to his protégé's plight and eventually succeeded in securing him the post of Second Kapellmeister at the Weimar Hoftheater from the beginning of the 1889–1890 season. While provincial Weimar lacked the appeal and glamour of Berlin or Vienna, it was a means of escape for Strauss, whose urge to leave the 'beer bog' of Munich had escalated from a strong desire to an all-consuming obsession.

Directing *Robert le diable*/Enthusiasm at the climax

CHAPTER 3

Enfant terrible

WEIMAR (1889–1894) AND *DON JUAN*

If Strauss's patience was tested to its limits by the actions of Perfall and Fischer at the Munich Hofoper, he must have felt encouraged by the prospect of pursuing his musical passions as Second Kapellmeister at the Weimar Hoftheater from September 1889.[1] For a German musician of Strauss's gener ation, Weimar was of particular significance. With its links to Bach, Goethe, Schiller and Liszt, its rich artistic heritage was the basis for a lively cultural environment that allowed Strauss to explore new musical avenues while discovering masterworks from the past. Working for a well-disposed Intendant, Hans Bronsart von Schellendorf,[2] and an amiable Hofkapellmeister, Eduard Lassen,[3] Strauss was able to develop musically in a secure environment that valued his abilities both as a creative and as a performer. His interest in *Zukunftsmusik* was nurtured at Weimar and with the help of Bronsart and Lassen, he was also able to explore some important works by Mozart and Beethoven. As Strauss had to balance responsibilities in the opera house and the concert hall for the first time, his new repertoire included not only opera but also symphonic music.[4]

SUBSCRIPTION CONCERTS WITH THE WEIMAR HOFKAPELLE (1889–1894)

Between 1889 and 1893, Strauss conducted sixteen Subscription Concerts with the Weimar Hofkapelle, of which eleven contained a work by Beethoven, the composer he conducted most frequently at the series.[5] Having 'encountered the full brilliance of Beethoven's Sun' at Meiningen with Bülow,[6] Strauss was keen to explore these works himself. Unable to pursue fully his symphonic interests during his tenure as Musikdirektor at Munich, he leapt at the chance to conduct Beethoven's music at Weimar. Although he never conducted an all-Beethoven concert there, he did perform five of the composer's nine symphonies at the Subscription Series, including two performances of the 'Eroica' and one performance each of Nos. 5, 6, 7 and 8.[7] Beethoven's overtures, concertos and incidental music also attracted Strauss and he used these as showcases for some of his colleagues at Weimar, including the former Liszt pupils Bernhard Stavenhagen and Margarete Stern, the leader of the Hofkapelle, Karl Halir, and Strauss's future wife, the soprano Pauline de Ahna.[8]

A committed Mozartian from an early age and a recent, but passionate, disciple of Wagner and Liszt, Strauss performed their works only intermittently at Weimar. Heard at three, five and seven concerts respectively, their music nevertheless remained of great importance to him; it was here, too, that he conducted his first symphony by Mozart, the 'Jupiter', on 12 January 1891.[9] At Weimar, he never conducted an all-Wagner programme but did devote half a concert to the composer's works on 26 January 1891. Having given over the first part of the concert to works by Beethoven,[10] Strauss concluded the programme with Wagner's *Siegfried Idyll*, the Bacchanale from *Tannhäuser* (Paris Version), and the Prelude and Liebestod from *Tristan und Isolde* (Pauline de Ahna, soprano). *Siegfried Idyll* was also heard on 9 December 1889 and on 4 December 1893, was the work by Wagner that Strauss conducted most frequently at the subscription concerts, and was the only composition by either Wagner or Liszt that he gave more than once at the series.[11] While all-Wagner concerts were rarities at subscription concerts in the German-speaking countries during the late nineteenth and early twentieth centuries, programmes devoted to Liszt's music were more frequent. Along with the three all-Liszt concerts that he conducted for the local Liszt-Stiftung (Liszt Foundation) between April 1890 and October 1892,[12] he included the composer's *Die Ideale*, *Totentanz*, *Eine Faust-Sinfonie*, *Ce qu'on entend sur la montagne*, *Les Préludes*, *Mazeppa*, *Festklänge* and some Lieder at his concerts with the Hofkapelle.[13]

DON JUAN AND THE AVANT-GARDE

Keen to promote his own works and eager to be seen as a successor of Liszt and Wagner, Strauss performed his own compositions at Weimar from the beginning of his tenure. After accompanying the tenor Heinrich Zeller[14] in a performance of his 'Ständchen' at his first Subscription Concert on 28 October 1889,[15] he then conducted the world première of his 1888 tone poem *Don Juan* at his second.[16] At the time of its first performance – 11 November 1889 – the work was considered the product of a musical revolutionary. Having made his first tentative steps into programme music with *Aus Italien* and *Macbeth*, Strauss confronted the genre with confidence in *Don Juan*, prompting some commentators to argue that the work was something of a watershed. Previously, he had been considered a musician of potential, but with this new work he was regarded as a leader of music's avant-garde, a distinction that he dismissed in later life. Reflecting on the term's implications in 1907, he wrote:

> I loathe such expressions with my whole heart. . . . The most audacious works of artists have never created as much confusion as the printed statements of their

opponents who try to combat these works with words. I leave such statements now and in the future to those who cannot live without such slogans, or who are sufficiently misguided to think that they can stop the natural process of progress with dogmatic prohibitions . . . [Then] I finally asked the question: in general is there an 'avant-garde'? The only answer that I could give was a definite no![17]

The followers of Brahms and Wagner were locked in fierce aesthetic battle during the late nineteenth century and this had a direct impact on Strauss's approach to composing. While the influence of Brahms can be detected in some of Strauss's early works, it was the principles of Wagner and Liszt, along with his understanding of eighteenth-century musical structures, that shaped his mature compositional style. In the case of *Don Juan*, it has been suggested that the work's true foundation is the literary programme and that its form is a direct outcome of the text, implying a degree of formal freedom not dissimilar to Liszt's approach in his symphonic poems. The German theorist Theodor Adorno agreed with this and wrote:

> The young Strauss, who wrote the *Don Juan* fantasy, wanted to grasp life in all its immediacy as the psychological subject of his music, and he began at a point where form followed life in a disinterested, unproblematic way – in the symphonic poem of Liszt. As he matured, he discovered that the pure formlessness of the prelude-like variation of forms . . . was the least effective means of securing that aesthetic sphere.[18]

Strauss was responsible, at least in part, for this naïve analysis of his evolving aesthetic, because in a letter to Bülow on 24 August 1888 he stressed the importance of a work's programmatic content:

> From the F minor Symphony onwards I have found myself in a gradually ever increasing contradiction between the musical-poetic content that I want to convey and the ternary sonata form that has come down to us from the classical composers. . . . what was for Beethoven a 'form' absolutely in congruity with the highest, most glorious content, is now, after 60 years, used as a formula inseparable from our instrumental music (which I strongly dispute), simply to accommodate and enclose a 'pure musical' (in the strictest and narrowest meaning of the word) content, or worse, to stuff and expand a content with which it does not correspond.
>
> If you want to create a work of art that is unified in its mood and consistent in its structure . . . [then] this is only possible through the inspiration by a poetical idea, whether or not it be introduced as a programme. I consider it a legitimate artistic method to create a correspondingly new form for every new subject. . . . Of course, purely formalistic, Hanslickian[19] music-making

will no longer be possible, and we cannot have any more random patterns, that mean nothing either to the composer or the listener.[20]

When Strauss wrote this letter, he was making his way as a composer and it is possible that he was keen to show that his thoughts and actions reinforced his ever-growing public image as a 'modern'. It is also likely that his comments were intended to appeal to Bülow's lingering affection for the music of Wagner and Liszt, a slightly misguided act of homage as it happens, because by the time of the note his mentor had broadened his musical interests to include the works of their aesthetic nemesis, Johannes Brahms. Strauss, too, later shied away from these views and in maturity wrote that a 'poetic programme may well suggest new forms, but whenever music is not developed logically from within, it becomes "literary music" . . . [and] [i]n reality, of course, there is no programme music so-called. This is merely a term of abuse used by all those who are incapable of being original.'[21]

Strauss's evolving compositional aesthetic during his early years can be confusing, but to suggest that Don Juan's structure is simply the result of his attempt at representing a programme in sound underestimates both his interest in and his reliance on Classical structures. Strauss's relatively recent conversion to Zukunftsmusik, along with his love of Mozart, began to shape his compositional language and approach to performance in the years following his Meiningen appointment. His intertwining of new and existing styles in his compositions, and the essential relationship between creation and interpretation, were soon apparent to some contemporary writers. The critic Alfred Kalisch[22] wrote:

One of the cardinal dogmas in [Strauss's] musical faith is his love of Mozart, whom he claims as a 'modern' in the sense that his music expresses ideas which appeal to men of this day more than Beethoven's work. His interpretations of Mozart are criticized in some quarters as being too modern because they impart into his compositions these very ideas.[23]

The exact nature of Don Juan's form has been a source of lively musical debate, prompting some commentators such as Richard Specht to describe it as a rondo, while others such as Norman Del Mar and Michael Kennedy call it an example of sonata form. Both propositions have some merit since in Don Juan Strauss hedged his bets, using a modified version of the sonata principle while alluding to rondo form. Even though the composer did not 'create a correspondingly new form for [the] new subject' in Don Juan, he did reshape an existing structure by craftily integrating the new with the traditional.

By approaching his 'subject' in this manner, Strauss seems to have made his programmatic works more accessible than those of Liszt. His canny moulding of programme and structure created a type of composition that has proved enduringly attractive to performers and audiences alike. Orchestral musicians and conductors have always enjoyed the challenges presented by Strauss's works and the public has never lost interest in them. In the average London concert season, for example, the inclusion of an orchestral work by Liszt is the exception rather than the rule, while Strauss's tone poems are programmed regularly. This is not just a recent trend. Between 1897 and 1942, for example, the Royal Philharmonic Society programmed nine performances of Liszt's symphonic poems, while Strauss's tone poems were heard on twenty-nine occasions.[24] It seems that by manipulating existing musical syntax and formal codes, combined with accessible programmes, Strauss not only challenged the listener within established musical boundaries but also continued to engage them.

Performing Don Juan

Composed with a virtuoso orchestra in mind, Don Juan tested the local Hofkapelle to its limits. Nevertheless, Strauss was able to report to his parents on 8 November [1889] that 'Yesterday, I directed the first (part proof-reading) rehearsal of "Don Juan".... even though it is terribly difficult, everything sounded splendid and came across magnificently. I really felt sorry for the poor horns and trumpets. They blew themselves completely blue... it's fortunate that the piece is short.... the oboe's passage in G major, with the double-basses divided into four parts, sounded especially beautiful. The divided cellos and violas, who play with mutes, along with the horns, who also play with mutes, sounded absolutely magical.'[25] While the rehearsal on 9 November proved no less challenging for the orchestra, Strauss remained optimistic and was able to inform his parents that 'yesterday's two-hour rehearsal of "Don Juan" went off splendidly; the piece sounded wonderful; Lassen was visibly moved. He felt that a work such as this will not be written again for another ten years. The orchestra puffed and gasped for breath but, nonetheless, did a wonderful job. A marvellous joke! After "Don Juan" one of the horn players, who was dripping with sweat and completely out of breath, asked: "Dear God, in what way have we sinned so as to cause you to send this scourge!" ... We laughed till we cried.'[26] Fortunately, the orchestra's good will continued to the first performance, prompting Strauss to write jubilantly that ' "Don Juan" was a great success. The piece sounded enchanting and went wonderfully. For Weimar, it unleashed an unprecedented storm of applause.'[27]

After that famous première, Don Juan remained central to Strauss's conducting repertoire for the rest of his career and it was given regularly by him as both a tenured and a guest artist. There are multiple radio and studio recordings of his interpretation of it dating from 1916, 1922, 1929, 1936, 1944 and 1947, and these readings are remarkably consistent in their approach. As consistency was a defining feature of Strauss's performance style, his recordings of *Don Juan* indicate not only his method for this work but also his approach when interpreting his other major tone poems. Curiously, no marked up scores of his own works have yet been found. Of course, it could be argued that as he was their creator, his response to them as a performing artist would have been a natural development of their initial compositional phase and would have required little or no supplementary information. When interpreting works by Mozart, Beethoven and Wagner, however, he marked his performing scores in detail and set out his intentions with great care. While the disciplines of composer and conductor are clearly different, Strauss was one of the last great artists to bridge that gap and considered them mutually dependent. As no annotated performing score of *Don Juan* exists, there is only a handful of written clues to his interpretative ideas, but in the six extant recordings the results of those intentions abound.

Two issues that set the 1922 recording of *Don Juan* apart from those made in 1929, 1936 and 1944 are Strauss's cut from bar 208 to bar 232 and his modifications to the existing orchestration.[28] In general, he was against the use of cuts, both in his own works and in those of others, as he once wrote famously about *Der Rosenkavalier*:

> After I had put up with Schuch's impossible cuts for long enough, I wrote to him and pointed out that he had forgotten one important cut. As the trio in the third act only held up the action, I suggested that he should make the following cut: D major, '*Ich weib nix, gar nix*', to G major, the beginning of the final duet! This insulted him but finally he was partially cured of the Dresden disease [Dresdner Krankheit]. Schuch's predecessor approached Draeseke and said: 'I hear, Herr Draeseke, that your new opera is ready.' Draeseke: 'Sure, the opera itself is ready but I still have to compose the cuts.'[29]

Excisions were common in early recordings and the cut in *Don Juan* was made so that the music could fit on to four, rather than five, sides of a 78 r.p.m. set. As the work is now part of the standard repertoire, the cut is unsettling for modern listeners. The sudden shift to G major at bar 232, rather than the repetition of the G minor passage from bar 208, as first heard in bars 197 to 200, disturbs both the tonal and structural symmetry of the section.

Textual fidelity was a burning issue for conductors from the nineteenth and twentieth centuries and the exact extent to which a score should be modified varied greatly from performer to performer. Strauss's great contemporary, Gustav Mahler, for example, is reported to have said that 'if, after my death, something doesn't sound right, then change it. You have not only a right but a duty to do so'[30] and that 'at first, of course, you will conduct the work [Beethoven's Symphony No. 6] as it is written. But later on you will see that some instrumental retouching has to be done.'[31] Mahler's disciple, Bruno

Walter,[32] agreed, writing that 'whatever can be adduced against [retouching] on the grounds of *literary fidelity*, I must declare myself against the radical rejection of retouching. . . . [While Wagner's] suggestions about the performing of Beethoven's Ninth . . . seem to go too far . . . [in Schumann's symphonies] instrumental retouching becomes an unavoidable duty . . . [because] the original orchestration is unable to do justice either to the spiritual content of the work or to its thematic clarity, either to the spirit or to the letter.'[33] Conversely, Otto Klemperer,[34] another Mahler acolyte, argued that 'the retouching of Beethoven, Schumann and others was an essential feature of Mahler's interpretation of their works . . . [but] I cannot go all the way with him on this point. He retouched in the spirit of his age. I believe it was unnecessary, and that one can bring out the full content of such music without retouching.'[35] Wilhelm Furtwängler,[36] on the other hand, agreed with Walter and wrote in 1930 that the 'literal rendering plays a major role in the practice and reception of music today . . . and placing the creator above the private person is naturally quite self-evident'. Furtwängler concludes that it would be a mistake 'to propagate literal rendering as such as an "ideal". If it is an ideal, it is at best a pedantic one.'[37]

Strauss did not share fully the views of Mahler, Walter, Klemperer or Furtwängler but was more pragmatic in his approach. In his marked scores of Mozart, for example, there are no alterations to the printed text but in his scores of Beethoven's symphonies there are some modifications. In general, though, his approach was more literal than that of Mahler and he was more faithful textually to scores by others. Why, then, in the 1922 recording of *Don Juan*, did he feel it necessary to alter the printed orchestration? The answer is simple: it was an acoustic recording. During this period, conductors were often required to make certain modifications to the work's orchestration for reasons of clarity. These adjustments, however, should not be viewed in the same way as those of the artists mentioned above, because Strauss's alterations were responses to limited acoustic imperatives while theirs were attempts at textual improvement.

The most obvious modifications to *Don Juan*'s orchestration in the 1922 recording are the doubling of the basses by a bass trombone in selected passages throughout the score[38] and the strengthening of the violas and cellos by a clarinet between bars 197 and 200. These represent an understandable attempt at greater clarity, but his reorchestration of bars 201 and 202 is more puzzling. Here, the woodwind material is doubled by the brass. From an extant photograph of the 1922 session, it seems that the recording was made in a small hall and that some adjustments to the orchestra's usual seating arrangements were necessary. That being so, the position of the woodwind may have caused an acoustic problem and Strauss's reorchestration of those bars might have been an attempt at resolving this dilemma.[39]

While caution has to be paramount when commenting on orchestral balance in early recordings, they do provide some useful information. As the

1922 discs were made using the acoustic method, their value is limited, but from the 1929 and 1944 recordings a clearer picture emerges. It might be assumed from Strauss's witty remarks concerning the brass in his *Ten Golden Rules* of conducting that he would have reduced the trumpets' dynamic in key passages.[40] This was not the case and Strauss's strict observance of the brass markings is a feature of his 1929 recording. In passages such as bars 353 to 355, where the first trumpet is marked '*Solo. con sord. giocoso*', its melodic role is undiminished. Equally, in bar 542 (beat 3), where the second and third trumpets' fanfare-like figure is marked forte, he follows the printed dynamic. Some conductors, such as Strauss's former assistant, George Szell, give this motif greater prominence.[41] For Strauss, however, the figure is of textural, rather than of melodic, importance and by observing the printed *forte*, he maintains the motif's function. Similarly, in bars 85 to 89 inclusive, the balance between the first bassoon and the first violins presents a problem for the interpreter, but from the 1944 recording it is clear that Strauss weights the balance in favour of the bassoon. The balance from bar 90 also needs careful handling and has been described by Del Mar as a love scene.[42] His assertion is not without merit and it seems to be confirmed by Strauss's orchestration, where the 'female' first clarinet and 'male' first horn come together musically, as if in a passionate duet. For Strauss, however, this duet is a one-sided affair, because the first clarinet is clearly the dominant figure, perhaps a prescient musical allusion to what would later be realized in his own domestic arrangements.

A central feature of Strauss's performance style was the way in which he manipulated and integrated tempo to clarify the micro- and macrostructures of the works that he was interpreting. A close comparison between his recordings of the music of Mozart and Beethoven and his annotated scores of these works suggests that he had highly organized method, that he could reproduce metronomic speeds at will, and that he used tempo to define musical structure. This method was adopted commonly in the readings of other conductors from the Central European tradition and was not unique to Strauss. Furtwängler was particularly organized in his approach to Beethoven's Ninth Symphony and from his various live recordings it is clear that his highly structured tempo plan was the foundation upon which the rest of the interpretation was built. Klemperer also subscribed to this method and when the critic Peter Heyworth asked whether he thought that 'one tempo can be right for one performance and another tempo right for a different performance?', Klemperer replied 'It could be, yes. But generally one sticks to the same tempo.'[43]

In *Don Juan*, Strauss looks to tempo as the foundation for his interpretation, uses speed to clarify the work's form, and is largely consistent in his approach across his various recordings. The structure of *Don Juan* can be summarized as follows: first subject, bars 1 to 36; transition passage, bars 37 to 89; second subject I, bars 90 to 159; transition passage, bars 160 to 231;[44] second subject IIa, bars 232 to 312; second subject IIb, bars 313 to 350; development, bars 351 to 473; recapitulated first subject, bars 474 to 509; recapitulated second subject IIb, from bar 510; coda, from bar 586. This cursory structural overview differs from some commentators' understanding of the work by incorporating the G major section (bars 232 to 350) into the second subject group, rather than as part of an extended development. By making this distinction, the Carnival Scene (bars 351 to 473) is defined as the true development section. Two other important issues are rationalized with this plan: first, the ambiguous tonality of the first subject group, caused by the juxtaposition of C major and E major in the opening bars, is balanced tonally by a two-part second subject that uses the conventional keys of B major and G major respectively, and, secondly, the restatement of second subject IIb, from bar 510, acts as a recapitulated second subject in the traditional manner. This interpretation of *Don Juan*'s structure seems to be verified by the way in which Strauss performed sonata structures by other composers. In his readings of sonata movements from the late eighteenth and the early nineteenth centuries, he applied a *meno mosso* at the onset of the second subject in fast movements.[45] At these points in his marked scores of Mozart, he regularly annotated either an *espressivo* or a *molto espressivo*. If the printed score of *Don Juan* is compared with Strauss's recordings of the work, it is clear that he applies these criteria to both parts of the second subject of his own work.[46]

From the evidence gleaned from Strauss's recordings, his tempi for second subject I are ♩=72 in 1922 and ♩=63 in 1929 and 1944. Although the earlier discs differ from the later recordings, it is clear that he wanted a reduced tempo at this point and that his preferred speed became ♩=63. As the 1929 and 1944 readings were made under more favourable circumstances than that of 1922,[47] the later recordings can be considered more representative of his approach as a whole. In contrast to second subject I, his tempo at second subject IIa is consistent in all three recordings, and by adopting ♩=60 rather than his own printed metronomic speed of ♩=76 he not only rejects the tempo marked in the text, but also indicates precisely how '*a tempo ma tranquillo*' (bar 232) and '*sehr getragen und ausdrucksvoll*' (bar 235) should be interpreted. From bar 447, Strauss again discards the printed ♩=72 in favour of either ♩=63 (1929) or ♩=60 (1944). As this passage is derived from second subject I, it seems clear that Strauss is attempting to underline the melodic similarities of the material by linking their tempo. That is harder to apply to the problematic 1922 recording, however, where second subject I is taken at ♩=72 and the passage from bar 447 is taken at ♩=63. Nevertheless, whenever the figure of Don Juan is being depicted,[48] Strauss interweaves the musical and poetic elements of the work by always observing ♩=84. By applying this speed to both the first subject and second subject IIb, Strauss not only underlines the symmetry of the work's musico-poetic argument, but also eases the transition from the speed at bar 232 (♩=60) to that of the development (♩=92).

Table 1: Strauss's speeds as found in his 1922, 1929 and 1944 recordings of *Don Juan*

Bar/Section	Printed metr. mark	Superscription and printed instructions	1922	1929	1944
1 [first subject]	♩=84	*Allegro molto con brio*	♩=84	♩=84+	♩=84
71 [transition passage]		*tranquillo/dolce* [woodwind and brass]	♩=76	♩=63	♩=63
90 [second subject I]		*tranquillo/molto espress.* [clarinet I and horn I]	♩=72	♩=63	♩=63
149 [second subject I]	♩=60	*un poco più lento*	♩=60	♩=60	♩=60
153 [second subject I]	♩=76	*a tempo, vivo*	♩=76	♩=76	♩=76
156 [second subject I]	♩=72	*poco sostenuto*	♩=66	♩=63	♩=63
166 [transition passage]	♩=84	*a tempo, molto vivace*	♩=84+	♩=84+	♩=84
197 [transition passage]	♩=92	*a tempo/molto appass.* [violas and cellos]	♩=92	♩=92	♩=92(–)
232 [second subject IIa]	♩=76	*a tempo ma tranquillo sehr getragen und ausdrucksvoll* [oboe I from bar 235 second half]	♩=60	♩=60–	♩=60
305 [transition passage]	♩=69		♩=56 [bar 306]	♩=56 [bar 306]	♩=56 [bar 306]
313 [second subject IIb]	♩=84	*a tempo/molto espr.* [horns from bar 314 second half]	♩=84	♩=84	♩=84
351 [development]	♩=92	*a tempo, giocoso*	♩=92	♩=92	♩=92
421 second half [development]	o=63	*sempre molto agitato*	o=60–3	o=60–3	o=60
447 [development]	♩=72	*molto tranquillo*	♩=63	♩=63	♩=60
457 [transition passage]		*a tempo primo*	♩=84+	♩=84	♩=84
474 [recap. first subject]			♩=84+	♩=84+	♩=84+
510 [recap. second subject IIb]		*molto espr.* [horns and cellos bar 510 second half]	♩=84	♩=84+	♩=84

| 569 [transition passage] | 𝅗𝅥=100 | stringendo [from bar 570] | 𝅗𝅥=100 [from bar 564] | 𝅗𝅥=100 [from bar 564] | 𝅗𝅥=96 |
| 586 [coda] | 𝅗𝅥=72 | tempo primo, poco a poco più lento (ma sempre alla breve) | 𝅗𝅥=76 | 𝅗𝅥=63 | 𝅗𝅥=58 |

THE DON JUAN FACTOR

With the success of Don Juan, Strauss took his first steps towards being seen as the 'Leader of the Moderns', a description that he came to dislike intensely.[49] Nevertheless, his triumph with Don Juan meant that Bronsart and Lassen allowed him to perform his newly-composed works at the Subscription Concerts on a regular basis. Of the sixteen subscription and two pension fund concerts that he conducted, eight included a work or works by him. Along with performances of songs and the première of Don Juan,[50] Strauss conducted the first or local first performances of his tone poems Macbeth (13 October 1890) and Tod und Verklärung (12 January 1891), a second outing for Don Juan on 11 January 1892, and a reading of Aus Italien on 4 December 1893. As the darling of the avant-garde, Strauss also worked actively on behalf of other contemporary composers at Weimar and although Bronsart was concerned that Strauss's first season was dominated by the music of Wagner, Liszt and Berlioz, he largely supported Strauss's interest in new music and allowed him to include a raft of recent works at the subscription and non-subscription concerts throughout his tenure.[51]

The concerts that Strauss gave with the Hofkapelle and the popularity of Don Juan did much to increase his public profile both within and without the Duchy and helped to secure his reputation as one of Germany's most versatile young musicians. The agent Hermann Wolff had always kept a close eye on his development and when it seemed possible that Bülow might not continue as conductor of the Philharmonic Concerts in Berlin, he looked briefly to Strauss. Ever loyal to Bülow, Strauss later mentioned the approach to his mentor and salved his conscience in a letter:

> I did not tell you anything at that time about Herr Wolff's enquiry in the matter of my taking over the Berlin concerts; because I did not feel justified, on the strength of this *mere enquiry*, in disturbing a relationship in which you, most revered Herr von Bülow, apparently had the greatest confidence; now, however, when so much seems to be changing in the Berlin circumstances,

when I read in the newspapers that you do not want to take on the Berlin concerts again next year, when I almost dare hope that these hostile influences which have so often tried to destroy your belief in my honour as a man and as an artist, may be disappearing from the society of my glorious master . . . I assure you, most truly and faithfully, that nothing, nothing in the world was ever able, or could ever be able to kill, or even to diminish my unbounded affection, respect and deepest gratitude towards you.[52]

Bülow was only too aware of the machinations that were an ever-present part of artistic life, and although he no longer continued as principal conductor of the Philharmonic Concerts after the 1891–1892 season, he underplayed Strauss's concerns and wrote by return of post that '*If you care to* we can, "round about" this year's intercalary day, chat in more detail over – politics. There stands with the utmost willingness at your service to this end. Your old, true, respectful admirer, Hans von Bülow.'[53]

Opera Performances at the Weimar Hoftheater (1889–1894) and the Première of *Guntram*

While Strauss was pleased that his activities in the concert hall were beginning to open some impressive doors, his principal duty at Weimar was to conduct operas at the Hoftheater, where he gave a staggering 201 operatic performances between 22 September 1889 and 1 June 1894.[54] The red threads that ran through the fabric of his performances were the operas of Mozart (thirty-three performances) and Wagner (fifty-one performances). Having made his Weimar début with *Die Zauberflöte* on 22 September 1889, Strauss then conducted fifty-four performances of sixteen operas by nine composers during his first season.[55] Of those, only works by Méhul and Auber were not from the emerging Austro-German tradition, and in contrast to the sometimes tedious repertoire that he conducted at Munich, most of the operas that he was allocated at Weimar were more substantial musically and more challenging technically. Keen to demonstrate his versatility and eager to underline his allegiance to new German music, he conducted Ritter's two one-act operas *Wem die Kron?* and *Der faule Hans* in a double-bill in June 1890.[56] A fiercely loyal musician, Strauss valued Ritter's ability and friendship highly and repaid his support by giving a further five performances of *Wem die Kron?* and *Der faule Hans* during his Weimar tenure.[57] Strauss's first season at the Grand Duchy also saw him take his first steps as a Wagnerian with performances of *Lohengrin* and *Tannhäuser*, works that he conducted annually there.[58] While operas by Mozart, Weber and Wagner accounted for nearly half of Strauss's operatic output during his first season, eighteen of the fifty-four performances that he gave were of operas and operettas by popular composers, such as Lortzing, Marschner and Flotow.

The repertoire that Strauss conducted during his second and third seasons at Weimar was similar to that of his first. In 1890–1891 he conducted forty-six performances of fifteen operas by nine composers, and in 1891–1892 he conducted fifty performances of nineteen operas by eleven composers.[59] The only works that were new to his Weimar repertoire during his second and third seasons were Wagner's *Rienzi* and *Tristan und Isolde*, Gluck's *Iphigenie en Aulide*, Kreutzer's *Das Nachtlager in Granada*, Auber's *La Muette di Portici*, Mozart's *Die Entführung aus dem Serail*, Beethoven's *Fidelio*, Cherubini's *Les deux journées* and Sommer's *Loreley*. Bronsart wisely allowed Strauss to add only four new operas in his second season and five in his third, ensuring that the young conductor established his personal repertoire in a systematic manner. As with his first season, the overwhelming majority of the works performed were from the emerging Austro-German canon; the only operas not from that tradition were *Les deux journées* and *La Muette di Portici*.

Having suffered a bout of pneumonia in 1891, Strauss was prone to infection and in June 1892 had to abandon work for a period because of an attack of pleurisy. He resumed his duties briefly that autumn, conducting Kreutzer's *Das Nachtlager in Granada* on 20 September and *Der Freischütz* on 27 October. His health remained fragile, however, and he was given leave to convalesce for the remainder of the season.[60] After returning to Weimar in the autumn of 1893, he began a busy period that included forty-nine performances of seventeen operas by ten composers.[61] As in previous years, the majority of these were already in his repertoire, but he did tackle seven operas that were new to him: Mozart's *Bastien und Bastienne*, Metzdorff's *Hagbart und Signe*, Wagner's *Die Meistersinger von Nürnberg*, Humperdinck's *Hänsel und Gretel*, Mottl's *Fürst und Sänger*, Fiebach's *Bei frommen Hirten* and his own *Guntram*. Of those seven operas, four – *Hagbart und Signe*, *Hänsel und Gretel*, *Fürst und Sänger* and *Guntram* – were world premières. While the first performance of *Hänsel und Gretel* was probably of greatest importance historically,[62] the première of Strauss's flawed first opera, *Guntram*, was the most significant personally.

Strauss conducted the world première of *Guntram* at Weimar on 10 May 1894. As this was his first opera and as he was a fervent Wagnerian, it came as no surprise to all in his circle that he looked to the Master of Bayreuth as his model. A true disciple, Strauss felt it necessary to copy Wagner's creative method in full and to write his own libretto. Much of the work on the text and the score was done at Weimar and during his trip to Italy, Greece and Egypt, which he undertook between November 1892 and June 1893. That journey was partly a means by which to recuperate from the bouts of illness that plagued him in 1891 and 1892 and partly a way of satisfying his lifelong interest in all things ancient. In tiny Weimar, Strauss's attempts at realizing his Wagner-like orchestration were inevitably doomed and he later acknowledged his 'incredible naïveté' by demanding so much of an orchestra that 'consisted of six first and five second violins, four violas, three celli [sic] and three double basses'; he had to look to the local military band to supplement its brass section.[63] Strauss also acknowledged in later life that he was no librettist and although *Guntram* 'scored a *success d'estime* . . . it vanished completely from the stage' after a few performances. While it was not a total failure at Weimar, the local musicians, audience and critics realized that *Guntram* was a far less convincing work than *Don Juan* and they were happy to dismiss it as the product of a fledgling theatre composer who had yet to find his operatic feet.

In the spring of 1893, Strauss was headhunted by the Munich Hofoper. It was clear that Hermann Levi's health was failing and that the theatre needed a dynamic young musician who could work side by side with him and who could absorb some of his duties. As a native of Munich and as a former member of the Hofoper's music staff, Strauss seemed the logical choice. Levi approached Strauss's father in March 1893 and enquired whether his son's health would permit such an appointment and whether Richard could free himself from Weimar.[64] If so, he would be employed in Munich as Levi's peer and would have complete artistic freedom. While he had been given scope by Bronsart and Lassen to explore some of his interests at Weimar, Strauss was still a relatively junior conductor there and believed that he was often allocated operas that Lassen was unwilling to take on himself. Strauss had been feeling restless for some time and had written to Bülow on 30 June 1892 that he had been

> Fretting . . . over my dear *Generalintendant* [Bronsart], with whom I have now so far fallen out (he has turned down a by no means unjustified request of mine to improve my position, because I cannot sit around for ever as a fifth wheel to old Lassen behaving as if he had a junior employee before him), that I shall soon be shaking the dust of the old Weimar tradition off my feet and recommending Herr von Bronsart to look for a thoroughly subservient mediocrity who does not treat *his* Beethoven so subjectively, etc. I am for another change of place, and am really curious to see where I get to this time.[65]

The Munich offer was timely, therefore, and under the conditions offered by Levi, Strauss would be able to programme freely, to engage singers of his choice and to work with an orchestra of the front rank. Moreover, since he was now a senior conductor at one of Central Europe's finest theatres, his international reputation would grow and the chance to promote his own works would improve substantially. With little reason to stay in Weimar, Strauss decided to accept Levi's offer and to return to the 'beer bog' of Munich from the beginning of the 1894–1895 season.

PART 2

MATURITY AND CULTURAL LEADER

CHAPTER 4

A Mozart Missionary

SECOND MUNICH PERIOD (1894–1898) AND MOZART STYLE

MARRIAGE

Before heading back to Munich and his new post at the Hofoper, Strauss stopped off at Marquartstein to marry Pauline de Ahna on 10 September 1894. The daughter of Major General Adolf de Ahna, Pauline was something of an emotional spitfire. Having met Richard in the summer of 1887, she was coached by him in Munich[1] before following him to Weimar where their on-again, off-again relationship was the talk of the local theatre. Stories about the exact circumstances of their engagement abound. The most commonly told tale involves Pauline hurling a score at Richard at a rehearsal for *Guntram*, followed by a slanging match in a dressing room that, in turn, was followed by the couple emerging hand-in-hand with the news that they had decided to marry. In reality, they had become engaged secretly during the early spring of 1894 and had been involved happily well before the première of *Guntram* that May. Their wedding was held at the Schlosskapelle St Veit and the ceremony was conducted according to the Catholic rite. Amongst the witnesses were his friends Ludwig Thuille, Friedrich Rösch[2] and Eugen Spitzweg. Pauline then became a muse to Strauss, who dedicated the *Vier Lieder* Op. 27 to her as a wedding present. Although she was famously direct to the point of rudeness, her devotion to her husband remained unshakable to the end of their long lives. To some outsiders, her behaviour towards him often appeared offensive, but he was largely unconcerned by it and generally dismissed her peccadilloes with the shrug of a shoulder. The support that she provided was clearly important to him and the domestic stability that she created was a necessary antidote to his busy professional life.[3]

SECOND MUNICH PERIOD (1894–1898)

After honeymooning in Italy, Strauss began work at the Munich Hofoper on 1 October 1894.[4] As in Weimar, he made his local début as Kapellmeister with Mozart's *Die Zauberflöte* six nights later. That reading was the first of 272 performances of thirty-five works by twenty-four composers that he conducted at the theatre between 7 October 1894 and 18 October 1898.[5] Unafraid of new challenges, Strauss continued to add works to his repertoire throughout his second Munich period, and of the operas performed, eighteen of the thirty-five had not been conducted previously by him. As a champion of modern music, he continued to challenge audiences by conducting the world premières of Thuille's *Theuerdank* and Hausegger's *Zinnober* on 12 March 1897 and 19 June 1898 respectively. Eager to introduce *Guntram* to Munich, Strauss gave the work at the Hofoper on 16 November 1895. In contrast to its reception at Weimar, *Guntram* provoked hostility from the start at Munich, causing the singers to rebel, the orchestra to demand to be freed of 'this scourge of God [Gottesgeibel]',[6] the critics to take a hostile stance and Wagner's family to consider the opera a betrayal of the Master's principles.[7] *Guntram* never recovered fully from this blow and it has remained on the periphery of the operatic repertoire ever since. The opera's reception had a devastating effect on Strauss; consequently, his courage to write for the theatre deserted him for the next six years.[8]

New works inevitably attract wide attention, but performers' reputations are made or lost according to their ability to interpret established masterpieces. Strauss was well aware of this and, as Kapellmeister in Weimar, he laid the foundations for his increasing reputation as an interpreter of the emerging Central European canon with his readings of Mozart's and Wagner's operas and music dramas. He then consolidated that reputation during his second Munich period by directing ninety-eight operatic performances of the former and eighty-five of latter. He had been a passionate advocate of these works since early in his operatic career, and in view of his senior position at Munich, he was able to explore them more fully. With the producer Ernst von Possart,[9] Strauss established in 1895 an annual series of Wagner performances that began each August and continued until either the following autumn or winter. At the first of those discrete seasons, Possart and Strauss mounted thirteen performances of *Rienzi, Tannhäuser, Tristan und Isolde* and *Die Meistersinger von Nürnberg*. These operas then formed the bases for the following three summer seasons, during which twenty-nine further performances of operas by Wagner were heard.[10]

BERLIN PHILHARMONIC AND MUNICH HOFKAPELLE (1894–1896)

In 1894, Hermann Wolff engaged Strauss to lead the prestigious Philharmonic Concerts in Berlin. As Bülow's protégé, and having gained considerable concert experience with the Weimar Hofkapelle, Strauss seemed the right man for the job. With programmes that were wide-ranging, Strauss offered Berlin audiences a well-balanced series of concerts that regularly juxtaposed the new with the familiar. Central to his Berlin repertoire were the works of Beethoven, with seven of the ten concerts containing a work by him.[11] Modern music was also a regular feature of Strauss's concerts in the German capital, and he continued to signal his interest in the compositions of his contemporaries by including works by Saint-Saëns, Schillings, Rubinstein, d'Albert, Ritter, Gernsheim, Stenhammar, Sauret and Mahler.[12] Curiously, Strauss's own orchestral works were not part of his Berlin programmes, with only extracts from *Guntram* being heard at his last Philharmonic Concert on 18 March 1895.[13] Even though Wolff had allowed Strauss the opportunity to present imaginative programmes in Berlin, his season with the Philharmonic was far from successful. Unable to fulfil his obvious potential, Strauss was not invited to return the following year and was replaced by the charismatic Hungarian, Arthur Nikisch.[14]

Commuting between Prussia and Bavaria for much of the 1894–1895 season, Strauss conducted the first of eight Subscription Concerts that year with the Munich Hofkapelle on 16 November 1894.[15] For practical reasons, some of the works that he performed in Berlin were also heard in Munich. In general, however, the content and character of Strauss's Hofkapelle concerts were different from those that he gave with the Philharmonic. That said, he was no less demanding of the Munich public than he was of the Berlin audience, with six of his eight concerts containing music by a contemporary composer.[16] While Strauss continued to programme new works with the Hofkapelle during the 1895–1896 season,[17] the music of Beethoven dominated his second year with the orchestra. That season, he gave his first cycle of the symphonies, which he conducted in numerical order.[18] As in Berlin, he failed to convince fully as an orchestral conductor and after his second season as director of the Hofkapelle's Subscription Concerts, he restricted his activities in Munich to the opera pit.

MOZART STYLE

When Strauss was promoted to the post of Hofkapellmeister on the retirement of Hermann Levi in 1896, the content of the Hofoper's summer seasons was extended to include operas by Mozart. That year, Strauss and Possart staged a highly acclaimed new production of *Don Giovanni*, which was followed by new productions of *Die Entführung aus dem Serail, Così fan tutte* and *Die Zauberflöte* during the summers of 1897 and 1898.[19] Those readings were influential in reawakening public interest in the operas of Mozart, with Munich soon being recognized as a centre of Mozartian excellence. But to understand fully the breadth of Strauss's efforts in revivifying and promoting the works of Mozart, it is necessary to consider his performances in relation to contemporary musical trends.

At the Paris Opéra, for example, Mozart's operas were all but ignored during
the late nineteenth century, with only two performances of them being given
there between 1885 and 1914.[20] At the opera house in Cologne, the situation
was similar with only three Mozart operas being performed between 1902 and
1912.[21] In London during the late nineteenth and the early twentieth centuries,
his works were performed more frequently, with the Royal Opera House,
Covent Garden, mounting ninety-six performances of them between 1886 and
1914.[22] During the same period, Strauss conducted 234 performances of
Mozart's operas, the vast majority of which were at Munich and Berlin, cities
where he held senior positions.[23] Strauss, as an individual, therefore gave more
than twice as many performances of Mozart's operas than the combined
conducting staff of London's major international opera house. Interestingly,
the repertoires of the Royal Opera House, Covent Garden, and the houses at
which Strauss worked were remarkably similar but the volume of Mozart
performances that he gave was much greater. While the number of performances of *Don Giovanni* are comparable – Strauss directed sixty-eight performances of *Don Giovanni* to the Royal Opera's sixty-seven – he gave considerably
more performances of *Le nozze di Figaro* – forty-eight to Covent Garden's
twenty-five – and of *Die Zauberflöte* – thirty-four to Covent Garden's one.
Curiously, *Bastien und Bastienne*, a rarity even today, was heard three times
at Covent Garden in 1907 and conducted by Strauss at Weimar on 7, 9 and
10 January 1894 and at Berlin on 1 February 1901.[24]

Strauss also extended his personal repertoire to include *Così fan tutte* and *Die
Entführung aus dem Serail*, works that remained on the periphery at Covent
Garden until well into the twentieth century. During the course of his career,
Strauss gave *Così* seventy-one times and *Entführung* thirty-three times and was
the first major conductor to champion *Così fan tutte*. The neglect of this opera can
be demonstrated by the statistics for the Royal Opera House, where it was not
given until 1947[25] and even then it was as part of the touring repertoire of the
Vienna Staatsoper. The first production of *Così fan tutte* as part of the standard
repertoire at Covent Garden was delayed until 1968, when it was given by Georg
Solti.[26] *Die Entführung aus dem Serail* faired only marginally better: after its
première there in 1827, it remained unperformed at the Royal Opera until 1927.[27]

When staging Mozart's operas at Munich in the late 1890s, Strauss and
Possart introduced a series of theatrical and musical innovations that have
since been called the 'Munich Reforms'.[28] At the Residenztheater, Munich's
ornate rococo theatre in the Hofburg, they used an orchestra of twenty-six
musicians, sets and costumes characteristic of the eighteenth century,
Hermann Levi's revised translations of the libretti, orchestral and vocal material based on Mozart's autographs, an electrically operated revolving stage for
the first time, the Prague version of *Don Giovanni*[29] and a fortepiano for the
recitatives, played by Strauss, who acted as both conductor and continuo

player. In later years, Strauss looked back on those performances with affection and in 1928 he recalled that the 'Mozart Festivals, which I inaugurated together with Possart . . . stand out among the truly wonderful memories of my life'.[30] The personal significance of those Festivals remained with him well into old age and in 1949 he wrote that 'at other times I would remember the enchanting Residenztheater in which Mozart had conducted his *Idomeneo* and where, 120 years later, I was able to initiate a Mozart renaissance and particularly to interpret, with Possart as an inspired producer, *Così fan tutte*, previously so often misunderstood, to native and even foreign admirers'.[31]

REASSESSING *DON GIOVANNI*

The opera by Mozart that Strauss conducted most frequently was *Don Giovanni*. It seems that he performed the work from at least two scores during his career, the second of which is housed currently at the Richard Strauss-Archiv in Garmisch-Partenkirchen.[32] That score was part of his complete set of Breitkopf und Härtel's *Gesammtausgabe*,[33] which he marked according to his performance intentions. Strauss makes a number of corrections and insertions that can be divided into two main areas. First, dynamic adjustments, phrasing and articulation, designed to meet the rigours of a live performance, and, second, corrections based on information found in the autograph. The annotations based on the autograph can again be divided into two areas: those that conform to Alfred Einstein's[34] research, as found in his revised 1930 edition for the publishers, Ernst Eulenburg, and those not confirmed by Einstein. The partial revisions that Strauss and Einstein ascribed to the autograph may be due to the incomplete nature of the material from which they worked. This raises a number of issues about Strauss's access to the autograph material.

According to Einstein, the autograph of *Don Giovanni* remained in private hands until it was bequeathed to the Paris Conservatoire in 1910. In 1923, the Munich publisher Drei Masken Verlag intended to publish a facsimile of the autograph at Einstein's instigation, a project that remained unrealized at the time of the Eulenburg score's publication.[35] Einstein did have access to a number of facsimile pages, however, on which he partially based his new edition and, as Strauss's references to the autograph are minimal,[36] it seems likely that he, too, only had access to the facsimile pages held in Munich. Had Strauss examined the autograph during his visits to France after the score was placed in a public collection, it would be reasonable to assume that he would have inserted many more changes. This appears not to have been the case, so it is safe to say that Strauss worked from incomplete material in Munich. He was living only a short distance away in Garmisch, so this would have been easily available to him from 1923 onwards.

In the Act 1 Finale, Scene XX, bar 408,[37] for example, Strauss writes that in Mozart's autograph, notes similar to those played by the violas are missing. He is not specific as to which instrument or voice is concerned but adds the same material down an octave to Don Giovanni's stave and writes 'fällt in Autograph' ('missing in the autograph'). In bars 412 to 413 with the quaver upbeat, Strauss then pencils in another addition to Don Giovanni's stave that corresponds to the harmonic material of those bars.[38] In bars 411 to 412, Strauss notes 'Bemerkung von Mozart fehlt bei Da Ponte' ('Remark by Mozart missing from Da Ponte'), an annotation that might have been prompted by Possart's statement[39] that F. P. Lyser copied a fragment of a German translation of *Don Giovanni* that was possibly approved by Mozart at a meeting with the composer's son, Wolfgang, at Dresden in 1834.[40] Although Possart's comments relate specifically to the Finale of Act 2, Strauss was obviously concerned that there might have been other inconsistencies in the libretto and that this was possibly one of them.

The majority of Strauss's markings relating to the autograph appear in Act 2. Following Donna Elvira's B flat major recitative and aria 'Mi tradì quell'alma ingrata' (Act 2, Scene Xe, No. 8c),[41] he notes 'fehlt in Autograph bis No. 24'[42] ('missing in the autograph until No. 24'). This reference applies to the recitative 'Ah ah ah ah, questa è buona!' (Act 2, Scene XI), which Einstein also notes as missing in its entirety from the autograph.[43] Nevertheless, this recitative is found in both Einstein's edition and the *Gesammtausgabe* and is based on material contained in the Donaueschingen manuscript of the opera.[44] Strauss then queries the personal pronoun 'mia' in bar 11 of Act 2, No. 10, which Einstein argues inhibits the flow of the recitative.[45] Unlike the other corrections contained in Strauss's score that correspond to Einstein's researches, this annotation appears to have been used for information only, as Strauss's performances regularly used Hermann Levi's translation. Einstein was also impressed by Levi's translation and used it in refining the text for his edition of *Don Giovanni*.[46]

For their new production of *Don Giovanni* at the Residenztheater on 29 May 1896, Strauss and Possart reinstated the *Scena ultima*. This scene was often omitted during the late nineteenth and early twentieth centuries because conductors from that period felt it weakened the opera's demonic qualities. Strauss, on the other hand, considered it central to the dénouement of the work and clearly believed that its inclusion was necessary if symmetry and balance were to be achieved. Within the context of a multi-movement finale, Mozart sought tonal symmetry by concluding each of the finales of his late operas in the key in which they began. The inclusion of the *Scena ultima* fulfils that function while strengthening the tonal core of the opera: D major. The nature of the tonal relationships within the Finale also highlights the need for the inclusion of the *Scena ultima*. Mozart does not maintain D minor to the end of Act 2, Scene XV, No. 11, but moves to the tonic major from bar 594. With this shift, the relationship to the ensuing tonalities takes on a symphonic character. At bar 603 (Allegro assai), Mozart moves to the subdominant (G major), then to A major, before returning, finally, to D major at the Presto. In the context of the Finale's greater tonal structure, these relationships effectively create an arch with Scene XV as its fulcrum, a device commonly used by Mozart in his symphonic output. The interactive nature of these relationships was seminal to Strauss's understanding of Mozart's finales, for he noted that whole sections of these movements 'are pure concert music'. Of course, Strauss was not alone in stressing the symphonic character of these passages: later, both H.C. Robbins Landon and Charles Rosen pursue similar ideas.[47]

By ending the opera with Don Giovanni's descent to Hell (Act 2, Scene XV), the eponymous villain might well be disposed of, but a number of important dramatic questions are left unresolved. The *Scena ultima* tackles these issues and resolves the status of the future marriage of Donna Anna and Don Ottavio, the reconciliation of Masetto and Zerlina, the emotional future of Donna Elvira, and Leporello's future employment. The last of these is particularly apt in any discussion of symmetry within the opera, since both acts begin with Leporello grumbling about Don Giovanni. For Strauss, these aspects of dramatic symmetry would have required resolution and were a necessary complement to his musical aims. The reinstatement of the *Scena Ultima* not only fulfils this function but also ensures that the opera concludes in the Italian *opera buffa* tradition.[48]

REVIVIFYING COSÌ FAN TUTTE

While Strauss's overriding concern for *Don Giovanni* was to rescue it from the mire of nineteenth-century performance traditions, for *Così fan tutte* it was more about presenting it as a coherent whole. Having witnessed the wholesale mutilation of the work by those who considered it frivolous, Strauss ensured 'that the blue pencil' should not be 'allowed to run amok' for his performances.[49] He argued that works that were traditionally considered theatrically weak had always been at the mercy of ruthless directors and producers. For him, the most distressing excesses of such people manifested themselves in what he referred to as 'making a play'. This is where producers and directors manipulated material, even cutting complete scenes, to create what they considered a stronger theatrical entity. What distressed Strauss still further was the habit of tradition-bound conductors cutting material that they deemed below Mozart's best work. Strauss cites the E flat major aria of Dorabella, Act 1, No. 11, Ferrando's B flat aria, Act 2, No. 24,[50] and Guglielmo's aria in G, Act 2, No. 26, with 'their connecting and extremely charming recitatives' as being 'invariably cut' because they were considered to be 'musically inferior'. But for him 'in reality they are all the most [sic] interesting and important from the dramatic point of view'.[51]

The salvaging of this material was central to Strauss's revivification of *Così fan tutte*. He believed that this opera was anything but a theatrical absurdity; rather, it was a carefully crafted psychological examination of human nature. As the British scholar Edward J. Dent[52] notes, the 'libretto [of *Così fan tutte*] was denounced throughout the nineteenth century . . . [and] various attempts were made in Germany and elsewhere to "improve" it, or even to substitute an entirely fresh libretto on a totally different subject. . . .'[53] Even the distinguished Austrian conductor Herbert von Karajan later dismissed the dramatic qualities of the opera by saying that 'I would not stage it at all! Wonderful music, but in the theatre – well, I must say it is not to my taste.'[54] Strauss took a different stance, prompting Donald F. Tovey[55] to note that it was Strauss's efforts at the turn of the twentieth century that led to the opera being regarded as 'a masterpiece of parody and irony'.[56]

That said, Strauss did indicate some cuts in his marked score,[57] which he generally marked with the letters 'vi–de' in pencil above the stave. These annotations might appear to run contrary to his views about presenting the work complete, but when conducting an opera at a house for the first time, the cuts that a conductor finds are often those that are considered 'traditional' and it is those cuts that Strauss has marked. It is unlikely that he made these excisions but added them for reference only. In Dorabella's aria 'Smanie implacabili' (Act 1, No. 11), for example, he marks 'vi–de' in pencil above the stave, between the second half of bar 15 and the second half of bar 55. If this excision had been made, more than a third of the aria would have been be lost, making a nonsense of Strauss's argument that this number was of particular importance to the work as a whole.[58]

CONTINUO STYLE

Of all the reforms that Strauss instigated at the Hofoper, his accompaniments of the recitatives caused greatest comment. Although his great mentor, Hans von Bülow, had led performances of Mozart operas from the keyboard at Hanover, he used a modern piano to accompany the recitatives. Strauss, on the other hand, used a fortepiano that had probably been housed at the Residenztheater since Mozart's time. The distinguished Strauss scholar Franz Trenner[59] recalled that a fortepiano was kept at the theatre but had fallen into disuse. He then argued convincingly that Strauss might have chosen this instrument over a harpsichord because it had three advantages. First, the fortepiano would have allowed Strauss a greater degree of dynamic freedom than is possible on the harpsichord. Second, the instrument would have resembled more closely the action of a modern piano, and third, Strauss was aware that a fortepiano would have been used by Mozart at the Residenztheater for the première of *Idomeneo*.[60]

The variety of dynamic available on a fortepiano would have suited Strauss's more elaborate continuo style and the delicate musical shadings that he sought when realizing the recitatives in his beloved *Così fan tutte*. Strauss was quick to point out the unique nature of these passages in this opera, their dramatic importance, and the complementary musical nuances that Mozart had added.[61] For Strauss, therefore, the fortepiano with its hammer action and more rounded sound would have been more supportive to the voices than the cutting sound of the plucked action harpsichord. But he was also aware that directing the opera from the keyboard had a very real theatrical purpose: dramatic control. In his correspondence with his librettist, Hugo von Hofmannsthal,[62] concerning *Der Rosenkavalier*, an opera whose conceptual inspiration was heavily influenced by *Le nozze di Figaro*, he wrote that comedy should make the audience '*Laugh*, not just smile or grin!'[63] In making the audience '*Laugh*', Strauss used motifs derived from his own works when realizing the recitatives. Trenner stressed that these were incorporated in a 'natural manner' and were used to underline key dramatic moments on stage. Wolfgang Sawallisch confirmed Trenner's observations and he was struck by the reverential manner with which Strauss interpolated the quotations from his own works into the recitatives. [64] In his autobiography, Sawallisch recalled these in more detail:

What [Strauss] played on the cembalo during the recitatives could not be repeated today. From the outset, Strauss's Mozart was a total surprise, but then, after a few moments, I grasped that every theme that he charmingly interwove had an exact reference to the action somewhere on the stage. When there was a joke, witticism or some other form of humour on stage, there suddenly appeared a touch of *Till Eulenspiegel*, or when, between Fiordiligi and Ferrando, there was a romantic exchange, a touch of *Don Juan* would ring out! But one knew exactly that each of the situations was correctly represented. Eventually, one waited for what would come next! So, suddenly, one was confronted with a completely different style which made Mozart live, a topical style of Mozart interpretation, even though Strauss was at least seventy years old.[65]

SYMPHONIC STYLE IN MOZART AND THE 'JUPITER' SYMPHONY

Given the monumental importance of Strauss's activities as a conductor of Mozart's operas, it defies belief that he recorded nothing from those works commercially apart from the Overture to *Die Zauberflöte*.[66] His readings of the symphonies were better documented, however, and these recordings indicate Strauss's approach clearly. During his lifetime, he was considered an outstanding interpreter of Mozart's symphonic works and was much admired by many of his contemporaries.[67] The British conductor Sir Adrian Boult[68] heard Strauss perform Symphony No. 40 at the Queen's Hall, London, with the Queen's Hall Orchestra on 26 June 1914 and reported that 'he polished off his three works in an hour and spent the remaining five hours on the Mozart. It sounded like it – the end movements were amazing: for 10 bars you thought it was slow; it was, but you forgot it after 10 bars because the rhythm and accentuation were so astonishingly light and lively.'[69]

Strauss's 'astonishingly light and lively' Mozart was the result of a clearly defined interpretative approach that was based on a set of well-considered practices and principles. Unlike Mahler, Strauss shunned any re-orchestration of Mozart's symphonies and operas. Instead, he looked to the autographs of works such as Symphonies Nos. 29 and 40 when preparing his performances. He then merged his study of the original sources with his own understanding of the structures and interpretative practices of the eighteenth century and developed a method that was both pragmatic and literalist. He looked critically at the performing material of the scores available and, in the case of Symphony No. 40, always opted for the version without the clarinets. A technique that defined Strauss's Mozart symphonic style was his highly organized approach to tempo. When interpreting movements in sonata form, he clarified the architectonics of the structure by adjustments in tempos, coupled with suitable complementary dynamic, expression and articulation marks in his annotated scores. In his recordings of these movements, he often differentiated between the first and second subjects by slowing the speed at the arrival of the latter. This approach was not unique to Strauss, but unlike many of his contemporaries, he made his speeds part of a wider plan. In slow movements, he invariably performed the first and second subjects at the same speed but manipulated the bridge passage instead. When performing a minuet and trio, he defined the internal architecture by conducting the middle section at a slower tempo, and when creating a cohesive symphonic whole, he linked the tempi of the various movements.[70]

Central to Strauss's readings of Mozart's symphonies was the way in which he integrated tempos within the symphonic whole. H.C. Robbins Landon states that Strauss used the idea of an '*Urtempo*' with respect to 'the underlying unity of the Viennese classical style', which was 'first examined and then put into practice by Richard Strauss when he was conducting at the Munich Opera'.[71] While Strauss undoubtedly relates his tempos both within individual movements and across the work as a whole, an underlying *Urtempo* is harder to detect. If Strauss's speeds in his recording of Symphony No. 41[72] are examined closely, it is clear that he treats tempo organically, building on each ensuing movement. It could be argued from his choice of speeds in the 'Jupiter' Symphony – Allegro vivace, $\downarrow$=84–88 (first subject) and $\downarrow$=80+ (second subject); Andante cantabile, $\downarrow$=84–88; Menuetto, $\downarrow$.=52 Molto allegro, $_{o}$=80 – that they confirm Landon's assertion. But for a more convincing explanation of these speeds, it is helpful to cite Nikolaus Harnoncourt,[73] a musician who, like Strauss, has not only performed Mozart's symphonies widely, but has also written about them as a practitioner. Harnoncourt claims that in Symphony No. 41 'each movement is somewhat faster than the previous one', creating effectively a form of 'composed accelerando' towards the Finale. He goes on to note that 'the ♩ in the first movement, the ♪ in the second movement, the ♩ in the third movement, and the 𝅗𝅥 in the fourth movement are all somewhat faster, respectively'.[74]

If Harnoncourt's tempos – Allegro vivace, 𝅗𝅥=72; Andante cantabile, ♪=84–88; Menuetto, 𝅘𝅥.=52; Molto allegro, o=72–76[75] – are compared with those of Strauss, the relationship is obvious. From these, it seems that there is a clear link between Strauss's and Harnoncourt's individual speeds in the first and last movements, the points of departure and arrival for the 'composed accelerando'. But when Harnoncourt's performance is considered movement by movement as he suggests, it is immediately apparent that he does not strictly follow his own stated ideals. Strauss's tempo in the finale, however, is in line with Harnoncourt's theories and in aural terms reflects somewhat more accurately Harnoncourt's tempo plan. By applying the concept of a 'composed accelerando' from the second movement, Strauss prepares the way for directing the finale in semibreves rather than minims. Moreover, by conducting the finale in one in a bar, Strauss hints at a related work. The opening theme can also be heard in, amongst others, the Sanctus of the Mass, K. 257, where Mozart sets the words 'Sanctus, Sanctus' syllabically. By conducting the last movement of Symphony No. 41 in semibreves, Strauss not only replicates the syllabic treatment of the material as found in the Mass, but also alludes to the liturgical origins of the counterpoint that dominates this Finale. By treating the tempi of the symphony as a 'composed accelerando', Strauss creates a classical arch that underlines the interactive nature of sonata form, reinforces the symmetrical qualities of Mozart's phrasing, and clarifies both the internal and external relationships that form the basis for the work's overall tempo structure.

An issue that has been the subject of lively musicological debate is the tempo relationship that exists between the Minuet and the Trio. Citing Hummel and Czerny, the distinguished Mozart scholar Neal Zaslaw argues against a slower tempo for the Trio.[76] Strauss takes a different stance in his recordings and differentiates between the courtly minuet and the bucolic trio with its links to the *Ländler* by reducing the tempo at the arrival of the latter. Harnoncourt reflects Strauss's practice:

> In Austria, a specifically alpine flavor is added. The Ländler – or the group of
> duple- and triple-time dances which went by this name – was added to the

family. Typical yodeling motifs . . . were thus added to these common dance forms. . . . These alpine dances, the triple-time forms of which soon were called waltzes because the dancers turned or revolved. . . . They are the true ancestors of the waltz. Very different social classes came together musically in these late minuets as a result of the amalgamation of the stylized minuet – which was no longer closely related to the dance – with these folk dances. . . . Should Mozart not have indicated such a significant shift in tempo? Absolutely not; on the contrary, it would be ridiculous to expect him to impart such obvious instructions to musicians who had these dance forms in their blood. It only becomes a problem centuries later, for us, who are convinced that a composer should spell out exactly what we are supposed to do. . . . We are therefore justified in juxtaposing the two different forms of the minuet and need not feel that we must try to force them onto the procrustean bed of an apparently correct, unified tempo. The trio should be played in a comfortable yodeler tempo, which it requires, and the minuet in a quick 'one'.[77]

It should be remembered that Strauss was a man of the mountains and even before he built his villa at Garmisch from the funds accrued after the spectacular success of *Salome* in 1905, he stayed for many years at the alpine home of his in-laws at Marquartstein, experiencing at first hand the folkloric style of the *Ländler*. Even to this day, the traditions of alpine music can be heard in the towns and villages of Bavaria and Upper Austria. Equally, Mozart, whose formative years were divided between the sub-alpine environment of Salzburg and the great courts of Europe, would have considered the diverse character of the two dance forms when pitting them against each other. Strauss, of all conductors, would have been aware of the relationship that existed between the waltz, *Ländler*, and Minuet, and marked the difference in his recordings between the courtly and the rustic by a distinction in tempo.

In his 1926 recording of Symphony No. 39, for example, he decreases the speed from ♩.=58 in the Minuet to ♩.=50 in the Trio, in his 1927[78] and 1928[79] recordings of Symphony No. 40 from ♩.=60/63 to ♩.=56, and in his 1926 recording of Symphony No. 41 from ♩.=51/2 to ♩.=50. For each of these interpretations, Strauss takes into consideration the underlying character of the music. In Symphony No. 39, where the Trio is based on an actual *Ländler* theme and where Mozart wittily alludes to the bucolic by treating the clarinets in a rustic manner, Strauss decreases the tempo sharply. In Symphony No. 41, on the other hand, where the differences in the orchestration are less distinct, he reduces the speed only marginally. Even so, his slight reduction in tempo at the beginning of the Trio in Symphony No. 41 is coloured by a clever use of rubato. In bars 1, 5, 21 and 25 of that section, he complements his *rallentandos* in the recording with *diminuendos* in the marked score, creating the brief illusion of a general easing of the tempo that underlines both the cadential nature of these bars and the onset of the new section.[80]

Even though Strauss was clearly committed to presenting Mozart's music in an objective manner, he occasionally indulged himself when performing movements that appealed to him. He was particularly fond of the Trios from the last three symphonies and at concerts he regularly followed the *da capo* of the Minuet with a second reading of the Trio. Understandably, this curious approach divided the critics and when Strauss repeated the Trio of Mozart's Symphony No. 40 at the Queen's Hall on 26 June 1914, the critic for *Musical Opinion* wrote:

> But the great Richard, however, was reticent to the verge of boredom; indeed, he seemed to lack interest in these works of his youth [*Don Juan* and *Tod und Verklärung*]. In conducting Mozart's Symphony in G minor, he did not win one's admiration, for he ended the famous Minuet with the trio and he tampered with the tempo of the last movement quite unnecessarily.[81]

In contrast, the critic for *The Musical Times* was much more positive:

> Mozart's G minor Symphony a master-work of a master of whom Strauss is well known to be an ardent admirer and a specially gifted exponent. The performance of the Symphony was perfect in its rhythm and graceful phrasing. We could not fully approve of the liberties taken with the tempo of the last movement, but another individual idea – the finishing of the Minuet with a repetition of the G major Trio – was much to our taste.[82]

In his article 'Dirigentenerfahrungen mit klassischen Meisterwerken' Strauss mentions tempo and stresses the importance of a *meno mosso* at the second subject.[83] His approach to the subject was influenced by Wagner, who wrote in *On Conducting* 'that since Beethoven there has been a very considerable change in the treatment and the execution of instrumental music . . . things which formerly existed in separate and opposite forms, each complete in itself, are now placed in juxtaposition, and further developed, one from the other, so as to form a whole . . . we may consider it established that in classical music written in the later style *modification* of *tempo* is a *sine qua non*'.[84] Moreover, 'the second theme . . . [in Weber's Overture to *Oberon*] does not in the least partake of the character of the allegro . . . but, as soon as the true character of the theme is brought out, it becomes apparent that a composer must think such a scheme capable of considerable modification if it is to combine both principles (*Hauptcharactere*)'.[85] Wagner then extended this thesis to include the second theme of Weber's Overture to *Der Freischütz*, which he felt should be performed at a slightly slower speed than the first. Similarly, when interpreting Beethoven's Overture to *Egmont*, he was in favour of a reduced tempo at the second subject (bar 82) and argued that a *meno mosso* was particularly effective at that point. When his protégé and Strauss's mentor, Hans von Bülow, followed his suggestion and 'firmly arrested and very slightly modified' the speed at that section, it 'brought about a new reading of the overture – the *correct* reading'.[86]

Conductors after Wagner were impressed by these arguments and applied his approach not only to music 'since Beethoven', but also to the works of Mozart. In the first movement of Symphony No. 41, for example, Strauss was vigilant in preserving both the homophonic texture and the lyrical quality of the second subject. At this section in his recording, he reduces the pulse from ♩=84–8 to ♩=80+, a tempo that is directly related to the speed of the Finale. In his marked score,[87] Strauss has made complementary annotations and inserts '*espr.*' (*espressivo*) in bars 56 and 58. These are characteristic of Strauss, who regularly adds *espressivo* markings at similar passages in his other annotated scores of Mozart's symphonies. Equally, his markings at the first violins' descending motif in bar 58, and the measures that follow, are indicative of his method when interpreting these often symmetrical, periodic sections. This motif is based on the dominant seventh of G major and is coloured by Strauss' annotation, '*grazioso*'. In practice, this has a dual function: first, to balance, in terms of inflection, the restatement of the initial rising figure in the cellos, and, second, to reinforce the symmetry of the first violins' phrase between bars 56 and 61. The homophonic character of the overall subject is further enriched by the reduced dynamic in the lower strings at bars 60 and 61, bars 66 to 69, and bars 77 to 79. This, too, is characteristic of Strauss, who, elsewhere in his interpretations of Mozart, ensures his desired balance by similar reductions. More important, however, is his manipulation of the material between bars 70 and 73 and between bars 75 and 77. In these passages, Mozart imports material derived from the first subject and uses it as a kind of melodic bridge that both links and unifies the first violins' thematic material. At these points, Strauss lifts the lower strings' dynamic to *piano* (bars 71 and 75). The new dynamic played *espressivo* is prepared with *crescendos* that are later balanced by *diminuendos*. This creates an arched dynamic that has direct interpretative links with his reading of the first subject. By inserting these dynamics, Strauss has reinforced the sense of line, has underlined the *espressivo* quality of the section, and has balanced the cantabile second subject against both the rhetorical first subject and the sudden dramatic shift to C minor at bar 81.

In slow movements, Strauss avoids slowing at the second subject but manipulates the tempo at the bridge passage instead. At this section in his recording of the 'Jupiter' Symphony's Andante cantabile (bars 19 to 27), Strauss takes a quicker pulse, increasing the speed from ♪=84 to ♪=92, followed by a return to the *tempo primo* at the dominant at bar 28. The *più mosso* at the bridge, marked '*agitato*' in the annotated score,[88] is designed to trick the listener, suggesting that the second subject was played slower than the first. This aural sleight-of-hand creates an impression of unity in his approach to sonata form movements in both fast and slow tempi and it was used by him in each of his recordings of Mozart's andantes. The *più mosso* is also musically satisfying because it not only reinforces the dramatic character of the music but also draws attention to Mozart's use of the dominant minor from the second half of bar 18. Especially when Mozart's marking – Andante cantabile – is taken into consideration, a reduction in pulse at the second subject would have been inappropriate, depriving the line of its *cantabile* element.

As in the first movement, Strauss's tempo manipulations in his recording are confirmed by detailed markings in the score.[89] The interplay between the first oboe and bassoon with the first violins (bars 18 to 26) is an important feature of the bridge passage. To secure the musical line, Strauss adjusts the first violins' dynamic throughout this section, allowing their descending figure to act as a foil to the ascending motif in the woodwind. He does this by crossing out the *piano* of the first violins' *forte-piano* in bars 19, 21, 23, 24 and 25 and by marking *piano* at the second beat of bars 20 and 22. Strauss continues to secure the line by adjusting the first violins' dynamic in the two bars that precede the second subject. In bars 26 and 27, he creates an arched dynamic, lifting the first violins to *fortissimo* at the first beat of bar 27. The harmonic support at the start of bar 26 is based on a diminished chord that finds resolution in the next bar. Strauss also marks a *diminuendo* in bar 27 (beats 5 and 6) that leads the listener effortlessly to the arrival of the dominant key and the second subject at bar 28. Here, Strauss emphasizes the melodic line by instructing the first violins to play *forte* and *molto espressivo*. The remainder of the strings retain the printed dynamic, *piano*, reinforced in pencil, while the woodwind are reduced to *pianissimo*, even though they mirror the first violins' melody.

Strauss's use of tempo modification as a means of architectonic definition was extended to include other structurally important passages. In 'Dirigentenerfahrungen mit klassischen Meisterwerken', he argues that

> In some cases, and particularly in quick movements, I recommend the tempo should be broadened before the end so that continuity can be achieved. The final fugue of the *Jupiter* symphony . . . [is a] good example. Mozart's final fugue is one of the works that Wagner wanted played 'as fast as possible'. At the beginning of the second part, after the development and at the start of the third part I modify [the tempo] strongly. So that the fugue retains its shape when played *presto*, it is imperative to reduce the dynamics of the brass and timpani, which should be clearly marked [in the parts and score].[90]

In keeping with this plan, Strauss reduces his tempo at 'the beginning of the second part' in his recording of Symphony No. 41.[91] The opening bars of the development – 'the second part' – are treated in a *misterioso* fashion, which he achieves by adding '*meno mosso*' above bar 158 in his marked score and by slowing down in the recording to bar 166, the movement's slowest point ($_o$=63), before restoring the original speed at the second half of bar 172. As with the beginning of the development, the arrival of the recapitulation is defined by a modification to the movement's overall speed.[92] From the second half of bar 219, Strauss annotates clearly the adjustments heard in the recording: '*poco calando*' in bars 220 and 221, and '*tempo primo*' in bars 223 and 224. His tempo adjustments are complemented by a general *diminuendo* in bar 218, leading to a tutti *piano* in bar 219. A further *diminuendo* follows in the woodwind, cellos and bass in bar 222, and the brass and woodwind are reduced to *pianissimo* in bar 223, thus colouring the '*poco calando*' with what is effectively a *poco a poco diminuendo*.

Following the double bar, bars 356a–356b,[93] 'the start of the third part [or Coda]', Strauss actively draws the listener's attention to the imaginative treatment of the counterpoint. At bar 360, Mozart inverts the first subject and manipulates it sequentially and canonically. Strauss emphasizes the passage in his marked score by inserting a '*poco meno mosso*' at bar 356b (second half) and a '*tranquillo*' five bars later. He realizes those annotations on the recording by an ethereal reduction in speed. At bar 372, he announces the counterpoint with a strident attack on the horns. The tempo at this point, $_o$=76, is pivotal to his reading of the coda, and his qualification above bars 373 to 382, '*A tempo aber bis zum Schluss bedeutend breiter als das Anfangs tempo*' ('A tempo but at a clearly slower speed than at the beginning'), signals a staged return to $_o$=80 with the 'tempo I' being restored at bar 402 (beat 1, second half).

For some modern commentators, Strauss's approach to Mozart's symphonies can be both confusing and disconcerting. The critic Lionel Salter seems to be at odds with Strauss's method. In the December 1991 issue of *Gramophone*, Salter wrote:

> His [Strauss's] approach is certainly unsentimental – he makes no easing-up into the recapitulation of the G minor Symphony's first movement, for example (though he does into that of the *Jupiter* finale) – but there is nothing bandmasterly about his readings. On the contrary, a good deal stricter discipline would have been very welcome . . . its ['Jupiter's'] *Andante* is taken very slowly, though immediately faster at the second subject (1′26″) and with a most unconvincing suddenly slower tempo at bar 39 (2′50″); the very much slower coda to the finale could be attributable to a side-break in the original set.[94]

Had Salter compared Strauss's recordings with his marked scores and his writings on performance, he might have come to a different conclusion. Annotated scores and treatises are essential guides to the intentions of performers, while recordings are valuable tools in establishing results. With Strauss, modern commentators have the opportunity of examining these documents and it is immediately apparent from them that he met all his interpretative objectives in his commercial recordings. When these documents are compared with those of later Mozart conductors, such as Otto Klemperer, Fritz Busch, Sir John Pritchard and Wolfgang Sawallisch,[95] it is clear that he was a crucial figure. His interpretations of Mozart's music were at the very heart of his activities as a creative and as a recreative artist and he considered them to be of didactic significance. While some aspects of his approach were inimitable, it is not an overstatement to suggest that the readings of later conductors would have been less rich artistically without the influence and example of Richard Strauss.[96]

CHAPTER 5

Cause Célèbre

ERSTER KÖNIGLICHER KAPELLMEISTER AT
BERLIN (1898–1908) AND *SALOME*

By the end of nineteenth century, Germany was seen increasingly by Germans and non-Germans alike as the political and cultural powerhouse of continental Europe. At its head was Wilhelm II, who was hailed and reviled in equal measure. Representing all that was best about the new Empire for many Germans and all that was worst for many foreigners, Wilhelm placed great emphasis on cutting-edge technology, the arts, the procurement of overseas colonies and militarism. His ambitions for Germany were boundless, demanding that it compete openly for political, scientific, cultural and artistic superiority in Europe. At the heart of his artistic quest was the Berlin Hofoper, one of the world's best-known theatres. The plaything of Wilhelm until the demise of the monarchy at the end of World War One, it was in many ways a conservative institution. Nevertheless, it was Germany's leading opera house and was considered by many Prussians to be a cultural Mecca that had the resources necessary to attract some of the finest conductors, singers, producers, designers and choreographers of the age. It was almost inevitable, therefore, that Strauss as Germany's most-discussed musician would be engaged by the Berlin theatre and when he was eventually offered a senior post there in 1898, he seized the opportunity.

EIN HELDENLEBEN AND COMPOSERS' RIGHTS

In the period directly preceding his Berlin appointment, Strauss was particularly busy as a performer, composer and champion of artists' rights. He continued to conduct throughout much of the summer and the early autumn of 1898, and gave his farewell performance at the Munich Hofoper with Beethoven's *Fidelio* on 18 October. In tandem with his conducting duties, he was occupied with the composition of *Ein Heldenleben*, which he completed in December 1898,[1] a year to the month after finishing the work's companion piece, *Don Quixote*. In contrast to *Till Eulenspiegel* and *Don Quixote*, which were given first by Franz Wüllner in Cologne, Strauss conducted the world première of *Ein Heldenleben* at the Frankfurt Museum Concerts on 3 March 1899. Often criticized heavily for its biographical content, the tone poem has been at the centre of a debate that continues to this day. With its extended musical panorama and its enlarged orchestration, *Ein Heldenleben* was considered by many as the ideal musical manifesto for Wilhelm II's Era. Its rhythmic swagger and its uncompromising demands on performers and audiences alike have left some commentators uneasy. Even so, its popularity has never wavered and it has remained firmly in the repertoires of most virtuoso orchestras since its first performance.

By the time of *Ein Heldenleben*'s completion, Strauss had become embroiled in a row over composers' rights and their copyright entitlements. In contrast to some other European countries, Germany's copyright law only allowed authors' exclusivity to extend for thirty years after their death.[2] For Strauss, this was an unacceptably short period and needed to be addressed urgently. Publishers were outraged by the idea and were keen for any attempt to change the situation to be stopped. Strauss was aware that some of his composing colleagues had been short-changed by their publishers and that they had benefited little from their labours. Eager to ensure that a fair and an equitable system should be established, he enlisted the help of his friends Friedrich Rösch and Hans Zincke.[3] Although Rösch was a lawyer and Zincke was a scientist, they were also composers and were committed to a longer period of copyright protection, higher fees and an organized system of distributing royalties. Together, they drafted a letter that was sent to their artistic colleagues outlining their proposals and were delighted when they received a positive response from the majority of composers approached. Consequently, the Genossenschaft deutscher Tonsetzer (Fellowship of German Composers) was later formed in 1901 and the Anstalt für musikalische Aufführungsrechte (Institute for Performing Rights in Music) was finally established in 1903. While these organizations did much to ensure the financial wellbeing of many German composers, their foundation left Strauss exposed professionally. *Ein Heldenleben* was an early victim of his crusade and after it was rejected by his long-standing publisher, Eugen Spitzweg (of Joseph Aibl), because of the possibility of reduced income under the proposed new copyright laws,[4] he placed it with the Munich-based publisher Leuckart in 1899.

BERLIN HOFOPER (1898–1902) AND *FEUERSNOT*

At the time of Strauss's appointment at the Berlin Hofoper, the theatre and its orchestra boasted some of Europe's foremost performing musicians, including two outstanding Wagner conductors, Karl Muck and Josef Sucher, and Strauss's great rival, Felix Weingartner. Born at Döbör, Hungary, on

23 November 1843, Sucher was the most senior of the three. After a period with the Wiener Sängerknaben (Vienna Boys Choir), he continued his studies in Vienna with Simon Sechter, the teacher of Anton Bruckner, before being appointed Director of the Wiener academischen Gesangsverein (Vienna Academic Choir). In 1870, he joined the staff of the Vienna Hofoper as répétiteur, in 1871 he moved to the Komische Oper, and in 1876 he was engaged by the legendary impresario Angelo Neumann as conductor at the Leipzig Stadttheater. Described by Hans von Bülow as 'a strikingly good and temperamental conductor, particularly of Wagner',[5] Sucher gave a complete cycle of *Der Ring des Nibelungen* at Leipzig in 1878. On moving to the Hamburg Stadttheater, he reinforced his Wagner credentials by giving the local première of *Tristan und Isolde* in 1882 before being appointed to the Berlin Hofoper in 1888, where he conducted *Rienzi*, *Der fliegende Holländer*, *Tannhäuser*, *Lohengrin*, *Tristan und Isolde*, *Die Meistersinger von Nürnberg* and the *Ring* in the summer of 1889. He was married to the renowned Wagnerian soprano Rosa Sucher,[6] who was feted in London, Bayreuth and Berlin for her interpretations of the Master's principal roles. Given Rosa's success at Bayreuth, and given her husband's place in the pantheon of great Wagner conductors, it is curious that he never performed there. Sucher retired from the Hofoper in 1899 and died in Berlin in 1908

Fifteen years Sucher's junior, Karl Muck was born at Darmstadt on 22 October 1859. A fascinating character who gained a doctorate in philology from the University of Heidelberg in 1880, Muck started his musical career as a pianist before rising through the ranks of the Central European opera-house system with appointments in Salzburg, Brno and Graz. As a Wagnerian, he began to attract attention after being appointed to the Deutsches Landestheater in Prague in 1886 by Angelo Neumann, the man who had appointed Josef Sucher and the young Arthur Nikisch to the Leipzig Stadttheater in 1876 and 1878 respectively and who would later appoint the youthful Otto Klemperer to the Prague theatre in 1907. Along with his duties at the Landestheater, Muck was engaged by Neumann to conduct his touring Wagner company, with which he gave the Russian première of *Der Ring des Nibelungen* at St Petersburg in 1889. At the Bayreuth Festival, he regularly conducted *Parsifal* between 1901 and 1930,[7] gave *Lohengrin* in 1909, and conducted *Die Meistersinger von Nürnberg* in 1925. He joined the Berlin Hofoper in 1892 and remained there until 1912, the year that he was appointed Music Director of the Boston Symphony Orchestra. The appointment proved disastrous, and when he refused to conduct *The Star Spangled Banner* after the United States entered World War One in 1917, he was thrown in gaol under the Alien Enemies Act. After spending the remainder of the war as a prisoner at Fort Oglethorpe, Georgia, he was deported to Germany, where he was appointed conductor of the Hamburg Philharmonic in 1922. He remained at Hamburg until his retirement in 1933 and died at Stuttgart in 1940

Of the Hofoper's and the Hofkapelle's three tenured conductors, it was Felix Weingartner who was most often at loggerheads with Strauss. Born a year before Strauss on 2 June 1863 at Zara in Dalmatia, Weingartner was raised by his mother, Karoline, after the death of his father, Guido, in 1868. Guido's death had a devastating effect on Felix and his mother, who relied on the good will of family and friends to survive. Virtually destitute, they were forced to lodge with relatives at Voitsberg, Baden and Vienna before finally settling in Graz. After leaving the Graz Gymnasium in 1881, Felix entered the Leipzig Conservatorium, where he encountered Carl Reinecke, Anton Seidl and Arthur Nikisch. It was Franz Liszt, however, who helped shape Weingartner's early career by arranging for Eduard Lassen to perform Weingartner's first opera, *Sakuntala*, at the Weimar Hoftheater in 1884. Hermann Levi was also impressed by the young Weingartner and on 3 June 1886 he gave the first performance of the fledgling composer's next opera, *Malawika*, at the Munich Hofoper. Weingartner, like Muck, rose through the ranks of the Central European opera-house system and after engagements at Königsberg (now Kaliningrad), Danzig,[8] Hamburg and Mannheim, was appointed to the Berlin Hofoper in 1891, where he later took charge of the Hofkapelle's subscription concerts with which he made a considerable impact.

Many commentators considered Weingartner's work in the concert hall far superior to his activities in the opera house. This was certainly true of his first period in Vienna, where he replaced Mahler as Director of the Hofoper in 1908. By opting to reverse some of Mahler's reforms, Weingartner came into direct conflict with his colleagues and the press, and he was forced to leave in 1911. In 1919, he returned to Vienna as Director of the Volksoper, where he remained until 1924, the same period that Strauss was Co-Director with Franz Schalk of the Staatsoper.[9] Faced with a theatre in financial chaos caused largely by the fiscal uncertainty that scarred Austria in the years immediately following the Great War, Weingartner struggled to convince unions and workers' councils that radical change was necessary if the theatre was to become viable financially and artistically. In 1935, he returned to the Vienna Staatsoper as Director for a second time, but that stint was even more disastrous than the first and he left the following year. While his tenures in the theatre were often troubled, his activities as an orchestral conductor were feted widely. His relationship with the Vienna Philharmonic was particularly long and fruitful, and after being appointed its conductor in 1908, he remained in post until 1927. During that time, he gave no fewer than 432 concerts with the orchestra in Vienna and elsewhere.

Having been overlooked by Bülow in 1885 as Mannstädt's replacement in Meiningen,[10] Weingartner never forgave Strauss for being appointed in his stead. Nor did he forgive Strauss for his remarkable success as a composer. Embittered by his ultimate failure as a creative artist, Weingartner felt that he was 'an unrecognised genius'[11] who had been overlooked by history. Sir Henry J. Wood,[12] a close associate of both Weingartner and Strauss, shared history's judgement and wrote some four years before Weingartner's death on 7 May 1942 in Winterthur that 'he and I had always been good friends, especially in his young days; but I must say his conducting interests me more now than his compositions. Perhaps his great orchestral technique, though it must naturally be responsible for his clever scoring, was his undoing; at all events, the inspiration of the composer did not always seem to be there.'[13]

Whether it was an example of one-upmanship or an act of artistic belligerence, Strauss's decision to introduce himself as Erster Königlicher Kapellmeister (First Royal Conductor) of the Berlin Hofoper with *Tristan und Isolde* was certainly brave. As Strauss had been the assistant to Hans von Bülow, the conductor who gave the work's première in 1865, as the music drama had been given first at his hometown, and as he had given a critically acclaimed uncut performance of *Tristan* at Weimar, the piece was clearly of some personal and artistic importance to him. Even so, with two of the world's leading Wagner interpreters already on the staff and a third who had fixed views about the Master's compositions, Strauss catapulted himself headlong into the artistic lions' den by choosing to introduce himself to the Berlin public with a work associated closely with Sucher and Muck. Never one to turn his back on a challenge, Strauss must have been aware that comparisons would be made and that battle lines would be drawn. Nevertheless, he was keen to be seen as *Zukunftsmusik's* most devoted advocate in Berlin and was determined to achieve that status whatever the cost.

Having taken up his duties on 1 November 1898, Strauss began rehearsals with Act 1 of *Tristan* on 3 November and Acts 2 and 3 the following day. His house début took place on 5 November, and near the end of the month he was able to report to his father that 'my success with "Tristan" appears extraordinary'.[14] Within days of his inaugural performance, Strauss was thrown into the musical deep end with seven performances of six operas without rehearsal between 8 and 21 November.[15] Luckily, all the operas were in Strauss's repertoire, so any challenge that he might have faced by tackling such a diversity of composers and styles within such a limited time-span was made more bearable through familiarity. On New Year's Day 1899 he conducted *Fidelio* at the request of the Emperor, and on 3 January he began rehearsals for Chabrier's unfinished opera, *Briséis*. Strauss gave the first Berlin performance of this novelty in a double-bill with d'Albert's *Die Abreise* conducted by Karl Muck on 14 January. The quality of Chabrier's score impressed Strauss, but he realized quickly that the work had little public appeal. Any allure that the composition might have had was severely hampered by its being coupled with a piece by d'Albert, a musician who was widely considered a great pianist but an inferior composer.

The hectic schedule that Strauss faced during his opening weeks at the Hofoper continued for the rest of the season. Between the first day of his tenure (5 November 1898) and his last day before going on holiday (28 June 1899), he gave no fewer than sixty-eight performances of twenty-five operas by sixteen composers. With the exceptions of Auber's *La Muette de Portici*, Rossini's *Il barbiere di Siviglia*, Mascagni's *Cavalleria rusticana*, Chabrier's *Briséïs* and Le Borne's *Mudarra*, all the operas performed were by German-speaking composers. Of the works given, forty-four were by nine composers from that group, eighteen were by four French-speaking composers, four were by two Italian composers and one was by a Czech composer.[16] It could be argued that this balance reflected the natural interdependence of creation, recreation and reception at an opera house positioned strategically at the centre of the new German Empire, but it could equally be seen as yet another example of Wilhelminian swagger at a time when national tensions were rising. Whatever the case, it meant that Strauss was able to explore some works that were new to him. Along with the local premières and new productions of operas by Chabrier, Le Borne, Johann Strauss II and Weber,[17] he conducted Wagner's *Der Ring des Nibelungen* for the first time in June 1899.[18] Given without rehearsal, he performed *Das Rheingold* on 19 June, *Die Walküre* on 20 June, *Siegfried* on 22 June and *Götterdämmerung* on 24 June. For Strauss, this must have been one of the greatest moments of his performing career, because by adding the tetralogy to his repertoire, he had conducted all of Wagner's major available stage works from *Rienzi* onwards,[19] an important milestone for such a committed Wagnerian.

With the 1898–1899 season behind him, Strauss spent the remainder of the summer composing vocal music at Marquartstein.[20] He was back in Berlin to restart his duties at the Hofoper with a performance of Humperdinck's *Hänsel und Gretel* on 2 September 1899. Strauss must have experienced a sense of *déjà vu* on returning to Berlin, because the new season bore a striking resemblance to the previous one. Again, he performed works by sixteen composers, many of which were carried over from the last season. The number of performances that he undertook increased substantially, however, meaning that he was seen in the pit on no fewer than ninety-six occasions that year. As in the previous season, he conducted three new productions – Lortzing's *Der Wildschütz* on 22 September 1899, Mozart's *Così fan tutte* on 12 October, and Auber's *Le cheval de bronze* on 5 May 1900 – but no local premières. Of particular artistic importance to him was the inclusion of Mozart's operas in his Berlin schedule for the first time, and along with the new production of *Così fan tutte*, which he performed five times that season, he gave eight performances of *Don Giovanni*, two of *Die Entführung aus dem Serail*, four of *Le nozze di Figaro* and three of *Die Zauberflöte*, leaving Berlin audiences in no doubt of his commitment to Mozart's music.[21]

With the exception of a concert at Elberfeld on 8 July,[22] Strauss spent most of the summer of 1900 dividing his time between Marquartstein and Pontresina. No compositions were completed during that summer and only after he returned to Berlin for the beginning of the 1900–1901 season did he finish the Lieder Opp. 48 and 49. Concurrent with the completion of those songs was a series of performances that he gave of operas by Auber, Wagner, Nicolai, Mozart and Berlioz during September and October. Of these, the Hofoper's new production of Berlioz's *Benvenuto Cellini* on 10 October was of particular importance to Strauss. Having heard Bülow perform the overture from this opera with the Meininger Hofkapelle on 27 February 1884 at Berlin, and having performed only the overture and one aria previously,[23] Strauss was eager to explore the whole opera and was able to report to his parents that the new production was a success.[24]

French opera then became something of a feature of Strauss's remaining duties that season; along with the three performances that he gave of *Benvenuto Cellini*, he conducted Auber's *Le cheval de bronze*, Bizet's *Carmen* and Saint-Saëns *Samson et Dalila*. As a boy, Strauss was enchanted by Auber's music and later he admired Bizet's and Saint-Saëns's operatic mastery. His fondness for French repertoire is also reflected in his approach to programming over the next few years. During the first full season of the new century, Strauss conducted eight-five performances of twenty-eight works by fifteen composers. Of these, nine were Austro-German, four were French and two were Italian, a ratio that was out of keeping with Germany's increasingly nationalistic stance. What makes those statistics even more remarkable is that of the four living or recently deceased composers represented in Strauss's schedule that year – Kienzl, Humperdinck, Verdi and Saint-Saëns – one was Italian and another was French. Were this approach to programming simply the consequence of the Hofoper's repertory system, then few eyebrows would have been raised, but as Verdi's *Falstaff* and Saint-Saëns's *Samson et Dalila* were two of four new productions that year[25] and as Saint-Saëns's opera was given by Strauss at least thirty-six times during his tenure as Erster Königlicher Kapellmeister, any suggestion that Strauss was a cultural chauvinist can be dismissed easily.

If the accusation of chauvinism finds Strauss's critics on shaky ground, then perhaps the case for parochialism is stronger. Five years after the failure of *Guntram*, Strauss returned to composing opera in 1901 with *Feuersnot*. Having started to discuss the work as early as 1899 with the opera's librettist, Ernst Freiherr von Wolzogen,[26] Strauss completed the score in Berlin on 22 May 1901. Based on a Flemish legend, the opera is set in medieval Munich and revolves around a sorcerer who extinguishes all the fires in the city after being

rejected by the object of his affections, only allowing them to be relit after his
amorous approaches are returned sexually. The score is witty and full of life,
and it draws on a rich palette of adventurous harmonies and melodic effects.
Feuersnot challenges the sexual *mores* of the time and is much tighter dramatically than *Guntram*. Wolzogen's liberal use of Munich dialect and his witty
references to Wagner and Strauss as victims of local artistic philistinism in
the text have often given rise to the accusation of parochialism. Considered
by some contemporary commentators as salacious, the opera did much to
reinforce the view that Strauss was an artistic subversive who liked nothing
better than to challenge the cultural and moral status quo. The fuss this opera
caused, and the technical problems that it presented, later prompted Strauss to
recall that the 'good Ernst von Schuch had accepted *Feuersnot* and, in spite of
some moral objections, it was very successfully performed [first] in Dresden
[on 21 November 1901]. . . . Its subsequent fate – especially in Berlin, where
it had to be removed from the repertoire after the seventh performance at
the instance of the Empress, whereupon the honest Generalintendant
Count Hochberg[27] handed in his resignation – is well known. Unfortunately,
Feuersnot is comparatively difficult . . . which [has] always been a handicap in
repertoire performances.'[28]

The opera's content also proved problematic elsewhere, and when
Gustav Mahler accepted it for the Vienna Hofoper, he encountered trouble
with the local censor. In June 1901, Mahler wrote optimistically to Strauss that
'*Feuersnot* is at the censor's' and 'once he passes it the agreements will be
concluded'.[29] Later that month, Mahler's optimism began to falter, causing
him to write that 'concerning *Feuersnot*, the *censor* seems, *horribile dictu*, to be
making difficulties . . . [and] I fear you may have to accept changes. At any rate
the "lirum larum"[30] will need changing, not only the words themselves but
probably more widely! Alas, there is still no placating these powers. I shall of
course pursue the matter and save what I can'.[31] On 6 July, matters deteriorated,
causing Mahler to sigh 'now as regards your *Feuersnot*! I have heard in a round-
about way that the censor is not releasing the work. Whether he is just making
difficulties, or banning it, I have not yet found out. . . . At any rate, I shall not
give in.' Mahler's perseverance seems to have paid dividends and by the end of
November he was able to report triumphantly that 'your *Feuersnot* . . . has
finally been passed here, and . . . I want to perform [it] at the beginning of
January'.[32] Strauss was overjoyed by the news and after attending the first
Vienna performance under Mahler, given on 29 January 1902, he wrote to his
friend from Berlin at 8 p.m. on 4 February 1902: 'I do not know a finer hour
than this, when you are conducting the second performance of *Feuersnot*, to
send you once more my most heartfelt thanks for the incomparably beautiful
rendition you gave of my work last week, and will, I hope, often give again. I still
revel in the recollection of the magical sound of the orchestra, the magnificent

décor created by the genius of Brioschi[33] and Löffler [sic][34] [and] the glorious poetry of sound with which the soloists and chorus delighted my ear.'[35]

After a summer walking in the Swiss resorts of Rigi-Kulm, Interlaken and Mürren, Strauss stopped briefly at Marquartstein before returning to Berlin to open the 1901–1902 season at the Hofoper with *Carmen* on 1 September. Bizet's opera was a work that he had conducted regularly every year since taking up his post in the Prussian capital in 1898, and with the exceptions of Meyerbeer's *Robert le Diable*, Auber's *Fra Diavolo* and Lortzing's *Der Waffenschmied*, all the operas that Strauss performed that season had been given previously by him in Berlin. His schedule was only marginally more demanding than the previous year with eighty-three performances of twenty-eight works by fourteen composers. Increasingly a victim of the repertory system, Strauss must have found his day-to-day routine somewhat repetitive. Composition provided no diversion from the sameness of his theatre routine: the only music that he wrote between *Feuersnot* and the first song of Op. 51 in December 1902 was the group of Lieder Op. 49, completed in September 1901.[36] His appointment as conductor of the Berlin Tonkünstler-Orchester that year, however, was an exciting development and the variety of new and colourful works that were the basis for its repertoire were a welcome distraction from his duties at the Hofoper.

Berlin Tonkünstler-Orchester (1901–1903)

Following his less than glorious seasons with the Berlin Philharmonic and the Munich Hofkapelle in the mid 1890s, Strauss was engaged only as a guest conductor with leading orchestras in Britain and on the Continent. Concert life in Berlin was dominated by the Philharmonic under Arthur Nikisch and the Hofkapelle under Felix Weingartner. Strauss was invited by both conductors to give concerts with their orchestras, but these either were outside the main subscription series or were shared programmes where he performed his own works.[37] Strauss's relationships with Nikisch and Weingartner were at best shaky and he seems to have been particularly dismissive of Nikisch, who had abandoned composition in favour of performance, causing Strauss to have doubts about his ability to understand Central European music fully. In his letter of 20 February 1905 to Mahler after Nikisch conducted the Berlin Philharmonic première of Mahler's Symphony No. 5 the same day, Strauss wrote:

Your Fifth Symphony again gave me great pleasure in the full rehearsal, a pleasure only slightly dimmed by the little Adagietto. But as this was what pleased the audience most, you are getting what you deserve. The first two movements, especially, are quite magnificent; the Scherzo has a quality of genius but seemed rather too long; how far the somewhat inadequate performance was responsible, I was unable to judge. At the final rehearsal your work had a great and unclouded success. The concert audience, by contrast, showed themselves somewhat more indolent intellectually, which is nothing new to you or me. Nikisch set to work with much zeal and, as far as German music suits him at all, in my opinion acquitted himself very well.[38]

Formed in 1900, the Berliner Tönkunstler-Orchester made an inauspicious start under the baton of Karl Gleitz, a musician now largely forgotten by history, and it posed no threat to either the Philharmonic or the Hofkapelle in terms of either prestige or quality.[39] Of the conductors who performed with the orchestra before Strauss, only Bruno Walter later distinguished himself internationally. Having taken up a post with the Hofoper in the autumn of 1900, Walter took charge of the orchestra's Third Subscription Concert in November that year. His enthusiasm seems to have had a positive effect on the orchestra's precision, but the programme was criticized heavily for being over-long.[40] Walter's impact on the orchestra was short-lived, however, and it was clear to its benefactors that a musician of stature was needed at the helm if it was ever to join the front-rank of Berlin ensembles. As Strauss was without an orchestra of his own, was one of the leading orchestral composers of his age and had been the protégé of the master orchestral trainer, Hans von Bülow, he seemed the logical choice. Very little is known about Strauss's negotiations with the orchestra's directors, but from his letter to Mahler dated 3 July 1901 it can be assumed that he was approached by the orchestra's management sometime earlier that year. He wrote:

Dear Friend,

I shall conduct six concerts of new works in Berlin next winter and in the second, on 18 November, I shall perform your Third or – Fourth Symphony. [Max von] Schillings told me in Munich that you are writing a Fourth that needs fewer performers than No. III.

Is that right? And if it is, would you let me have the Fourth for 18 November? I'll tell you why! The concerts are *on* the stage in the new Royal Opera House (Kroll) and I do not yet know whether I can position the boys' choir at the proper height, get hold of the six bells, etc. I should certainly be able to procure the orchestra, and I have three weeks of rehearsals at my disposal.

. . . So please send me a line to say whether I might have your Fourth for 18 Nov. *this* year, assuming, of course, that is really more convenient to perform than your Third.[41]

Although Mahler was able to confirm on 6 July that the 'Fourth [was] at the printer's'[42] and that it was likely to come 'out in *October*',[43] he intended to give the world première of the work himself with the Kaim Orchestra in Munich on

25 November. Keen to give the first Berlin performance, Strauss continued to press his friend about the work and eventually conducted it on 16 December at the Kroll.[44]

Performing for a fee of 500 Marks a performance, Strauss led seven concerts with the orchestra at the Kroll and one each in the provincial centres of Posen, Halle, Hanover and Stettin between 21 October 1901 and 24 March 1902.[45] As a committed follower of Liszt, he used his position with the orchestra to champion his hero's cause by presenting a work by the composer at ten of the eleven concerts.[46] Bruckner's rarely heard Symphony No. 3 was given at five concerts, as was Strauss's *Don Juan*. While Strauss led performances of his own music at seven concerts, he was equally concerned that music by less-known composers should be played for the Berlin public. Works by Blech, Ertel, Sgambati, Rabl and Neitzel peppered his programmes, leaving his audiences in no doubt of his support for his contemporaries. While Strauss's commitment to new music was less obvious the following season, his efforts on behalf of *Zukunftsmusik* remained constant. Liszt's works were played at five of his six Berlin concerts, while four of his own compositions were also given. But it was his twenty-five concert tour of twenty-one cities with the orchestra between 28 February and 23 March 1903 that dominated the season. With a series of interchangeable programmes that included works by Bruckner, Strauss, Liszt and Wagner, Strauss and the orchestra performed night after night in centres of both major and minor cultural importance in Germany, Austria, Italy, France and Switzerland.[47]

Even though Strauss's model must surely have been the protracted tours of Bülow and the Meininger Hofkapelle during the early 1880s,[48] international travel of this type was far from pleasurable during the first decade of the twentieth century. Strauss and his players often travelled to new venues on the day of the concerts and occasionally gave performances in different cities on the same day. The logistics of moving a full symphony orchestra that was performing major works by composers from the late nineteenth and early twentieth centuries must have been a nightmare for the orchestral porters. Even today, with modern transport and shifting equipment, touring can at best be a challenge. The punishing schedule must have left Strauss and the orchestra exhausted. From Cologne on the afternoon of 5 April 1903, where he was engaged to conduct Mozart's Requiem and Beethoven's Symphony No 9 that evening with the Gürzenich Orchestra, Strauss wrote to his parents about the trip and his concerns about the Tonkünstler Orchestra's shortcomings. While it did not disgrace itself on tour, its performances were not an unqualified success. Nevertheless, Strauss was optimistic that the group had a future and, if the management were prepared to engage better soloists and wind principals and to provide better instruments, he would be willing to continue working with it. Ever the pragmatist, Strauss was aware that this could only be achieved with a substantial injection of cash, so he asked his friend Willy

Levin[49] to drum up financial support. Backers failed to materialize, however, and after his concert with the orchestra on 7 April 1903, Strauss resigned.

BERLIN HOFOPER (1902–1908) AND THE *SALOME* SENSATION

Throughout his time with the Tonkünstler-Orchester, Strauss maintained his usual busy schedule at the Hofoper. In many ways, the 1902–1903 season resembled previous years with many of the works being carried over from the past.[50] While the operas by Wagner and Mozart were the backbone of his schedule, he did manage to chip away at his conservative Berlin audience by conducting the world première of Bernhard Scholz's 'patriotic opera "1757" ',[51] which he found less than appealing, and the Berlin premières of Max von Schillings's *Der Pfeifertag* and his own contentious *Feuersnot*. Launching the season with Meyerbeer's *Robert le Diable* on 3 September 1902, Strauss threw himself into a heavy schedule of rehearsals for Schillings's opera the next day. After two weeks of intensive preparation, Strauss mounted the podium for the first Berlin performance of *Der Pfeifertag* on 17 September. From his home in Charlottenburg, he wrote to his parents on 3 October that 'the preparation of "Pfeifertag" went splendidly, was a wonderful success and has done well at the box office. Our performance made a huge impression on Schillings; he was impressed by the vocal, choral and orchestral standard, the long rehearsals and the Prussian discipline! All of a sudden, he finds annoying Berlin a "wholly beautiful city" Yea, yea!!'[52]

Having given Schillings's opera in September, Strauss devoted much of October to *Feuersnot*. Again, there was an exhaustive period of preparation that lasted three weeks. After conducting the first concert of the Tonkünstler-Orchester's 1902–1903 season on 6 October, Strauss took a piano rehearsal of *Feuersnot* the following afternoon and gave the first Berlin performance on 28 October. That evening, *Feuersnot* was given on a double-bill with Saint-Saëns's ballet *Javotte*, also conducted by Strauss. This was the first of twenty performances that he gave of *Feuersnot* during the 1902–1903 and 1903–1904 seasons, a statistic very different from the seven performances that he mentions in his memoirs.[53] With few exceptions, Strauss usually coupled *Feuersnot* with a work by another composer and, between 1902 and 1904, it was heard regularly alongside *Javotte*, d'Albert's *Die Abreise*, Leoncavallo's *I Pagliacci* and Mascagni's *Cavalleria rusticana*.[54] By programming the opera in this way, Strauss not only placed himself firmly within a European context but also managed to placate his critics at Court, whose palates were far more in tune with artistic delicacies from Italy and France than with the more challenging *nouvelle cuisine* of his own music.

With the Tonkünstler-Orchester tour over and the Berlin première of *Feuersnot* behind him, Strauss spent much of the summer of 1903 at Marquartstein working on his third opera, *Salome*, and on his new tone poem, *Sinfonia domestica*. Back in Berlin, he opened the new season with a performance of *Don Giovanni* on 22 September. But it was the new production of *Die Meistersinger von Nürnberg* on 3 October that was the highlight of the season. The work dominated Strauss's duties that year and, of the thirty-eight performances he gave that season at the Hofoper, twelve were of *Die Meistersinger*. What is striking from those statistics is the reduction in the number of performances given by him in Berlin that season compared with earlier years. In the past, he had normally led between sixty-five and ninety-six performances each season and planned his guest engagements around his Berlin roster. In the 1903–1904 season, however, the situation was reversed, with his Hofoper duties taking second place to his major tours of Great Britain and the USA, which took him away from Berlin for four months.[55] Although the next two seasons saw him conduct sixty-one and fifty-four performances respectively at the Hofoper, he continued to tour widely with visits to Britain, the Netherlands, France, Austria and provincial Germany, a consequence of his increasing fame both as a composer and as a conductor.

With the world première of *Salome* at Dresden on 9 December 1905, Strauss's international fame skyrocketed, making him both a musical megastar and the most talked about musician of his age. The impact of *Salome* was massive, prompting outrage and disgust in some and awe and amazement in others. After the first performance under Ernst von Schuch, the theatre rocked to the sound of thirty-eight curtain calls, while the local bars and cafés trembled from the shaking of critics' heads. The unflappable Strauss delighted in the mixed response and later wrote:

As soon as Schuch had had the courage to undertake to produce *Salome*, the difficulties began: during the first reading rehearsal at the piano, the assembled soloists returned their parts to the conductor with the single exception of Mr. Bur[r]ian,[56] a Czech, who, when asked for his opinion last of all, replied: 'I know it off by heart already'. Good for him. After this the others could not help feeling a little ashamed and rehearsals actually started. During the casting rehearsals Frau Wittich,[57] entrusted the part of the sixteen-year-old Princess with the voice of Isolde (one just does not write a thing like that, Herr Strauss: either one or the other), because of the strenuous nature of the part and the strength of the orchestra, went on strike with the indignant protest to be expected from the wife of a Saxon Burgomaster: 'I won't do it, I'm a decent woman'.[58]

With a plot that depicted the severed head of John the Baptist and a dance that was sure to titillate, the opera soon proved contentious and a magnet for the censors. Wilhelm II initially banned the work in Berlin until the

Hofoper's Intendant, Baron Georg Hülsen-Haeseler,[59] 'had the bright idea of signifying the advent of the Magi at the end by the appearance of the morning star!'[60] When Mahler scheduled *Salome* for performance in Vienna, the ironically named censor, Cardinal Piffl,[61] put his foot down, causing the work's Austrian première to be shifted to Graz, where Strauss conducted it on 16 May 1906 before an audience that included Gustav and Alma Mahler, Arnold Schoenberg, Alexander Zemlinsky, Alban Berg, Giacomo Puccini, Wilhelm Kienzl and the young Adolf Hitler, who was outraged by the opera's decadence. In New York, *Salome* was considered so salacious that after its first performance at the Metropolitan Opera House on 22 January 1907 it was not heard there again until 1933. In London, the work 'had been banned . . . for its religious implications,'[62] which inevitably meant that the great, if not the good, were keen to hear it. The distinguished Polish pianist Arthur Rubinstein, an early and passionate advocate of *Salome* who knew Strauss and who was also able to play the entire score from memory, recalled in his memoirs:

> King Edward VII had expressed curiosity to hear [part of] it. . . . The concert and the reception took place at three in the afternoon. There were not more than thirty guests, and the King was the last to arrive. Four of the ladies present were pointed out to me as sometime mistresses of His Majesty. He had good taste, I must admit – all four of them were beautiful . . . . [A] small platform [had been] built at one end of the room, with a fine Bechstein grand rented especially for me. The King settled down in front, quite close to the platform, and the others sat around him. My performance of the 'Dance of the Seven Veils' was well received; at least, they listened to this modern music in silence. . . . Olive Fremstad[63] . . . [then] sang the difficult long lament of Salomé with perfect intonation and in a grand style. . . . [A]ll the while she was singing, the King puffed at a big cigar and blew the smoke right into her face; it was something short of a miracle that she was able to overcome such a handicap. After the concert tea was served, Madame Fremstad and I were introduced to His Majesty. . . . The King had a sonorous voice and spoke with a slight German accent. He had some warm words of praise for Madame Fremstad and then turned to me for a discussion about the merits of Strauss's opera. 'I did not notice anything shocking in what I heard, and I cannot understand why our censors objected to it', he said. Obviously, he expected to be a little scandalized and was secretly disappointed.[64]

Paris also succumbed to *Salome* fever and even before the local première was given, the city was alive with speculation about the opera, prompting Strauss's good friend, the writer Romain Rolland,[65] to write 'Your *Salomè* is creating the devil of a row in that little provincial town, the Paris-that-matters of the theatres and boulevards. You should know about it: the question which is being discussed at the moment is much less a question of Art than a question of actresses, who are quarrelling in advance over the part of *Salomè*. Each has her adherents. And what is comic is that both sides, fancying (I can't think why) that I have some influence with you, have come to see me to ask me to bring my influence to bear on you the way they wish.'[66]

As *Salome* prompted such a seismic response, it was almost inevitable that managements would be clamouring for Strauss to conduct it at their theatres. In the first year after the Dresden première, the opera was staged by no fewer than sixteen theatres and Strauss was keen to be involved with as many productions as possible. After leading the first Munich production of *Feuersnot* on 23 December 1905,[67] Strauss conducted a total of sixty performances of *Salome* at Graz, Prague, Cologne, Berlin, Turin, Paris, Amsterdam, Rotterdam, Arnhem, Naples and Warsaw between 16 May 1906 and 20 February 1908.[68] Not all met Strauss's expectations. Of the Dutch performances, he recalled that

> What I was to find in Amsterdam beggars all description. I had at my disposal for *one* dress rehearsal a miserable Italian troupe hardly capable of managing more than a sixth-grade performance of *Il Trovatore* and which did not know its parts, and a beer garden orchestra. . . . It was dreadful and yet I could not resign without risking an enormous indemnity. In the circumstances, it had to be carried through to the bitter end. I concluded the evening full of shame and annoyance. . . . My old friend Justizrat Fritz Sieger . . . had by chance attended the performance [and] told me afterwards that it had been quite a good performance and he liked it very well indeed. Can it be that the hypnotism of my baton was such that even a connoisseur overlooked the shortcomings of the performance, or is it simply impossible to kill the opera? I think the latter must have been the case.[69]

The Paris production was a far more positive experience and amongst the audience was Strauss's friend Romain Rolland, who was bowled over by the work. Still reeling under the impact of the third local performance, he wrote:

> If I have not yet seen you, it is because I was shaken by so many tumultuous and diverse emotions after hearing your *Salomé* for the first time, that I did not want to speak to you about it before hearing it again. . . . Your work is a meteor, the power and brilliancy of which commands the attention of everyone, even those who don't like it. It has conquered the public. It has even got the better of certain antipathies of temperament. I saw a well-known French musician who hated it, but who had just heard it for the third or fourth time: he couldn't tear himself away from it; he was grumbling, but he was caught. I don't think that one could find a more manifest proof of your

power. That power is, so far as I am concerned, the greatest in musical Europe today.[70]

Having agreed the staggering sum of 60,000 Marks for *Salome* with his publishers, Fürstner, and having struck lucrative deals with the managements of the houses in which he conducted it, Strauss wanted to reduce his commitments at the Hofoper. Never fully at ease with the repertory system, he cut the number of opera performances that he gave there by a quarter in the 1906–1907 and 1907–1908 seasons and began to turn more of his attention to the concert platform.[71] After the experiment of the Tonkünstler-Orchester, Strauss was keen to be associated only with the best Berlin ensembles and signed an initial three-year contract on 14 April 1908 to replace Felix Weingartner as conductor of the Berlin Hofkapelle's Subscription Concerts from the beginning of the 1908–1909 season. On 23 April 1908, he left with the Berlin Philharmonic on a thirty-one concert tour of Germany, France, Spain, Portugal and Switzerland.[72] But Strauss's shift of emphasis might well not have been possible had *Salome* failed. It marked a watershed in his career and provided him with the financial security to explore new musical avenues and to enjoy a lifestyle that was the envy of the musical world. Of the income that the opera provided, the composer famously recalled 'William the Second once said to his Intendant [Hülsen-Haeseler]: "I am sorry Strauss composed this *Salome*. I really like the fellow, but this will do him a lot of damage". The damage enabled me to build my villa in Garmisch.'[73]

CHAPTER 6

At the Summit
GENERALMUSIKDIREKTOR AT BERLIN (1908–1920)
AND BEETHOVEN STYLE

BERLIN HOFKAPELLE (1908–1920)

When Strauss took charge of the Berlin Hofkapelle in 1908, the orchestra had already gained a formidable reputation as one of the world's most distinguished ensembles. Competing openly with the newly reconstituted Berlin Philharmonic from the late 1880s,[1] the Hofkapelle had a proud heritage that could be traced back to the time of Prince-Elector Joachim II of Brandenburg in the late sixteenth century. When it was established by Joachim in 1570, its role was solely that of a court orchestra, but with the founding of the Hofoper by Frederick the Great in 1742, it began its metamorphosis into the orchestra that it is today.[2] From the middle of the nineteenth century, its Subscription Concerts were conducted for lengthy periods by Wilhelm Taubert, Robert Radecke, Ludwig Deppe, Heinrich Kahl and Josef Sucher, before being taken over by Felix Weingartner in October 1891.[3] Weingartner was unimpressed by the orchestra's playing at his Hofoper début the previous May[4] and he later recalled that the musicians had a habit of playing with 'an indeterminate mezzoforte, to which they seemed to have become addicted'.[5] Determined to drag the players out of their mire of artistic apathy, he went back to the musical drawing board and insisted that by 'conscientiously following all the dynamic instructions and by rhythmical phrasing',[6] they could begin the slow process of artistic reconstruction. Weingartner's simple but meticulous approach paid off quickly and the orchestra's playing soon began to be compared favourably with that of the Philharmonic.

When Weingartner was appointed Mahler's successor as Director of the Vienna Hofoper on 1 January 1908, he withdrew from the Berlin Hofkapelle, leaving the way open for Strauss to take charge of the orchestra from the 1908–09 season, the same season in which Strauss was elevated to the rank of Generalmusikdirektor.[7] That year, he conducted seven of the Hofkapelle's eleven concerts, with the remainder being led by Leo Blech, Robert Laugs, Edmund von Strauss and Hugo Rüdel.[8] With the exception of Berlioz's 'Le Roi

Lear' Overture at his third concert on 6 November, all the works were from the Austro-German repertoire. Ranging chronologically from Bach's Brandenburg Concerto No. 1 to his own *Sinfonia domestica*, Strauss explored the music of his great Central European predecessors, including works by Haydn, Mozart, Beethoven, Weber, Schumann, Liszt, Wagner and Mahler.[9] On 15 January 1909, Strauss conducted Mahler's Symphony No. 4, a work that he had first performed with the Berlin Tonkünstler-Orchester. Over the next ten years, he went on to give two performances of Mahler's Symphony No. 1 ('Titan') and one each of Symphonies Nos 2 and 3 and *Das Lied von der Erde*. Of those performances, that of the Third Symphony on 11 December 1911 was of particular personal significance to Strauss, as it was the first work by Mahler that he gave after his friend's tragically early death. Strauss had been in contact with Mahler throughout his illness and tried to cheer him up before he died by inviting him to conduct the work with the Hofkapelle. From Garmisch on 11 May, Strauss wrote optimistically 'I read with great pleasure that you are feeling better and are recovering from your long illness. . . . in early December, I shall perform . . . your Third Symphony. If you would like to conduct your-self . . . it will be a pleasure to hear your lovely work under your own direction again. . . . With the heartfelt wish that you may have completely recovered soon, and with very best wishes from my wife too, who follows the news of your condition with deepest sympathy.'[10]

Sadly, Mahler's condition was too advanced for any recovery to be possible and he died in Vienna on 18 May 1911. His death had a devastating effect on Strauss, who confided to his diary:

> Gustav Mahler died on 19 May [*sic*] after a grave illness. The death of this aspiring, idealistic, energetic artist is a heavy loss. . . . The Jew Mahler could still be uplifted by Christianity. The hero Richard Wagner descended to it again as an old man, under the influence of Schopenhauer. It is absolutely clear to me that the German nation will only find new strength through liberation from Christianity. Are we really once again as we were at the time of the political union of Charles V and the Pope? Wilhelm II and Pius X?
>
> I will call my *Alpine* Symphony the Antichrist, because in it there is: moral purification by means of one's own strength, liberation through work, worship of glorious, eternal nature.[11]

Given Strauss's interest in the great figures of Central Europe's musical past and given the Prussian court's lack of cultural adventure, it was entirely under-standable that he should inaugurate his tenure with the Hofkapelle with a season consisting largely of established masterpieces. Apart from the *Sinfonia domestica* and Mahler's Symphony No. 4, the compositions were all standard fare that did little to challenge the expectations of his conservative local audience. From the 1909–1910 season, however, that changed sharply after Strauss adjusted the content of the Abonnement Concerts to include his own music, works by his contemporaries and novelties from the past. Between 5 October 1909 and 26 March 1910, he programmed music by five living composers – Gernsheim, Mahler, Hochberg, Schillings and Strauss – at his twelve concerts.[12] Of these works, three were Hofkapelle first performances and one was a world première. Strauss's passion for the new and the colourful continued throughout the rest of his tenure: he conducted all his own tone poems from *Macbeth* to *Eine Alpensinfonie*, a staggering thirty-six Hofkapelle first performances and an impressive eighteen world premières by fifteen composers.[13] He believed fully that 'great music and kitsch will make their own way, Masters of the second rank need promoting. What I perform must please not me alone but also the public. Let time be the judge. Better to overestimate twenty than bar the way to one. With me, nobody had better try to subscribe to conservatism.'[14]

Understandably, works by composers such as Rüfer, Scheinpflug, Böhe, Kaun and Atterberg were unfamiliar to Berlin audiences, but it seems remarkable today that some important compositions by Bach, Handel, Haydn, Weber and Bruckner had not previously been given at the Hofkapelle's Subscription Concerts. For musicians of Strauss's generation, the arch of music history effectively began with J. S. Bach and ended with their contemporaries. Their involvement with the pre-Bach repertoire was minimal and was considered a niche interest. As a child of his time, Strauss rarely ventured into the dark historic mists of the early Baroque and beyond, but he was concerned that his Berlin public should hear unfamiliar masterpieces by Bach and Haydn and that his orchestra should experience the music that was the basis for the emerging canon. During Weingartner's tenure, the Bach repertoire consisted of the Orchestral Suites Nos. 1, 2 (edited by Bülow) and 3, the Concerto for Two Violins in D minor, the Keyboard Concerto in D minor and Brandenburg Concerto No. 3, while the Haydn repertoire was restricted to the ever-popular last twelve symphonies. Strauss took a slightly different tack by presenting all six Brandenburg Concertos and by conducting an overview of Haydn's symphonic output ranging from the early Symphony No. 7 ('Le midi') to No. 104 ('London').

The works that dominated Strauss's subscription schedule, however, were those of Mozart and Beethoven. As a passionate advocate of Mozart from his earliest years, Strauss jumped at the chance to present familiar and unfamiliar works by Mozart to his Berlin audience. During the nineteenth and early twentieth centuries, conductors shied away from much of Mozart's output and only performed regularly some of the composer's most famous music. The works heard annually at most subscription series were the last thee symphonies and little else. Mozart's piano concertos were virtually boycotted by pianists: during Weingartner's tenure with the Hofkapelle, no Mozart piano concerto was played, while in Vienna only two performances of them were programmed by the Philharmonic during its first hundred years, 1842 to 1942.[15] Dismissed as insignificant, the concertos struggled in the concert hall, prompting the great Austrian pianist Artur Schnabel[16] to recall that 'in Vienna, Albert J. Gutmann,[17] . . . a very enterprising and rather influential [impresario] . . . arranged a private concert for me [when I was eight], to arouse interest in my talent. It was given in a small hall connected with his piano salesrooms. I played the D minor concerto by Mozart, still considered a work accessible chiefly to children . . . a traditional misconception . . . [with] an astonishing longevity.'[18] Strauss shared Schnabel's passion for the piano concertos and he gave three of them during his time with the Hofkapelle.[19]

It was Beethoven's music, however, that occupied Strauss most with the Hofkapelle. Of the 125 concerts that he led with the orchestra between 2 October 1908 and 2 March 1920, 106 contained a work by Beethoven. Today, that figure seems remarkably high, but in the context of the Hofkapelle's history as a whole it is not particularly significant and was in keeping with the schedules of previous principal conductors. For Strauss, Beethoven's works were pivotal and were the programmatic core around which other works revolved. In general, he liked to place them side by side with novelties and masterworks from the past and he restricted complete cycles of the symphonies to the 1914–1915 and 1915–1916 seasons. Even then, the works were not performed in numerical order and only four concerts during those two seasons were all-Beethoven. While Strauss performed all nine symphonies regularly during his Berlin period, the work that he gave most often was the Ninth, which he usually conducted at the last concert of the season, a practice that was common in Germany at that time.

Less common was Strauss's fondness for conducting the symphony twice on the same day, a practice that bore a striking resemblance to Bülow's habit of giving the work twice at the same concert. Bülow pioneered this method at Meiningen on 19 December 1880 and repeated the experiment with the Hofkapelle on 2 April 1881 and 2 April 1884[20] before extending it to the Berlin Philharmonic on 6 March 1889. Bülow's bizarre approach to programming the Ninth Symphony must have been taxing for musicians and audiences alike, but they were warned in advance of his intentions: the programme for the 1880 performance and the posters for the 1881 and 1884 concerts stated clearly that the symphony would be heard twice. Bülow's double performances of the work soon became an accepted part of his performance style at Meiningen and only a handful of listeners left the auditorium after the first reading. While Strauss's approach to the Ninth Symphony was not quite as challenging as that of Bülow, his double performance of it on 26 March 1910 must have stretched both the orchestra and the choir to their limits. For variety, however, the companion piece at the matinee was Schumann's Symphony No. 2, while at the evening concert Beethoven's Overtures to *Coriolan* and *Leonore* No. 3 were played. More taxing still was Strauss's *penchant* for conducting two different programmes on the same day to mark the end of a subscription season. Often, the first concert would contain the Ninth Symphony and the second would involve either the 'Eroica' or Symphony No. 5 – a work that Strauss famously recorded with his Berlin orchestra in 1928 for Deutsche Grammophon and of which he was considered a master interpreter.

BEETHOVEN STYLE AND SYMPHONY NO. 5

Beethoven's Symphony No. 5 was a work of special significance to Central European conductors and was afforded a special place in their performance style. Strauss was particularly smitten with the piece and in an attempt to penetrate its content and that of the other eight symphonies, he annotated two sets of scores.[21] The first was edited by Friedrich Chrysander[22] and was published by the firm of Rieter-Biedermann of Leipzig and Winterthur. This set is heavily worn, marked extensively in lead and blue pencil, and it was probably used by Strauss until the end of his Berlin period. Owned originally by his father, the scores were given to Franz as a thank-you present by the Intendant of the Munich Hofoper, Baron Karl von Perfall, on 19 April 1873, after he took part in a performance of Wagner's *Rienzi* on 2 April 1873.[23] The second set was edited by Wilhelm Altmann and was published by the firm of Ernst Eulenburg. This set contains tempo, phrase and expression marks inserted by Strauss largely in red ink. The Eulenburg scores include hand-written comments that relate to Strauss's performance style in general, his acceptance of some of Wagner's ideas on retouching, and his recollection of some of Bülow's practices and principles as a conductor of Beethoven's symphonies. Strauss's reasons for annotating the Eulenburg scores so heavily are unclear but, as the comments are often didactic, it is possible that he intended them for publication. What is clear, however, is that when he inserted an annotation it usually remained unaltered: while there were a few small exceptions, once Strauss had decided upon an interpretation, it remained fixed.

The articulation of the four-note motif in the first movement of the Fifth Symphony was of particular importance to Strauss and on the first page of his Eulenburg score he writes dramatically that 'this movement must be stormy throughout and played with the highest excitement and thundering character. I also reject the idea of broadening the opening bar. The first of each quaver group (or second respectively) must be accented. At the beginning, I recommend that no up-beat is given, because the first crotchet beat might be taken too quickly, resulting in .[24] It is unsurprising that he commonly

adds an accent above the first note of the motif throughout much of the movement. For Strauss, this accent not only ensured greater clarity of articulation
but also provided a means by which to control the potentially unstable
rhythmic figure when played in *accelerando* passages. He was also aware that
the first movement had other potential articulation hazards, so at bar 33 he
also inserts accents above the third and fourth quavers, ensuring that 'the two
last quavers of each group should not be garbled'.[25] Characteristically, Strauss
took great care over the interpretation of the first movement's second subject
and, at bar 63 in the Eulenburg score, he draws attention to the *tenuto* mark
that he inserted above the bar's first crotchet and notes that no *crescendo*
should be made in bars 64 and 65. The *tenuto* is also added in the Chrysander
score and, again, it is clear that the centre of the asymmetrical three-bar phrase
should be considered within the line as a whole and that it should not be
interrupted unnecessarily.[26]

In general, Strauss was restrained when adding bowing to his scores and he
stands in sharp contrast to conductors such as Sir John Barbirolli and Clemens
Krauss,[27] who marked their scores and parts in detail. When performing
Mozart, for example, Strauss bowed selected movements in Symphonies
Nos. 29 and 40 but none in the 'Jupiter'.[28] In his scores of the Beethoven
symphonies, Strauss again bows sparingly and, in his Chrysander and the
Eulenburg scores of Symphony No. 5 he annotates only one passage specifically: bars 198 to 207 of the first movement, in which he inserts a series of
repeated down-bows.[29] There are, however, a number of implied bowings in
the scores, especially in the first and last movements. From bar 38 in the first
movement, for example, Strauss inserts accents above the last two quavers of
each bar, suggesting that he wants two consecutive up-bows, both of which are
to be articulated by stopping the bow on the string. At bar 48 in the last movement, Strauss marks a slur over the second half of the first beat and the first
half of the second beat, indicating that the triplets and the following crotchet
are to be articulated by a single bow.[30] Like Weingartner, Krauss and other
conductors whose practical knowledge of woodwind and brass playing was
limited, Strauss makes very few changes to the printed phrasing of those parts,
but does stress that each of the rising piccolo figures in the last movement from
bar 330 in the Eulenburg score and bar 346 in the Chrysander score should be
played *legato*.[31]

In his 'Ten Golden Rules' for young conductors, Strauss wrote famously
'Never look encouragingly at the brass, except with a short glance to give an
important cue', 'never let the horns and woodwind out of your sight: if you can
hear them at all they are still too strong' and 'if you think that the brass is not
blowing hard enough, tone it down another shade or two'.[32] Although written
with tongue firmly in cheek, Strauss's suggestions were a statement of policy
that he adhered to for much of his career. For him, the balance between the

brass, the percussion and the other orchestral voices was of paramount importance and he regularly reduced the dynamics of the brass and the percussion
to secure the work's 'melos', which John Barbirolli later defined as 'the unifying
thread of line that gives a work its form and shape'. Between bars 6 and 12 in
the last movement, for example, he inserts in both scores a series of *fortepiano*
markings followed by *crescendos* to *forte* that ensures not only that the musical
line in the woodwind and the first violins is heard clearly, but also that the
dynamic direction of the *fortepiano* bars is distinct. In the Eulenburg score,
Strauss makes clear the importance of this gesture by writing that 'the afore-
mentioned dynamic reduction in the brass in this movement seems absolutely
essential'.[33]

Of Beethoven's Ninth Symphony, Strauss wrote at the beginning of his
Eulenburg score:

> Everything that we know about this symphony comes from Rich. Wagner.
> Concerning Wagner's orchestrational retouchings, I personally counsel against
> the alteration to the trumpet part at the beginning of the last movement. The
> original is characteristic and sounds 'modern' enough![34] I completely reject
> the aforementioned coarse alterations of Gustav Mahler (although they were
> made with the best of intentions!).[35]

Although Strauss felt that Mahler's wholesale adjustments to Beethoven's Ninth
Symphony went too far, he subscribed happily to most of Wagner's suggestions
on retouching this symphony and the others in the set. Nevertheless, he exer-
cised prudence when altering the text of Symphony No. 5. The only example in
the first movement is in the bars directly preceding the recapitulation of the
second subject. Here, Strauss strengthens the bassoons with the horns, an
adjustment that was common well into the twentieth century.[36] In the second
movement, his alterations are more extensive because he adds the oboes to the
rest of the woodwinds between bars 185 and 190, and strengthens these instruments further in bars 245 and 246 by adding the trumpets and horns.[37] In the
last movement, Strauss's modifications to the text are again minimal, the only
adjustment occurring from bar 391, where the bass and later tenor trombones
double the lower strings and the bassoons.[38]

For Central European conductors from the late nineteenth and early twentieth centuries, tempo was a means by which to define the structure of individual movements and to unify works as a whole. Strauss was a keen advocate
of this approach and, in his 1928 recording of the Fifth Symphony, linked the
tempo of the opening four-note motif, ♩=88, to the speed of the second movement from bar 22 and the core tempo of the last movement. Similarly, the speed
of the first movement from bar 6, ♩=92, is linked to that of the central section
of the third movement, while the opening tempo of the third movement, ♩=96,

is heard again when the material is repeated after the fourth movement's development and at the transition passage in the last movement from bar 294. Within each movement of Symphony No. 5, Strauss establishes a series of core speeds around which his interpretation revolves. In the first movement, his principal tempos are $\boldsymbol{J}$=88, $\boldsymbol{J}$=92 and $\boldsymbol{J}$=100, while in the last movement they are $\boldsymbol{J}$=76, $\boldsymbol{J}$=84, $\boldsymbol{J}$=88 and $\boldsymbol{J}$=96. In keeping with contemporary trends, Strauss reduces the speed of the second subject of sonata form movements in quick tempi. In the first movement, he deceives the ear by increasing the tempo of the bridge passage to $\boldsymbol{J}$=100 before reducing the speed at the second subject to $\boldsymbol{J}$=92, the tempo of the first subject from bar 6, while in the last movement he reduces the speed of the second subject marginally from $\boldsymbol{J}$=88 to $\boldsymbol{J}$=84.

Central to Strauss's interpretation of Symphony No. 5 is his approach to the pauses. In the first movement, he treats the pauses metrically and indicates his desired length for each fermata in his Eulenburg score. In general, the pauses are held for six beats with the exceptions of bar 21, which is held for four beats, and bars 479 and 482, which are each held for eight beats. For the pause and cadenza in bar 268, Strauss was clearly influenced by Wagner's comment that 'I have since found it impossible . . . to permit the touching cadence . . . to be played in the customary timid and embarassed way',[39] and by writing 'sehr langsam Fermata' ('very slow pause') above the cadenza in his score, Strauss makes clear not only his debt to Wagner but also the importance of nine-teenth-century techniques to his interpretation as a whole.

BERLIN HOFOPER (1908–1919)

Strauss remained active as an opera conductor throughout his tenure with the Hofkapelle, but from 1908 onwards he reduced sharply the number of performances he gave annually. In the 1908–1909 season, he led only eight performances of six works by four composers, considerably less than the eighty or so performances that he regularly conducted each season during his early years at the Hofoper. During his eleven years as Generalmusikdirektor from 1908 to 1919, Strauss led only 234 performances in contrast to the 688 that he had given during his period as Erster Königlicher Kapellmeister. With the exceptions of the 1909–1910 and 1912–1913 seasons, when he conducted thirty and twenty-eight performances respectively, his schedule leading up to World War One was relatively light. In the 1911–1912 season, for example, the number of performances dipped to five, but with the outbreak of war his commitment rose and during the four years of hostilities he led on average twenty-seven performances a season. Of the fourteen composers presented during those years, only Strauss and Schillings were living and only Bizet, Auber, Rossini and Verdi were not from the German-speaking countries.

The core of Strauss's wartime and immediate post-war schedules were his own works and those of Wagner and Mozart. The bulk of his Wagner performances involved *Der fliegende Holländer, Lohengrin, Tristan und Isolde, Die Meistersinger von Nürnberg* and *Die Walküre*, all good patriotic fare. No complete cycle of the *Ring* was given, but *Parsifal* was added to his personal repertoire on 29 March 1917. Mozart's works also continued to occupy him, and even during the darkest days of the War and the political chaos that ensued in its immediate aftermath he led new productions. On 5 December 1917, the 126th anniversary of Mozart's death, for example, the Hofoper's new production of *Die Entführung aus dem Serail* was given its première. Considered the pre-eminent Mozart interpreter of his age, Strauss was praised widely for his sensitive handling of the opera, prompting one critic to write 'yesterday, in the Royal Opera House, "Entführung" reappeared on the programme for the first time since the departure of [Frieda] Hempel.[40] . . . Richard Strauss, from whom we have already had such an exquisite "Figaro" and "Così fan tutte", returned to the podium, and in whose refined hands, with his tender love of Mozart, created some interesting effects. The aria "Marten aller Arten" could be heard once again without its customary cuts.'[41]

Seventeen months later, Strauss conducted a new production of *Don Giovanni* on 25 April 1919. Given for the first time only two months after the founding of the new republic at Weimar, and at a time when Berlin was being torn apart by warring political factions,[42] Strauss seems to have detached himself from the capital's troubles by looking back to the halcyon days of his second Munich period when political stability reigned and when musical innovation was the principal source of dissent in an opera house. Many of the Mozart reforms that he championed in Munich with Possart in 1896 were incorporated into the new production, causing one critic to report: '. . . the poster noted the revised translation of Hermann Levi . . . [who] has, in undertaking this task, attempted to translate the original Italian as closely as possible. The frequent scene-changes that are required here are made simple by the revolving stage . . . the lighter Finale (Sextet) concludes the work within a Buffo context . . . Dr. Richard Strauss is an accomplished Mozart interpreter.'[43]

Strauss's innovative continuo style with its carefully chosen references to his own works also caught the attention of the Berlin critics:

Now the [political and artistic] obstacles and dangers that have gradually become so inevitable in the Opera House have been overcome, the new production of *Don Giovanni* finally appeared yesterday. We had been threatened with the new prize-winning translation, but then heard no more of it; Hermann Levi's edition was finally used, a version which preserves with the greatest care what is to be regarded, to judge by the model before us, as the intention of the author of the text and also of the composer. Musical direction was under Richard Strauss, so that there came from the orchestra an abundance of most exquisite sound, quite impossible to describe. Indescribable in the truest sense of the word were all the fine features of nuance, the changes of tempo, and the muting and swelling of the orchestra. In addition, there was the inimitable style of accompaniment of the secco recitative, a sheer pleasure to listen to in itself. . . . But the orchestra also demanded its share of attention with its fine strings and glorious wind instruments and over them all the magic baton wielded by Richard Strauss. [44]

The sharp reduction in the number of performances given by Strauss in Berlin from 1908 was the result of a perceived *volte-face* that he experienced after his triumph with *Salome*. No longer was he considered a conductor-composer but, rather, a composer-conductor. That change of perception was reinforced by the spectacular success of his next three operas *Elektra*, *Der Rosenkavalier* and *Ariadne auf Naxos*, all of which were composed to librettos by the celebrated Vienna poet Hugo von Hofmannsthal. Completed at Garmisch on 22 September 1908 and first performed in Dresden under Ernst von Schuch on 25 January 1909, *Elektra* was considered by some to be a flawed masterpiece and the last work of importance to come from Strauss's pen. Alfred Einstein held this view and wrote in 1934:

[*Elektra*] is one of the most grandiose of Strauss's works . . . [and] it is one of the most unevenly proportioned, since the climax comes at the beginning, in Electra's [*sic*] first monologue. It is one of the least satisfying, since from the moment of the murder of Clytaemnestra [*sic*] it is no longer Electra [*sic*] who is the principal figure, but the matricide Orestes. . . . Everything that Strauss wrote without Hofmannsthal, everything in which he depended on his own resources – *Schlagobers* (Whipped Cream), *Intermezzo* and other works – was an absolute failure and a catastrophe. Everything that Strauss has written since *Elektra* outside the field of opera is not only work of secondary importance but second-rate, from the *Alpine Symphony* to the piano concerto.[45]

Strauss was certainly aware of *Elektra*'s contentious qualities and the extent to which it challenged existing notions of tonality, prompting him to recall wittily in his memoirs that 'during one of the first orchestral rehearsals Schuch, who was very sensitive to draughts, noticed in the third balcony of the empty theatre a door which had been left open by a charwoman. Full of annoyance, he shouted: "What are you looking for?" I replied from the front stalls: "A triad".'[46]

Elektra soon became the talk of the musical world and it was quickly taken up by theatres around the globe. Within days of the Dresden première, it had its first New York performance at the Metropolitan Opera under Cleofonte Campanini[47] on 28 January 1909. The opera houses of Munich, Berlin, Hamburg, Vienna and Milan were the next to fall under the work's spell with local premières over the next three months.[48] While Strauss attended the Berlin, Vienna and Milan performances, he only conducted the opera for the first time on 13 October 1909 in Berlin. That was the first of twenty-two performances of it that he gave during his Hofoper tenure. From 1915, he often preceded the opera with one of his tone poems on the same evening,[49] a practice that he initiated when he coupled *Tod und Verklärung* with *Salome* on 26 November 1914.[50]

The success that Strauss enjoyed as a theatre composer with *Salome* reached its peak with his fifth opera, *Der Rosenkavalier*. First given at the Dresden Hofoper under Schuch on 26 January 1911, the work again caused a sensation with its morally challenging opening scene and its sexually explicit use of horns in the Prelude to Act 1, playing erotically charged whooping figures moments before the ageing Marschallin and the young Octavian are exposed on stage enjoying a moment of post-coital bliss. Strauss must have known that censors around the world would be scrambling for their rulebooks. In some theatres either the bed had to be removed or the lovers were detached from it, and in others the language had to be altered because it was considered coarse. But with this came notoriety, and so eager was the public to be scandalized after the première that extra trains had to be scheduled between Berlin and Dresden to meet the demand. Within weeks of that famous first performance, Europe's leading theatres competed for the privilege of shocking their audiences. First came Nuremberg on the day after the Dresden première and, within weeks, productions in Mainz, Zurich, Hamburg, Milan and Prague followed.[51] Conservative Berlin was slow to accept the work, and after yet more alterations were made to appease the sensibilities of the Empress it was finally given on 14 November 1911 under Karl Muck. Nearly a year passed before Strauss conducted it for the first time at the Hofoper[52] but he quickly went on to give a further thirty performances over the next seven seasons.

Within months of *Der Rosenkavalier*'s première, Strauss completed his next opera, *Ariadne auf Naxos*, at Garmisch on 22 July 1912. Heard for the first time at the Stuttgart Hofoper under his baton on 25 October 1912, the opera followed Hofmannsthal's adaptation of Molière's *Le bourgeois gentilhomme* on the same evening. Even though some continuity was achieved by having Strauss compose incidental music for the play, it was immediately clear that plays and operas did not necessarily appeal to the same audiences and that the juxtaposition of both genres on the same night does not guarantee a satisfying theatrical experience. To the chagrin of Strauss, who uncharacteristically conducted the world première, the play took some three hours to perform and the King of Württemberg then held an interval reception that lasted three-quarters of an hour before he could begin the opera. The evening was a disaster, prompting Strauss and Hofmannsthal to reassess their theatrical experiment and to revise the work in 1916 with a new Prologue and a shortened Opera. The new version was given first at the Vienna Hofoper by Franz Schalk on 4 October 1916 and was an instant success. Both versions were performed widely by Strauss, and of the seventeen performances of them that he gave at the Berlin Hofoper by the end of his tenure, eleven were of the 1912 version and six were of the 1916 revision.[53]

By the time Strauss first conducted the 1916 version of *Ariadne auf Naxos* at the Berlin Hofoper on 17 February 1917, it was clear that Germany had little chance of winning the war and that the privations suffered by the public would have an impact on artistic life. Matters worsened considerably at the beginning of 1918, and by the middle of the year Strauss had decided to abandon Berlin in favour of Vienna. The Austrian capital had a special place in Strauss's affections and when he was offered the post of joint Director of the Vienna Hofoper with Franz Schalk, the temptation to accept was overwhelming. He discussed the offer with Hofmannsthal, who advised him that he was not the right man for the job. Even though Strauss 'would add outward lustre to the Opera',[54] his librettist was concerned that he 'would put [his] own personal convenience, and above all the egoism of the creative musician, before the uphill struggle for the ultimate higher welfare of [the theatre]'.[55] Strauss accepted Hofmannsthal's objections and recognised 'that [he] neither could, nor would want to, accept this post today in the way Mahler filled it[,] [as] that would [only] have been possible fifteen or twenty years ago'.[56] But he 'could well imagine [himself]' participating in 'the necessary new engagements of singers and young conductors' and 'the reorganisation and rejuvenation of the magnificent orchestra'[57] and 'since I am generally regarded as a very good Mozartian and Wagnerian conductor, the works of these masters (in addition to Gluck and Weber) would be the first to be chosen for revival'.[58] Clearly determined to accept the post whatever Hofmannsthal's advice, Strauss signed a contract on 11 October 1918 to undertake joint artistic direction of the Vienna Hofoper from the beginning of 1919–1920 season.

One month later, Strauss' world ended. With the defeat of Germany on 11 November 1918, many of the social and political systems that had supported him effectively ceased. Chaos reigned on the streets of Berlin and disorder threatened the opera house. Workers' councils and unions replaced Court officials and the Hofoper was transformed into the Staatsoper. On the day of the Armistice, Strauss and the producer, Georg Dröscher,[59] accepted interim control of the Berlin theatre but within weeks of that arrangement being formalized, Strauss withdrew from its administration. On 25 November, Dröscher was appointed sole Director of the new Staatsoper, and two days later

Strauss's Vienna contract was ratified by the Austrian authorities. Over the next twelve months, Strauss honoured the remainder of his Berlin agreement, conducting twenty-eight opera performances and thirteen concerts. But it was clear to all that these engagements were the dying embers of a musical fire that had once burned so brightly. Strauss had set his sights firmly on Vienna and he was soon to be the last great composer-conductor to lead the jewel in Austria's cultural crown.

CHAPTER 7

A Poisoned Chalice

VIENNA STAATSOPER AND THE PERFORMING VERSION OF MOZART'S *IDOMENEO*

VIENNA STAATSOPER (1919–1924)

If Strauss thought that he had escaped revolutionary turmoil by exchanging Berlin for Vienna, he was sadly mistaken. With the collapse of the monarchy in Austria at the end of 1918, the newly proclaimed republic did little to quell the wildly radical behaviour of either the left or the right.[1] For the average Austrian, life in the immediate aftermath of World War One was one of financial misery, famine, disease, lack of accommodation and political uncertainty. With the pall of anarchy descending fast over Vienna, a glimmer of democratic hope occurred when a new city council was elected by universal suffrage on 4 May 1919, the first election of its kind in the capital after the fall of the monarchy. The victorious party was the Social Democrats and the Austrian capital was soon known as 'Red Vienna'. Inevitably, the new politics found its way into the recently renamed Staatsoper, which became increasingly unstable professionally and politically, reinforcing its image as a musical poisoned chalice rather than an artistic holy grail. The events following November 1918 had a toxic effect on the theatre, which quickly became a cultural and political minefield that few could negotiate safely. Even though Strauss was a battle-hardened musician who had worked his way up through the ranks of the opera-house system, he was still surprised by the wave of opposition that his appointment caused in Vienna and was taken aback when he fell victim to the machinations of the local press so soon after taking up his post as joint Director with the infamous Brucknerian, Franz Schalk.

A native of Vienna, Schalk was born on 27 May 1863 and studied composition with the great Austrian symphonist Anton Bruckner. As a member of Bruckner's inner circle, Schalk had a decisive influence on the composer and he has been attacked vigorously by many commentators for his cuts and changes to Bruckner's Fifth Symphony. Having started work as Kapellmeister at what was the Vienna Hofoper in 1900, he took charge of the Gesellschaft der Musikfreunde in 1904, was made Director of the Staatsoper in 1918, and became its joint Director with Strauss from 1 December 1919, two months after conducting the world première of Strauss's seventh opera, *Die Frau ohne Schatten*, at the Staatsoper. Composed to a libretto by Hofmannsthal and completed at Garmisch on 24 June 1917, the opera was described by Strauss as 'a child of sorrow . . . as it was completed in the midst of trouble and worries during the war, which [might have been] responsible for a certain irritation in the score, especially halfway through the third act, which was to "explode" in melodrama'.[2] The opera, the circumstances of its first performance on 10 October and the joint directorship were clearly unhappy experiences for many in the company, causing the distinguished German soprano Lotte Lehmann[3] to recall that 'the revolution was infectious: a bad crisis broke out in our Opera-house too. [The Director, Hans] Gregor[4] resigned, and in his place came the double directorate of Strauss–Schalk. Richard Strauss lent the Opera-house the lustre of his great name, and gave some wonderful evenings. But Franz Schalk devoted his life and soul and entire strength. . . . One could have safely predicted that the joint rule of two such dissimilar natures couldn't last. It soon led to great misunderstandings between the two, and this did not do the Opera any good.'[5]

Strauss was an easy target for the local press. Angry that he accepted work as a guest conductor elsewhere, the newspapers took him to task over his frequent absences from the Staatsoper. These complaints were not without foundation and he probably did not help matters much by leaving for an extended tour of South America during the first year of his appointment. Departing from Genoa on 12 August 1920, he arrived in Santos on 31 August, where he took a train to Rio de Janeiro by way of São Paolo. In Rio, he gave three concerts on 14, 16 and 18 September before moving on to Buenos Aires, where he conducted at least thirteen concerts between 14 October and 11 November. This was only the start of an extensive touring schedule during his Vienna years that took Strauss to Berlin, Linz, Donaueschingen, Graz, Prague, Freiburg, Hamburg, Munich, Innsbruck, Nuremberg, Bern, Zurich, Trieste, Breslau, Dresden, Rome, Amsterdam, Karlsruhe, Bremen, the USA, Great Britain and South America. The second tour of South America, in 1923, was with Franz Schalk, the Vienna Philharmonic and the Staatsoper, and it was intended to raise funds for the cash-strapped Viennese. In fairness, that trip could be hardly held against him, but the average local operagoer was in no mood to be placated by financial arguments and felt that Strauss wanted to have his Sacher Torte and eat it too.

Back at the Staatsoper, Strauss's schedule did little to reassure the Viennese that he was not simply going through the motions rather than applying himself with his usual missionary's zeal. With the exceptions of *Die Frau ohne Schatten*, Pergolesi's *La serva padrona*, Weber's *Abu Hassan* and Rimsky-Korsakov's *Scheherazade*, all the operas and ballets that he performed there had been in his repertoire for years. Some of his critics might have been impressed by his new production of *Così fan tutte* on 26 May 1920, while others might have considered it an indulgence, simply shrugging their shoulders in the knowledge that many conductors of Strauss's generation regularly staged their own productions. From the nature and number of the works performed, however, it seems that Hofmannsthal was right to have been concerned by Strauss's programme policy,[6] because eighty-eight of the 216 opera and ballet performances that he conducted at the Staatsoper between 1919 and 1924 were of his own works.[7] Consequently, he came under fire from all sides. The press inevitably led the attack by arguing that when Strauss deigned to be present in Vienna, all he was interested in was the performance of his own music.[8]

Much of the grumbling was probably sour grapes and today it would seem almost bizarre if Strauss had not championed his own compositions. With his appointment, Vienna had secured the world's most famous musician and it was only natural that he should explore artistic avenues that were seminal to him. The mistake was to have two Directors and to expect them to see eye-to-eye on all matters theatrical. From the outset, the division of labour was unfair, with Strauss acting as a kind of artistic adviser while Schalk was responsible for the day-to-day running of the theatre. To many, it seemed as if Schalk shouldered the burden of responsibility while Strauss basked in the glory. As the acrimony between the two Directors increased, politicians and civil servants were drawn into the dispute, and by the end of 1924 the crisis had reached its peak, and after unsuccessfully demanding Schalk's dismissal, Strauss resigned. Although his time as joint Director of the Staatsoper ended unhappily, he returned regularly to the theatre in later years and remained smitten with Vienna for the rest of his life.

STRAUSS'S PERFORMING VERSION OF MOZART'S *IDOMENEO*

One of the most contentious works to flow from Strauss's pen after resigning from the Staatsoper, but destined for its stage, was his performing version of Mozart's *Idomeneo*. All but forgotten until relatively recently, Strauss's version was not only a significant landmark in his relationship with Mozart but also an important means of resurrecting a much-neglected masterpiece. In its original form, *Idomeneo* was heard first at the Munich Residenztheater on 29 January 1781, the same theatre in which Strauss and Possart instigated their 'Mozart renaissance' in 1896. Some ten years later, Vienna also saw a revival of interest in Mozart's operas when Mahler and the designer Alfred Roller[9] created a sensation with their new productions of *Don Giovanni, Die Zauberflöte, Le nozze di Figaro, Die Entführung aus dem Serail* and *Così fan tutte*. While these Vienna performances were edited heavily by Mahler, they were also described as a 'Mozart renaissance' by his friend, the distinguished musicologist Guido Adler,[10] and as 'revolutionary' by the historian Ilsa Barea.[11]

As a Mozart interpreter, Mahler had more in common with the traditions of the nineteenth century than the more forward-looking, historically-aware approach of Strauss. In *Le nozze di Figaro*, for example, Mahler inserted, and set to music, a whole additional scene from Beaumarchais in Act 3, while in *Così fan tutte* he reworked the recitatives, altered the orchestration and dynamics, inserted and omitted passages, used parts of the overture elsewhere in the score, and interpolated other works such as divertimenti.[12] The style and extent of Mahler's alterations in Mozart's late operas cannot be found in Strauss's scores of these works, but even though his approach was usually that of a literalist who strove to strip the operas of their nineteenth century patina and to restore them to their original form, he did feel the need to resort to drastic editorial measures in returning *Idomeneo* to the stage.

After its première at Munich, *Idomeneo* was heard with revisions at the Auersperg Palace in Vienna on 13 March 1786. Although that was its last performance during Mozart's lifetime, it was resurrected occasionally during the nineteenth and early twentieth centuries with modifications. According to Gernot Gruber, the impresario and composer Anton Wilhelm Florentin von Zuccalmaglio[13] presented the opera to the public in the early nineteenth century, but altered the score and rewrote the libretto. He transferred the action from Antiquity to the period of the Hundred Years' War, gave it a new title, *Der Hof in Melun*, and replaced the recitatives with dialogue. The rest of the music remained intact, however, allowing Zuccalmaglio to boast that 'no bar has been transposed, no note has been altered'.[14] Apparently, this version met with little success, and a century later the opera fared only marginally better. After productions in Karlsruhe in 1917 and Dresden in 1925,[15] *Idomeneo* was heard in Dessau and Brunswick in 1931 to mark the 175th anniversary of Mozart's birth,[16] and the same year in new performing versions at Munich and Vienna by Ermanno Wolf-Ferrari[17] and Richard Strauss.

Strauss's version was suggested by his friend and collaborator, Clemens Krauss. It was translated and adapted into German from rhymed verse to prose by the producer Lothar Wallerstein[18] and it was later supported by a commission from the publishers, Bote & Bock.[19] The version was published by Heinrichshofen's Verlag in 1931 and the copy of the full score that was used by Strauss at the première in Vienna on 16 April 1931 is housed at the British Library.[20] The published score was subsequently revised and it was a copy of this score that was used for the 1941 Vienna revival.[21] The autograph of Strauss's interpolations and newly-composed recitatives is held at the Richard Strauss-Archiv, Garmisch-Partenkirchen,[22] and is a mine of information. Written on twenty-eight stave *"Sünova" No. 12* paper and numbered pages 1 to 65,[23] it is a useful guide to Strauss's approach, both as a performer and as a composer-editor. The cover page simply notes the title of the opera and records that the performance rights are reserved. On the inside cover, there are a number of instructions in point-form for the copyist and printer as well as details of the orchestration. This autograph is a model of practical calligraphy and it contains no major alterations or revisions, with only a handful of penciled-in rehearsal numbers and stage directions that are not found in the 1941 score. In the published score, Mozart's original material can be distinguished from that of Strauss by Heinrichshofen's Verlag's use of Breitkopf & Härtel's original plates from the *Gesammtausgabe*.[24] In the autograph, Strauss gives the relevant page numbers from the latter for each of his interpolations[25] and notes simply that the version was composed between 14 and 28 September 1930, some seven months before the first performance.

While the timeline of composition to publication is relatively clear,[26] a letter of provenance accompanying the British Library score raises other questions. Writing in German to A. Hyatt King, the publisher and antiquarian dealer Hans Schneider recalled:

Regarding the provenance of the *Idomeneo* score, let me say the following: the previous owner was F. C. Adler, the former proprietor of Edition Adler in Berlin, who, in conjunction with Heinrichshofen of Magdeburg, partly undertook responsibility for the stage-material. Herr Adler, a personal friend of Richard Strauss, directed the preparatory rehearsals for the original performance. Later, the score was given to him by R. Strauss. Herr Adler confirms that the musical insertions ['Orestes und Ajas'], and especially those marked in blue pencil, unlike those in pencil, are in the hand of the master. The latter [blue], in contrast to the former [those found in 'Orestes und Ajas'], were not made at his desk, but were added when he was on the podium. After access to comparative material, the declarations of Herr Adler are undoubtedly true.[27]

Adler was a rare combination of conductor, publisher and record company executive. Born in England in 1889, he was the chorus-master for the world première of Mahler's Symphony No. 8 at Munich in 1910 before working as an assistant conductor at the Bayreuth Festival. After conducting, publishing and administrative duties at Ljubljana, Düsseldorf and Berlin between 1911 and 1931, he moved to the United States in 1933, where he became co-founder and artistic director of the Society of Participating Artists record company.[28] The full extent of Adler's contribution either to the genesis or to the performance of Strauss's version may never be fully known, but his name does appear in the autograph.[29] Adler's reported comments seem to be open to question, since it is clear from the British Library score that Strauss inserted his markings on at least two occasions, with the majority of his insertions being made in blue pencil. These marks were then supplemented with annotations in lead pencil, some of which were later confirmed in blue. From those that were confirmed in this way, it is clear that both sets of markings were inserted by the same person, so Adler was probably mistaken when he claimed that the lead pencil annotations were not in Strauss's hand. It is also unlikely that Strauss inserted the blue pencil markings while he was actually 'on the podium', since the sheer number of these precludes that possibility, but it *is* likely that the manuscript insertion (British Library score, p. 140) containing dynamic annotations and interpolations in black ink to 'Orestes und Ajas' was made last.

The annotations found in both the British Library and the 1941 scores reveal something of Strauss's working practice, both as a creative and as a performing artist. From the detailed nature of the corrections and from the sheer volume of tempo, bowing, dynamic and expression marks that he inserted, it is clear that he was a meticulous proof-reader. When annotating a dynamic that applies to the whole orchestra, Strauss avoids the possibility of misinterpretation by marking each of the instruments and voices individually, a practice common to many of his extant performance scores. When two or more dynamics are in play, he marks each of the instruments or voices separately but often abbreviates his annotations. When he reduces the dynamic from *piano* to *pianissimo*, for example, he often simply adds a second *P* to that which already exists in print. There are a number of essential differences and omissions between the British Library and 1941 scores, including bowing, dynamic and expression marks. A curious feature of the British Library score is the way in which Strauss marks a down-bow. Unlike elsewhere in his annotated scores, he uses the inverted form of the symbol ⌐, a short-lived practice, since he reverts to his customary method of indicating a down-bow in the 1941 score. In that score, there is also a French translation of Wallerstein's text that is particularly puzzling. This is not in Strauss's hand and there is no evidence to suggest that any French performance of it was ever staged during his lifetime. Equally puzzling are the metronome marks in the 1941 score, which are also not by Strauss and do not correspond to his recorded tempos from his performance the same year.[30]

Central to Strauss's new version was his approach to the recitatives. In general, he either transformed secco recitatives into accompanied recitatives or modified the content of existing accompanied recitatives. As a champion of eighteenth-century music throughout much of his professional career, he studied closely the works of composers who made fundamental changes to the musical landscape. One such composer was Christoph Willibald von Gluck, whose operas Strauss conducted for the first time at Weimar, where he also created a performing version of *Iphigénie en Tauride* in 1890. Entitled *Iphigenie auf Tauris in drei Aufzügen für die deutsche Bühne bearbeitet* (*Iphigenie on*

Tauris in a three act reworking for the German stage), the new version reduced the opera from four acts to three, included a new translation into German by Strauss himself, reworked the recitatives, repositioned various musical numbers, and extended the final scene. The première of the version was not conducted by Strauss but by Rudolf Krzyzanowski[31] at the Weimar Hoftheater on 9 June 1900, some six years after Strauss had left the Grand Duchy. Strauss's interest in Gluck's music then remained life-long and he conducted the composer's works in the concert hall, the opera house and the recording studio. Moreover, in the Preface to his last opera, *Capriccio*, Strauss makes mention of Gluck's reforms, while in the opera itself, he develops those issues further.[32] It seems, then, that in his new version of *Idomeneo*, Strauss combined his knowledge of Gluck's reforms[33] with both existing and new material as the basis for many of the recomposed recitatives.

A feature of Mozart's approach in *Idomeneo* was his use of motif, which Strauss retains in his new performing version. Strauss regularly used motif as a fundamental tool for underpinning the dramatic unity of his own stage works, but often handled it in a different manner from either Mozart or Wagner. Strauss's biographer, Ernst Krause, believed that

> In contrast to Wagner's 'leitmotiv' Strauss developed a *motif technique* which was more a matter of feeling than of construction. . . . Strauss guided [the growth of the psychological characterization] from the germ cell of the motif. He did not employ this motif as a mere formula intended as a guide to make the contents of the dramatic situation clear to the audience. Instead he varied and transformed it, making it serve the cause of psychological elucidation like a red thread leading into the instrumental and vocal structure.[34]

Norman Del Mar developed this issue further and argued that

> Mozart's use in *Idomeneo* of interrelated thematic references is almost unique in his own work and was far ahead of its time. It was, of course, a source of continual fascination to Strauss who, in the course of turning all the *secco* recitatives into continuous symphonic structures, transformed many of the more prominent themes into something verging on Wagnerian *leit-motif*.[35]

While both Krause and Del Mar acknowledge Strauss's use of motif, they differ sharply on his approach to it, but, when both arguments are examined within the contexts of Strauss's activities as a Mozartian in general and his treatment of the recitatives in *Idomeneo* in particular, Krause's argument is persuasive.[36] In other accompanied recitatives, he preserved much of Mozart's original but reduced many of them in length. In Mozart's late operas, where the drama would be weakened by cuts, Strauss avoided them,[37] but in *Idomeneo*, where he believed dramatic tension to be at a premium, the use of judicious cuts in the accompanied recitatives and elsewhere arguably strengthens the drama and tightens the musical structure.[38]

For some commentators, Strauss's interpolations were controversial, but for others they were simply a logical means to a necessary end. The Strauss scholar Franz Trenner argued that the inclusion of Strauss's own 'Interludio' and the extensions to both the Temple Scene and the 'Scena Ultima' were in keeping with the concept of *pasticcio*.[39] The orchestration of Strauss's newly-composed material using the same forces as Mozart's original displays Strauss's textural fingerprints and these insertions are clearly identified by him and do not purport to be by Mozart. Reinhard Strohm defines *pasticcio* as a genre that 'arose in the late 17th- and early 18th-century opera house . . . selections of which ['favourite arias'] were assembled in 'new' works. In this way the required novelty was assured and the risk of failure diminished. . . . The librettist adjusted the recitative texts and altered (or parodied) the aria texts; the musical director set the recitatives anew and undertook transpositions and other adaptations. . . . An existing score is interspersed with new pieces, some of which may be by the compiler himself.'[40] Strohm's criteria certainly add weight to Trenner's thesis, which is compelling both by definition and by intent.

While Strauss notes on the title page that his version is a *'Vollständige Neubearbeitung'* ('completely new edition'), much of Mozart's original is retained and these extensively marked passages in the score provide a clear insight into Strauss's recreative process. Of the seven Mozart operas that he performed during his career, only three – *Idomeneo, Così fan tutte* and *Don Giovanni* – give any clear indication of his interpretative intentions and of these only *Idomeneo* is edited heavily.[41] The scores of *Don Giovanni* and *Così fan tutte* avoid any major alterations and differ little from the text of the *Gesammtausgabe*, Strauss's preferred edition. Although altered considerably, his *Neubearbeitung* of *Idomeneo* makes clear what is Mozart's original, Strauss' autograph clearly defines the material composed by him, and the 'Interludio' bears his name on page 193 of the 1941 score. As the publishers used Breitkopf & Härtel's original plates from the *Gesammtausgabe* for the main text of the new version, the distinction between Mozart's original and Strauss's revisions is obvious. Strauss clearly felt that as *Idomeneo* had been so neglected, his efforts on behalf of it were an extension of his Mozart renaissance, and that a kind of *pasticcio* technique was the best way to revive the work.

One of the most significant alterations to Mozart's original is Strauss's transformation of Princess Elettra (Electra/Elekra) into Ismene, a High Priestess of Poseidon. Ismene is an even less attractive figure than Elektra and is a woman of vengeance and extreme racial hatred. The reason for the change of identity probably stemmed from Strauss's long association with the character of Electra. In the summer of 1881, aged fifteen, he composed a work for chorus and orchestra based on an excerpt from Sophocles's *Electra*, which was given its first performance during his years at the Ludwigs-Gymnasium. Three decades later, in 1909, his *Elektra* received its première at the Dresden Hofoper. Its phenomenal success and the public's perception of Strauss's relationship with the character suggest that he was avoiding any direct comparison between his treatment of her and that of Mozart, a hypothesis shared by Krause:

Wallerstein's libretto transformed Elektra, with her outbursts of unbridled passion, into a priestess named Ismene, . . . The character of Ismene is undoubtedly [dramatically] weaker than that of Elektra. The change is probably due to the fact that having once solved the problem of Elektra at great depth, Strauss did not want to tackle it again in another man's work.[42]

In keeping with the Munich première in 1781, Strauss used a soprano for the character of Idamante,[43] but when the new version was revived at the Vienna Staatsoper in 1941,[44] he toyed with the idea of giving the role to a tenor. Although he finally decided against the change, his reasons for considering this possible modification make for interesting speculation. Perhaps he knew that the role of Idamante was sung by a tenor[45] at the only Vienna performance during Mozart's lifetime, or perhaps he might have felt that the proposed alteration was in keeping with the broader tenets of Mozart's revisions. Whatever the case, Strauss seems to have thought deeply about the issue but eventually opted for his first vocal love, the soprano voice. Conversely, in some of the other roles, Strauss altered or qualified the *tessitura* and made a number of changes to the material. The role of Arbaces was hardest hit with the excision of both his arias and his transformation from a tenor into a baritone. The High Priest, also a tenor in Mozart's original, becomes a bass, Ilia remains a soprano but with the qualification '*lyrischer Sopran*', while Ismene retains her original *tessitura* but is designated a '*hochdramatischer Sopran*'. With these qualifications, Strauss brings into sharp focus the difference in their characters, which he underlined further by casting the more lyric Elisabeth Schumann[46] as Ilia and the Hungarian dramatic soprano Maria Németh as Ismene[47] for the first performance in 1931.

For much of his career, Strauss was celebrated for his readings of Mozart. In the critiques of his version of *Idomeneo*, however, the tone is less reverential and the emphasis shifts from Strauss the performer to Strauss the artistic collaborator. Of the new *Neubearbeitung*, Gruber reported that Strauss's version of *Idomeneo* 'was sharply criticized for being sacrilegious, a criticism which was exaggerated, even though not without basis'.[48] This reflects Alfred

Einstein's view that the Strauss version was a 'gross act of mutilation'.[49] Other critics developed this idea, with one describing it as 'Mozart with whipped cream',[50] a clear reference to Strauss's 1922 ballet *Schlagobers* (*Whipped Cream*), and a second writing 'it is no advantage that one constantly recognizes when it is Mozart's turn to speak and when Strauss's – it is one of the weaknesses of this version'.[51] This hints at Strauss's use of *pasticcio* as the basis for his version, a catalyst for much discussion in the German and Austrian presses. One critic wrote:

> 'Idomeneo' is the boundary between the early works of Mozart and his masterpieces. It is Mozart's summation of the important operatic styles of his day: *opera seria* and the music dramas of Gluck. 'Idomeneo' has remained unknown to the public. The audience does not warm to the Cretan King. . . . The music is magnificent. There are moments of both passion and solemnity, but this does not move us personally, nor grip us in the manner of 'Figaro', 'Don Juan [Don Giovanni]' or 'The Magic Flute'. 'Idomeneo' is a product of the eighteenth century, rather than an individual creation of Mozart. But now Richard Strauss has come on the scene. He replaces all the secco recitatives throughout with accompanied recitatives. The latter make use of motifs. He writes an intermezzo [*Interludio*], bringing forth a sea monster, and adds a brilliant new finale. Strauss does not try to disguise himself as Mozart, he composes as Richard Strauss, quoting his 'ägyptische Helena'.[52] His style is often chromatic, using modulations that would have terrified the eighteenth century. This aspect of the current 'Idomeneo' is very intellectual. This change of style, from that of Mozart, will aggravate most music historians. More important, however, Strauss binds Mozart's arias tightly together, though these linking passages are often more substantial than the subsequent aria. . . . Strauss conducted and Elisabeth Schumann proved to be an expert Mozartian. . . . The audience experienced this work as an interesting experiment and expressed their respect for both Mozart and Strauss.[53]

Alfred Kalmus, writing from Vienna for the British journal *Musical Opinion*, also considered the issue of Strauss's creative involvement:

> Mozart's 'Idomeneo,' in the revised Strauss-Wallerstein version, has at last been given at the State Opera, and with great success. . . . Probably the libretto hindered previous success. In the Wallerstein version, many secco recitatives are omitted and others added: changes which have given Strauss an opportunity for the display of his art and the incorporation of much new music. Only a musician such as Strauss could attempt a like task with any hope of success, and he has achieved it. The arias remain for the most part unchanged, though they do not always retain their original position. The

ensembles and choruses are retained, though sometimes interwoven skilfully by Strauss with his own work.[54]

When the work was given its first German performance at Magdeburg on 24 April 1931[55] one critic wrote '*Idomeneo* by Mozart–Strauss: the perform-ance of Mozart's first major opera, *Idomeneo*, on Friday was an unparalleled success. *Idomeneo*, an *opera seria*, was composed for Munich in 1781. In Magdeburg, it was performed in an energetic revision by Richard Strauss (libretto: Lothar Wallerstein). Strauss, through his modern reshaping of this work, has restored it to the German stage.'[56] Another reviewer reported:

Idomeneo by Mozart–Strauss

The Magdeburg Theatre gave the German première . . . the world's attention was focused on the new version by Richard Strauss and the Vienna Staatsoper's producer, Lothar Wallerstein. Strauss's goal in this revision is to challenge historical preconceptions and to create a new entity. Strauss, an experienced man of the theatre, did not wish to conserve or change a museum piece. His god is the living theatre, not an historical experiment. He can see the eternal power of Mozart's music. However, it was necessary to revise completely this work, if it is to be made relevant to our time. The work had to be polished and concentrated. Wallerstein accomplished this with a feeling for language and an excellent sense of drama.[57]

A central theme of the two Magdeburg reviews was not simply the notion of revivification but revivification through contemporary relevance. From these reviews, there emerges a feeling of expectation based on the hope that the efforts of Strauss and Wallerstein would secure a place for *Idomeneo* in the repertoire in its revised form, a sentiment shared by Strauss, who wrote that 'if we succeed in putting this unique *opera seria* back on to the German stage, I will personally answer for my impiety to the divine Mozart if I ever actually get to Heaven!'[58]

While Strauss's version was originally intended to be part of the events held in Vienna in 1931 to mark the 140th anniversary of Mozart's death, his hope was that it would eventually take its place in the standard repertoire. After further performances at the Berlin Staatsoper in 1933 and Vienna Staatsoper in 1941,[59] he mentioned it in a letter to his young friend, the conductor Karl Böhm,[60] in which he outlined his 'artistic legacy'.[61] Even though his version has never been accepted fully, and even though it is ironic that Strauss's modifica-tions are now considered as anachronistic as Mozart's original was during the first half of the twentieth century, it has been revived in recent years in New York, London, Salzburg and Garmisch-Partenkirchen. More important, it alerted Strauss's acolyte, Fritz Busch, and his disciple, Sir John Pritchard, to a forgotten masterpiece. This eventually led to heavily-cut performances and recordings of Mozart's original score by the Glyndebourne Festival Opera in the 1950s, and the 1960s and a recording of it by Sir John with Luciano Pavarotti and the Vienna Philharmonic in the 1980s.[62] But, of course, their efforts on behalf of Mozart's original score might not have been possible without Strauss's groundbreaking work.

PART 3

A WORLD FIGURE

CHAPTER 8

A German Abroad
TOURING (1885–1914)

When Strauss resigned from the Vienna Staatsoper in 1924, he turned his back on tenure. Over the years, he had used his permanent posts at Weimar, Munich, Berlin and Vienna to support an international career that took him to some of the world's great cities. As early as the mid-1880s, his music had begun to capture the attention of the musical world on both sides of the Atlantic with his challenging works, and by the late 1890s he had become something of a superstar with his revolutionary readings of the emerging Austro-German canon of masterworks. Like Hans von Bülow before him, he used the railway and shipping networks to cross the world and to appear in city after city. A keen traveller who enjoyed the sights and sounds of the places he visited, Strauss loved attending galleries and museums and was a true child of the Baedeker age.

EARLY TOURS AND BAYREUTH

From near the beginning of his professional career, Strauss was courted openly by some of Germany's leading impresarios who competed vigorously to attract him to their series. While still an apprentice at Meiningen, he conducted the Munich première of his Symphony in F minor at the Second Subscription Concert of Munich Hofkapelle at the Odeon on 25 November 1885, and he was the pianist at the world première of his Piano Quartet in C minor with the Halir Quartet at Weimar on 8 December 1885.[1] The prestigious Frankfurt Museum Concerts then engaged him as a conductor in January 1887, where he conducted the F minor Symphony from memory. The concert was a spectacular success, prompting the renowned pianist Clara Schumann to congratulate him personally.[2] From Frankfurt, he took the symphony to Leipzig before including it at concerts in Milan in December 1887, his first as a conductor outside Germany. The response to the work in Italy was beyond his wildest dreams, and after the second performance he wrote to his father that 'today, as for Thursday, a great success: immense! The symphony was received with storms of enthusiasm. The Scherzo had to be repeated. After the symphony, four curtain calls. From the orchestra after the symphony, I was given a splendid silver baton.'[3] From Italy, he travelled back to Germany, where within weeks of his Milan concerts, he performed the work at Mannheim in January 1888.[4]

Audiences at some of those early concerts might have been forgiven for thinking that they had just experienced the first symphonic flowering of a young but traditionally-minded musician. If that was the case, Strauss quickly dispelled that notion by performing his most recent works, *Aus Italien* and *Macbeth*, at Frankfurt, Munich, Berlin, Meiningen, Cologne and Wiesbaden. Those audiences were left in no doubt that he had shifted his loyalties from absolute music to programme music and that he had become *Zukunftsmusik*'s newest apostle. *Aus Italien* was of particular importance in establishing his credentials as a modern composer, and after getting off to a rocky start at its world première,[5] it was soon heard at some major musical centres. Self-deprecating as ever when writing to Bülow, he wrote in a letter to his mentor on 11 March 1887 that the first performance was not a success because the audience could not come to terms with its formal structure and that he was unable to do the work justice with only two rehearsals. Apparently, 'lively booing broke [out] in the hall' after the last movement, but that was soon 'drowned by applause'. Strauss relished the reaction and was aware that contentious music attracted attention. *Aus Italien* was no exception, and keen to hear what all the fuss was about, impresarios and artistic directors promptly invited Strauss to perform music's newest *cause célèbre* with their orchestras. Consequently, he gave the work twice in Berlin in the first half of 1888 and once each at Meiningen, Cologne, Frankfurt and Wiesbaden between 23 January 1888 and 28 June 1889.[6]

Travelling direct from Wiesbaden where he conducted in temperatures of '28 degrees in the shade',[7] Strauss arrived at Bayreuth on the morning of 30 June. For any young Wagnerian, the chance to participate in the festival there must have been an overwhelming experience. He immediately threw himself into the hurly-burly of Bayreuth life by acting as a rehearsal pianist for *Parsifal* and lapped up all that the festival had to offer. He was thrilled to be taken under the wing of Cosima Wagner, whom he had met that March and was honoured to be the only person other than Hermann Levi and Felix Mottl[8] to be allowed to take piano rehearsals.[9] Along with *Parsifal* under Levi, Strauss was able to hear *Die Meistersinger von Nürnberg* conducted by Hans Richter[10] and *Tristan und Isolde* performed by Mottl. With the insensitivity of youth, he reported to his father on 7 July that 'yesterday and today "Tristan" was wonderful' and on 31 July 'the last "Tristan" was impressive', comments that probably would have made the arch-anti-Wagnerian Franz grimace with embarrassment and anger. Of Richter's *Meistersinger*, Strauss was less impressed and least good of all was Levi's

Parsifal, which was 'so execrable ("so scheusslicher") that Frau Wagner was beside herself'.[11]

Over the next four years, Strauss made no fewer than twenty-two guest appearances in seven cities. At many of these, he performed works such as *Aus Italien, Don Juan, Macbeth, Wanderers Sturmlied* and *Tod und Verklärung* in mixed programmes under the general direction of the orchestra's resident conductor. But in Berlin, Braunschweig, Leipzig and Hamburg he took charge of whole concerts and expanded his touring repertoire to include works by Liszt, Spohr, Davidoff, Berlioz, Berger and Beethoven. While the guest engagements given during this period were often routine, three were of particular personal and musical significance to him. After having the honour of deputizing for an indisposed Hans von Bülow at the Seventh Hamburg Subscription Concert on 22 January 1894, little did he know that within a month of that performance, his great mentor would be dead and that he would be conducting a concert in his memory with the Leipzig Gewandhaus Orchestra on 21 February 1894.[12] When Strauss mounted the podium for the Tenth Philharmonic Concert in Berlin on 19 March 1894, memories of his teacher must have come flooding back, because at that concert he gave his first performance of Beethoven's Symphony No. 9, a work that he always associated with Bülow.[13]

In June 1894, Strauss 'shook the dust of the old Weimar tradition off [his] feet' by treading his now-familiar summer path to Bayreuth. Unlike previous years when he was simply either a visitor or a junior member of the music staff,[14] at the 1894 festival he was engaged for the first time as a conductor. Along with Hermann Levi and Felix Mottl, who conducted *Parsifal* and *Lohengrin* respectively, Strauss led performances of *Tannhäuser* on 22 and 30 July, and 6 August. These engagements were an act of homage for the young Wagnerian, who was overjoyed at the prospect of performing one of the Master's middle works in front of his widow, acolytes and disciples. Nevertheless, he had strong reservations about the acoustic properties of the Festival Theatre and the ways in which those properties affected his reading. He felt that the covered pit was only effective for performances of *Parsifal*, but robbed the other works of the 'many . . . inexhaustible riches of the score'.[15] As he pointed out, the enduring attraction of any opera was not the libretto but the elaborate harmonic, melodic and orchestral detail of the score. Being able to hear a lyric work's text time after time never filled an opera house, but the opportunity of experiencing fully the sound world created by expert composers was a sure way of delighting audiences.

London Début

At the end of 1897, Strauss undertook an extensive tour of Europe that involved concerts in Barcelona, Brussels and Paris.[16] At the end of the trip, he also conducted in London for the first time, a city that quickly became central to his touring schedule. Attracted by its prosperous middle-class and its cosmopolitan character, Strauss was quick to exploit many of the musical and financial possibilities that London had to offer. Fêted by the city's well-to-do and culturally influential German community, he soon found a musical home from home and happily accepted numerous engagements at the sumptuous Queen's Hall. Opened in 1893 at Langham Place just north of Oxford Circus, the Hall attracted a wide audience thanks to the pioneering work of the manager, Robert Newman,[17] and the conductor, Henry J. Wood. After establishing an annual series of promenade concerts there in 1895, they challenged existing trends in concertgoing by aiming both to entertain and to educate. Newman and Wood were not alone in realizing the artistic and commercial potential of the Queen's Hall and they were soon competing with other impresarios for a share of the market. Prominent amongst these promoters was Alfred Schülz-Curtius who was something of a musical wheeler-dealer and who recognized the importance of attractive programming. Aware that Londoners were besotted by the music of Wagner and that Strauss was the musician on everybody's lips, he cannily engaged Strauss to conduct one of his 'Wagner concerts' there on 7 December 1897.

The billing for Strauss's London début in *The Times* was a masterstroke of publicity that trumpeted a 'Grand Wagner Concert [conducted by] . . . Richard Strauss, of Munich and Bayreuth, The eminent Composer and Conductor . . .'.[18] Of course, Schülz-Curtius knew that he was stretching the truth by linking Strauss closely to Bayreuth, but he was a wily impresario who clearly intended to exploit the public's passion for Wagner's music. That said, the overall shape of the programme was indicative of Strauss's wider performance aesthetic and included works with which he was associated closely elsewhere. Presumably at the conductor's suggestion, the first half of the concert began with Mozart's *Eine kleine Nachtmusik*, continued with *Tod und Verklärung* and concluded with the English première of *Till Eulenspiegel*. After the interval, Strauss returned to conduct the Preludes to *Tristan und Isolde* and *Die Meistersinger von Nürnberg*, 'Karfreitagzauber' from *Parsifal*, and the Overture to *Tannhäuser*.

Even though Schülz-Curtius had tried to add lustre to the evening by marketing it as a 'Grand Wagner concert', the critic for *The Musical Times* was unimpressed and dismissed 'the second part [because it] consisted of the inevitable Wagner selection.'[19] Mozart's Serenade fared little better and was considered by reviewers in *The Musical Times* and *The Times*[20] to be nothing more than a 'delicious' filler. Of Strauss's own works and podium manner, however, the critic for *The Times* was less dismissive and reported:

The concert given last night in the Queen's-hall gave English amateurs an opportunity of becoming acquainted with the most important works of Herr Richard Strauss. . . . *Tod und Verklärung* and *Till Eulenspiegels lustige Streiche*, were the principal features, the former of which was heard for the first time in London, though it came out a good many years ago in Germany. . . . The first and earlier work is supposed to portray, with that attention to detail which marks the modern orchestral writer, the demise of a wretched man in a garret. . . . A prodigious noise is occasionally made, and the entire stock-in-trade of the theatrical music-maker is employed; but when that portion of the composition is reached which treats of the regeneration of the after-life the strains become almost conventional in their suavity. There is much use of leading themes, but few of them have either individuality or convincing beauty. It is only necessary to mention Berlioz's 'Symphonie fantastique' as an example of the entirely successful treatment of what is virtually the same subject. . . . Here the symphonic-poem form is used with happiest results. . . . The two works, and, indeed, all the programme, were conducted with great skill by Herr Strauss, who, in spite of a not very inspiring beat, secured an admirable performance of his immensely difficult works, the second of which, it will be remembered, was publicly declared by Mr. Manns[21] to be the hardest composition he had ever had to conduct.[22]

During the 1898–1899 season, Strauss conducted a punishing schedule of guest engagements that took him to Leipzig, Chemnitz, Plauen im Vogtland, Aachen, Amsterdam, Dresden, Paris, Weimar, Bremen, Heidelberg, Frankfurt, Strasburg, Düsseldorf and London.[23] As Strauss was at the height of his powers as an orchestral composer, many of these concerts contained music by him. The Amsterdam concert was held at the Concertgebouw on 30 October 1898 and he was thrilled to find that his name had been added to the interior wall in gold paint beside those of Wagner and Liszt.[24] Greeted enthusiastically by the orchestra, Strauss reported to his parents that *Tod und Verklärung* was 'conducted fabulously' by Willem Mengelberg and that his own account of *Also sprach Zarathustra* 'was the most beautiful performance of the work that he had yet experienced'. Clearly overjoyed by the response to his music, he summed up the whole event as 'wonderful' and a 'great triumph'.[25]

Strauss continued to harbour a lingering affection for some of his early works during the late 1890s and along with recent compositions such as *Don Quixote* and *Ein Heldenleben*, he either performed, or suggested for performance, his Symphony in F minor. These programmes were also peppered with the music of his heroes, Mozart, Beethoven and Wagner, whose importance to his performance grew with each passing year. At the Paris concert on 22 January 1899, he juxtaposed *Also sprach Zarathustra* with Beethoven's Symphony No. 7 and Wagner's Preludes to *Lohengrin* and *Die Meistersinger von Nürnberg*. The orchestra for that concert was the Orchestre Lamoureux, which had been founded by Charles Lamoureux in 1881 and which later gave the world premières of Debussy's *Nocturnes* and *La Mer*. Strauss was impressed with the standard of its playing, which he described as 'wonderful'.[26] As an ensemble, it must have been remarkable, because Strauss's friend Sir Henry Wood recalled in 1938 that when Robert Newman engaged

> Lamoureux and his . . . Orchestra for six concerts . . . in 1896 we were all excited, I remember, at the chance of hearing forty classical works rehearsed by this great Frenchman. The way in which he had trained his strings alone was a revelation to me. Lamoureux was himself a violinist and had been educated under Gérard, Tolbecque, Leborne, and Chauvet. By the absolute unanimity of bowing, and the *exact place of the bow on the strings*, he obtained a colour and variety of tone I could not hope to achieve in those early days, having no chance of extended rehearsals. The one blot in Lamoureux's string quality resulted from his players using modern instruments made by one firm. They were very red-looking, I remember, and *new*. It may have been that he wanted to help the French violin industry, but I was sorry about it at the time. Our English players take pride in possessing the best instruments money can buy. Those belonging to any of our great orchestras are worth thousands of pounds. On the other hand, Lamoureux's woodwind was composed of magnificent instruments – but French-made woodwind instruments are the finest in the world.[27]

PHILHARMONIC SOCIETY OF LONDON: A LESSON IN NEGOTIATING

In June 1899, Strauss returned to England to conduct for Philharmonic Society of London.[28] Founded by professional musicians in 1813, the Society is Britain's oldest concert organisation[29] and is probably best known outside the United Kingdom for its association with Beethoven in his final years. During its history, it has played host to many of music's important figures and amongst those who conducted its orchestra were Louis Spohr, Felix Mendelssohn, Hector Berlioz and Richard Wagner. Even though prominent British musicians directed the organisation's concerts during the late nineteenth century,[30] Continental artists continued to fascinate London audiences and it was this fascination, along with the Society's interest in new music, that made an invitation to Richard Strauss almost inevitable.

The interest generated by the *enfant terrible* of new music after his London début in 1897, prompted the directors of the Philharmonic Society to contact Strauss in October 1898.[31] Keen to capitalize on audience curiosity, they suggested that he might like to conduct his new tone poem, *Don Quixote*. Given that the Society was managed by jobbing musicians, their initial approach was clumsy and unprofessional. Hoping that Strauss would be impressed by an offer from one of Europe's leading concert societies, their first letter to him seems to have underestimated his sense of professional worth.[32] This is clear from the Society's second letter,[33] which elicited a sharp response from Strauss, who considered their offer of '£30 for expenses'[34] derisory. In an attempt to win him over, and in a failed attempt to impress him, the directors then listed artists of stature who had worked for the organisation for no 'monetary profit'.[35] This attempt at bargaining with the ever-savvy Strauss was at best ham-fisted and at worst insulting. As the Society regularly paid fees higher than that offered to him, and as musicians are notorious gossips, it is highly likely that he had already been alerted to their negotiating tactics. In 1897, for example, the Society invited Engelbert Humperdinck 'to come & conduct some of his music at the Third Autumn Concert[36] for the fee of £100',[37] while 'it was resolved also to go as high as £50 to secure [the pianist, Moritz] Rosenthal, for [15 June] 1899',[38] the same concert at which Strauss was to perform his tone poem. Of course, both musicians were known to Strauss and it is reasonable to assume that he was aware of their fees.

After the Society's second letter to Strauss, negotiations were continued on his behalf by Schülz-Curtius, who had been engaged as his sole representative in the United Kingdom after the 1897 concert. Given the level of expertise associated with an agent of Schülz-Curtius's standing, his first, unauthorized, approach to the Society was mishandled. It seems that Schülz-Curtius assumed that his agreement with Strauss entitled him to undertake the negotiations from the outset. Strauss took a different view, preferring to commission the agent personally. Having resolved the question of representation, the Society and Schülz-Curtius then began to haggle over three important issues: the size of Strauss's fee, the choice of solo cellist, and the number of rehearsals available.

Central to any agent's role is the negotiation of fees. As '£30 for expenses' was unthinkable for a musician of Strauss's stature, Schülz-Curtius dismissed the sum in his letter of 19 October 1898 and suggested a fee of £75 instead. Ever the businessman, the agent supported his proposal by offering to market the Society's 'special concert' through his own subscription lists. Both were unacceptable to the Society, so in his letter of 28 October 1898 he reduced the fee to £50, a figure that the directors approved on 4 November 1898. Aware of the financial advantages of exclusivity, the Society was concerned that the agent might prevent Strauss from accepting their invitation or, more worrying, involve him in another venture during his visit.

Schülz-Curtius placated the directors by stressing that he had 'no intention to "block the way" or to treat your invitation to Herr Strauss in a narrow sense of competition'.[39] Unconvinced, the Society's Honorary Secretary, Francesco Berger, raised the issue again on 20 November 1898 and wrote: 'we rely upon your not arranging any appearance for him in London before our date'.[40] In reply, Schülz-Curtius confirmed that he was willing to comply with their request.[41]

Worried that the Society's principal cellist might find the solo part in *Don Quixote* too difficult, Strauss suggested that it should engage 'a cellist of firstclass [*sic*], preferably Hugo Becker'.[42] The directors were offended: Berger defended his colleague and argued that Strauss 'is probably not aware that our first viol[o]ncello is an [*sic*] sol[o]ist of repute . . . and quite competent to deal with the Solo-part in Don Quixote'.[43] Although supportive of their front-desk colleague, the directors 'resolved to order a copy of [the] score of Don Quixote and to be guided by the report of [their conductor] Sir A. C. Mackenzie[44] as to the neccessity [*sic*] of engaging a special 'Cellist for it in the event of its being performed, for which the name of Mr. [W. H.] Squire was suggested'.[45] For Strauss, however, the question of the solo cellist could not be considered in isolation and he linked it directly to the thorny issue of rehearsal time.

London orchestras have always been proud of their ability to read difficult scores at sight. As state, county and local subsidies to orchestras in the United Kingdom were, and are, generally less than to arts organizations on mainland Europe, the ability of British musicians to sight-read expertly grew out of necessity. In the last years of the nineteenth century, the Philharmonic Society relied heavily on their musicians' ability to read and to respond quickly, and with dwindling funds the organization was in no position to be generous with rehearsal time. But lack of preparation eventually lowers performance standards, and in October 1897 a staff critic for *Musical Opinion* took the Philharmonic Society to task over the matter. Angered by the comments, Berger issued a brusque rebuttal:

> Sir, — Your issue for October contains the following statement: 'Foreign conductors cannot understand how one day's rehearsal is considered sufficient for the concerts of our leading musical society, – the Philharmonic.' Permit me to correct this error on the part of 'Common Time.'
>
> For *many* years past each concert has been preceded by *two* rehearsals; and the directors have never allowed the question of expense (though a heavy one) to stand in the way of their granting a *third* rehearsal whenever their appointed conductor has seen fit to ask for one. I shall feel obliged by your kindly giving this letter, or the facts that it embodies, the same publicity as you have given to the less accurate version.

Aware of the Society's rehearsal policy, Schülz-Curtius challenged them from the start and in his letter of 12 November 1898, in which he also confirmed 15 June 1899 as the date of the concert, he reminded Berger that 'as I already mentioned to you, I gave Herr Strauss <u>three</u> Rehearsals [sic] on the occasion of his last visit'.[46] To add weight to his argument, Schülz-Curtius enclosed a note from Strauss that made clear that a successful performance of Don Quixote would be completely dependent on sufficient rehearsal time. Writing in the strongest terms, Strauss argued that 'with only 2 rehearsals, Don Quixote is impossible. . . . I require at least 3 rehearsals, as [sic] also a cellist of firstclass [sic], preferably Hugo Becker who has already played the piece quite unsurpassably [sic]. Don Q. is a very diff[icult]. & very risky work which can only have effect . . . thro' a faultless rendering'.[47]

Considered preconditions by the directors, Strauss's comments prompted an unwelcome response. It was decided at the next directors' meeting[48] that unless Strauss withdrew his demands for a guest cellist and three rehearsals, then 'the Directors . . . must decline to entertain them' and 'under these circumstances . . . the matter must be considered to have fallen through'.[49] Worried that a commission was slipping away, Schülz-Curtius contacted Berger by letter on 19 November 1898 and suggested a compromise. The agent stressed that Strauss had not made the engagement of Becker a condition and if the Society's orchestra could read through the tone poem 'at one of your earlier rehearsals . . . [this] I think would remove the difficulty about the third rehearsal'.[50]

Having put the suggestion to Berger, Schülz-Curtius needed Strauss's approval. He was not convinced, however, and from the agent's letter of 13 December 1898 it is clear that Strauss was unwilling to perform Don Quixote under those conditions.[51] Neither the former nor the latter was prepared to forgo the engagement, however, and it was proposed that Strauss could perform one of his earlier works instead. As alternatives, he suggested that either ' "Don Juan", "Eulenspiegel" or "Tod und Verklärung" . . . might be managed in two rehearsals' or the Society might 'prefer to do an older Symphony[, that] in . . . F. minor op. 12 . . . which . . . is still in the "<u>classic style</u>" '. Eventually, Tod und Verklärung was considered suitable and it was with this work that Strauss gave his first, and last, performance with the Philharmonic Society on 15 June 1899.[52]

BRUSSELS, PARIS AND FIRST LONDON STRAUSS FESTIVAL

The next season, Strauss's schedule was as busy as ever with guest engagements in Munich, Augsburg, Brussels, Berlin, Chemnitz, Krefeld, Cologne, Paris, Mannheim and Hamburg. With the exception of his visits to Brussels and Paris, the programmes for the majority of these concerts were based either wholly or largely on his own music. At the Brussels concert on 5 November 1899 for an indisposed Joseph Dupont,[53] Strauss paid homage to his musical heroes by performing *Don Juan* side by side with works by Berlioz, Beethoven and Wagner.[54] The composers featured in that concert were heard again during his two-week visit to Paris at the beginning of 1900,[55] when he conducted two concerts with the Lamoureux Orchestra.[56] Between those engagements, he dazzled his Paris audience with an evening of chamber music and song,[57] spent much time with his friend, the author Romain Rolland, popped in to art galleries and visited the *Exposition universelle* (World's Fair).

By the end of the season, Strauss must have been exhausted, but before abandoning the podium for the summer he conducted two concerts at the North Rhine Music Festival in Aachen, programming some of his own works along with those by Berlioz, Cornelius, Beethoven, Schillings and Wagner.[58] At the second concert, Strauss was appointed to the management committee of the Allgemeiner deutscher Musikverein, one of Germany's most influential forums for the dissemination of new music. Founded in 1861 by Franz Liszt and Franz Brendel,[59] the ADMV was active until 1937, when it was dissolved by the Nazis for political reasons. Over its seventy-six year history, it was linked closely with some of world's leading composers and it honoured Strauss on 7 June 1934 by marking his seventieth birthday with an all-Strauss concert.[60]

When Strauss returned to Britain in 1902 after concerts at Düsseldorf and Bremen,[61] he spent a few days relaxing on the Isle of Wight before starting a gruelling series of concerts in London. He wrote to his father from Sandown on 27 May 1902:

After a splendid crossing (without sea-sickness), I have been experiencing since Thursday the most wonderful weather here on the island, where everything I see is an expression of beauty. The green meadows of Switzerland, the deciduous trees of central Germany, the blossoming fruit-trees of the Tyrol, the wonderful coastal formations of the Riviera, the colourful Mediterranean Sea and, not least, the English hospitality, come together to provide mind and body with a really invigorating experience. I spend the whole day in the open air. Before midday, I lie on the beach and marvel at the in-coming tide. After midday, I take an extensive walk on the coastal rocks and the wonderful paths through the meadows. . . . In every garden there is greenery and blossoms; a scene that would please our beloved mother. My next concerts with Possart, on 31 May and 6 June, are, to a greater or lesser degree, Kitsch. The first concert, on 31 May, includes 'Manfred'; the second concert, on 2 June, has 'Enoch Arden'; the third concert, on 4 June, involves 'Don Juan', 'Eulenspiegel', 'Tod und

Verkl[ärung]'; while the fourth concert, on 6 June, includes the violin sonata and melodramas with piano.[62] I will remain here until Thursday. Then I will go to sooty London, where I will stay for part of the time at the Langham Hotel and part of the time in the country with Edg[ar] Speyer.[63] I have already relaxed in these two wonderful days; the sea-air is enormously invigorating. I am already burnt brown. 7–10 June I will be going to the Tonkünstlerversammlung in Krefeld; 11/12 June again in Berlin, to perform the six hundredth performance of 'Don Juan';[64] and, on 13 June, I am, God willing, in Munich, where I hope to find you all well and dearest Mama completely recovered.[65]

The four concerts mentioned by Strauss were organized by Hugo Görlitz. Like Schülz-Curtius before him, Görlitz was an experienced agent and impresario who handled, amongst others, the violinist Jan Kubelík[66] and the pianist Wilhelm Backhaus.[67] Görlitz was a master publicist, who cleverly billed the series as a 'Grand Musical and Lyric Festival'. Along with a complete performance of Schumann's *Manfred* with Ernst von Possart in the title role at the first concert,[68] Görlitz programmed *Enoch Arden* with Possart and Strauss at the second.[69] Based on Tennyson's poem of the same name, *Enoch Arden* was melodrama in German that was composed by Strauss in 1897[70] and that was performed widely by him in Germany. The third concert[71] was billed as a 'Grand Orchestral and Heine Night' at which Possart recited some of Heine's best-known poems in German and Strauss gave performances of *Don Juan*, *Tod und Verklärung* and *Till Eulenspiegel*. The final evening[72] was given over to extracts from works by Schiller and Goethe recited by Possart in German, two melodramas performed by Possart and Strauss, and a performance of the latter's Violin Sonata played by the composer and the leader of the Queen's Hall Orchestra, Elkan Kosman.[73]

Unconcerned that much of the 'Lyric' element of the Festival was given in German, *The Times* reported on 2 June 1902 that 'Under Herr Strauss the Queen's-hall orchestra played finely' and on 4 June 1902 that 'the experiment [*Enoch Arden*] was the greatest possible success, both pianist, composer, and reciter covering themselves with glory'. Strauss was overjoyed at the success of the first two concerts and in a letter to his father from the Langham Hotel, London, probably written on 3 June 1902, he rhapsodized about Edwardian city life, his recent triumphs and his hopes for the future:

I am in the swim of the hurly-burly [Trubel]! Since yesterday, the armistice,[74] the life on the streets is fantastic. It defies description; the street and townscapes are rather intoxicating. In addition, the wonderful weather brings [London's] approximately two million people, from all classes, out and about! And the sound and the wagon traffic! My concerts are going splendidly, and it seems to bode well for my future, both here and in America.[75] For the time being, I have four orchestral concerts in London. Today, I have been offered concerts in Glasgow and Edinburgh, for 22 and 23 December: I am also considered here as the leading living composer; I cannot fail. You need no longer worry![76]

While Strauss's 1902 concerts contained some novelties, it is curious that his three most recent works for orchestra, *Also Sprach Zarathustra, Don Quixote* and *Ein Heldenleben*, were missing from the programmes. The tone poems heard at the third concert were composed between 1888 and 1895, and in the intervening years they had become increasingly familiar to both listeners and musicians alike. As his latest tone poems presented new technical problems for the orchestra and as Görlitz's 'Festival' was a commercial enterprise, it is possible that their absence was due simply to limited rehearsal time.

The London public did not have to wait long to hear *Ein Heldenleben*, however, because it received its British première on 6 December 1902. Performed as part of the Saturday Symphony Concert series at the Queen's Hall, the tone poem was conducted by Strauss for a fee of '75 Guineas',[77] with Henry Wood directing the rest of the programme.[78] Even though the overall management of the concert was handled by Robert Newman, the advertisement in *The Times* bore the hallmark of Strauss's newly appointed sole agent, Hugo Görlitz:[79] 'To-day, at 3, Richard Strauss will conduct his Tone-Poem, "Ein Heldenleben," ten rehearsals of which have already been held this week by Mr. Henry J. Wood. The final rehearsal and the performance will be conducted by The Composer.'[80] As the attention of the average concertgoer was sure to be captured by Görlitz's flamboyant marketing and as Strauss was still the darling of British audiences, a capacity house was assured. The concert was a triumph, as he reported to his father:

'Heldenleben' was, in London (where I stayed in some style with the wealthy E. Speyer, and in whose electric automobile I travelled; he has a house that is modelled after the old Italian style), a fabulous success! 3500 people attended the concert and there were unheard of cheers for London! All the papers were full of it! Next Sunday I will be returning to England [*recte* Scotland] (Thank God I had two good crossings by way of Vlissingen) – on 22 and 23 December [I have] two concerts in Glasgow and Edinburgh, which means that I will not be home for Christmas Eve.[81]

A second successful London performance of *Ein Heldenleben* soon followed under Wood at the Queen's Hall on 1 January 1903. Again, Strauss was delighted by the response of the audience and wrote to his father in buoyant mood:

The second performance of 'Heldenleben' in London, on 1 January, under [Henry] Wood, where Halir was the solo violinist,[82] again inspired spirited cheering; [the work] seems to be succeeding at an impressive rate. At the beginning of June, I will be conducting the Amsterdam Orchestra in four all-Strauss concerts in London, the programmes will, perhaps, contain all my works; Pauline will sing my Lieder. . . .[83]

The London engagements mentioned by Strauss in his letter took place later that summer, and after arriving there with his family on 1 June he quickly despatched another of his customary notes:

Today, we arrived punctually at 8.03 in London. The bright weather made yesterday's journey, on Whit Sunday, rather warm; the crossing was effortless. Bubi,[84] in enthusiastic mood, was awake throughout the whole crossing because of the ship and the sea. Sadly, his thirst for knowledge is so great that he was unable to sleep on the journey. We will be staying with the Speyers at a seaside resort . . . two wonderful houses with gardens, four butlers, a maid, horses and an electric car are all at our disposal, we can live like princes without any social pressures . . . Today, London is completely deserted. Pauline is asleep and Bubi likewise. After lunch we will go to Hyde Park for a walk; we will be accompanied by that charming couple, the Tschirchs (the critic),[85] who will also attend our concert and travel with us to [the Isle of] Wight! On Wednesday morning, we have the first rehearsal and, in the evening, the first concert. We are now taking a necessary rest, as the last few days were a great strain. After four months of packing and making our apartment ready,[86] along with a performance every evening, I have had enough.[87]

Organised by Hugo Görlitz, the concerts were held at St. James's Hall and were billed as a 'Richard Strauss Festival'. Strauss was joined by the Concertgebouw Orchestra of Amsterdam and its conductor, Willem Mengelberg.[88] The festival opened with a concert on 3 June. After the National Anthem played by Percy Pitt on the organ,[89] Mengelberg conducted *Till Eulenspiegel*, while Strauss performed *Also Sprach Zarathustra*, three songs with orchestra,[90] three songs with piano[91] and the Love Scene from *Feuersnot*. The next day's concert followed a similar pattern, with *Don Juan* conducted by Mengelberg and three songs with orchestra,[92] *Don Quixote*, three songs with piano[93] and *Tod und Verklärung* performed by Strauss. The third concert on 5 June again saw a juxtaposition of his tone poems and songs with orchestra, and it included *Macbeth*, *Also Sprach Zarathustra*, two songs for baritone and orchestra[94] and *Ein Heldenleben*, all conducted by the composer. Demand for tickets soon outstripped supply and an extra concert was hastily arranged for 6 June. Unlike the other performances, the additional concert was not restricted to the works of Strauss but also included music by Beethoven, Stanford, Chopin, Elgar and Liszt. *Till Eulenspiegel* opened the concert under Strauss and Beethoven's Piano Concerto No. 3 was played by the young American pianist, Richard Platt, under Mengelberg. Platt then played Chopin's *Berceuse*, *Mazurka* Op. 7 No. 3, *Grand Valse* Op. 42 and *Ballade* Op. 47, followed by Liszt's *Fantasie über ungarische Volkweise* conducted by Strauss. The remainder of the programme was given by Mengelberg, who performed Stanford's Irish Rhapsody No. 2 and the incidental music from *Grania and Diarmid* by Elgar. The Festival's final concert was given on 9 June. It included excerpts from *Aus Italien* under Mengelberg and *Burleske, Ein Heldenleben* and a selection from *Guntram* under Strauss.[95]

While the Festival was a success, the stress it caused had an effect on Strauss's health. In a letter to his parents written the day after the last concert he wrote:

> My concert, held yesterday, which contained 'Guntram' and 'Heldenleben', turned out splendidly. The success was brilliant, especially for Pauline, who has already been engaged for seven *Liederabende* in America. All the newspapers praised her unanimously. However, a battle between the critics has broken out over me: the majority are in line with the critic from the 'Times', who is London's answer to Hanslick. We have a further five concerts in England in December, with Pauline giving a complete *Liederabend*. My stomach has been playing up. I have cancelled Basel and will go direct to Sandown with the family to relax. We have spent some lovely peaceful days in Speyer's wonderful home. Yesterday, after the concert, Speyer gave a splendid supper, to which Mengelberg, Tschirch and the first desks of the Dutch orchestra were also invited.[96]

Strauss's description of the critic for *The Times* as 'London's answer to Hanslick' was no exaggeration. Eduard Hanslick's Vienna reviews of Strauss's tone poems were often scathing and of *Tod und Verklärung* he wrote the 'composer of *Don Juan* has again proved himself a brilliant virtuoso of the orchestra, lacking only musical ideas. . . . A dreadful battle of dissonances, in which the wood-winds come screaming down in chromatic thirds, while the whole brass section thunders and the fiddles rage.'[97] *The Times* review of 4 June 1903 was strikingly similar to that of Hanslick:

> Whether the public, by which we would be understood to mean the public that matters, will accept Herr Strauss as the great man his friends think him, or will refuse the feast of cacophony spread for them, remains to be seen. . . . At present the mere fact that these larger compositions are a great deal uglier than anything else in music does not itself constitute what is called individuality of style; for there are so many ways of being ugly, and Herr Strauss is a

master of them, with the single exception that he never writes ineffectively for the orchestra.

A more balanced discussion of both the Festival and Strauss's music was published by a critic in the July issue of *Musical Opinion and Music Trade Review*:

> On the whole, the London press has done well over Strauss. There has been an earnest desire to set forth the merits and demerits of his work to the best of the writers' capabilities. More than this cannot be asked of any musical critic. . . . Strauss is certainly a revolutionist compared with Wagner, – for good or evil. I will not say which it is. . . . Another point I notice is that many amateurs and critics would complain that Strauss does not write in a certain style. Some of these complainants would have him pen symphonies. 'If only he would write a real symphony!' But why should he if the symphony does not appeal to him now? . . . It seems to me that certain musicians would prescribe one style for all composers. Thus, to some minds a little stretch of sentiment not of the heroic order is tantamount to an artistic crime. . . . Wagner thought in 'heroics:' it was natural to him, and he was a child of the romantic movement. Strauss is of to-day; perhaps he is too much of to-day to be a great composer. We shall see.[98]

From London, Strauss travelled to the Isle of Wight for an extended holiday.[99] Never one to lie idle for long, he took the opportunity to finish the draft sketch of the *Sinfonia domestica*. During his stay on the island, he was informed by the University of Heidelberg that he was to be conferred with an honorary doctorate. Strauss was proud of this degree, and from that day forward he preceded his signature with 'Dr.' and insisted on being called 'Herr Doktor Strauss'. Unable to contain his pride, he wrote immediately to his father:

> I have the pleasure of telling you the following, which must be kept secret (only dearest Mama may, for the time being, be told): I will, at the beginning of August, receive an honorary doctorate from the University of Heidelberg. The indefatigable and faithful Wolfrum[100] has had this honour bestowed upon me by the Philosophy Faculty. Today, Dr. Thode,[101] Frau Wagner's son-in-law, told me that the Faculty unanimously approved my elevation as part of the University's centenary celebrations; this is excellent news. I will dedicate 'Taillefer' to the University as my 'Doktorarbeit'. The first performance should take place at the Heidelberg Music Festival at the end of October.[102] I would like you to be there! Heidelberg is not much further than Würzburg. . . . We are having a wonderful time here. We have already swum twice in the sea and Bubi runs barefoot all day in the hot sand, alternating between the sand and the sea. We go for many walks. The weather is changeable and fresh. We have

only had one really bad rainy day. . . . I am working and have, today, just finished the sketch for my 'Sinfonia domestica'.[103]

Later that year, Strauss was back in the United Kingdom for performances in Glasgow,[104] Edinburgh, Birmingham[105] and two concerts in London, where he gave a *Liederabend* with his wife and conducted an all-Berlioz programme with the Queen's Hall Orchestra. His first London appearance that visit was at St. James's Hall on 9 December 1903 with a programme consisting entirely of songs composed by Strauss. While the audience reaction was enthusiastic, the critical response was disappointing. The reviewer for *The Times* found the evening particularly tedious and wrote:

> It is given to very few composers to be able to sustain the interest of an audience through a programme of their own works, yet, although Frau Strauss De Ahna sang nothing but her husband's songs at her recital at St. James's-hall last night, there was no waning of the public enthusiasm as group of songs followed group. . . . For ourselves, we found the ordeal trying, since so often the idea came home that pure lyricism was being sacrificed either for a new effect or in order that an ordinary cadence might be avoided.[106]

The second concert was given at the Queen's Hall on 11 December 1903 and was part of that year's Berlioz centenary celebrations.[107] Managed by Strauss's sole agent, Hugo Görlitz, it was held for 'the Benefit of the Relief Fund of the National Society of French Teachers in England'.[108] The extent of Strauss's interest in the well-being of French teachers in England may never be known, but his regard for the music of Berlioz is well documented. The French composer's works were a regular feature of Strauss's programmes at home and abroad, and he also edited and revised the German edition of Berlioz's *Treatise on Instrumentation and Modern Orchestration*.[109] The evening included the *Rêverie et Caprice* for violin[110] and the song-cycle *Nuits d'Été*, which were sung by a German soprano, Alice Holländer, in an English translation. The concert was poorly attended and the celebrations as a whole failed to attract large audiences. It appears that the public had grown tired of Berlioz's music and that works such as 'his *Faust* and his *Enfance du Christ* . . . [had] vanished from the general repertoire'.[111] Nonetheless, Strauss considered his visit to Britain a success and was particularly pleased with the Scottish and Birmingham concerts. In his letter to his parents from Warsaw, dated 18 December 1903,[112] he reported:

> In England [*recte* Scotland], I had a great success with the outstanding Scottish Orchestra in Glasgow and Edinburgh. In Birmingham, I played my Piano Quartet and Violin Sonata, accompanying Herr Mossel[113] in the Adagio from the Violin Concerto; the provincial English audience seemed to

be pleased. In London, I conducted an all-Berlioz evening with Wood's Queen's Hall [Orchestra]. They played faultlessly before a French audience who attended; the concert was given on behalf of a French charity. Owing to my post in Berlin, I felt unable to conduct the French national anthem, the *Marseillaise*, as requested. . . .[114]

NEW YORK DÉBUT AND FIRST NORTH AMERICAN TOUR

In 1904, Strauss toured the United States for the first time and even before leaving the dock at Hoboken, New Jersey, on 24 February, he managed to set the cat among the pigeons with his comments about the Metropolitan Opera House's 1903 production of Wagner's *Parsifal*. As the work was still protected by the 'Bayreuth copyright', Strauss was furious that New York's leading opera house had performed the music drama, and he minced no words in his defence of the unique status of Wagner's last work. The *Tribune's* headline on 25 February thundered: 'RICHARD STRAUSS HERE. *Says Religious Side of "Parsifal" Has Been Profaned'*. The main body of the text was no less strident and complained that Strauss 'had no compliments ready for either America or the Americans, and one of his first remarks, through his press agent,[115] was that the religious side of 'Parsifal' had been profaned by its production in this city. He then advanced the opinion that, through the example of its production in this city, it would be performed within ten years in every city in Germany. He said that his only feeling on approaching the city were those of curiosity and interest, and his coming to America had awakened no other emotion.'[116]

This early encounter coloured Strauss's opinion of the American press for the rest of his stay, and in a letter to his parents from New York on 2 March 1904 he complained that he was often misreported by the newspapers.[117] Nevertheless, by the time of that letter, he had started to warm to the United States and had become something of a fan of the New World. It was soon evident that he was experiencing more than just 'curiosity and interest' and that he was impressed by the country's architecture, transport system, orchestral standards and food. In numerous letters to his parents, he reported his experiences in detail and left them in little doubt of the deep impact that America had made on him culturally, musically and personally.

Having started controversially, Strauss settled down to a series of thirty-six public and private concerts of orchestral music, Lieder and chamber music that started in New York with the Wetzler Symphony Orchestra on 27 February and continued in Philadelphia, Boston, Cleveland, Pittsburgh, Morgantown, Chicago, Milwaukee, Detroit, Cincinnati, Minneapolis, Buffalo, and in Washington, where he performed at the White House for President Theodore Roosevelt.[118] With his wife as principal soloist, he was fêted wherever he performed and he was greeted with particular enthusiasm by the German-speakers along his route. At Cleveland he was given an impressive silver bowl by the local German community, at Morgantown he was awarded the key to the city, and in Cincinnati he was made an honorary member of the local music society. In Boston he was impressed by the standard of the orchestra, and in Chicago he was pleased to spend time with Theodore Thomas, the conductor who had given the first performance of his Symphony in F minor twenty years earlier.

Aside from the world première of *Sinfonia domestica* with the Wetzler Orchestra at Carnegie Hall on 21 March, Strauss's reading of Mozart's Symphony No. 41 with the New York Philharmonic at the same hall five days later prompted the most extensive comment. Known to be a committed and an innovative Mozart interpreter, Strauss inevitably divided the New York press by programming the composer's last symphony. Gustav Kobbé wrote in the *The New York Telegraph* on 27 March 1904:

> From Mozart to Strauss! Everything that has been accomplished in music from 1791 to 1904, three years more than a century, lies between the two names. Is that why Richard Strauss elected to open yesterday afternoon's Philharmonic concert with a Mozart symphony? He chose the so-called 'Jupiter,' which was considered very grand and even pompous, in its day. Now it sounds like a limpid, graceful and pretty piece of symphonic writing. This suggests the query whether audiences a century from now will look upon 'Heldenleben,' which seems so stupendous to us, as a charming trifle; and regard 'The Ring of the Nibelung' as a comic opera involving four after-theatre suppers. Strauss read the Mozart symphony neatly. But the sound he evoked, compared with the volume he draws from an orchestra when conducting his own tone poems, made one think of a man who, after finishing a set of exercises with Indian clubs, goes through them with tooth-picks. There are many men less great, who could have conducted the symphony as well. One point about it was worth noticing. Strauss looked less frequently at the score than when he is leading one of his own works and, in the repeats, didn't even take the trouble to turn back the pages.

The critic for *The Herald* was more responsive to Strauss's approach to Mozart in a review published on 26 March 1904:

> Public acquaintance with Richard Strauss as conductor was at once improved and given a somewhat new direction yesterday afternoon, when, holding the baton at the final matinee concert of the Philharmonic Society, he interpreted for the first time during his visit here a work not of his own composition. . . . As a whole, the concert did not prove the most interesting of

the Philharmonic's series under foreign conductors,[119] and it is somewhat significant that Mr. Strauss' reading of the Mozart symphony should have won only perfunctory applause. . . . In the first movement of the symphony Mr. Strauss sustained his reputation as a sane reader of the classics, giving a conservative, clear cut interpretation, free from affectations or eccentricities. More individuality was noticeable in the second and third movements, which were subjected to some radical departures from the tradition in the matter of pace, and were marked by the use of unusually vigorous accents. The finale was taken at top speed and was, perhaps, over noisy at times. Considered as a whole, the reading was a powerful one.

The New York Evening World was more in sympathy with Strauss's vision of the work and reported on 26 March 1904:

At yesterday's public rehearsal of the Philharmonic Society Dr. Richard Strauss conducted this orchestra for the first time. . . . Also was it the first time that this conductor has led any work other than his own during his stay here. The exceptional composition was none other than Mozart's big C major symphony, called by admiring writers 'Jupiter,' which work headed the programme yesterday afternoon at Carnegie Hall. Strauss has great reputation abroad for his Mozart interpretations, so that the interest of the huge audience was tense with expectation. Strauss did not disappoint them, for he read this work with commendable daintiness and also with masterly attention to details of phrasing and characteristic effects. The one movement that sounded least interesting was the andante, with its heavenly beauty. Here the playing of the orchestra was highly unsatisfactory, so that the audience drew but little enjoyment from this portion of the work. But the first and especially the last movements Strauss conducted admirably.

The Sun on 26 March 1904 took a more cynical tone and carped:

The mighty one of Munich deemed it his duty to show on this occasion that he could read other scores than his own. So he elected to place at the head of the programme no less a composition than Mozart's 'Jupiter' symphony. It was a proud day for Mozart, to be on the same programme with Richard Strauss and to be conducted by him. It made one recall that story which Gounod tells on himself in his memoirs. He says that he had from his youth a tremendous admiration for Mozart. When he was young he used to say, 'I and Mozart.' When he was older he said, 'Mozart and I.' When he was an aged man and had written 'Faust' and 'Romeo et Juliette' he said, 'Mozart.' Why did Mr. Strauss conduct Mozart? One sceptic said because it was easy. Another

said in order to show the contrast between that music and his, not necessarily
to prove that his was the better, but just to give a lesson in musical history and
a glimpse of the development of orchestral composition from 1788 till today.
Let us credit Mr. Strauss with a sincere admiration for Mozart. He has
expressed it often. Sometimes he even writes a little like Mozart. It is very
little, but for even a fragment of Mozartian cantilena in a Strauss tone poem
a man would forgive much immoderate modulation and many deferred reso-
lutions toward a diatonic life. Mr. or Dr. Strauss conducted Mozart's 'Jupiter'
symphony as if he honestly believed pure melody to be a good and whole-
some thing in music and that it was possible to be an artist without being
perennially cerebral. It was a sincere, straightforward, unaffected reading that
Dr. Strauss gave, a little rigid in the matter of tempo, but not in that of
nuance. The voice parts were brought out well and the vigorous polyphony of
the finale lost nothing at his hands.

But it was an unidentified and undated review that had greatest respect for
Strauss's interpretation:

It was the first time Dr. Strauss had conducted anything besides his own
compositions in New York, though even so there was only one piece on the
programme not signed by his own name. That was Mozart's C major
symphony, to which custom has given the title of 'Jupiter.' Dr. Strauss has the
name of being a special admirer and authoritative exponent of Mozart, whose
music stands in so many respects at the opposite pole from his own, and his
choice of this symphony for the programme of his Philharmonic concert
came as a confirmation of it. His performance of it gave still more confirmation. There was by no means the technical finish and perfect clarity of articulation in it that this music, more than all other, so insistently demands; nor
did the tone of the orchestra, especially of the violins, seem as fine as it
usually does for some reason with which the weather may have had to do. But
the reading of the symphony was strikingly beautiful. There was no injection
of the unquiet modern spirit into its serene and lovely utterance; but there
were subtle touches that gave animation, spirit, vivacity, to it, and there was
an understanding of the music as a vital expression of emotion, in the
eighteenth century idiom, it is true, but yet charged with a meaning that a
rigid and a routine playing of the notes could not set forth. All this was deli-
cately and suggestively realized in the spirit of Mozart. There was everywhere
a finely felt balance and adjustment of all the parts, a free and broad exposition of the melody, finely phrased and eloquently expressed. There was a
shade of rubato in the andante, now and again a minute swelling upon a
significant phrase or the salient point of a phrase in the andante, and in the
final allegro there were delicate modifications of tempo that gave the whole

an elasticity and a buoyancy, lucidly setting forth the contrapuntal structure and seeming the inevitable interpretation of its meaning.[120]

It is possible that it was not Strauss's approach to the symphony that divided the critics so sharply but the fact that he programmed it at all. When the schedules of leading orchestras of that period are examined closely, it seems clear that audiences, impresarios and musicians generally liked the idea of Mozart's music rather more than the music itself. In the German-speaking countries, the composer's last two symphonies were generally given once only in a season and the piano concertos were hardly, if ever, performed at subscription concerts. In America, the situation was similar and when Arthur Nikisch was engaged as Music Director of the Boston Symphony Orchestra between 1889 and 1893, only twelve performances of Mozart symphonies were heard at his 190 Subscription Concerts. Similarly, when Gustav Mahler took charge of the New York Philharmonic between 1909 and 1911, only three performances of Mozart's symphonies were given at the sixty-seven concerts that he conducted with the orchestra at Carnegie Hall. It seems that for Victorian and Edwardian audiences, the 'divine' Mozart was a composer to be adored from afar, rather than at close quarters in contemporary concert programmes.

COVENT GARDEN, *ELEKTRA*, *JOSEPHSLEGENDE* AND SIR THOMAS BEECHAM

In December 1904, Strauss made a brief visit to Britain for concerts in London, Edinburgh, Birmingham and Manchester,[121] and on 25 February 1905 Henry Wood conducted the London première of the *Sinfonia domestica* at the Queen's Hall with the Queen's Hall Orchestra. As the work was a success, Strauss was invited to perform it later that year. En route to the British capital, he gave two performances of the work in Holland[122] and conducted it in London on 1 April 1905.[123] *The Times* had mixed feelings about the piece but considered Strauss's interpretation valuable:

Whether from the fact that the 'Symphonia Domestica' was conducted by Herr Richard Strauss in person last Saturday, or from the wholly excellent quality of the rest of the programme, it is undeniable that the work made a more favourable impression on the general public than it did at its first performance. As a matter of course, the band played a good deal better; and in one way, if in no more, the composer's direction was a gain, since he disguised some of the least original passages in his work by taking them at a very different pace from that of the pieces that suggested them. The loans from Mendelssohn's 'Gondellied,' Beethoven's piano concerto in G, and all the others were less obvious than before. . . . The two movements by which the work will live come out with real effect, and both the scherzo and slow movement, as well as some of the connecting passages, are of distinct value. To enjoy them to the full the hearer must submit to receive an impression of hopeless ineptitude from the introductory portion, and from much of the rest, but this is worth while for the sake of the portions which are the best things the composer has yet done.[124]

Strauss was pleased with the public's reaction and the orchestra's playing, and in a letter of gratitude he wrote:

> I cannot leave London without an expression of admiration for the splendid Orchestra which Henry Wood's master hand has created in such a short time. He can be proud indeed of this little colony of artists, who represent both discipline and quality of the highest order. After the thirty performances of the *Sinfonia Domestica* which I have conducted this winter, and of which only very few indeed can compare to the masterly rendering of the new and, in that sense, youthful Queen's Hall Orchestra, I can well appreciate what an amount of hard work, expert knowledge and sympathetic comprehension of my intentions have been expended on this performance through the energy and self-effacing labours of Mr. Wood. Performances such as these mark days of rejoicing in a composer's life.[125]

This encomium was not simply post-concert euphoria; in a letter to his parents from Berlin on 5 April 1905, Strauss again expressed his admiration for Wood's orchestra:

> The few days rest that I had in Holland and London, where I had splendid weather, did me the world of good. I had a tremendous success with the 'domestica' (played in an exceptional manner by the Queen's Hall Orchestra).[126]

The relationship between Strauss, Wood and the Queen's Hall Orchestra was strengthened when the composer returned to London to direct a further performance of the tone poem on 4 November 1905 at the Queen's Hall.[127] Again, the *Sinfonia domestica* was greeted enthusiastically by the general public but was received coolly by the critics. The press coverage was minimal, with *The Musical Times* noting simply that 'The last-named work was conducted by the composer'.[128] *The Times* critic recognized the quality of the playing under Strauss but was relieved that the performance 'was happily five minutes shorter than some previous ones'.[129]

After visiting Britain for a performance of *Don Quixote* with the Queen's Hall Orchestra at the Queen's Hall on 3 May 1906, Strauss returned to London for performances of *Elektra* at the Royal Opera House, Covent Garden, in 1910. As the local première approached, the excitement of the press and the opera-going public rose to near fever pitch. Stories of the lurid nature of Hugo von Hofmannsthal's libretto and Strauss's decadent music abounded in many of the capital's leading publications. This free publicity was a godsend for the opera's conductor, Thomas Beecham, who relished the coverage that *Elektra* was receiving. As a direct result of the publicity, the first night (19 February) attracted an audience that included the King, the Queen and other members of the Royal Family. For the opening performances, Beecham assembled a formidable cast that included Edyth Walker (Elektra), Anna Bahr-Mildenburg (Klytämnestra), Frances Rose (Chrysothemis) and Hermann Weidemann[130] (Orest). In the reviews that followed, a war of words broke out between two of London's leading music commentators. In *The Nation*, Ernest Newman[131] grumbled 'that much of the music is as abominably ugly as it is noisy',[132] while George Bernard Shaw[133] fired back by arguing that Newman's comments were ill-considered and unwarranted.[134] Whatever the case, the opera was so successful that Beecham extended the season and invited Strauss to conduct two of the nine performances – 12 and 15 March – at his usual fee of £200. According to Beecham, the composer only agreed to perform if he could have two extra orchestral rehearsals and recalled with pride that 'in the middle of the first of them – that is after about three-quarters of an hour – he quitted the desk, expressing the highest satisfaction with the work of the players'.[135] Inevitably, Strauss attracted the interest of leading members of society and the arts, with the Queen attending his second performance and receiving him in her box. Still on an emotional high, he then with members of the cast to the Savoy Hotel, where a dinner was held in his honour.[136]

After a flying visit to London during which he conducted *Don Juan, Tod und Verklärung* and Mozart's Symphony No. 41 with the Queen's Hall Orchestra at the Queen's Hall on 9 April 1910, four years passed before Strauss returned to England. Travelling direct from Munich, Strauss arrived in Britain on 20 June 1914, where he was honoured at a reception by the Music Club of London the next day. Described by the Chairman of the Club, Alfred Kalisch,[137] as ' "the greatest musician of the present day" ',[138] Strauss was greeted at the Grafton Galleries by some of Europe's leading artists, including Arthur Nikisch, Emil Mlynarski, Sir Charles Stanford and Sir Frederic Cowen.[139] A concert followed the speeches with a programme that included some of Strauss's earlier works and Wagner's *Siegfried Idyll*. Strauss's compositions were intended to reflect ' "the hero's works of peace" ',[140] a clear reference to *Ein Heldenleben* and the growing political tension in Europe. Nikisch opened the concert with Strauss's Suite for Wind in B flat major and he was then joined by the soprano Elena Gerhardt for a selection of the composer's songs.[141] Strauss also performed at the concert when he accompanied his friend 'Lady Speyer in his well-known sonata for piano and violin in E flat'.[142] The evening continued with Strauss's melodrama *Das Schloss am Meere*, in a translation by Kalisch, performed by the actress Lena Ashwell and the pianist Stanley Hawley,[143] and ended with Nikisch's interpretation of *Siegfried Idyll*.

The main reason for Strauss's visit to London in 1914 was to conduct his new ballet, *Josephslegende*. Written for Serge Diaghilev's Ballets Russes, the work received its première at the Paris Opéra that year on 14 May.[144] The idea for the ballet was suggested by Hofmannsthal and Count Harry von Kessler.[145] At first, Strauss showed some interest in the subject but soon found it tedious. Nevertheless, the first night was a success, and Strauss and Hofmannsthal were called back for ten curtain calls. The Paris triumph was reported widely in the British press and a capacity audience flocked expectantly to Drury Lane for the London première on 23 June. But many of those who attended were disappointed by what they heard and most of the critics were dismissive of the score. As might be expected after the *Elektra* exchange, Ernest Newman and George Bernard Shaw locked horns over the ballet. Newman's scathing review in *The Nation* on 27 June 1914 declared that 'the music of The Legend of Joseph is bad enough to ruin any man's reputation [and Strauss] . . . is now one of the dullest and at the same time one of the most pretentious composers in Germany', while Shaw replied on 4 July: 'as before, I flatly contradict Mr Newman. . . . If the Nation could devise some means of printing the opinions which Mr Newman will have some years hence, instead of his first impressions, your readers would be spared the irritation of being told, at the moment when a masterpiece is being performed, that it is not worth hearing . . .'.[146] That said, the score is hardly Strauss's best work and even Thomas Beecham, the man responsible for bringing the Ballets Russes to London,[147] was less than thrilled by it. Writing some thirty years later, he complained:

> The German master revealed no talent for this sort of thing [ballet]; in spite of a few vivid and picturesque moments the piece went with a heavy and plodding gait which all the resource and ingenuity of the troupe could not relieve or accelerate.[148]

The response to *Josephslegende* in London must have upset Strauss, but the reaction to his concert with the Queen's Hall Orchestra at the Queen's Hall on 26 June 1914 probably made up for any disappointment. With a programme that included *Don Juan, Tod und Verklärung, Till Eulenspiegel*, 'Morgen', 'Wiegenlied' and 'Cäcilie', the Countess's Cavatina from Mozart's *Le nozze di Figaro* (with Elena Gerhardt) and Symphony No. 40, Strauss was on familiar ground and was received with enthusiasm. Two days earlier, he was made an honorary Doctor of Music at the Oxford Encaenia and was perhaps surprised to learn that of the five doctorates conferred that day, two were to Germans and one was to a German of British birth.[149] For many, artistic and academic life continued to operate normally during the early summer of 1914. But political tensions had already begun to divide Europe and four days after Strauss received his degree from Oxford, the heir to the Habsburg throne, Franz Ferdinand, was shot in Sarajevo.[150] For Strauss, as for millions of others, the next four years proved catastrophic and by the end of the Great War, the world that had nurtured Strauss as a musician had disappeared, never to return.

Strauss conducting the Olympic Hymn at the Olympic Games, Berlin, 1 August 1936

CHAPTER 9

A Tarnished Icon?

TOURING AND RECORDING (1914–1947)

After Germany mobilized in 1914, Strauss threw his patriotic weight behind the Kaiser's war machine and cheered on the troops. It quickly became apparent, however, that war was more than an abstract concept and that life as he knew it would be affected badly. A little over two months after hostilities were declared, he wrote disconsolately to Hofmannsthal:

> Amidst all the unpleasant things which this war brings with it – except the brilliant feats of our army – hard work is the only salvation. Otherwise the incompetence of our diplomacy, our press, the Kaiser's apologetic telegram to Wilson[1] and all the other undignified acts that are being committed would be enough to drive a man to distraction. And how are the artists treated? The Kaiser reduces the salaries at the Court Theatre, the Duchess of Meiningen turfs her orchestra out into the street, Reinhardt stages Shakespeare, the Frankfurt theatre performs *Carmen, Mignon, The Tales of Hoffmann* – who will ever understand this German nation, this mixture of mediocrity and genius, of heroism and obsequiousness? . . . We're bound to win, of course – but afterwards, Heaven knows, everything will be bungled again![2]

For Strauss, the impact of the war on his professional life was immediate and some of the freedoms that he had previously taken for granted were curtailed overnight. As he was no longer able to visit London, Paris and New York, his touring was restricted to Germany during the second half of 1914[3] but was extended to include the other German-speaking countries, their allies, the occupied territories and neutral states by 1916,[4] the year in which he made his first gramophone records and some eleven years after he made his first piano rolls.

PIANO ROLLS AND FIRST GRAMOPHONE RECORDS

Aged only thirteen when the American inventor Thomas Edison first publicly demonstrated his recitation of 'Mary had a little lamb' on his 'phonograph' in

1877, Strauss was a child of the recording era. While it would be wrong to suggest that he was an audiophile, he was the only major composer-conductor born in the mid nineteenth century to record on piano rolls, shellac and magnetic tape. Without Edison's pioneering technology those transitions might well have been much delayed. An uneasy mix of visionary, entrepreneur, businessman and inventor, Edison captured on wax cylinders the voices not only of Johannes Brahms and Sir Arthur Sullivan, but also of Strauss's friend and mentor, Hans von Bülow, in a concert of Austro-German music before a packed Metropolitan Opera House with a battery of recording horns in New York on 2 May 1889. Sadly, none of the cylinders from that historic event has survived, but as Bülow willingly participated in Edison's experiment, Strauss can be placed firmly in a performance tradition that engaged actively with a technical process that did much to shape the ways in which music was created, performed and received by succeeding generations.

As recording technology was primitive at the beginning of the twentieth century, cylinders and flat discs often failed to inspire confidence in contemporary performers. Recorded by horns with extremely restricted acoustic ranges, pianos sounded like banjos, singers sounded harsh and orchestras sounded like second-rate school bands. It was understandable, then, that many leading musicians preferred to record on piano rolls, of which there were two distinct types, those for player pianos and those for reproducing pianos. The rolls used in manually operated player pianos (pianolas[5]) were less capable of reflecting the interpretative gestures of the performer, while those for electrically operated reproducing pianos responded to pianistic nuances with remarkable accuracy. More important, the music came straight from the instrument for which it was intended rather than through an acoustically inadequate horn. While the technology of reproducing pianos was a revelation for musicians and audiences alike, it came at a cost: the instruments were expensive to buy and even more expensive to repair. Only the middle class and above could afford to own and maintain these instruments, and with the advent of microphones in 1925 and the Wall Street Crash four years later, their attraction came to a clattering halt. Middle-class consumers began to count their pennies and turned instead to good-quality gramophones, which were cheaper to own and easier to maintain.

During their short but fascinating history, reproducing piano rolls were manufactured by three main companies: Welte-Mignon in Germany, and Duo-Art and Ampico in the United States. Many of the leading artists of the day recorded their music for these organizations, including the pianists Teresa Carreño, Ignaz Friedman, Myra Hess, Josef Hoffman and Rudolf Serkin, as well as the composers Gustav Mahler, Edvard Grieg, Eugen d'Albert, Engelbert Humperdinck and Sergei Rachmaninoff. Strauss also recorded on this medium and made his first rolls for Welte at the company's Freiburg studios towards the end of 1905. The works that he recorded at those sessions were selections from *Feuersnot* and *Salome*, the 'Love Scene' from *Ein Heldenleben*,[6] and four of his Lieder specially arranged for solo piano. His recording of the 'Tanz' from *Salome* was particularly timely as the opera was heard for the first time at the Dresden Hofoper later that year. A publicity photo of the recording session was released by Welte shortly after the roll was made that shows Strauss at the piano with the score in front of him surrounded by members of the recording company. Keen to capitalize on Strauss's international fame, the firm then invited him to endorse their product. Careful not to overstate the value of the process, Strauss wrote on 16 February 1906 that the 'Mignon is a quite extraordinary invention, and of all such mechanisms the only one which can lay claim to artistic significance. To the inventors I extend my sincere admiration.'

Strauss made a further set of rolls in 1914, but unlike those from 1905, these were for player pianos. In contrast to reproducing pianos, which were only within the financial reach of the affluent, player pianos were designed to appeal to a wider demographic. One of the leading manufacturers of these instruments was Hupfeld of Leipzig, which made rolls for the mass market. Although more accessible financially, they were less satisfying musically, as they were incapable of replicating articulation and dynamics with any degree of accuracy. Nevertheless, Strauss recognized that they were an effective way of disseminating his music to a wide audience and another means by which to document key aspects of his performance style. For Hupfeld, he recorded excerpts from the 1912 version of *Ariadne auf Naxos*, the 'Love Scene' from *Ein Heldenleben* and an extract from *Josephslegende*.

In 1916, Deutsche Grammophon invited Strauss to record some of his shorter works on shellac through an acoustic horn. For a musician renowned for his understanding of orchestral colour and nuance, this must have been an unsettling experience. Nevertheless, he entered the recording studio for the first time that December[7] and documented *Don Juan*, the suite from *Der Bürger als Edelmann*, the Overture to *Ariadne auf Naxos*, *Till Eulenspiegel* and waltzes from *Der Rosenkavalier*, all with 'der Königlichen Kapelle, Berlin' ('the Royal Orchestra, Berlin').[8] While it might seem strange that Deutsche Grammophon commissioned a protracted series of recordings at a time when German troops were fighting on all fronts, most Berliners probably would not have thought twice about it and would have considered it a normal extension of cultural life. Unlike in London, where the Royal Opera House, Covent Garden, was closed during the hostilities,[9] the Hofoper in Berlin continued to present a full programme of events. Not only did Strauss maintain his usual heavy schedule during this period, but the war years also saw German audiences increase with most forms of professional music-making being sought out by the public. Although resources were scarce and fewer new productions were mounted, people attended concerts and opera in unprecedented numbers, hoping, perhaps, to forget the rigours of their increasingly depressing lives. The relatively recent medium of sound recording also attracted the public's interest, and while the market for gramophone records was limited, they provided a further means of escape. As Strauss's music was a regular feature of concert life in the German capital and as he was considered by many to be the quintessential modern German artist, Deutsche Grammophon's decision to record these works was timely.

Not all of the 1916 sessions accredited to Strauss were recorded by him, however, and in later years, the exact extent of his involvement became a contentious issue. As his former assistant, George Szell, had recorded sides 1 and 2 of *Don Juan* in lieu of Strauss, he was eventually dragged into the row, prompting his discographer, Jack Saul, to recall:

> In the late 'sixties . . . [Szell] wanted me to locate performances of Mozart's Symphony No. 39 and two sides of *Don Juan*, released under Richard Strauss' name by the Polydor Company of Germany. These works were recorded by George Szell in 1917, but being an apprentice conductor he received no credit on the labels for them. The Berlin State Opera Orchestra was listed as being conducted by its chief conductor, Richard Strauss. It is my regret that to this day I have as yet not located them.[10]

In the May 1968 issue of *The Gramophone*,[11] the question of Szell's involvement was raised again by Roger Wimbush:

> The recording of Strauss' *Don Juan* issued in either 1916 or 1917 and labelled as the work of the composer was in fact conducted by his young assistant. The great man had this session, and being busy had asked young Szell to go down to the studios and prepare the orchestra and generally to make ready, which included the cutting of the music on to four sides. When all was prepared and there was still no sign of Strauss the recording director instructed Szell to take the session, since he was not prepared to waste his company's money. After much protest the young man launched the orchestra into the greatest manifestation of a young man ever written. After completing the third side he saw Strauss standing in the doorway in his overcoat, his face wreathed in smiles. Both he and the director were delighted with the way things were going 'and that is how my first records appeared under the name of Dr Richard Strauss'.[12]

Wimbush's remarks did not correspond with the recollections of Szell himself:

> May I say that I very definitely remember having conducted only sides 1 and 2 of that 1917 recording of 'Don Juan' which came out under the name of

Richard Strauss. He himself did sides 3 and 4. If The Gramophone writes that Strauss was in the recording studio at the end of side 3, it may be a misprint or a mistake. I very clearly remember that he had arrived when I was approaching the end of side 2.[13]

SWITZERLAND AND THE UNITED STATES

In 1917, Strauss extended his touring schedule to include Scandinavia and Switzerland.[14] His first Swiss visit involved performances of his own works, while his second also included Mozart's *Don Giovanni* and *Die Zauberflöte*.[15] With stellar casts that included Josef Geiss, Lillian von Granfeldt, Hans Erwin Hey, Barbara Kemp, Paul Knüpfer and Elisabeth Schumann-Puritz, and with an orchestra that comprised the combined Hofkapellen of Meiningen and Dessau, Strauss restaged the famous 1896 Munich production of *Don Giovanni*. Thrilled by what he saw and heard, the critic for the *Zürcher Post* wrote:

If anyone has penetrated right into the soul and spirit of Mozart, it is Richard Strauss. The performance of 17 May [at the Zurich Municipal Theatre] for which we have to thank both him and the combined Meiningen and Dessau Hofkapellen, has brought evidence of this, which cannot be more convinc ingly and more beautifully conceived. This was evident to all who filled the theatre down to the last seat. If ever the acclaim occasioned by the many guest performances of recent weeks has been the expression of genuine enthusiasm, it was so after this performance of *Don Giovanni*. . . . For the correct rendition of Mozart's works a particular blend of instruments is necessary. This must be neither too strong nor too weak. The right balance between strings and woodwind instruments is of the utmost importance, for only thus do the nuances emerge as they should without any danger of the dramatic emphases being weakened. In this respect the conductor has had, thankfully, the most fortuitous touch, as his inspired excellence was percep- tible at every possible stage. If one can say of a Mozart performance that not one single word was lost, then this is just as much praise for the orchestra as for the singers. The orchestra, about 50 strong, played with an accuracy and purity which could not be surpassed. . . . Nowhere was there excess or defi- ciency; each *ritenuto* was well rounded in its sentiment – in a word, a classic rendition. . . . Never before has one felt so strongly that Mozart's greatness and depth speak to us most powerfully precisely in his simplicity. No one understands how to reveal this secret as convincingly in the theatre as Richard Strauss. His achievement in this unforgettable performance extends not only to the musical direction but also to the selection of soloists and with these, he was decidedly fortunate.[16]

In the years immediately following the end of the war, Strauss restricted his activities to Berlin, Vienna and a few local trips. But with the collapse of the German and Austrian economies, he was forced to look to the Americas for hard currency. Having had much of his fortune sequestrated by the British government at the outbreak of war in 1914,[17] Strauss tried to re-establish himself financially by making extensive tours of South America[18] and the United States in the early 1920s. His tour of the USA between 26 October 1921 and 3 January 1922 involved a punishing schedule of orchestral, Leider and chamber concerts in New York, Chicago, Pittsburgh, Boston, Wheeling, St Louis, Kansas City, Indianapolis, Philadelphia, Washington, Detroit, Madison, Milwaukee, Cincinnati and Reading. Of the concert with the Chicago Symphony Orchestra on 16 December,[19] a local critic wrote:

> Richard Strauss tarried a little in Chicago to give a profound and moving elucidation of his art through the medium of the Chicago Symphony. It was an afternoon of sheer beauty, in which a capacity audience at the Auditorium passed from one ecstasy to another as Strauss led the [Frederick] Stock[20] forces through a splendid program. The composer did not seek to impose anything new on the players who had his music at their finger tips. He conducted quietly, tranquilly, almost subordinating himself to the enthusiasm of the men. Only in the climaxes did he seem to conjure up new fires and colorings with his swift beat. At the end of each number there was a tumult of applause . . . 'Also sprach Zarathustra,' one of the monumental Strauss works, opened the orchestral program. There was a clear revelation of the music, and colorings rich and harmonious to fit the changing ideas. 'Tod und Verklärung' was done majestically. The Love Scene from the opera 'Feuersnot' brought an enchanting bit of melody to the program, with rich sentiment in its interpretation.[21]

Before leaving the United States, Strauss made discs of the 'Tanz' from *Salome* and the 'Menuett' and 'Intermezzo' from *Der Bürger als Edelmann*[22] for Brunswick with an unnamed orchestra in New York on 30 and 31 December 1921,[23] and recorded the accompaniments to 'Zueignung', 'Allerseelen' and 'Traum durch die Dämmerung' on reproducing piano rolls for Ampico. Intended for domestic use, these rolls allowed aspiring singers to be accompanied by the composer in the comfort and seclusion of their front parlours.

BRITAIN, *DER ROSENKAVALIER* FILM, AND ELECTRICAL RECORDINGS

After leaving the United States, Strauss travelled to Britain, where he gave concerts in London and Manchester, and recorded a number of his own works for Columbia.[24] In the capital, he conducted the London Symphony Orchestra on 17 January 1922 in a programme that included a selection of his songs with orchestra, *Don Juan, Till Eulenspiegel* and *Tod und Verklärung*.[25] The concert was poorly attended and the stalls of the Royal Albert Hall were only partially occupied. As Strauss was one of the first major German artists to visit Britain after the war, it is possible that anti-German feeling and a familiar programme dissuaded the public from attending. At least one critic was disappointed that Strauss felt either unwilling or unable to perform any of his more recent works, such as *Eine Alpensinfonie*,[26] a sentiment probably shared by many who attended the concert that night.

During his stay in London, Strauss was interviewed by a 'Special Correspondent' for *The Times* who asked him about his thoughts on accompanying 'cinematograph films with good music' and whether he 'had ever considered the possibility of writing original music to accompany films'.[27] Somewhat bewildered by the question, Strauss 'replied emphatically that he had never entertained such an idea, and declared that good music was quite able to stand on its own, without the adventitious help of the film producer'. It is ironic, then, that during his next visit to London he was involved in a performance and a recording of his specially adapted music for Robert Wiene's[28] 1925 silent-film version of *Der Rosenkavalier*. At first, Strauss had serious concerns about the project, but Hofmannsthal soon convinced him of its potential. As the original music required substantial rearrangement, Karl Alwin[29] and Otto Singer[30] were engaged to make the necessary changes. Somewhat bizarrely, the première of the film was given at the Dresden Staatsoper on 10 January 1926 under Strauss, who then conducted it in London on 12 April and again in Zurich on 16 July.[31] While the 'audience [at the Tivoli[32] in London] applauded enthusiastically'[33] the critics had decidedly mixed feelings about it. *The Times* critic wrote:

> The general production was excellent ... the photography of a high standard ... it was delightful to hear the old tunes.... The first appearance of the Prince was the occasion for a brilliant piece of military music in the 18th-century vein. It might almost have been written by Dr. Arne,[34] and yet bears the characteristic stamp of Strauss's style. The reduction of the score to an orchestra of 40 naturally detracted from the richness to which we are accustomed, and justified, negatively, the large forces employed by the composer in the first instance. The performance was adequate in the best sense of the word without attaining to real brilliance. We suppose it is not possible to obtain absolute synchronization of the music with the action, and must be grateful for the one or two places where a really dramatic effect was obtained by the unanimous entry of a character and a new theme.[35]

Conversely, the critic for *Musical Opinion* grumbled:

People who still need to be told what a strange admixture of boy, extraordinary genius and huckster Richard Strauss is can be sated at the Tivoli, where they will see a meandering 'Rosenkavalier' film flickering along to music which, without the singing voices and operatic compactness of construction, is like a nigger troupe without the bones and banjo and jazz without the kettle and mutes. I know that this metaphor is a descent from the sublime to the ridiculous; but Strauss set the fashion. Think of his callow self-consciousness in 'Feuersnot;' his infantile puerilities in his Domestic Symphony, 'Whipped Cream;' and that recent opera on his alleged conjugal affairs, his Fat-Boy-in-Pickwick freakishness in 'Salome;' and now this Tivoli affair, which is neither opera, comedy, music, nor plain, unadulterated 'movie' thrill. A great work of genius – probably Strauss's greatest – first disembowelled, then stuffed in order that it may leer like some mythical hybrid in the gilded shop window of a fashionable taxidermist.[36]

Clearly, the critic for *Musical Opinion* was not a fan of Strauss or his music, and while his tone was harsh, his opinion was prophetic: the film was a failure.

Shortly before visiting London in 1926, Strauss made his first electrical recordings. The shift from horn to microphone towards the end of 1925 was one of the great watersheds of music history. With the inception of the microphone the record industry flourished and, with the broadening of the acoustic spectrum, orchestras no longer needed to huddle around the recording device and retouching the orchestration was no longer necessary for linear clarity. As the length of the discs was approximately the same, cuts were still common, but turntable speeds were standardized at 78 r.p.m.. This meant that pitch was more stable and recordings were more representative of artists' intentions. Cinematographers were also quick to exploit the microphone when they combined moving pictures with sound to create the 'talkies'. While audiences were amazed and delighted by the new medium, musicians faced the greatest crisis of their long history. No longer needed to accompany silent films, cinema musicians were thrown on to the ever-growing human scrapheap of unemployment that did much to define life in late 1920s. The first conductor to record a piece of western art music using a microphone was Strauss's friend Leopold Stokowski,[37] who documented Saint-Saëns's *Danse macabre* with the Philadelphia Orchestra for Victor in 1925. Those discs were the first of a flood of new recordings that swamped the market within a few years, with record companies revisiting works that had already been documented and selecting new repertoire to explore. With an eye firmly focused on the bottom line, firms were keen to publish material that was commercially viable, which inevitably meant works from the Austro-German canon in general and the Beethoven symphonies in particular.

As one of the leading Beethoven interpreters of his age, Strauss was an obvious choice to record a symphony using the new technology. Symphony No. 7 was a piece that he had conducted frequently throughout his career and it was with that work that he made his first electrical recording with the Berlin Staatskapelle on 24 February 1926.[38] At the sessions, Deutsche Grammophon used the Brunswick 'Light-Ray' Method, a process that involved a photoelectric cell. A curious feature of the recording is Strauss's approach to the last movement, where he observed all but one repeat,[39] but excised bars 247 to 421. As a rule, Strauss objected to cuts but seems to have agreed to this excision for commercial reasons, so that the record set could be issued on eight, rather than nine, sides. Cuts were common in recordings of the period[40] and contemporary commentators were not particularly disturbed by them. What interested those writers more were the ways in which the new technology influenced interpretations. This was certainly true of *The Gramophone* magazine's founder, Compton Mackenzie,[41] who wrote:

This is the first 'new method' issue of this symphony, and very tasty it is. . . . The wood-wind at the start appears to me a little less full and round than in English recordings by the new process; the strings balance well, and the bass runs are far more effective than in the old records. Scarcely enough is made of the *PP* work – again the old gramophonic defect, but less pronounced than it used to be. In side 2 the strings do not come out so well against the high woodwind, as in side 1, and their tone rather lacks fatness. The metallic quality is not so pronounced as in the earlier British records, but the 'body' is somewhat light. The rhythmic swing is well kept up, though the whole is too much on a few dynamic levels. We do not want contrast merely for the sake of excitement, but there are legitimate opportunities for making it that are rather neglected. On page 30 the bassoon is out of truth. . . . The last movement, apart from the cut, is very effective. This is an extremely difficult thing to record well. Strauss, with his present not very subtle methods, brings this off well enough. I personally do not mind the cut very much. There are possibilities in this last movement that no conductor I have heard (except Weingartner) really explores. Under him the work is a great joy. Under Strauss it is a moderately stimulating pleasure, a piece of quite adequate conducting without any hidden marvels. He does not take you by the hand, but conducts the party like a Cook's man. He has, I fear, done it a little too often![42]

On the other hand, the American critic Harold C. Schonberg, writing some forty years later, had little interest in the recorded sound and was appalled by the cut:

[Strauss's] recording of the Beethoven Seventh, made in the middle 1920s with the Berlin State Opera Orchestra, is amazing. There is almost never a ritard or a change of expression or nuance. The slow introduction is almost as fast as the following vivace; and the last movement, with a big cut in it, is finished in four minutes, twenty-five seconds. (It should run between seven and eight minutes.) . . . the records leave a bad impression. They are disgraceful, and certainly no testimony to Strauss's probity.[43]

In many ways, it is hard to reconcile Schonberg's comments with either the marks found in Strauss's score of the symphony or the recording itself, but by the 1960s the musical world had changed drastically and expectations of what recordings should represent had shifted markedly. For better or for worse, recordings had become highly manufactured commodities that were representative of the age.

Two days after recording Symphony No.7, Strauss was back in the studio with the Berlin Staatskapelle to set down Mozart's Symphony No. 39 for Deutsche Grammophon. On hand to discuss the discs after they were released in Britain was Compton Mackenzie, who argued:

The new process is at work in the recording, and a rather too ancient one, I think, in the conducting. This seems to me a workmanlike performance, but not a very poetical one. Strauss is not subtle here. . . . The strings have an edginess that helps to bring the lower tone out, but grates a little in the upper ranges. One of the best boons of the new system is that little wood-wind bits have taken on a new and vivid life. In those three bars at the top of page 16, for example, that lead in the recapitulation, the instruments' tone is charmingly fresh and limpid. Some of the tone-levels are ill-considered – that at the start of the slow movement, for example. This is not *piano* playing. The players are a bit careless, rhythmically, in several places. The delicacy of this movement's step is not well caught. Fineness matters immensely in such a work. It is possible, for example, to get much more out of the last movement than Strauss does. The best one can say of this is that the march-discipline is good – better than one often finds it; but the finer dynamic shades are not attempted. There is enough musicianship in the playing to make the records acceptable, especially as the music is bodied forth so much more fully than ever before (this is the first 'new process' recording of the symphony). But I wish Strauss had treated it more thoughtfully and 'inwardly.' It has not the dramatic life of the *G minor*, but there is a lot of sweetness and emotion in it, for the right man to awaken.[44]

Mackenzie's rather Hoffmanesque view of the symphony would probably have baffled Strauss, whose understanding of poetic content was very different from that of the critic.[45] Mackenzie's cloying language had more in common with the aesthetic of Bruno Walter than that of Strauss, who tended to view the interpretative process through objective glasses.

The next work that Strauss recorded for Deutsche Grammophon was his own *Ein Heldenleben*, which he documented with the Berlin Staatskapelle on 4 and 5 March 1926. The sessions were held in the German capital and were sandwiched between engagements in Hamburg and Vienna. Having conducted an all-Strauss programme at Hamburg on 3 March that included *Ein Heldenleben*,[46] Strauss arrived in Berlin on the morning of the fourth and conducted the first session that afternoon. The next morning, he conducted the second session before catching the night train to Vienna. Within months of completing the discs, they were released in England, where Mackenzie reviewed them that August. Pulling no punches, he wrote:

> Is it all worth doing? Most of us, I think, will agree that parts of it are not worth while; but take away these, and you have a singularly strong and in places moving picture of a great man. The recording of such a work presents enormous difficulties. I like best the consistency of the work where there is no really weak spot, though experience of the work 'at first ear' reminds one that still greater clarity might perhaps yet be achieved; and of course, the sonority is nothing like that of the real thing. Otherwise the tone-colours are so faithfully laid before us that the work really lives.[47]

With *Ein Heldenleben* safely in the can, Strauss then turned his attention to Mozart and recorded the 'Jupiter' Symphony with the Berlin Staatskapelle for Deutsche Grammophon on 1 November. As for Strauss's other three recordings for the company, the new discs were made using the Brunswick 'light-ray' method. The Staatskapelle's playing is often breathtaking and the recorded sound is better focused than in the earlier discs. Peter Morse argues that the November sessions were held in a more confined space,[48] which the improved acoustic quality seems to support. Mozart's Symphony No. 40 followed in 1927 with the Staatskapelle and was recorded again a year later with the same orchestra.[49] These discs are something of an enigma, as no concrete reason has yet emerged as to why Strauss recorded the work twice. But the answer to the riddle may lie partly in the recording technique used in 1927 and partly in Strauss's expectations as to how these discs would promote his Mozart style.

Along with his recordings of *Ein Heldenleben*, Beethoven's Symphony No. 7 and Mozart's Symphonies Nos. 39 and 41, Strauss also documented *Tod und Verklärung* and excerpts from *Intermezzo* and *Der Rosenkavalier* with the Berlin Staatskapelle for Deutsche Grammophon in 1926. Each of those discs was made using the 'light-ray' method before it was scrapped by the company in 1927 in favour of the Western Electric microphone method. As Strauss re-recorded the excerpts from *Intermezzo* and *Der Rosenkavalier* with the Staatskapelle immediately after his first recording of Symphony No. 40, this suggests that the first group of excerpts was made using the 'light-ray' method and that the second group was made using the Western Electric microphone method. If that is true, then by extension the earlier recording of the symphony must have been made using the first method and the later recording using the second. It would seem, then, that Deutsche Grammophon was simply experimenting with improved technology and that Strauss was a willing musical guinea pig. Even though both sets of Symphony No. 40 used the leaner version without the clarinets, the 1927 recording was released on six sides and lacks acoustic definition, while the 1928 recording was released on seven and has clearer focus. From all perspectives, the second set is the more satisfying acoustically and interpretatively, and it is more representative of Strauss's Mozart style as a whole.

At the end of 1926, Strauss returned to Britain for concerts for the BBC in London and for the Hallé Concerts Society in Manchester.[50] In the capital, he conducted a programme that included *Eine Alpensinfonie, Don Juan*, the 'Tanz' from *Salome* and the *Festliches Präludium*[51] at the BBC's Third National Concert with an 'orchestra of its musicians' on 9 November. As *The Times* critic had been keen to hear *Eine Alpensinfonie* under Strauss in 1922, it might be assumed that he would write a sympathetic review of the 1926 concert. This was certainly not the case and in a blistering attack he carped that when Strauss 'contemplated the mountains, the experience brought little more eloquence to his pen than it brings to the lips of the average German tourist who goes up in the funicular, exclaiming "Wundershoen!" and "Kolossal!" '[52] The critic for *The Musical Times* was equally unimpressed and felt that 'the best thing in the Symphony is near the beginning. . . . The rest is very long, and sometimes shamelessly bad – mere pot-boiling, in fact.'[53] Of the performances, the critic for *The Times* was of the view that 'neither work [*Eine Alpensinfonie* and *Don Juan*] was perfectly played . . . [and there were] some audible wrong notes and out-of-tune playing on the wind.'[54] Conversely, *Musical Opinion* felt that in *Eine Alpensinfonie* 'the tone-quality was often lovely' and that in *Don Juan* Strauss gave 'a fine performance . . . [that] pulsated with ardour and again with languor and passion.'[55]

Strauss then returned to Germany by way of the Netherlands. Over the years, he had become a regular and welcome visitor to Amsterdam, where he conducted the Concertgebouw Orchestra on no fewer than nineteen occasions. The orchestra's Music Director, Willem Mengelberg, was a close associate of Strauss and it was to the Dutch conductor and orchestra that he had dedicated *Ein Heldenleben*. With the exceptions of trips to provincial German cities, a visit to Milan and a concert in Rome,[56] Strauss spent much of the late 1920s conducting in Berlin and Vienna and making gramophone records.

Among the discs that he made that during period was his last commercial recording of a work by Mozart, the Overture to *Die Zauberflöte* with the Berlin Staatskapelle in 1928. As he was never one to adopt a ponderous tempo, his speeds were often contentious and regularly divided the critics. Writing in the November 1932 issue of *The Gramophone*, W. R. Anderson felt that Strauss

> makes a capital *Flute* record, mellow and yet youthful, as the music must sound. There is a moment or two of slackish rhythm, which pulls us up, apparently for the instruments' sake, in clear speaking. This should not be necessary. Though one feels the players are on their toes, the recording, for once, does not quite convey the mountain-top spirit.[57]

Harold Schonberg, writing in the 1960s, was less sympathetic and dismissed the discs: 'the *Magic Flute* Overture is also taken at a terrific clip . . . the only thing that explains such conducting is the suggestion that Strauss considered those sessions merely a paying assignment'.[58] Lionel Salter writing in 1991 was also far from impressed with the recording and was quick to point out that 'not only are there ragged entries galore – one is the change to the *Allegro* in the *Zauberflöte* Overture – but ensemble is conspicuously touch-and-go throughout . . . (the Overture, taken so fast that it almost falls over itself – though the flute solo, 2'00", has his own ideas about the proper tempo)'.[59] Nevertheless, Strauss's recordings of Mozart were pivotal aesthetically and as Morse rightly pointed out they 'cut away a great deal of romantic excess which had accumulated during the nineteenth century and restored to Mozart's music the coolness and clarity of the original . . . [and did much to secure Strauss's place as] . . . one of the modern founders of the new orchestral style'.[60] The British composer Colin Matthews also recognized their importance and recalled that 'I well remember the first time I heard his recording of Mozart's G minor symphony, and compared it directly with a supposed modern master of Mozart (though only Strauss's junior by 30 years). There *was* no comparison, the later interpretation sounding merely mechanical and unimaginative'.[61]

Along with his second recording of Symphony No. 40 and the Overture to *Die Zauberflöte* in 1928, Strauss re-recorded his 'Tanz' from *Salome* and a series of works by Gluck, Weber, Cornelius and Wagner with the Berlin Philharmonic and Beethoven's Symphony No. 5 with the Staatskapelle.[62] Released in Britain in 1930, the Beethoven discs immediately caught the attention of the critics, prompting W. R. Anderson to write:

> Strauss has fine qualities of symphonic thought. One is struck at the start by the accentual phrasing of the opening four-note *motif*. The urgency in speed

is perhaps a little strong, but I like the dramatic tingle in it. Later, I begin to feel a little routinism in some of the effects, which are like many of those the German orchestras and that from Vienna have lately been showing us; still, these things come off: only, there is a little too much regimentation about them, and an inclination in the players, one feels, to peep round and see if you are noticing their neat little effects. The slow movement is broadly done; but again I seem to want rather more gracious stroking than Strauss appears to be using. I fancy his emotion runs less warmly than it used to do. I recollect feeling this when I heard him at his first London appearance after the war. . . . [The third] movement seems almost too well held in, though it gets a good head of steam as it goes on, and the incisiveness of the playing pleases me well. It just lacks the authentic demonic touch. . . . On the whole, a really good 'cool head' reading and recording. All I miss is a bit more 'warm heart,' and the Beethovenian devilry; but where is perfection to be found?[63]

Strauss's recording of Beethoven's Fifth Symphony is curious for two reasons: first, from the non-consecutive numbering of the matrices it could be argued that it was recorded on two separate occasions, and second, the discs were not released in Britain until 1930, two years after they were made. While Strauss was in the studio four times in 1928, the working practices of both conductor and orchestra make it unlikely that the symphony was recorded at different sessions, and as the reading is a model of tempo integration and tempo manipulation, it is more probable than not that it was documented on the same day. Concerning the release date in Britain, it is possible that Deutsche Grammophon held back the discs for commercial reasons. As recordings by Felix Weingartner, Wilhelm Furtwängler and Eduard Moerike were already available, and as Moerike's recording for Parlophone was also with the Berlin Staatskapelle,[64] it is possible that Polydor was unwilling to release the discs at a time when the market was saturated with recordings of the symphony.

In 1929, Strauss and the Berlin Staatskapelle returned to the studio to record *Don Juan* and *Till Eulenspiegel* for Deutsche Grammophon. The sessions were part of a twelve-day festival held in the German capital that June to mark the composer-conductor's sixty-fifth birthday. At an age when most people consider retirement, Strauss was as active as ever and in less than a fortnight conducted *Salome*, *Elektra*, *Der Rosenkavalier*, *Die Frau ohne Schatten*, *Intermezzo*, *Die ägyptische Helena*, recorded *Don Juan* and *Till Eulenspiegel*, and gave the world première of his *Gesänge des Orients* with the Hungarian tenor Koloman von Pataky.[65] From the non-consecutive matrix numbers, it seems that *Till Eulenspiegel*[66] was recorded before *Don Juan*[67] and that the recordings were made on separate occasions. The possibility of multiple sessions is again unlikely as Strauss can only be confirmed in the studio on 5 June. More important, the discs were his first electrical recordings of *Don Juan* and *Till Eulenspiegel*, an innovation that did not elude the critic for *The Gramophone*:

> It is a boon to have Strauss' own interpretation [of *Don Juan*]; and how easy and natural that sounds, after some we have heard! I remember with pain a wireless performance the other day, which started off so fast that there never was any hope. We do well, I think, to remember that this music goes well back into last century, when Wagner had not been long dead, and Brahms was still going strong: and that the composer of it was only twenty-four. I doubt whether any recording will give the full perfection of detail among the brass. This one has particularly clear wood-wind, and a harp that you can easily trace. With a little reservation about the reverberation, the records are highly commendable.[68]

When *Till Eulenspiegel* was released on long-playing discs in Britain in 1960, Strauss's imprimatur was less important than it had been some thirty years earlier and the early sheen of electric recording had faded considerably:

> This recording, made ten days after the outbreak of war,[69] is a rarity in this country (even the B.B.C. Library does not have a copy) and it is good to have it now in so convenient a format. The recording is very dated, of course, and the transfer appears to have been made for copies that were 'swingers' so that some of the slow passages are rather painful in their pitch variation. . . . All in all perhaps one's surprise is that the performance as a whole is not more personal, but when Strauss marked his scores so well there is not so much room for new revelations. Apart from the fact that speeds are on the fastish side . . . and that in particular he does not linger over the return of the opening theme in the Epilogue, there is little unusual to note.[70]

By the time of the 1929 sessions, Strauss had completed all his major tone poems, but had only recorded *Don Juan, Tod und Verklärung*,[71] *Till Eulenspiegel* and *Ein Heldenleben*.[72] The majority of his other recordings of his own music were given over to excerpts from his operas and the suite from *Der Bürger als Edelmann*. The lack of interest shown by both the composer and the record industry in documenting works such as *Don Quixote* and the *Sinfonia domestica* at that time is puzzling. The public's interest in these tone poems had not diminished and the Berlin orchestra's expertise in realizing Strauss's intentions was not in question. Perhaps record producers felt that the length and complexity of the works made them unviable commercially, yet they are neither longer nor more complex than *Ein Heldenleben*.

BBC Symphony Orchestra and Thoughts on Conducting Technique

In June 1930, Strauss re-recorded *Der Bürger als Edelmann* with the Berlin Staatskapelle for Deutsche Grammophon[73] before travelling to Paris for opera and concert performances that autumn. Then, on 18 and 21 October 1931, he returned to London for two concerts for the BBC, the first of which was part of the Sunday Orchestral Concerts series and was broadcast from a converted wine warehouse. This unlikely setting was the home of the BBC Symphony Orchestra for a number of years[74] and during the transmission Strauss conducted *Macbeth, Don Juan, Tod und Verklärung,* 'Morgen' and 'Cäcilie' with the German Soprano Margarete Teschemacher as soloist.[75] The second concert was also broadcast and was given at the Queen's Hall, where Strauss and the BBC Symphony Orchestra were again joined by Teschemacher. The programme consisted of Mozart's Symphony No. 39, the first English performance of *Drei Hymnen von Friedrich Hölderlin,* and the *Sinfonia domestica.*[76] The *Radio Times* prepared the listeners for the broadcasts by commissioning an article from Percy Scholes,[77] who examined the programmatic nature of Strauss's symphonic writing in detail.[78] The magazine also published a detailed description of the Queen's Hall concert[79] and a listing for the studio broadcast.[80] Apart from the *Drei Hymnen* and the Mozart symphony, the other works given by Strauss were a familiar part of his London repertoire. It is understandable, then, that the critics focused on the novelties when they came to discuss his podium manner and interpretative style. Impressed by what he heard, the critic for *Musical Opinion* wrote:

> On October 21st, Dr. Strauss conducted the B.B.C. Symphony Concert. . . . On this occasion the Mozart symphony was the famous E flat. Strauss, a Mozart worshipper, regards the composer from a broad human point of view, so that the performance was singularly warm and intimate, with little of that elegance and finicking refinement indulged by several Mozart interpreters. . . . The 'Symphonia Domestica' an *enfant terrible* . . . has now grown and developed into an unusually happy and cheerful adult. To say so much implies that the performance was a triumph for the B.B.C. Orchestra. The real novelty on this occasion was the first London performance of Three Hymns for soprano and orchestra, written by the German poet, Hölderlin. Into his music Strauss has reflected the deep brooding of the visionary poet in three magnificent and rapturous orchestral poems. . . . There was much friendly excitement at the close of the concert.[81]

The Times, however, was not quite so impressed. Its critic reported:

> Dr. Richard Strauss was the hero of the symphony concert given by the B.B.C. at Queen's Hall last night. As a conductor of Mozart his reputation has always

stood high, and he began the programme, which otherwise consisted of his own works, with Mozart's lovely Symphony in E flat (No. 39). His view of the function of a conductor of the classics is the very opposite of that of the modern virtuoso conductor. He has no personal interpretation to impress on the players, and he makes no appeal to the eyes of the audience. He believes in time, which his right hand indicates with precision. He uses his left hand chiefly to turn the pages of his score. Most of all, he believes, as a musician should, in Mozart's power to create his own impression if his music is played aright, and that the conductor is there to secure rightness of time, of tone, of phrasing – an unprofitable servant who, when all has gone right, has done only what it was his duty to do. Dr. Strauss's own compositions in this programme were the 'Three Hymns of Hölderlin' for soprano voice and orchestra (Op. 71), never before given in this country, and the 'Domestic Symphony' (Op. 53) for orchestra, which has not been played here for a number of years. . . . Love and Home and Love once more are the deities hymned. Each [Hymn] begins with a musical theme which is undeniable Strauss: each becomes laboured before the poem is half declaimed. That is the drawback of practically all Strauss's music, apart from the theatre. . . . Each work begins with an originative impulse which becomes exhausted long before the end. [The *Sinfonia domestica*] lags and halts and attempts to make up by elaborateness what it lacks in development. It was brilliantly played, except for some raggedness in the rapid wind passages, and the composer received an ovation when it reached its vociferous end[82]

From the reviews, it is clear that Strauss's podium manner continued to fascinate British critics. But for him, the function of the conductor was simply that of 'an unprofitable servant' of the music and in an interview for *The Observer* published ten months before his 1931 visit, he explained that 'the audience . . . desires the "acting" manner of the conductor. . . . [but] gradually musical education will progress, and gestures in conducting will be looked upon as a matter of secondary importance'. More important, 'the musicians in the orchestra dislike the conductor who attempts to conjure them by mystic gestures. . . . Nowadays . . . the orchestra does not want the gesture of an Imperator; it knows by itself what it wants, and seeks connection only with the conductor's personality'.[83]

POLITICAL UNCERTAINTY AND THE IMPACT OF THE NAZIS

From his home in Garmisch, Strauss criss-crossed large parts of mainland Europe in 1932 by rail and along with performances in Italy and Germany, he conducted operas and concerts in Salzburg and Budapest. Having been one of the co-founders of the Salzburg Festival in 1920,[84] he returned there regularly to conduct operas and concerts. In 1932, he gave a programme of his own works, a second of music by Mozart, Beethoven and Weber, and two performances of Beethoven's *Fidelio*.[85] While his visits to Salzburg decreased sharply over the following years, he gave his last Mozart performance at the festival on 6 August 1943[86] and he attended the general rehearsal of his fourteenth opera, *Die Liebe der Danae*, under Clemens Krauss on 16 August 1944.[87] In Budapest, Strauss conducted a series of his operas and orchestral works between 21 and 31 October 1932 that included *Salome, Der Rosenkavalier, Die ägyptische Helena, Don Juan, Tod und Verklärung, Wanderers Sturmlied* and *Till Eulenspiegel*.[88] These performances amounted to a mini festival of Strauss's music, a format that had become increasingly popular throughout much of western European after the turn of the twentieth century.

With the Nazis' victory at the German elections in January 1933, Strauss's life changed for ever. As one of the country's cultural icons, he quickly became an unwitting propaganda tool and he was soon engulfed by controversy. When Bruno Walter was ousted as conductor of the Berlin Philharmonic's concert on 20 March, Strauss was nominated as his replacement. The concert was given by Strauss at the suggestion of the Nazis, according to Walter, who was shocked that 'the composer of *Ein Heldenleben* actually declared himself ready to conduct in place of a colleague who had been forcibly removed. This made him especially popular with the upper ranks of Nazism. Later, to be sure, for reasons unknown to me, Strauss was said to have fallen out with the government.'[89] Perhaps unsurprisingly, Walter's recollection of the event differs sharply from that of Strauss, who maintained that he performed as a favour to the orchestra and that he donated his fee to it. His international image then suffered another blow when he replaced Toscanini for performances of Wagner's *Parsifal* at Bayreuth that summer.[90] As the music drama was given in the presence of Hitler and as Toscanini had walked out as an anti-fascist protest, the Italian never forgave Strauss for replacing him and never missed an opportunity to take the moral high ground. Strauss's reputation was further damaged when he was appointed President of the Reichsmusikkammer by the Minister for Propaganda, Dr. Joseph Goebbels, on 15 November. Even though Strauss and his Vice-President, Wilhelm Furtwängler, had little choice but to accept the appointments, history has never considered their plight sympathetically and has often tarred them with the same brush as those who actively supported the regime.

In 1933, Strauss also recorded *Don Quixote* with the Berlin Staatskapelle for Deutsche Grammophon. Presumably made during his visit to Berlin where he conducted the Philharmonic in a programme that included *Don Quixote*, some orchestral songs with Viorica Ursuleac[91] and *Ein Heldenleben* on

13 October, the much-anticipated recording was greeted warmly when it was released in Britain in 1934. In a lengthy review for *The Gramophone* one critic argued:

> Music is still the greatest evocative force. Compare Strauss's tone poem . . . with the film in which Robey and Chaliapin appeared – a failure, in spite of singing and comedy.[92] It failed largely because it left too little to the imagination. Strauss failed slightly from the same cause: those sheep, amusing though they are, show where he was beginning to go wrong. Yet is by far the more successful, subtle interpretation of Cervantes, who had to wait just about three centuries for the bodying forth in music (spiriting forth, rather) of his universal figure. There have been plenty of *Don Quixote* operas, most of which we do not hear; but if they had really got hold of the Don, we should have known it beyond a peradventure. One quality that always lifts the great man above the crowd is his perception of appropriate *form*, and, as I have often urged, our appreciation of this powerful element, and of a composer's handling of it, is what most surely gives us a place as true 'appreciators' of music. Strauss has always been a wonder in that respect. His use of free variation form for *Don Quixote* is yet another of his triumphs in the shaping of material to dramatic ends. . . . The eloquent 'cello of Enrico Mainardi[93] is admirably at the service of the music. In the composer's interpretation, and this modest-scaled recording, I find it satisfying (with steel), although some will doubtless wish for bolder tone. I prefer to have a little left to do, even if it means mentally supplying things that only the score gives the true hint of. And will not any recording of this tone-poem have wrought an additional good work upon us if it sends us back to Cervantes's great fantasy, in which is so much of philosophical truth?[94]

Never one to kowtow completely to dogma, Strauss was unwilling to relinquish his relationships with Jewish artists who had been isolated by the Nazis. With the death of Hofmannsthal on 15 July 1929, Strauss lost his most valued artistic collaborator but hoped that he had found a suitable replacement in Stefan Zweig.[95] The son of a wealthy Jewish textile manufacturer, Zweig was a much-respected biographer, novelist and playwright, and the librettist for Strauss's eleventh opera, *Die schweigsame Frau*. As Zweig was unacceptable racially to the regime, Strauss had to negotiate hard to secure the authorities' approval for Zweig to act as his librettist. After much haggling, the work was eventually composed and scheduled for performance at the Dresden Staatsoper on 25 June 1935. When Strauss arrived for the première under Karl Böhm, he demanded a copy of the poster and was shocked to see that Zweig's name had been omitted. Outraged by the insult, Strauss insisted that the poster be reprinted and that the librettist's name be included. If not, he would leave the next day and the première would have to go ahead without him. After much shuffling of anti-Semitic feet, Strauss's demands were met and Zweig's name was inserted. Nevertheless, it was clear that Strauss's and Zweig's professional relationship was not viable because of the existing political climate. While Strauss wanted to continue collaborating with Zweig, the writer was more pragmatic and tried to persuade Strauss to pursue other possibilities. Unwilling to relinquish Zweig without a fight, Strauss had sent him a letter eight days before the first performance that set out his feelings:

Dear Herr Zweig,

Your letter of the 15th is driving me to distraction! This Jewish obstinacy! Enough to make an anti-Semite of a man! This pride of race, this feeling of solidarity! Do you believe that I am ever, in any of my actions, guided by the thought that I am 'German' (perhaps, *qui le sait*)? Do you believe that Mozart composed as an 'Aryan'? I know only two types of people: those with and those without talent. 'Das Volk' exists for me only at the moment it becomes an audience. Whether they are Chinese, Bavarians, New Zealanders, or Berliners leaves me cold. What matters is that they pay full price for admission. . . . The comedy you sent me is charming . . . I won't accept it under an assumed name. . . . Just keep the matter a secret on *your* part and let *me* worry about what I will do with the plays. Who told you that I have exposed myself politically? Because I have conducted a concert in place of that greasy rascal Bruno Walter? That I did for the orchestra's sake. Because I substituted for that other 'non-Aryan' Toscanini? That I did for the sake of Bayreuth. That has nothing to do with politics. It is none of my business how the gutter press interprets what I do, and it should not concern you either. Because I act the part of president of the Reich Music Chamber? That I do only for good purposes and to prevent greater disasters! I would have accepted this trouble-some honorary office under any government, but neither Kaiser Wilhelm nor Herr Rathenau offered it to me. . . . The show [*Die schweigsame Frau*] here will be terrific. Everybody is wildly enthusiastic. And with all this you ask me to forgo you? Never ever![96]

Tragically, the letter never reached Zweig because it had been intercepted by the Gestapo shortly after it was posted. But by penning it, Strauss had snubbed the system and had to be ostracized. On 6 July, he was visited by Walter von Keudell, a Nazi official, who insisted that he resign immediately as President of the Reichsmusikkammer for health reasons. Strauss agreed without hesitation. By so doing, he had become *persona non grata* and was seen as a liability to the regime.

Nevertheless, Strauss accompanied the Dresden Staatsoper on their 1936 visit to London where the company of 194 musicians, singers, dancers and dressing-room attendants performed operas and concerts between 2 and 13 November. As the tour was sponsored by the German Government, the wider political implications of the event were not lost on the British press, with at least one journalist raising the issue of Nazi cultural suppression.[97] While the majority of the conducting was undertaken by Karl Böhm,[98] Strauss conducted a performance of _Ariadne auf Naxos_ and a concert with the Dresden Staatskapelle. For his only opera performance at Covent Garden since 1910, Strauss conducted the 1916 version of _Ariadne auf Naxos_ on 6 November. The critics considered the individual performances of the singers and the playing of the orchestra to be of a high standard and they were particularly impressed by Strauss's management of the ensemble. _The Times_, for example, found that 'what appealed most was the mollowness [_sic_] of most of this music and the ease with which in conducting it [Strauss] obtained what he wanted from singers and players without any apparent physical effort on his own part'.[99] On 7 November, Strauss conducted the Staatskapelle at the Queen's Hall in a programme that included _Till Eulenspiegel_, _Don Quixote_ and Mozart's Symphony No. 40. Once again, _The Times_ was fascinated by Strauss's podium manner and observed that 'formerly he was a demonstrative, though never an extravagant mannered, conductor; [but] now he seems to do little but set the time and watch the players all playing their best because his eye is on them. And that is enough.'[100]

During the visit, Strauss was no longer considered the leader of the avant-garde but music's elder statesman. Havergal Brian[101] published an article in _Musical Opinion_ that not only considered Strauss's performances with the Staatsoper and its orchestra but also his achievements as a composer. Brian, a Strauss admirer, argued that the composer's 'genius as a contrapuntist, melodist and orchestrator ... [was] unsurpassable'[102] and that he was ' the last of a great line of German composers'.[103] The Royal Philharmonic Society also held Strauss in high regard and awarded him the Gold Medal of the Society on 5 November. In his presentation speech, Sir Hugh Allen described the composer as 'the outstanding figure in the world of music of our time.'[104] As a gesture of gratitude, Strauss then presented the Society with an autograph copy of the first page of his tone poem _Macbeth_.

WAR WORLD TWO AND POLITICAL ISOLATION

After _Don Quixote_ in 1933, Strauss's interest in recording diminished for a period and the only sound documents of him as a conductor from the late 1930s to survive World War Two are radio recordings of _Don Quixote_ and a fragment of _Till Eulenspiegel_ from the Dresden Staatskapelle's Queen's Hall concert,[105] _Macbeth_ with the Orchester des Deutschlandsender Berlin

from 1936, and *Eine Alpensinfonie, Don Juan* and *Tod und Verklärung*
with the Orchester des Reichssender München from 1936 and 1937. Strauss's
interest in recording seems to have been reawakened four years later,
when he set down *Don Quixote, Ein Heldenleben, Eine Alpensinfonie,
Japanische Festmusik* and waltzes from *Der Rosenkavalier* with the Bayerisches
Staatsorchester for Deutsche Grammophon and Electrola between 1940 and
1941.[106] Of these works, only the *Japanische Festmusik* had not been recorded
previously by Strauss. Based on material sketched in 1915, the work was
completed at Merano on 22 April 1940. Composed for the 2,600th anniversary
of the Japanese imperial dynasty, it was given its first performance later
that year at Tokyo on 14 December. But the work had little personal appeal
for Strauss, who quickly dropped it from his performing repertoire after
recording it.[107]

During World War Two, Strauss made no commercial recordings, but his
performances were documented extensively by Reichssender Wien and by the
private enthusiast Hermann May, who recorded extracts from Strauss's
performing version of *Idomeneo* at the Staatsoper on 3 December 1941 and
excerpts from four performances of *Salome* under the composer in 1942.[108] As
May used an amateur recording machine, the quality of the original masters
was very poor and their subsequent use caused them to deteriorate further.
Nevertheless, these are extremely important sound documents, as they are the
only known recordings of Strauss conducting Mozart's vocal music. In the
1990s, Koch Schwann released the discs after they were re-mastered by
Christian Zimmerli,[109] who pointed out:

> Since the discs were played several times since they were made, a mechanical
> abrasion has impaired the disc with each playing. Herr May's recording
> equipment was not conceived for professional use – this is comparable today
> with the difference between a walkman cassette and digital studio tech-
> nology. This also explains the background noise . . . that arose when the
> recording stylus had not been sufficiently pre-heated, or the whoosh
> caused by a strip (cut-out material) which had not been properly siphoned
> off. Since the recording apparatus was behind the stage and the recording
> stylus picked up not only the signals from the microphone, but also the
> noises from the immediate vicinity, one can also hear noises from behind the
> stage.[110]

In 1942, Reichssender Wien recorded Strauss performing *Also sprach
Zarathustra* and *Till Eulenspiegel* with the Vienna Philharmonic and a selection of songs with leading singers from the Vienna Staatsoper. Then, in June
1944, Vienna mounted some of his operas at the Staatsoper and held a series
of concerts and radio recordings with the Philharmonic to celebrate his eight-

ieth birthday. Recording on magnetic tape for the first time, Strauss conducted *Also Sprach Zarathustra*, the suite from *Der Bürger als Edelmann, Don Juan, Ein Heldenleben, Sinfonia domestica, Till Eulenspiegel, Tod und Verklärung* and the Prelude to *Die Meistersinger von Nürnberg* for Reichssender Wien between 12 and 15 June.[111] During the celebrations, Strauss was also captured on film by Universum Film AG (UFA) conducting *Till Eulenspiegel* with the Vienna Philharmonic, the longest filmed example of him conducting and the most valuable extant snapshot of his late podium style.

Made at a time when the Third Reich was teetering on the brink of collapse, Strauss's Vienna recordings had a wider social and political significance. His activities during the Third Reich have been a source of interest to historians and musicologists alike, but given his association with Hugo von Hofmannsthal and Stefan Zweig and his concern for the well-being of the Jewish members of his family throughout the period, the hostility of some commentators seems difficult to justify. Moreover, during the course of World War Two, the Nazis actively set out to damage his credibility and on 24 January 1944, six months before the composer's eightieth birthday celebrations, Martin Bormann issued the following communiqué:

> The personal contact of our leading men with Dr. Strauss shall end. The Führer, to whom Reichsminister Dr. Goebbels has referred the matter, has decided, however, that the performance of his works should not be hindered.[112]

Even though Strauss's works continued to be played during the dying days of the Third Reich, his inability to associate with some senior colleagues caused him concern. Nevertheless, the Vienna Philharmonic was unaffected by the ban and fellow musicians continued to support him throughout this difficult period. At a time when public morale was declining sharply, Hitler's decision to allow Strauss's music to be played was shrewd. As Strauss was considered by many to be Germany's leading musician, the decision to permit his works to be heard did much to support the increasingly shaky illusion of social and artistic normality.

CONDUCTING SWANSONG

After the collapse of the Third Reich, Strauss took refuge for a time in Switzerland. As his health, financial circumstances and professional standing were in sharp decline in the period directly following the end of the war, his friends Dr. Ernst Roth[113] and Sir Thomas Beecham rallied around and organised a festival of his music in London in 1947. The festival involved six concerts and broadcasts, and was intended to be a forum for Strauss's works and a means by which to provide him with some urgently needed foreign currency. Travelling by air for the first time, he arrived in London from Geneva on 4 October. After landing at Northolt Airport, he was taken to the Savoy Hotel, where he was greeted by a large and curious press contingent. Asked about his plans for the future, Strauss replied simply 'To die, of course!' Keen to explore as many of his old haunts as possible, he reacquainted himself with the treasures of the National Gallery, played Skat with old friends, and visited Eton and Windsor.

The festival's first two concerts were held on 5 and 12 October with Beecham conducting the Royal Philharmonic Orchestra at the Theatre Royal, Drury Lane.[114] On 19 October, Strauss conducted the Philharmonia Orchestra at the Royal Albert Hall in a programme of works that included *Don Juan*, *Burleske* (Alfred Blumen, piano), waltzes from *Der Rosenkavalier*, and the *Sinfonia domestica*.[115] Roth recalls that Strauss was given three two-hour rehearsals for the performance and 'was somewhat anxious about [the *Sinfonia domestica*] because of his health' but 'refused to conduct the work sitting down'.[116] Fascinated by the return of a musician who had been such an important part of London's concert life for fifty years, the critics fell over themselves to publish their impressions of the great man. Inevitably, Strauss's baton technique was a central issue and much copy was given over to it. The critic for *The Times* wrote:

> Dr. Strauss has never been of the demonstrative school. His left hand rarely leaves his side, and his right seems to do no more than beat time. But how exact that beat is! How infinite the gradation of expression conveyed by variations in the movement of the stick! At 83 his command of the orchestra and his ability to obtain from it exactly what he wants remain undiminished.[117]

On 24 and 26 October, Beecham gave two performances of *Elektra* that were broadcast by the BBC,[118] and on 29 October the festival's last concert was held at the Royal Albert Hall. At that performance, Holst's *The Planets* and Mozart's 'Jupiter' Symphony were given by Sir Adrian Boult and the BBC Symphony Orchestra, while *Till Eulenspiegel* was conducted by the composer. As Strauss had performed the tone poem at his first London concert in 1897, its inclusion was an appropriate end to his visit. For many present at the Royal Albert Hall that night, it was obvious that they were witnessing Strauss's swansong and this sense of finality was captured poignantly by Neville Cardus:

> Yesterday in the vasty spaces of the Albert Hall Richard Strauss looked frail as well as very old as he bent and stumbled his way to the rostrum to conduct

'Till Eulenspiegel.' The thought came to me that on such a wintry night he would have been better in bed with a hot water bottle. . . . At the end the audience applauded affectionately; there was no rhetorical demonstration – just sustained and very English handclaps. The old man picked and tottered his way through the orchestra back to the front of the platform and bowed stiffly but with a rare courtesy. Then he disappeared from view and it is not in the nature of things that we shall see him again.[119]

Conclusion

When Strauss walked off stage at the Royal Albert Hall that 'wintry night' in 1947, his conducting career faded into history. Never again would he raise his baton professionally and never again would the musical world engage with such a versatile artist. From London, Strauss flew on 31 October to Switzerland, where he was reunited with his beloved Pauline, and from Montreux he moved back to Garmisch on 10 May 1949. Even though his health was failing during his final months, he was still passionately interested in theatre life, and when the young Georg Solti visited him at his villa that June, Strauss quizzed him about the most recent comings and goings at the Bavarian Staatsoper. The impact that meeting had on Solti was profound, and in old age he recalled vividly that 'when I rang the bell, the door was opened not by a servant but by Strauss himself. This was the first of two occasions in my life when I found myself reduced to utter silence. . . . I stood there tongue-tied, clutching my scores. He sensed my nervousness, and, to put me at my ease, he asked me to sit down and tell him the latest gossip at the opera.'[1] Eager to gain an insight into Strauss's scores, Solti quickly turned the conversation to musical matters and asked about the tempi in *Der Rosenkavalier*. Strauss quipped 'very easy . . . I set Hofmannsthal's text at the pace at which I would speak it, with a natural speed and in a natural rhythm. Just recite the text and you will find the right tempi.'[2] Ever the practical musician, Strauss then asked Solti if he had ever left the pit when rehearsing the opera to listen in the auditorium. When Solti replied 'No', Strauss said 'You really should . . . because what you hear from your place in the pit is totally different from what the audience hears.'[3] But probably the most important piece of advice that Solti was given that day concerned the conductor's response to the score. Objective to the last, Strauss stressed that one should 'not to get too involved with the music, but to stay somewhere outside it – not to lack passion, but to be dispassionate in the execution.'[4]

Of course, Solti was only one of a long list of conductors who sat at the Master's feet during his lifetime. Clemens Krauss, Fritz Busch, Karl Böhm, Fritz Reiner, George Szell and Herbert von Karajan all benefited from Strauss's wisdom and all remained devoted disciples to the end of their lives. For them, Strauss represented a purity of approach that less objective figures often lacked. Deeply saddened by his death on 8 September 1949, they all realized that they had lost not only a major performing artist but also the last great German composer. But thanks to modern technology, there is now available an arc of historical artefacts that spans half the composer's life, ranging from his earliest piano rolls in 1905 to the film footage of him conducting the final bars of Act 2 of *Der Rosenkavalier* at Munich's Prinzregententheater on 10 June 1949.[5] Given both the beauty and the majesty of these recordings and given the current interest in such objects as the basis for performance research, it seems odd that much of the available material has been overlooked by many scholars and performers. Heated discussions about how Stravinsky's and Elgar's recordings should be used to inform the approach of performers are commonplace, but the same kind of discussions rarely happen about Strauss's discs and films. In a recent excellent book that examined sound documents as vibrant research tools, Strauss's recordings were overlooked completely. This was a sad omission as his recorded legacy does more than just simply indicate the personal approach of a musician isolated by time and place. Strauss was a pivotal artist whose teachers and mentors could trace their heritage back to the era of Beethoven and whose protégés did much to shape current performance trends. Strauss's recordings and films are not only a treasure trove of information about his life and times but are also the key to a historical door that has yet to be unlocked fully.

APPENDICES

Rehearsal for the *Alpensinfonie* film, Munich, June 1941.

Autograph text: 'If you don't have the score in your head, put your head right in the score' [Hans von Bülow's advice to Strauss].

APPENDIX 1

Strauss's Performances as a Tenured Conductor

PART A: MEININGEN, 1885–1886[1]

1. 18.10.1885 (with the Meininger Hofkapelle conducted by Bülow): Beethoven. *Coriolan* Overture; Mozart: Piano Concerto No. 24 (Richard Strauss, piano); Strauss: Symphony in F minor (Richard Strauss, conductor); Beethoven: Symphony No. 7.
2. 06.12.1885 (with the Meininger Hofkapelle): Gluck: *Iphigénie en Aulide* Overture; Handel: unspecified aria from *Semele*; Mozart: Requiem; Brahms: *Schicksalslied*.
3. 25.12.1885 (with the Meininger Hofkapelle): Schubert: Symphony in D minor ('Unfinished'), Reif: Clarinet Concerto (Richard Mühlfeld, clarinet), Gluck: 'Ach ich habe sie verloren' from *Orpheus*; Princess Marie Elizabeth von Sachsen-Meiningen: 'Meine drei Freunde' (Fannie Schreiber, soprano); Schumann: *Manfred* Overture; Brahms: Symphony No. 3.
4. 08.01.1886 (chamber music concert with Strauss as pianist and members of the Meininger Hofkapelle): Haydn: String Quartet Op. 76 No. 1; Beethoven: Sonata for Violin and Piano in E flat major Op. 12 No. 3 (Friedhold Fleischhauer, violin); Strauss: Piano Quartet in C minor.
5. 29.01.1886 (with the Meininger Hofkapelle conducted by Bülow and Strauss): Rheinberger: *Der Widerspenstigen Zähmung* (Hans von Bülow, conductor); Rubinstein: Piano Concerto No. 3 (Hans von Bülow, piano; Richard Strauss, conductor); Bülow: *Nirwana* (Hans von Bülow, conductor); Liszt: *Fantasie über ungarische Volkweise* (Hans von Bülow, piano; Richard Strauss, conductor); Beethoven: Symphony No. 3 (Hans von Bülow, conductor).
6. 23.02.1886 (with the Meininger Hofkapelle): Beethoven: *Leonore* No. 1 Overture; Gluck: unspecified aria from *Alceste* (Amalie Joachim, soprano); Thuille: Symphony in F major;§[2] Lachner: Gavotte from Suite No. 6 Op. 150; Brahms: 'Allegretto' from Symphony No. 2, unspecified Lieder (Amalie Joachim, soprano), *Academic Festival Overture*.
7. 05.03.1886 (chamber music concert with Strauss as pianist and members of the Meininger Hofkapelle): Beethoven: Cello Sonata Op. 5 No. 1; Brahms: Horn Trio; Strauss: 'Zueignung', 'Nichts', 'Georgine' and 'Allerseelen' (Rudolf Engelhardt, tenor); Schubert: 'Trout' Quintet.
8. 18.03.1886 (with the Meininger Hofkapelle): Mozart: *Die Zauberflöte* Overture; Bach: *Gottes Zeit ist die allerbeste Zeit*; Brahms: *Gesang der Parzen*; Mendelssohn: *Die erste Walpurgisnacht*.
9. 26.03.1886 (chamber music concert with Strauss as pianist and members of the Meininger Hofkapelle): Gouvy: Clarinet Sonata in G minor; Volkmann: Piano Trio in B minor; Beethoven: Quintet for Piano and Winds Op. 16.
10. 02.04.1886 (with the Meininger Hofkapelle): Strauss: Concert Overture in C minor; Wagner: *Tristan und Isolde* Prelude and Liebestod (Therese Malten,[3] soprano); Weber: 'Ozean' aria from *Oberon* (Therese Malten, soprano); Brahms: unspecified Lieder (Therese Malten, soprano), Haydn Variations (Johannes Brahms, conductor), Symphony No. 4 (Johannes Brahms, conductor).

11. 09.04.1886 (chamber music concert with Strauss as pianist and members of the Meininger Hofkapelle): Mozart: 'Kegelstatt' Trio; Strauss: three piano pieces from *Stimmungsbilder*; Beethoven: String Quartet in C minor Op. 18; Saint-Saëns: Violin Sonata; Schumann: Piano Quintet.

PART B: MUNICH HOFOPER, 1886–1889

Composer	Work	Date

1886–1887 Season

	Composer	Work	Date
1.	Boieldieu	*Jean de Paris*	01.10.1886
2.	Boieldieu	*Jean de Paris*	12.10.1886
3.	Mozart	*Così fan tutte*	12.11.1886
4.	Boieldieu	*Jean de Paris*	16.11.1886
5.	Mozart	*Così fan tutte*	17.11.1886
6.	Rheinberger	*Des Thürmers Töchterlein*	26.01.1887
7.	Auber	*Le domino noir*	01.02.1887
8.	Auber	*Fra Diavolo*	08.02.1887
9.	Auber	*Fra Diavolo*	17.03.1887
10.	Goldmark	*Die Königin von Saba*	20.03.1887
11.	Goldmark	*Die Königin von Saba*	25.03.1887
12.	Auber	*Le domino noir*	29.03.1887
13.	Goldmark	*Die Königin von Saba*	15.04.1887
14.	Boieldieu	*Jean de Paris*	07.05.1887
15.	Cherubini	*Les deux journées*	13.05.1887
16.	Cherubini	*Les deux journées*	20.05.1887
17.	Cherubini	*Les deux journées*	24.05.1887
18.	Lortzing	*Die beiden Schützen*	17.06.1887
19.	Lortzing	*Die beiden Schützen*	21.06.1887
20.	Verdi	*Il Trovatore*	23.06.1887

1887–1888 Season

	Composer	Work	Date
1.	Mozart	*Così fan tutte*	03.11.1887
2.	Lortzing	*Die beiden Schützen*	08.11.1887
3.	Verdi	*Il Trovatore*	18.11.1887
4.	Lortzing	*Die beiden Schützen*	22.11.1887
5.	Lortzing	*Zar und Zimmermann*	29.11.1887
6.	Lortzing	*Zar und Zimmermann*	22.12.1887
7.	Lortzing	*Die beiden Schützen*	01.03.1888
8.	Cherubini	*Les deux journées*	22.03.1888
9.	Weber	*Der Freischütz*	17.04.1888
10.	Flotow	*Alessandro Stradella*	30.04.1888
11.	Weber	*Der Freischütz*	21.06.1888
12.	Cornelius	*Der Barbier von Bagdad*	24.07.1888
13.	Weber	*Der Freischütz*	31.07.1888

1888–1889 Season

	Composer	Work	Date
1.	Cornelius	*Der Barbier von Bagdad*	29.08.1888
2.	Weber	*Der Freischütz*	06.09.1888

3. Weber	*Der Freischütz*	13.11.1888
4. Lortzing	*Die beiden Schützen*	18.12.1888
5. Cornelius	*Der Barbier von Bagdad*	31.01.1889
6. Donizetti	*La favorite*	02.02.1889
7. Donizetti	*La favorite*	07.02.1889
8. Verdi	*Un ballo in maschera*	18.02.1889
9. Lortzing	*Die beiden Schützen*	21.02.1889

PART C: WEIMAR HOFTHEATER, 1889–1894

Composer	Work	Date

1889–1890 Season

1. Mozart	*Die Zauberflöte*	22.09.1889
2. Wagner	*Lohengrin*	06.10.1889‡[4]
3. Weber	*Der Freischütz*	20.10.1889
4. Mozart	*Die Zauberflöte*	23.10.1889
5. Mozart	*Le nozze di Figaro*	31.10.1889
6. Mozart	*Le nozze di Figaro*	09.11.1889
7. Mozart	*Die Zauberflöte*	13.11.1889
8. Méhul	*Joseph in Ägypten*	21.11.1889†[5]
9. Weber	*Der Freischütz*	26.11.1889
10. Lortzing	*Zar und Zimmermann*	01.12.1889
11. Weber	*Der Freischütz*	03.12.1889
12. Lortzing	*Zar und Zimmermann*	04.12.1889
13. Wagner	*Lohengrin*	08.12.1889
14. Weber	*Preziosa*	15.12.1889
15. Lortzing	*Zar und Zimmermann*	02.01.1890
16. Weber	*Der Freischütz*	03.01.1890
17. Mozart	*Le nozze di Figaro*	04.01.1890
18. Lortzing	*Der Waffenschmied*	05.01.1890
19. Wagner	*Lohengrin*	12.01.1890
20. Méhul	*Joseph in Ägypten*	15.01.1890
21. Méhul	*Joseph in Ägypten*	16.01.1890
22. Lortzing	*Der Waffenschmied*	22.01.1890
23. Marschner	*Hans Heiling*	26.01.1890†
24. Mozart	*Don Giovanni*	09.02.1890
25. Marschner	*Hans Heiling*	11.02.1890
26. Lortzing	*Der Wildschütz*	23.02.1890.
27. Weber	*Preziosa*	08.03.1890
28. Lortzing	*Der Wildschütz*	09.03.1890
29. Lortzing	*Der Wildschütz*	12.03.1890
30. Méhul	*Joseph in Ägypten*	18.03.1890
31. Mozart	*Le nozze di Figaro*	23.03.1890
32. Wagner	*Tannhäuser*	27.03.1890†
33. Weber	*Der Freischütz*	06.04.1890
34. Wagner	*Tannhäuser*	09.04.1890
35. Lortzing	*Der Wildschütz*	16.04.1890
36. Wagner	*Tannhäuser*	20.04.1890
37. Wagner	*Lohengrin*	24.04.1890
38. Wagner	*Tannhäuser*	27.04.1890
39. Flotow	*Alessandro Stradella*	01.05.1890

40.	Auber	*Le cheval de bronze* (arr. Humperdinck)	04.05.1890
41.	Lortzing	*Der Waffenschmied*	15.05.1890
42.	Auber	*Le cheval de bronze* (arr. Humperdinck)	20.05.1890
43.	Mozart	*Die Zauberflöte*	22.05.1890
44.	Wagner	*Tannhäuser*	25.05.1890
45.	Auber	*Le cheval de bronze* (arr. Humperdinck)	28.05.1890
46.	Auber	*Le cheval de bronze* (arr. Humperdinck)	30.05.1890
47.	Flotow	*Alessandro Stradella*	01.06.1890
48.	Lortzing	*Der Wildschütz*	04.06.1890
49.	Ritter	*Wem die Krone?*	08.06.1890*[6]§
50.	Ritter	*Der faule Hans*	08.06.1890*
51.	Ritter	*Wem die Krone?*	10.06.1890*
52.	Ritter	*Der faule Hans*	10.06.1890*
53.	Ritter	*Wem die Krone?*	17.06.1890*
54.	Ritter	*Der faule Hans*	17.06.1890*

1890–1891 Season

1.	Mozart	*Die Zauberflöte*	21.09.1890
2.	Ritter	*Wem die Krone?*	28.09.1890*
3.	Ritter	*Der faule Hans*	28.09.1890*
4.	Lortzing	*Der Wildschütz*	30.09.1890
5.	Wagner	*Tannhäuser*	05.10.1890
6.	Ritter	*Wem die Krone?*	07.10.1890*
7.	Ritter	*Der faule Hans*	07.10.1890*
8.	Marschner	*Hans Heiling*	08.10.1890
9.	Ritter	*Wem die Krone?*	15.10.1890*
10.	Ritter	*Der faule Hans*	15.10.1890*
11.	Mozart	*Die Zauberflöte*	16.10.1890
12.	Weber	*Der Freischütz*	19.10.1890
13.	Gluck	*Iphigénie en Aulide*	26.10.1890
14.	Wagner	*Lohengrin*	02.11.1890
15.	Mozart	*Die Zauberflöte*	09.11.1890
16.	Marschner	*Hans Heiling*	13.11.1890
17.	Wagner	*Tannhäuser*	16.11.1890
18.	Lortzing	*Der Waffenschmied*	25.11.1890
19.	Gluck	*Iphigénie en Aulide*	02.12.1890
20.	Weber	*Der Freischütz*	14.12.1890
21.	Wagner	*Lohengrin*	21.12.1890
22.	Wagner	*Rienzi*	25.12.1890‡
23.	Wagner	*Lohengrin*	28.12.1890
24.	Mozart	*Don Giovanni*	04.01.1891
25.	Kreutzer	*Das Nachtlager von Granada*	09.01.1891
26.	Mozart	*Don Giovanni*	14.01.1891
27.	Wagner	*Tannhäuser*	18.01.1891
28.	Mozart	*Le nozze di Figaro*	20.01.1891
29.	Auber	*La Muette de Portici*	25.01.1891
30.	Wagner	*Tannhäuser*	28.01.1891
31.	Kreutzer	*Das Nachtlager von Granada*	30.01.1891
32.	Wagner	*Tannhäuser*	04.02.1891
33.	Wagner	*Lohengrin*	08.02.1891
34.	Mozart	*Le nozze di Figaro*	11.02.1891
35.	Weber	*Der Freischütz*	15.02.1891
36.	Wagner	*Rienzi*	01.03.1891

37.	Weber	*Der Freischütz*	04.03.1891
38.	Lortzing	*Der Wildschütz*	08.03.1891
39.	Wagner	*Rienzi*	01.04.1891
40.	Mozart	*Don Giovanni*	05.04.1891
41.	Lortzing	*Der Waffenschmied*	09.04.1891
42.	Ritter	*Wem die Krone?*	14.04.1891*
43.	Ritter	*Der faule Hans*	14.04.1891*
44.	Lortzing	*Der Waffenschmied*	15.04.1891
45.	Wagner	*Rienzi*	19.04.1891
46.	Lortzing	*Der Wildschutz*	29.04.1891

1891–1892 Season

1.	Mozart	*Die Zauberflöte*	20.09.1891
2.	Wagner	*Lohengrin*	04.10.1891
3.	Gluck	*Iphigénie en Aulide*	07.10.1891
4.	Gluck	*Iphigénie en Aulide*	11.10.1891
5.	Wagner	*Rienzi*	25.10.1891
6.	Ritter	*Wem die Krone?*	17.11.1891*
7.	Ritter	*Der faule Hans*	17.11.1891*
8.	Weber	*Der Freischütz*	29.11.1891
9.	Mozart	*Die Zauberflöte*	03.12.1891
10.	Mozart	*Don Giovanni*	05.12.1891
11.	Lortzing	*Der Wildschütz*	08.12.1891
12.	Ritter	*Wem die Krone?*	09.12.1891*
13.	Ritter	*Der faule Hans*	09.12.1891*
14.	Lortzing	*Der Wildschütz*	10.12.1891
15.	Wagner	*Tannhäuser*	13.12.1891
16.	Wagner	*Lohengrin*	28.12.1891
17.	Lortzing	*Zar und Zimmermann*	12.01.1892
18.	Wagner	*Tristan und Isolde*	17.01.1892†
19.	Wagner	*Tannhäuser*	20.01.1892
20.	Wagner	*Tristan und Isolde*	24.01.1892
21.	Weber	*Der Freischütz*[7]	26.01.1892
22.	Lortzing	*Der Wildschütz*	28.01.1892
23.	Wagner	*Tannhäuser*	01.02.1892
24.	Ritter	*Wem die Krone?*	16.02.1892*
25.	Ritter	*Der faule Hans*	16.02.1892*
26.	Mozart	*Don Giovanni*	17.02.1892
27.	Weber	*Preziosa*	18.02.1892
28.	Lortzing	*Der Waffenschmied*	19.02.1892
29.	Wagner	*Lohengrin*	21.02.1892
30.	Mozart	*Die Entführung aus dem Serail*	23.02.1892
31.	Wagner	*Tristan und Isolde*	24.02.1892
32.	Weber	*Der Freischütz*	04.03.1892
33.	Wagner	*Tristan und Isolde*	08.03.1892
34.	Wagner	*Lohengrin*	11.03.1892[8]
35.	Kreutzer	*Das Nachtlager von Granada*	15.03.1892
36.	Wagner	*Tristan und Isolde*	20.03.1892
37.	Wagner	*Tristan und Isolde*	24.03.1892
38.	Wagner	*Lohengrin*	27.03.1892
39.	Mascagni	*Amico Fritz*	07.04.1892
40.	Beethoven	*Fidelio*	21.04.1892
41.	Mozart	*Die Zauberflöte*	24.04.1892

42.	Gluck	*Iphigénie en Aulide*	26.04.1892
43.	Cherubini	*Les deux journées*	28.04.1892
44.	Cherubini	*Les deux journées*	30.04.1892
45.	Mozart	*Die Entführung aus dem Serail*	12.05.1892
46.	Cherubini	*Les deux journées*	17.05.1892
47.	Wagner	*Tannhäuser*	22.05.1892
48.	Kreutzer	*Das Nachtlager von Granada*	25.05.1892
49.	Sommer	*Loreley*	03.06.1892‡
50.	Sommer	*Loreley*	12.06.1892

1892–1893 Season

1.	Kreutzer	*Das Nachtlager von Granada*	20.09.1892
2.	Weber	*Der Freischütz*	27.10.1892

1893–1894 Season

1.	Weber	*Der Freischütz*	24.09.1893
2.	Lortzing	*Der Waffenschmied*	26.09.1893
3.	Flotow	*Alessandro Stradella*	01.10.1893
4.	Mozart	*Don Giovanni*	10.10.1893
5.	Metzdorff	*Hagbart und Signe*	15.10.1893§
6.	Weber	*Der Freischütz*	17.10.1893
7.	Metzdorff	*Hagbart und Signe*	19.10.1893
8.	Mozart	*Don Giovanni*	25.10.1893
9.	Weber	*Preziosa*	28.10.1893
10.	Metzdorff	*Hagbart und Signe*	07.11.1893
11.	Wagner	*Tannhäuser*	12.11.1893
12.	Weber	*Der Freischütz*	16.11.1893
13.	Wagner	*Tannhäuser*	17.11.1893
14.	Wagner	*Lohengrin*	10.12.1893†
15.	Humperdinck	*Hänsel und Gretel*	23.12.1893§
16.	Wagner	*Lohengrin*	25.12.1893
17.	Wagner	*Tannhäuser*	28.12.1893
18.	Humperdinck	*Hänsel und Gretel*	31.12.1893
19.	Mozart	*Bastien und Bastienne*	07.01.1894*
20.	Humperdinck	*Hänsel und Gretel*	07.01.1894*
21.	Mozart	*Bastien und Bastienne*	09.01.1894*
22.	Humperdinck	*Hänsel und Gretel*	09.01.1894*
23.	Mozart	*Bastien und Bastienne*	10.01.1894*
24.	Humperdinck	*Hänsel und Gretel*	10.01.1894*
25.	Wagner	*Lohengrin*	31.01.1894
26.	Wagner	*Tristan und Isolde*	13.02.1894
27.	Mozart	*Die Zauberflöte*	15.02.1894
28.	Humperdinck	*Hänsel und Gretel*	23.02.1894
29.	Wagner	*Die Meistersinger von Nürnberg*	28.02.1894
30.	Humperdinck	*Hänsel und Gretel*	02.03.1894
31.	Mozart	*Don Giovanni*	04.03.1894
32.	Mottl	*Fürst und Sänger*	09.03.1894§*
33.	Fiebach	*Bei frommen Hirten*	09.03.1894*
34.	Mottl	*Fürst und Sänger*	15.03.1894*
35.	Fiebach	*Bei frommen Hirten*	15.03.1894*
36.	Wagner	*Lohengrin*	28.03.1894

37. Wagner	*Tristan und Isolde*	01.04.1894
38. Wagner	*Tannhäuser*	15.04.1894
39. Mozart	*Die Zauberflöte*	17.04.1894
40. Wagner	*Tristan und Isolde*	25.04.1894
41. Lortzing	*Zar und Zimmermann*	29.04.1894
42. Mozart	*Don Giovanni*	06.05.1894
43. Strauss	*Guntram*	10.05.1894§
44. Lortzing	*Zar und Zimmermann*	13.05.1894
45. Strauss	*Guntram*	15.05.1894
46. Wagner	*Tannhäuser*	20.05.1894
47. Strauss	*Guntram*	24.05.1894
48. Humperdinck	*Hänsel und Gretel*	31.05.1894
49. Strauss	*Guntram*	01.06.1894

PART D: WEIMAR HOFKAPELLE, 1889–1894

1889–1890 Season[9]

1. 28.10.1889: Beethoven: *König Stephan* Overture; Lalo: *Symphonie Espagnole* (Carl Halir, violin); Bülow: *Nirwana*; Ritter: *Sternen Ewig* (Heinrich Zeller, tenor); Lassen: 'Frühling', 'Frühlingsgruss' and 'Ich fühle deinen Odem' (Heinrich Zeller, tenor), Strauss: 'Ständchen';§ Liszt. *Die Ideale*.
2. 11.11.1889: Cherubini: *Les Abencérages ou L'Étendard de Grenade* Overture; Weber: *Ines de Castro*; Saint-Saëns: Cello Concerto Op. 33 (Leonhard Halir, cello); Schubert: *Die junge Nonne*; Lassen: *Die Musikantin*; Strauss: *Don Juan*;§ Beethoven: Symphony No. 6.
3. 25.11.1889· Beethoven: *Leonore* No. 1 Overture, Piano Concerto No. 3 (Bernhard Stavenhagen, piano); Stavenhagen: *Suleika*;[10] Liszt: *Totentanz* (Bernhard Stavenhagen, piano); Berlioz. *Symphonie fantastique*.
4. 09.12.1889: Schubert: Symphony in C Major ('Great'); Wagner: *Eine Faust-Ouvertüre*; Cornelius: aria from *Der Barbier von Bagdad* (Hans Giessen,[11] tenor); Wagner: *Siegfried Idyll*; Liszt: three unspecified songs (Hans Giessen, tenor); Wagner: *Huldigungsmarsch*.

1890–1891 Season[12]

1. 13.10.1890: Weber: *Oberon* Overture; Thuille: 'Botschaft' and 'Waldesgang' (Heinrich Zeller, tenor); Ritter: 'Erklärung', 'Ich möchte ein Lied dir weihn' and 'In Lust und Schmerzen' (Heinrich Zeller, tenor); Strauss: 'Seitdem dein Aug' in meines schaute', 'Nichts' (Heinrich Zeller, tenor), *Macbeth*;§ Beethoven: Symphony No. 3.
2. 17.11.1890: Smetana: *Lustspielouvertüre*; Beethoven: Violin Concerto (Karl Halir, violin); Schubert-Liszt: 'Die Allmacht' (Hans Giessen, tenor); Liszt: *Eine Faust-Sinfonie* (Hans Giessen, tenor).
3. 12.01.1891: Mozart: Symphony No. 41; Weiss: Piano Concerto (Josef Weiss,[13] piano); [unidentified] solo piano piece (Josef Weiss, piano); Liszt: *Ce qu'on entend sur la montagne*; Strauss: *Tod und Verklärung*.
4. 26.01.1891: Beethoven: Symphony No. 8, 'Die Trommel gerühret' and 'Freudvoll und Leidvoll' from *Egmont* (Pauline de Ahna, soprano), *Egmont* Overture; Wagner: *Siegfried Idyll*, Bacchanale from *Tannhäuser*, Prelude and Liebestod from *Tristan und Isolde* (Pauline de Ahna, soprano).

1891–1892 Season[14]

1. 19.10.1891: Haydn: Symphony No. 100; Mozart: 'Der Stern meiner Liebe strahlt tröstend hernieder' from *Così fan tutte* (Hans Giessen, tenor), Piano Concerto No. 20

(Muriel Elliot,[15] piano); Sommer: 'Abschied', 'Froh im Gesang' and 'Ganz leise' (Hans Giessen, tenor); excerpts from Berlioz: *Roméo et Juliette*; Liszt: *Les Préludes*.

2. 23.11.1891: Wagner: *Eine Faust-Ouvertüre*; Bruch: Violin Concerto No. 3 (Karl Halir, violin); Ritter: *Seraphische Fantasie*; Beethoven: Romance in F Major (Karl Halir, violin) and Symphony No. 5.

3. 07.12.1891: Schumann: Symphony No. 1; Liszt: *Mazeppa*; Schubert: 'Gretchen am Spinnrade', 'Du bist die Ruh' and 'Die Post' (Pauline de Ahna, soprano); Liszt: 'Bist du!' and 'Wo weilt er?' (Pauline de Ahna, soprano); Wagner: 'Der Engel' (Pauline de Ahna, soprano) and *Kaisermarsch*.

4. 11.01.1892 (Pension Fund Concert): Lassen: Symphony in D (Eduard Lassen, conductor); Gounod: 'Ich gäb' was drum, wenn ich nur wüsst' from *Faust* (Jenny Alt,[16] soprano); Mozart: Concerto for Two Pianos (Eduard Lassen and Richard Strauss, pianos; Karl Halir, conductor); Björn: *Ich möcht' ein Kind weihn*, Schubert: 'Die Forelle', Schumann: 'Frühlingsnacht' (Jenny Alt, soprano, Richard Strauss, piano); Strauss: *Don Juan*.

5. 30.01.1892: Schubert: Symphony in B minor ('Unfinished'); Beethoven: Piano Concerto No. 4 (Margarete Stern, piano); Humperdinck: *Wallfahrt nach Kevelaer* (Luise Tibelti,[17] contralto, Heinrich Zeller, tenor, Hoftheater Chor); [unidentified] piano pieces by Scarlatti, Chopin and Liszt (Margarete Stern, piano); Beethoven: *Die Weihe des Hauses* Overture.

1893–1894 Season[18]

1. 06.11.1893: Berlioz: *Le Roi Lear* Overture; Brahms: Violin Concerto (Karl Halir, violin); Berlioz: aria from *Benvenuto Cellini* (Hans Giessen, tenor); Halir: Violin Concerto (Karl Halir, violin); Strauss: four unidentified songs (Hans Giessen, tenor); Beethoven: Symphony No. 7.

2. 20.11.1893: Liszt: *Festklänge*; Mozart: Piano Concerto No. 26 (Bernhard Stavenhagen, piano); Méhul: aria from *Josef in Ägypten* (Heinrich Zeller, tenor); Stavenhagen: Piano Concerto (Bernhard Stavenhagen, piano); Schubert: 'Die böse Farbe', 'Trockne Blumen' and 'Rastlose Liebe' (Heinrich Zeller, tenor); Haydn: Symphony No. 103 ('Drum Roll').

3. 04.12.1893: Beethoven: *Corolian* Overture; Wieniawski: Violin Concerto Op. .22 (Eugen Donderer,[19] violin); Wagner: *Siegfried Idyll*; Strauss: *Aus Italien*.

4. 15.12.1893: Draeseke: Prelude to *Das Leben ein Traum*; Bazzini: Konzertstück for Cello (Hugo Becker, cello);[20] Weber: aria from *Euryanthe* (Fräulein Schwarz, soprano); Locatelli: Cello Sonata (Hugo Becker, cello); Sommer: 'Der Mönch' and 'O du seliges Wandern am Rhein' (Fräulein Schwarz, soprano); Schumann: 'Wohlauf noch getrunken' (Fräulein Schwarz, soprano); Beethoven: Symphony No. 3.

5. 05.01.1894 (Pension Fund Concert): Beethoven: Symphony No. 8; Mozart: Violin Concerto No. 5 (Joseph Joachim, violin), aria with the violin obbligato from *Idomeneo* (Pauline de Ahna, soprano; Joseph Joachim, violin); Bach: Andante in C major and Andante and Finale (Joseph Joachim, solo violin); Schumann: 'Stille Thränen', Jensen;[21] 'An der Linden', 'Und schläfst du, mein Mädchen' and 'Das Gedicht' (Pauline de Ahna, soprano; Richard Strauss, piano); Brahms: Three Hungarian Dances arr. Joachim (Joseph Joachim, violin; Richard Strauss, piano).

PART E: MUNICH HOFOPER, 1894–1898[22]

Composer	Work	Date

1894–1895 Season

	Composer	Work	Date
1.	Mozart	*Die Zauberflöte*	07.10.1894
2.	Lortzing	*Der Waffenschmied*	20.10.1894

3.	Weber	*Oberon*	21.10.1894
4.	Wagner	*Die Meistersinger von Nürnberg*	07.11.1894
5.	Weber	*Oberon*	13.11.1894
6.	Wagner	*Tristan und Isolde*	22.11.1894
7.	Humperdinck	*Hänsel und Gretel*	02.12.1894
8.	Mozart	*Die Zauberflöte*	13.12.1894
9.	Liszt	*Die Legende von der heiligen Elisabeth*	19.12.1894
10.	Brüll	*Das goldene Kreuz*	23.12.1894
11.	Brüll	*Das goldene Kreuz*	29.12.1894
12.	Liszt	*Die Legende von der heiligen Elisabeth*	06.01.1895
13.	Brüll	*Das goldene Kreuz*	05.02.1895
14.	Maillart	*Das Glöckchen des Eremiten*	07.02.1895
15.	Wagner	*Die Meistersinger von Nürnberg*	13.02.1895
16.	Maillart	*Das Glöckchen des Eremiten*	21.02.1895
17.	Weber	*Oberon*	24.02.1895
18.	Humperdinck	*Hänsel und Gretel*	28.02.1895
19.	Flotow	*Martha*	09.03.1895†
20.	Wagner	*Die Meistersinger von Nürnberg*	10.03.1895
21.	Humperdinck	*Hänsel und Gretel*	30.03.1895
22.	Bizet	*Carmen*	09.04.1895
23.	Bizet	*Carmen*	19.04.1895
24.	Brüll	*Das goldene Kreuz*	24.04.1895
25.	Humperdinck	*Hänsel und Gretel*	27.04.1895
26.	Wagner	*Tannhäuser*	28.04.1895
27.	Nicolai	*Die lustigen Weiber von Windsor*	30.04.1895
28.	Wagner	*Die Meistersinger von Nürnberg*	07.05.1895
29.	Wagner	*Tristan und Isolde*	12.05.1895
30.	Flotow	*Martha*	15.05.1895
31.	Brüll	*Das goldene Kreuz*	18.05.1895
32.	Wagner	*Rienzi*	22.05.1895†
33.	Wagner	*Rienzi*	25.05.1895
34.	Flotow	*Martha*	26.05.1895
35.	Verdi	*Il Trovatore*	04.06.1895
36.	Bizet	*Carmen*	09.06.1895
37.	Wagner	*Rienzi*	13.06.1895
38.	Wagner	*Rienzi*	16.06.1895
39.	Wagner	*Tannhäuser*	23.06.1895
40.	Humperdinck	*Hänsel und Gretel*	27.06.1895
41.	Kreutzer	*Das Nachtlager von Granada*	29.06.1895
42.	Wagner	*Rienzi*	09.08.1895
43.	Wagner	*Tannhäuser*	13.08.1895
44.	Wagner	*Tristan und Isolde*	25.08.1895
45.	Wagner	*Die Meistersinger von Nürnberg*	27.08.1895
46.	Wagner	*Tristan und Isolde*	29.08.1895
47.	Wagner	*Die Meistersinger von Nürnberg*	01.09.1895
48.	Wagner	*Rienzi*	09.09.1895
49.	Wagner	*Tannhäuser*	13.09.1895
50.	Wagner	*Rienzi*	23.09.1895
51.	Wagner	*Tristan und Isolde*	25.09.1895
52.	Wagner	*Die Meistersinger von Nürnberg*	27.09.1895
53.	Wagner	*Rienzi*	29.09.1895
54.	Wagner	*Tannhäuser*	04.10.1895

1895–1896 Season

1.	Mozart	*Die Zauberflöte*	07.10.1895
2.	Verdi	*Il Trovatore*	10.10.1895
3.	Lortzing	*Der Waffenschmied*	12.10.1895
4.	Bizet	*Carmen*	13.10.1895
5.	Zöllner	*Der Überfall*	15.10.1895‡†
6.	Flotow	*Martha*	17.10.1895
7.	Wagner	*Tannhäuser*	18.10.1895
8.	Zöllner	*Der Überfall*	20.10.1895
9.	Zöllner	*Der Überfall*	24.10.1895
10.	Wagner	*Der fliegende Holländer*	31.10.1895
11.	Zöllner	*Der Überfall*	02.11.1895
12.	Lortzing	*Der Waffenschmied*	03.11.1895
13.	Weber	*Der Freischütz*	05.11.1895
14.	Mozart	*Le nozze di Figaro*	06.11.1895[23]
15.	Wagner	*Der fliegende Holländer*	07.11.1895
16.	Humperdinck	*Hänsel und Gretel*	09.11.1895
17.	Wagner	*Rienzi*	10.11.1895
18.	Beethoven	*Fidelio*	12.11.1895
19.	Humperdinck	*Hänsel und Gretel*	13.11.1895
20.	Strauss	*Guntram*	16.11.1895‡†
21.	Rossini	*Il barbiere di Siviglia*	26.11.1895
22.	Beethoven	*Fidelio*	28.11.1895
23.	Brüll	*Das goldene Kreuz*	06.12.1895
24.	Flotow	*Martha*	09.12.1895
25.	Mozart	*Don Giovanni*	12.12.1895
26.	Verdi	*Il Trovatore*	14.12.1895
27.	Liszt	*Die Legende von der heiligen Elisabeth*	19.12.1895
28.	Verdi	*Un ballo in maschera*	20.12.1895
29.	Wagner	*Tannhäuser*	22.12.1895
30.	Mozart	*Don Giovanni*	26.12.1895
31.	Nicolai	*Die lustigen Weiber von Windsor*	29.12.1895
32.	Wagner	*Die Meistersinger von Nürnberg*	06.01.1896
33.	Humperdinck	*Hänsel und Gretel*	09.01.1896
34.	Gluck	*Iphigénie en Aulide*	11.01.1896†
35.	Wagner	*Tannhäuser*	12.01.1896
36.	Kreutzer	*Das Nachtlager von Granada*	14.01.1896
37.	Gluck	*Iphigénie en Aulide*	15.01.1896
38.	Kreutzer	*Das Nachtlager von Granada*	16.01.1896
39.	Wagner	*Die Meistersinger von Nürnberg*	18.01.1896
40.	Flotow	*Martha*	21.01.1896
41.	Lortzing	*Der Waffenschmied*	25.01.1896
42.	Adam	*Die Nürnberger Puppe*	06.02.1896‡†*
43.	Cornelius	*Der Barbier von Bagdad*	06.02.1896†*
44.	Adam	*Die Nürnberger Puppe*	08.02.1896*
45.	Cornelius	*Der Barbier von Bagdad*	08.02.1896*
46.	Bizet	*Carmen*	09.02.1896
47.	Kreutzer	*Das Nachtlager von Granada*	11.02.1896
48.	Adam	*Die Nürnberger Puppe*	22.02.1896*
49.	Cornelius	*Der Barbier von Bagdad*	22.02.1896*
50.	Wagner	*Die Meistersinger von Nürnberg*	27.02.1896
51.	Adam	*Die Nürnberger Puppe*	29.02.1896*
52.	Cornelius	*Der Barbier von Bagdad*	29.02.1896*

53.	Gluck	*Iphigénie en Aulide*	01.03.1896
54.	Beethoven	*Fidelio*	03.03.1896
55.	Wagner	*Rienzi*	08.03.1896
56.	Flotow	*Martha*	21.03.1896
57.	Wagner	*Tannhäuser*	22.03.1896
58.	Lortzing	*Der Waffenschmied*	25.03.1896
59.	Adam	*Die Nürnberger Puppe*	09.04.1896
60.	Lortzing	*Der Waffenschmied*	21.04.1896
61.	Rossini	*Il barbiere di Siviglia*	25.04.1896
62.	Bizet	*Carmen*	02.05.1896
63.	Liszt	*Die Legende von der heiligen Elisabeth*	05.05.1896
64.	Nicolai	*Die lustigen Weiber von Windsor*	09.05.1896
65.	Wagner	*Rienzi*	14.05.1896
66.	Wagner	*Tannhäuser*	17.05.1896
67.	Kreutzer	*Das Nachtlager von Granada*	19.05.1896
68.	Mozart	*Don Giovanni*	29.05.1896†[24]
69.	Mozart	*Don Giovanni*	31.05.1896
70.	Mozart	*Don Giovanni*	03.06.1896
71.	Kreutzer	*Das Nachtlager von Granada*	06.06.1896
72.	Mozart	*Don Giovanni*	10.06.1896
73.	Wagner	*Tristan und Isolde*	14.06.1896
74.	Mozart	*Don Giovanni*	17.06.1896
75.	Wagner	*Tristan und Isolde*	20.06.1896
76.	Mozart	*Don Giovanni*	21.06.1896
77.	Mozart	*Don Giovanni*	25.06.1896
78.	Wagner	*Tannhäuser*	27.06.1896
79.	Mozart	*Don Giovanni*	29.06.1896
80.	Mozart	*Don Giovanni*	05.08.1896
81.	Wagner	*Tannhäuser*	06.08.1896
82.	Mozart	*Don Giovanni*	12.08.1896
83.	Wagner	*Tannhäuser*	13.08.1896
84.	Mozart	*Don Giovanni*	19.08.1896
85.	Wagner	*Tristan und Isolde*	22.08.1896
86.	Wagner	*Rienzi*	25.08.1896
87.	Mozart	*Don Giovanni*	26.08.1896
88.	Wagner	*Die Meistersinger von Nürnberg*	29.08.1896

1896–1897 Season

1.	Wagner	*Tristan und Isolde*	01.09.1896
2.	Mozart	*Don Giovanni*	02.09.1896
3.	Wagner	*Tannhäuser*	03.09.1896
4.	Wagner	*Rienzi*	08.09.1896
5.	Mozart	*Don Giovanni*	09.09.1896
6.	Wagner	*Die Meistersinger von Nürnberg*	12.09.1896
7.	Mozart	*Don Giovanni*	16.09.1896
8.	Wagner	*Tannhäuser*	17.09.1896
9.	Mozart	*Don Giovanni*	23.09.1896
10.	Wagner	*Tristan und Isolde*	24.09.1896
11.	Mozart	*Don Giovanni*	30.09.1896
12.	Wagner	*Die Meistersinger von Nürnberg*	01.10.1896
13.	Mozart	*Don Giovanni*	04.11.1896
14.	Mozart	*Don Giovanni*	11.11.1896

15.	Liszt	*Die Legende von der heiligen Elisabeth*	14.11.1896
16.	Rossini	*Il barbiere di Siviglia*	17.11.1896
17.	Wagner	*Tannhäuser*	26.12.1896
18.	Humperdinck	*Hänsel und Gretel*	03.01.1897
19.	Adam	*Die Nürnberger Puppe*	09.01.1897
20.	Nicolai	*Die lustigen Weiber von Windsor*	14.01.1897
21.	Gluck	*Orfeo ed Euridice*	21.01.1897
22.	Schubert	Centenary performance	31.01.1897[25]
23.	Wagner	*Die Meistersinger von Nürnberg*	02.02.1897
24.	Mozart	*Die Entführung aus dem Serail*	03.02.1897†
25.	Mozart	*Die Entführung aus dem Serail*	10.02.1897
26.	Wagner	*Tannhäuser*	13.02.1897
27.	Mozart	*Die Entführung aus dem Serail*	14.02.1897
28.	Mozart	*Die Entführung aus dem Serail*	17.02.1897
29.	Mozart	*Die Entführung aus dem Serail*	26.02.1897
30.	Mozart	*Die Entführung aus dem Serail*	04.03.1897
31.	Thuille	*Theuerdank*	12.03.1897§
32.	Wagner	*Tristan und Isolde*	19.03.1897
33.	Thuille	*Theuerdank*	23.03.1897
34.	Wagner	*Die Meistersinger von Nürnberg*	25.03.1897
35.	Thuille	*Theuerdank*	27.03.1897
36.	Mozart	*Don Giovanni*	30.03.1897
37.	Smetana	*The Bartered Bride*	31.03.1897
38.	Wagner	*Tannhäuser*	01.04.1897
39.	Smetana	*The Bartered Bride*	06.04.1897
40.	Mozart	*Die Entführung aus dem Serail*	20.04.1897
41.	Thuille	*Theuerdank*	27.04.1897
42.	Mozart	*Die Entführung aus dem Serail*	29.04.1897
43.	Schillings	*Ingwelde*	08.05.1897‡†
44.	Mozart	*Don Giovanni*	13.05.1897
45.	Wagner	*Die Meistersinger von Nürnberg*	22.05.1897
46.	Wagner	*Tannhäuser*	27.05.1897
47.	Schillings	*Ingwelde*	30.05.1897
48.	Mozart	*Die Entführung aus dem Serail*	17.06.1897
49.	Mozart	*Così fan tutte*	25.06.1897†
50.	Mozart	*Così fan tutte*	27.06.1897
51.	Mozart	*Così fan tutte*	29.06.1897
52.	Mozart	*Die Entführung aus dem Serail*	04.08.1897
53.	Wagner	*Tristan und Isolde*	05.08.1897
54.	Wagner	*Tannhäuser*	10.08.1897
55.	Mozart	*Don Giovanni*	11.08.1897
56.	Wagner	*Tristan und Isolde*	12.08.1897
57.	Mozart	*Die Entführung aus dem Serail*	14.08.1897
58.	Wagner	*Tannhäuser*	17.08.1897
59.	Mozart	*Die Entführung aus dem Serail*	18.08.1897
60.	Wagner	*Tristan und Isolde*	19.08.1897
61.	Mozart	*Così fan tutte*	21.08.1897
62.	Mozart	*Così fan tutte*	25.08.1897
63.	Wagner	*Tristan und Isolde*	26.08.1897
64.	Wagner	*Tannhäuser*	31.08.1897

1897–1898 Season

1.	Mozart	*Don Giovanni*	01.09.1897
2.	Mozart	*Così fan tutte*	04.09.1897
3.	Wagner	*Tristan und Isolde*	05.09.1897
4.	Mozart	*Don Giovanni*	08.09.1897
5.	Mozart	*Così fan tutte*	11.09.1897
6.	Wagner	*Tannhäuser*	14.09.1897
7.	Wagner	*Tristan und Isolde*	16.09.1897
8.	Mozart	*Don Giovanni*	29.09.1897
9.	Mozart	*Così fan tutte*	02.10.1897
10.	Mozart	*Die Entführung aus dem Serail*	13.10.1897
11.	Wagner	*Tristan und Isolde*	14.10.1897
12.	Mozart	*Così fan tutte*	18.10.1897
13.	Mozart	*Così fan tutte*	09.12.1897
14.	Wagner	*Tristan und Isolde*	12.12.1897
15.	Mozart	*Così fan tutte*	22.12.1897
16.	Wagner	*Tannhäuser*	26.12.1897
17.	Mozart	*Don Giovanni*	05.01.1898
18.	Schillings	*Ingwelde*	20.01.1898
19.	Adam	*Die Nürnberger Puppe*	30.01.1898
20.	Nicolai	*Die lustigen Weiber von Windsor*	06.02.1898
21.	Mozart	*Die Entführung aus dem Serail*	14.02.1898
22.	Wagner	*Tristan und Isolde*	17.02.1898
23.	Mozart	*Così fan tutte*	18.02.1898
24.	Wagner	*Tristan und Isolde*	19.03.1898
25.	Beethoven	*Fidelio*	25.03.1898
26.	Wagner	*Tannhäuser*	27.03.1898
27.	Mozart	*Così fan tutte*	18.04.1898
28.	Beethoven	*Fidelio*	20.04.1898
29.	Mozart	*Così fan tutte*	23.04.1898
30.	Wagner	*Tristan und Isolde*	24.04.1898
31.	Mozart	*Die Zauberflöte*	30.04.1898†
32.	Mozart	*Die Zauberflöte*	01.05.1898
33.	Mozart	*Die Zauberflöte*	05.05.1898
34.	Mozart	*Die Zauberflöte*	07.05.1898
35.	Mozart	*Die Zauberflöte*	08.05.1898
36.	Mozart	*Die Zauberflöte*	19.05.1898
37.	Mozart	*Die Entführung aus dem Serail*	20.05.1898
38.	Wagner	*Tannhäuser*	24.05.1898
39.	Nicolai	*Die lustigen Weiber von Windsor*	25.05.1898
40.	Mozart	*Die Zauberflöte*	30.05.1898
41.	Mozart	*Die Zauberflöte*	09.06.1898
42.	Beethoven	*Fidelio*	11.06.1898
43.	Wagner	*Tannhäuser*	12.06.1898
44.	Hausegger	*Zinnober*	19.06.1898§
45.	Hausegger	*Zinnober*	26.06.1898
46.	Mozart	*Die Zauberflöte*	31.07.1898
47.	Mozart	*Don Giovanni*	01.08.1898
48.	Wagner	*Tannhäuser*	02.08.1898
49.	Mozart	*Die Entführung aus dem Serail*	03.08.1898
50.	Mozart	*Così fan tutte*	06.08.1898
51.	Wagner	*Tristan und Isolde*	11.08.1898
52.	Mozart	*Don Giovanni*	17.08.1898

53. Mozart	*Così fan tutte*	27.08.1898
54. Mozart	*Die Zauberflöte*	28.08.1898
55. Mozart	*Don Giovanni*	29.08.1898
56. Wagner	*Tannhäuser*	30.08.1898
57. Mozart	*Die Entführung aus dem Serail*	31.08.1898
58. Mozart	*Così fan tutte*	03.09.1898
59. Wagner	*Tristan und Isolde*	08.09.1898
60. Mozart	*Die Entführung aus dem Serail*	10.09.1898
61. Mozart	*Die Entführung aus dem Serail*	14.09.1898
62. Mozart	*Die Zauberflöte*	15.09.1898
63. Mozart	*Così fan tutte*	16.09.1898
64. Mozart	*Don Giovanni*	19.09.1898
65. Beethoven	*Fidelio*	04.10.1898
66. Wagner	*Tannhäuser*	09.10.1898
67. Beethoven	*Fidelio*	18.10.1898

PART F: MUNICH HOFKAPELLE, 1894–1896

1894–1895 Season

1. 16.11.1894: Berlioz: *Le Roi Lear* Overture; Schillings: Prelude to *Ingwelde*; Mozart: Violin Concerto No. 4 (Miroslav Weber,[26] violin); Paganini: solo pieces (Miroslav Weber, violin); Beethoven: Symphony No. 7.
2. 30.11.1894: Haydn: Symphony in G major; Rubinstein: Piano Concerto No. 4 (Fannie Bloomfield-Zeisler,[27] piano); Liszt: *Eine Faust-Sinfonie*.
3. 14.12.1894: Schumann: *Genoveva* Overture; Goetz: aria from *Der Widerspenstigen Zähmung* (Katharina Bettaque,[28] soprano); Schubert, Schumann: unspecified Lieder (Katharina Bettaque, soprano; Richard Strauss, piano); Rheinberger: Organ Concerto No. 2 (Josef Becht,[29] organ);§ Gilson: *La mer*;§[30] Beethoven: *Leonore* No. 2 Overture.
4. 25.12.1894: Mendelssohn: *Hebrides* Overture; Berlioz: *Nuits d'été* (Emanuela Frank,[31] soprano); Strauss: Preludes from *Guntram*; Beethoven: Symphony No. 2.
5. 08.02.1895: Rubinstein: Symphony No. 2 ('Ocean'); Dvořák: *Carnival* Overture; Bruch: Violin Concerto No. 1 (Betty Schwabe,[32] violin); Mozart: Symphony No. 38.
6. 22.02.1895: Bussmeyer: Overture C minor;[33] Schumann: *Dichterliebe* (Raoul Walter,[34] tenor; Richard Strauss, piano); Smetana: *Tábor*; Beethoven: Symphony No. 3.
7. 08.03.1895: Beethoven: *Coriolan* Overture; Raff: Symphony No. 5 ('Lenore'); Schubert: Symphony in B minor ('Unfinished'); Bungert, Chopin, Loewe, Moszkowski, Mozart, Schumann and Tchaikovsky: unspecified songs.
8. 22.03.1895: Wagner: *Eine Faust-Ouvertüre*; Liszt: *Die Ideale*; Beethoven: Symphony No. 1; Chopin: Piano Concerto [unspecified] (Teresa Carreño, piano); Schubert: Impromptu D899 No. 4 (Teresa Carreño, piano).

1895–1896 Season

1. 15.11.1895: Beethoven: Symphony No. 1; Bach: Brandenburg Concerto No. 1; Schubert: Symphony in C major ('Great').
2. 29.11.1895: Haydn: Symphony in C Minor; Strauss: *Till Eulenspiegel*; Beethoven: Symphony No. 2; Berlioz: *Benvenuto Cellini* Overture.
3. 13.12.1895: Weber: *Abu Hassan* Overture; Mozart: Symphony No. 40; Smetana: *Vltava*; Beethoven: Symphony No. 3.
4. 25.12.1895: Cherubini: *Ali baba* Overture; Schumann: Symphony No. 4; Beethoven: Piano Concerto No. 4 (Otto Neitzel,[35] piano), Symphony No. 4.
5. 07.02.1896: Mendelssohn: Symphony No. 4; Schillings: 'Meergruss' and 'Seemorgen'; Rameau: Musette, Tambourin and Rigaudon; Beethoven: Symphony No. 5.

6. 24.02.1896: Haydn: Symphony in E flat major; Smetana: *Šárka*; Beethoven: Symphony No. 6, *Leonore* No. 1 Overture.
7. 06.03.1896: Schubert: *Fierrabras* Overture; Ritter: *Sursum corda*; Mozart: *Maurerische Trauermusik* and *Eine kleine Nachtmusik*; Beethoven: Symphony No. 7.
8. 20.03.1896: Spohr: *Jessonda* Overture; Rezniček: *Donna Diana* Overture and Intermezzo; Brahms: Symphony No. 4; Beethoven: Symphony No. 8.
9. 27.04.1896 (extra concert): Beethoven: *Die Geschöpfe des Prometheus* incidental music, Symphony No. 9.

PART G: BERLIN PHILHARMONIC, 1894–1895

1. 15.10.1894: Wagner: *Eine Faust-Ouvertüre*; Brahms: Violin Concerto (Hugo Heermann,[36] violin); Schillings: *Ingwelde* Prelude to Act 2; Liszt: *Mephisto Waltz*; Beethoven: Symphony No. 7.
2. 29.10.1894: Berlioz: *Le Roi Lear* Overture; Rubinstein: Piano Concerto No. 4 (Fannie Bloomfield-Zeisler, piano); Schubert: Fantasy in F minor arr. Mottl; Johann Strauss II: *Perpetuum mobile*; Haydn: Symphony in E flat major.
3. 12.11.1894: Liszt: *Die Ideale*; Bruch: Violin Concerto No. 3 (Pablo de Sarasate,[37] violin); Widor: Symphony in A major; Saint-Saëns: *Introduction et Rondo capriccioso* (Pablo de Sarasate, violin); Beethoven: *Leonore* No. 2 Overture.
4. 26.11.1894: Wagner: *Tristan und Isolde* Prelude; Paganini: Violin Concerto No. 1 (Willy Burmester,[38] violin); Glazunov: *Spring*; Ritter: *Olafs Hochzeitsreigen*; Beethoven: Symphony No. 2.
5. 10.12.1894: Rubinstein: Symphony No. 2 ('Ocean'); Mozart: *Ch'io mi scordi di te* (Selma Nicklas-Kempner,[39] soprano); D'Albert: *Der Rubin* Prelude; Stenhammar: Piano Concerto in D minor (Wilhelm Stenhammar,[40] piano); Rubinstein, Schubert: unspecified Lieder; Wagner: *Die Meistersinger von Nürnberg* Prelude.
6. 14.01.1895: Dvořák: *Carnival* Overture; Gernsheim: Violin Concerto (Émile Sauret,[41] violin); Rameau: Musette, Tambourin and Rigaudon; Frederick the Great: Grave from a Flute Concerto; Sauret: *Elégie und Rondo* (Émile Sauret, violin); Beethoven: Symphony No. 3.
7. 28.01.1895: Smetana: *Šárka*; Liszt: Piano Concerto No. 2 (Ferruccio Busoni, piano), *Mazeppa*; Brahms: Symphony No. 4; Beethoven: *Egmont* Overture.
8. 18.02.1895: Tchaikovsky: Suite No. 3; Haydn: Cello Concerto in D major (Hugo Becker, cello); Bülow: *Nirwana*; Beethoven: Symphony No. 5.
9. 04.03.1895: Mendelssohn: *Hebrides* Overture; Saint-Saëns: Piano Concerto No. 4 (Josef Hofmann, piano); Mahler: Symphony No. 2, movements 1–3 (Gustav Mahler, conductor); unspecified piano solos (Josef Hofmann, piano); Weber: *Oberon* Overture.
10. 18.03.1895: Beethoven: *Coriolan* Overture; Spohr: *Gesangsszene* (Leopold Auer,[42] violin); Schumann: *Manfred* Overture; unspecified violin solos (Leopold Auer, violin); Strauss: *Guntram* Prelude to Act 2, 'Friedenserzählung' (Heinrich Zeller, tenor), Prelude to Act 1, Conclusion to Act 3.

PART H: BERLIN HOF- AND STAATSOPER, 1898–1919

1898–1899 Season

Composer	Work	Date
1. Wagner	*Tristan und Isolde*	05.11.1898
2. Bizet	*Carmen*	08.11.1898
3. Humperdinck	*Hänsel und Gretel*	11.11.1898

4. Nicolai	*Die lustige Weiber von Windsor*	12.11.1898
5. Auber	*La Muette de Portici*	13.11.1898
6. Beethoven	*Fidelio*	15.11.1898
7. Auber	*La Muette de Portici*	20.11.1898
8. Wagner	*Rienzi*	21.11.1898
9. Humperdinck	*Hänsel und Gretel*	01.12.1898
10. Bizet	*Carmen*	03.12.1898
11. Wagner	*Tristan und Isolde*	09.12.1898
12. Weber	*Der Freischütz*	18.12.1898
13. Bizet	*Carmen*	19.12.1898
14. Kreutzer	*Das Nachtlager von Granada*	23.12.1898
15. Auber	*La Muette de Portici*	26.12.1898
16. Humperdinck	*Hänsel und Gretel*	30.12.1898
17. Beethoven	*Fidelio*	01.01.1899
18. Humperdinck	*Hänsel und Gretel*	03.01.1899
19. Auber	*La Muette de Portici*	04.01.1899
20. Wagner	*Der fliegende Holländer*	05.01.1899
21. Mascagni	*Cavalleria rusticana*	07.01.1899
22. Humperdinck	*Hänsel und Gretel*	08.01.1899
23. Auber	*La Muette de Portici*	10.01.1899
24. Bizet	*Carmen*	12.01.1899
25. Chabrier	*Briséïs*	14.01.1899‡†
26. Wagner	*Rienzi*	15.01.1899
27. Nicolai	*Die lustige Weiber von Windsor*	02.02.1899
28. Wagner	*Die Meistersinger von Nürnberg*	03.02.1899
29. Wagner	*Der fliegende Holländer*	13.02.1899
30. Wagner	*Tristan und Isolde*	17.02.1899
31. Smetana	*The Bartered Bride*	19.02.1899
32. Smetana	*The Bartered Bride*	05.03.1899
33. Weber	*Der Freischütz*	07.03.1899
34. Auber	*La Muette de Portici*	10.03.1899
35. Nicolai	*Die lustige Weiber von Windsor*	13.03.1899
36. Bizet	*Carmen*	16.03.1899
37. Rossini	*Il barbiere di Siviglia*	17.03.1899
38. Auber	*La Muette de Portici*	19.03.1899
39. Wagner	*Lohengrin*	27.03.1899
40. Auber	*La Muette de Portici*	03.04.1899
41. Rossini	*Il barbiere di Siviglia*	05.04.1899
42. Humperdinck	*Hänsel und Gretel*	08.04.1899
43. Rossini	*Il barbiere di Siviglia*	11.04.1899
44. Nicolai	*Die lustige Weiber von Windsor*	15.04.1899
45. Le Borne	*Mudarra*	18.04.1899‡†
46. Le Borne	*Mudarra*	20.04.1899
47. Humperdinck	*Hänsel und Gretel*	03.05.1899
48. Johann Strauss II	*Die Fledermaus*	08.05.1899†
49. Bizet	*Carmen*	09.05.1899
50. Johann Strauss II	*Die Fledermaus*	10.05.1899
51. Johann Strauss II	*Die Fledermaus*	15.05.1899
52. Johann Strauss II	*Die Fledermaus*	16.05.1899
53. Johann Strauss II	*Die Fledermaus*	18.05.1899
54. Lortzing	*Regina, oder die Marodeure*	30.05.1899
55. Johann Strauss II	*Die Fledermaus*	31.05.1899
56. Wagner	*Der fliegende Holländer*	02.06.1899
57. Johann Strauss II	*Die Fledermaus*	04.06.1899

58. Kienzl	*Der Evangelimann*	06.06.1899
59. Johann Strauss II	*Die Fledermaus*	08.06.1899
60. Bizet	*Carmen*	09.06.1899
61. Humperdinck	*Hänsel und Gretel*	12.06.1899
62. Weber	*Euryanthe*	17.06.1899†
63. Wagner	*Das Rheingold*	19.06.1899
64. Wagner	*Die Walküre*	20.06.1899
65. Wagner	*Siegfried*	22.06.1899
66. Wagner	*Götterdämmerung*	24.06.1899
67. Weber	*Euryanthe*	26.06.1899
68. Wagner	*Der fliegende Holländer*	28.06.1899

1899–1900 Season

1. Humperdinck	*Hänsel und Gretel*	02.09.1899
2. Mozart	*Don Giovanni*	03.09.1899
3. Bizet	*Carmen*	05.09.1899
4. Rossini	*Il barbiere di Siviglia*	07.09.1899
5. Mozart	*Don Giovanni*	09.09.1899
6. Nicolai	*Die lustige Weiber von Windsor*	12.09.1899
7. Humperdinck	*Hänsel und Gretel*	13.09.1899
8. Smetana	*The Bartered Bride*	15.09.1899
9. Bizet	*Carmen*	17.09.1899
10. Mozart	*Don Giovanni*	18.09.1899
11. Lortzing	*Der Wildschütz*	22.09.1899†
12. Lortzing	*Der Wildschütz*	24.09.1899
13. Johann Strauss II	*Die Fledermaus*	27.09.1899
14. Lortzing	*Der Wildschütz*	02.10.1899
15. Wagner	*Die Meistersinger von Nürnberg*	03.10.1899
16. Johann Strauss II	*Die Fledermaus*	04.10.1899
17. Lortzing	*Der Wildschütz*	05.10.1899
18. Bizet	*Carmen*	07.10.1899
19. Auber	*La Muette de Portici*	10.10.1899
20. Beethoven	*Fidelio*	11.10.1899
21. Mozart	*Così fan tutte*	12.10.1899†
22. Rossini	*Il barbiere di Siviglia*	07.11.1899
23. Mozart	*Don Giovanni*	09.11.1899
24. Lortzing	*Der Wildschütz*	10.11.1899
25. Auber	*La Muette de Portici*	12.11.1899
26. Mozart	*Così fan tutte*	13.11.1899
27. Johann Strauss II	*Die Fledermaus*	17.11.1899
28. Wagner	*Die Walküre*	20.11.1899
29. Beethoven	*Fidelio*	24.11.1899
30. Gluck	*Orfeo ed Euridice*	26.11.1899
31. Johann Strauss II	*Die Fledermaus*	28.11.1899
32. Beethoven	*Fidelio*	30.11.1899
33. Mozart	*Così fan tutte*	05.12.1899
34. Verdi	*Aïda*	09.12.1899
35. Mozart	*Don Giovanni*	12.12.1899
36. Kreutzer	*Das Nachtlager von Granada*	14.12.1899
37. Beethoven	*Fidelio*	16.12.1899
38. Weber	*Der Freischütz*	18.12.1899
39. Bizet	*Carmen*	19.12.1899
40. Humperdinck	*Hänsel und Gretel*	20.12.1899

41. Lortzing	*Der Wildschütz*	26.12.1899
42. Wagner	*Die Meistersinger von Nürnberg*	01.01.1900
43. Wagner	*Der fliegende Holländer*	07.01.1900
44. Lortzing	*Der Wildschütz*	08.01.1900
45. Auber	*La Muette de Portici*	09.01.1900
46. Mozart	*Die Entführung aus dem Serail*	13.01.1900
47. Mozart	*Don Giovanni*	15.01.1900
48. Mozart	*Le nozze di Figaro*	24.01.1900
49. Mozart	*Die Zauberflöte*	25.01.1900
50. Wagner	*Rienzi*	27.01.1900
51. Bizet	*Carmen*	29.01.1900
52. Mozart	*Così fan tutte*	30.01.1900
53. Mozart	*Die Entführung aus dem Serail*	01.02.1900
54. Wagner	*Die Meistersinger von Nürnberg*	05.02.1900
55. Lortzing	*Der Wildschütz*	16.02.1899
56. Humperdinck	*Hänsel und Gretel*	17.02.1900
57. Auber	*La Muette de Portici*	21.02.1900
58. Lortzing	*Undine*	22.02.1900
59. Wagner	*Die Meistersinger von Nürnberg*	23.02.1900
60. Mozart	*Die Zauberflöte*	25.02.1900
61. Wagner	*Tannhäuser*	17.03.1900
62. Wagner	*Tristan und Isolde*	20.03.1900
63. Verdi	*Aïda*	23.03.1900
64. Johann Strauss II	*Die Fledermaus*	25.03.1900
65. Mozart	*Le nozze di Figaro*	28.03.1900
66. Wagner	*Tannhäuser*	30.03.1900
67. Wagner	*Tannhäuser*	08.04.1900
68. Gluck	*Orfeo ed Euridice*	11.04.1900
69. Weber	*Der Freischütz*	15.04.1900
70. Mozart	*Le nozze di Figaro*	16.04.1900
71. Mozart	*Così fan tutte*	17.04.1900
72. Wagner	*Tannhäuser*	18.04.1900
73. Johann Strauss II	*Die Fledermaus*	22.04.1900
74. Wagner	*Lohengrin*	25.04.1900
75. Mozart	*Le nozze di Figaro*	29.04.1900
76. Bizet	*Carmen*	30.04.1900
77. Kienzl	*Der Evangelimann*	04.05.1900
78. Auber	*Le cheval de bronze* (arr. Humperdinck)	05.05.1900†
79. Beethoven	*Fidelio*	06.05.1900
80. Nicolai	*Die lustige Weiber von Windsor*	07.05.1900
81. Lortzing	*Zar und Zimmermann*	09.05.1900
82. Wagner	*Das Rheingold*	10.05.1900
83. Wagner	*Die Walküre*	11.05.1900
84. Auber	*Le cheval de bronze* (arr. Humperdinck)	12.05.1900
85. Mozart	*Don Giovanni*	13.05.1900
86. Wagner	*Siegfried*	14.05.1900
87. Wagner	*Götterdämmerung*	16.05.1900
88. Wagner	*Lohengrin*	22.05.1900
89. Lortzing	*Der Wildschütz*	23.05.1900
90. Wagner	*Rienzi*	28.05.1900
91. Mozart	*Don Giovanni*	29.05.1900
92. Auber	*Le cheval de bronze* (arr. Humperdinck)	31.05.1900
93. Wagner	*Lohengrin*	07.06.1900
94. Bizet	*Carmen*	08.06.1900

95.	Mozart	*Die Zauberflöte*	11.06.1900
96.	Weber	*Der Freischütz*	13.06.1900

1900–1901 Season

1.	Auber	*Le cheval de bronze* (arr. Humperdinck)	16.09.1900
2.	Wagner	*Die Meistersinger von Nürnberg*	17.09.1900
3.	Mozart	*Don Giovanni*	20.09.1900
4.	Nicolai	*Die lustige Weiber von Windsor*	22.09.1900
5.	Kienzl	*Der Evangelimann*	25.09.1900
6.	Mozart	*Le nozze di Figaro*	27.09.1900
7.	Mozart	*Die Zauberflöte*	03.10.1900
8.	Wagner	*Die Meistersinger von Nürnberg*	05.10.1900
9.	Wagner	*Die Meistersinger von Nürnberg*	06.10.1900
10.	Mozart	*Le nozze di Figaro*	09.10.1900
11.	Berlioz	*Benvenuto Cellini*	10.10.1900†
12.	Berlioz	*Benvenuto Cellini*	15.10.1900
13.	Mozart	*Così fan tutte*	23.10.1900
14.	Berlioz	*Benvenuto Cellini*	02.11.1900
15.	Beethoven	*Fidelio*	03.11.1900
16.	Mozart	*Die Zauberflöte*	16.11.1900
17.	Mozart	*Le nozze di Figaro*	22.11.1900
18.	Mozart	*Così fan tutte*	25.11.1900
19.	Beethoven	*Fidelio*	02.12.1900
20.	Mozart	*Le nozze di Figaro*	06.12.1900
21.	Lortzing	*Der Wildschütz*	07.12.1900
22.	Beethoven	*Fidelio*	17.12.1900
23.	Mozart	*Die Zauberflöte*	20.12.1900
24.	Wagner	*Lohengrin*	25.12.1900
25.	Humperdinck	*Hänsel und Gretel*	05.01.1900
26.	Wagner	*Der fliegende Holländer*	07.01.1900
27.	Mozart	*Le nozze di Figaro*	09.01.1901
28.	Wagner	*Lohengrin*	11.01.1900
29.	Wagner	*Der fliegende Holländer*	13.01.1900
30.	Mozart	*Così fan tutte*	15.01.1901
31.	Wagner	*Der fliegende Holländer*	25.01.1901
32.	Weber	*Der Freischütz*	27.01.1901
33.	Wagner	*Die Meistersinger von Nürnberg*	28.01.1901
34.	Cornelius	*Der Barbier von Bagdad*	29.01.1901†
35.	Mozart	*Bastien und Bastienne*	01.02.1901*
36.	Mozart	*Die Entführung aus dem Serail*	01.02.1901*
37.	Bizet	*Carmen*	08.02.1901
38.	Verdi	*Falstaff*	09.02.1901†
39.	Wagner	*Rienzi*	10.02.1901
40.	Wagner	*Der fliegende Holländer*	11.02.1901
41.	Bizet	*Carmen*	14.02.1901
42.	Wagner	*Das Rheingold*	16.02.1901
43.	Wagner	*Die Walküre*	17.02.1901
44.	Bizet	*Carmen*	26.02.1901
45.	Wagner	*Die Meistersinger von Nürnberg*	11.03.1901
46.	Mozart	*Le nozze di Figaro*	17.03.1901
47.	Wagner	*Rienzi*	18.03.1901
48.	Rossini	*Il barbiere von Siviglia*	19.03.1901
49.	Saint-Saëns	*Samson et Dalila*	28.03.1901†

50. Rossini	*Il barbiere di Siviglia*	30.03.1901
51. Saint-Saëns	*Samson et Dalila*	31.03.1901
52. Saint-Saëns	*Samson et Dalila*	03.04.1901
53. Saint-Saëns	*Samson et Dalila*	07.04.1901
54. Weber	*Der Freischütz*	10.04.1901
55. Saint-Saëns	*Samson et Dalila*	12.04.1901
56. Saint-Saëns	*Samson et Dalila*	16.04.1901
57. Mozart	*Le nozze di Figaro*	18.04.1901
58. Saint-Saëns	*Samson et Dalila*	20.04.1901
59. Saint-Saëns	*Samson et Dalila*	22.04.1901
60. Bizet	*Carmen*	23.04.1901
61. Saint-Saëns	*Samson et Dalila*	25.04.1901
62. Saint-Saëns	*Samson et Dalila*	28.04.1901
63. Nicolai	*Die lustige Weiber von Windsor*	01.05.1901
64. Humperdinck	*Hänsel und Gretel*	02.05.1901
65. Saint-Saëns	*Samson et Dalila*	04.05.1901
66. Saint-Saëns	*Samson et Dalila*	09.05.1901
67. Humperdinck	*Hänsel und Gretel*	10.05.1901
68. Saint-Saëns	*Samson et Dalila*	13.05.1901
69. Saint-Saëns	*Samson et Dalila*	18.05.1901
70. Cornelius	*Der Barbier von Bagdad*	20.05.1901
71. Wagner	*Der fliegende Holländer*	22.05.1901
72. Bizet	*Carmen*	24.05.1901
73. Saint-Saëns	*Samson et Dalila*	26.05.1901
74. Wagner	*Lohengrin*	06.06.1901
75. Humperdinck	*Hänsel und Gretel*	07.06.1901
76. Bizet	*Carmen*	09.06.1901
77. Wagner	*Tristan und Isolde*	13.06.1901
78. Humperdinck	*Hänsel und Gretel*	14.06.1901
79. Wagner	*Lohengrin*	16.06.1901
80. Bizet	*Carmen*	17.06.1901
81. Wagner	*Tristan und Isolde*	19.06.1901
82. Wagner	*Das Rheingold*	22.06.1901
83. Wagner	*Die Walküre*	23.06.1901
84. Wagner	*Siegfried*	25.06.1901
85. Wagner	*Götterdämmerung*	28.06.1901

1901–1902 Season

1. Bizet	*Carmen*	01.09.1901
2. Saint-Saëns	*Samson et Dalila*	02.09.1901
3. Wagner	*Lohengrin*	05.09.1901
4. Saint-Saëns	*Samson et Dalila*	07.09.1901
5. Wagner	*Tristan und Isolde*	09.09.1901
6. Bizet	*Carmen*	10.09.1901
7. Saint-Saëns	*Samson et Dalila*	13.09.1901
8. Weber	*Der Freischütz*	15.09.1901
9. Wagner	*Tannhäuser*	16.09.1901
10. Bizet	*Carmen*	18.06.1901
11. Saint-Saëns	*Samson et Dalila*	22.09.1901
12. Mozart	*Le nozze di Figaro*	24.09.1901
13. Verdi	*Aïda*	26.09.1901
14. Smetana	*The Bartered Bride*	29.09.1901
15. Wagner	*Die Meistersinger von Nürnberg*	30.09.1901

16.	Bizet	*Carmen*	02.10.1901
17.	Wagner	*Tristan und Isolde*	05.10.1901
18.	Kienzl	*Der Evangelimann*	11.10.1901
19.	Saint-Saëns	*Samson et Dalila*	12.10.1901
20.	Wagner	*Der fliegende Holländer*	19.10.1901
21.	Saint-Saëns	*Samson et Dalila*	20.10.1901
22.	Weber	*Der Freischütz*	22.10.1901
23.	Auber	*Fra Diavolo*	27.10.1901
24.	Wagner	*Die Meistersinger von Nürnberg*	28.10.1901
25.	Lortzing	*Der Wildschütz*	29.10.1901
26.	Saint-Saëns	*Samson et Dalila*	01.11.1901
27.	Lortzing	*Der Waffenschmied*	04.11.1901
28.	Saint-Saëns	*Samson et Dalila*	10.11.1901
29.	Wagner	*Tristan und Isolde*	11.11.1901
30.	Saint-Saëns	*Samson et Dalila*	13.11.1901
31.	Auber	*Fra Diavolo*	14.11.1901
32.	Mozart	*Don Giovanni*	24.11.1901†
33.	Mozart	*Così fan tutte*	25.11.1901
34.	Wagner	*Das Rheingold*	07.12.1901
35.	Wagner	*Die Walküre*	08.12.1901
36.	Mozart	*Don Giovanni*	09.12.1901
37.	Wagner	*Siegfried (Act 3 only)*	11.12.1901
38.	Wagner	*Götterdämmerung*	14.12.1901
39.	Wagner	*Die Meistersinger von Nürnberg*	21.12.1901
40.	Mozart	*Don Giovanni*	22.12.1901
41.	Saint-Saëns	*Samson et Dalila*	26.12.1901
42.	Auber	*Fra Diavolo*	31.12.1901
43.	Wagner	*Lohengrin*	01.01.1902
44.	Humperdinck	*Hänsel und Gretel*	05.01.1902
45.	Wagner	*Tristan und Isolde*	06.01.1902
46.	Saint-Saëns	*Samson et Dalila*	07.01.1902
47.	Beethoven	*Fidelio*	17.01.1902
48.	Wagner	*Die Meistersinger von Nürnberg*	20.01.1902
49.	Saint-Saëns	*Samson et Dalila*	07.02.1902
50.	Mozart	*Le nozze di Figaro*	08.02.1902
51.	Wagner	*Tristan und Isolde*	13.02.1902
52.	Beethoven	*Fidelio*	15.02.1902
53.	Auber	*Fra Diavolo*	17.02.1902
54.	Wagner	*Tannhäuser*	23.02.1902
55.	Mozart	*Le nozze di Figaro*	27.02.1902
56.	Wagner	*Der fliegende Holländer*	03.03.1902
57.	Auber	*La Muette de Portici*	04.03.1902
58.	Saint-Saëns	*Samson et Dalila*	06.03.1902
59.	Wagner	*Siegfried*	12.03.1902
60.	Wagner	*Götterdämmerung*	15.03.1902
61.	Mozart	*Le nozze di Figaro*	16.03.1902
62.	Beethoven	*Fidelio*	23.03.1902
63.	Saint-Saëns	*Samson et Dalila*	26.03.1902
64.	Weber	*Der Freischütz*	02.04.1902
65.	Mozart	*Die Zauberflöte*	03.04.1902
66.	Wagner	*Die Meistersinger von Nürnberg*	07.04.1902
67.	Wagner	*Das Rheingold*	10.04.1902
68.	Wagner	*Die Walküre*	11.04.1902
69.	Wagner	*Siegfried*	14.04.1902
70.	Wagner	*Götterdämmerung*	16.04.1902

71.	Mozart	*Die Entführung aus dem Serail*	18.04.1902
72.	Wagner	*Der fliegende Holländer*	22.04.1902
73.	Nicolai	*Die lustige Weiber von Windsor*	24.04.1902
74.	Meyerbeer	*Robert le Diable*	26.04.1902†
75.	Nicolai	*Die lustige Weiber von Windsor*	01.05.1902
76.	Meyerbeer	*Robert le Diable*	03.05.1902
77.	Mozart	*Don Giovanni*	04.05.1902
78.	Mozart	*Le nozze di Figaro*	07.05.1902
79.	Meyerbeer	*Robert le Diable*	08.05.1902
80.	Wagner	*Tristan und Isolde*	09.05.1902
81.	Meyerbeer	*Robert le Diable*	14.05.1902
82.	Wagner	*Die Meistersinger von Nürnberg*	15.05.1902
83.	Mozart	*Don Giovanni*	12.06.1902

1902–1903 Season

1.	Meyerbeer	*Robert le Diable*	03.09.1902
2.	Mozart	*Die Entführung aus dem Serail*	05.09.1902
3.	Wagner	*Die Meistersinger von Nürnberg*	08.09.1902
4.	Mozart	*Le nozze di Figaro*	13.09.1902
5.	Wagner	*Der fliegende Holländer*	14.09.1902
6.	Schillings	*Der Pfeifertag*	17.09.1902‡
7.	Wagner	*Das Rheingold*	18.09.1902
8.	Wagner	*Die Walküre*	19.09.1902
9.	Mozart	*Don Giovanni*	21.09.1902
10.	Wagner	*Siegfried*	23.09.1902
11.	Wagner	*Götterdämmerung*	25.09.1902
12.	Schillings	*Der Pfeifertag*	26.09.1902
13.	Weber	*Der Freischütz*	28.09.1902
14.	Saint-Saëns	*Samson et Dalila*	01.10.1902
15.	Schillings	*Der Pfeifertag*	04.10.1902
16.	Schillings	*Der Pfeifertag*	08.10.1902
17.	Schillings	*Der Pfeifertag*	19.10.1902
18.	Mozart	*Die Entführung aus dem Serail*	21.10.1902
19.	Strauss	*Feuersnot*	28.10.1902‡*
20.	Saint-Saëns	*Javotte*	28.10.1902*
21.	Strauss	*Feuersnot*	01.11.1902*
22.	Saint-Saëns	*Javotte*	01.11.1902*
23.	Schillings	*Der Pfeifertag*	04.11.1902
24.	Strauss	*Feuersnot*	05.11.1902*
25.	Saint-Saëns	*Javotte*	05.11.1902*
26.	Schillings	*Der Pfeifertag*	08.11.1902
27.	Strauss	*Feuersnot*	09.11.1902*
28.	Saint-Saëns	*Javotte*	09.11.1902*
29.	Strauss	*Feuersnot*	14.11.1902*
30.	Saint-Saëns	*Javotte*	14.11.1902*
31.	Strauss	*Feuersnot*	20.11.1902*
32.	Saint-Saëns	*Javotte*	20.11.1902*
33.	Auber	*La Muette de Portici*	22.11.1902
34.	Mozart	*Don Giovanni*	23.11.1902
35.	Strauss	*Feuersnot*	25.11.1902*
36.	Saint-Saëns	*Javotte*	25.11.1902*
37.	Mozart	*Le nozze di Figaro*	09.12.1902
38.	Wagner	*Siegfried*	12.12.1902

39.	Mozart	*Don Giovanni*	14.12.1902
40.	Weber	*Euryanthe*	18.12.1902†
41.	Wagner	*Siegfried*	19.12.1902
42.	Weber	*Euryanthe*	25.12.1902
43.	Wagner	*Die Meistersinger von Nürnberg*	26.12.1902
44.	Strauss	*Feuersnot*	28.12.1902
45.	Meyerbeer	*Robert le Diable*	01.01.1903
46.	Wagner	*Lohengrin*	08.01.1903
47.	Strauss	*Feuersnot*	09.01.1903*
48.	Saint-Saëns	*Javotte*	09.01.1903*
49.	Weber	*Euryanthe*	14.01.1903
50.	Scholz	*Anno 1757*	18.01.1903§
51.	Strauss	*Feuersnot*	20.01.1903*
52.	Saint-Saëns	*Javotte*	20.01.1903*
53.	Scholz	*Anno 1757*	21.01.1903
54.	Meyerbeer	*Robert le Diable*	25.01.1903
55.	Saint-Saëns	*Javotte*	27.01.1903
56.	Strauss	*Feuersnot*	04.02.1903*
57.	d'Albert	*Die Abreise*	04.02.1903*
58.	Scholz	*Anno 1757*	06.02.1903
59.	Saint-Saëns	*Samson et Dalila*	11.02.1903
60.	Mozart	*Don Giovanni*	14.02.1903
61.	Strauss	*Feuersnot*	19.02.1903*
62.	Leoncavallo	*I Pagliacci*	19.02.1903*
63.	Wagner	*Die Meistersinger von Nürnberg*	20.02.1903
64.	Mozart	*Die Zauberflöte*	22.02.1903
65.	Wagner	*Der fliegende Holländer*	26.02.1903
66.	Strauss	*Feuersnot*	01.04.1903
67.	Wagner	*Die Walküre*	02.04.1903
68.	Wagner	*Tristan und Isolde*	08.04.1903
69.	Verdi	*Aïda*	12.04.1903
70.	Strauss	*Feuersnot*	14.04.1903*
71.	Leoncavallo	*I Pagliacci*	14.04.1903"
72.	Wagner	*Die Meistersinger von Nürnberg*	17.04.1903
73.	Wagner	*Lohengrin*	20.04.1903
74.	Weber	*Der Freischütz*	21.04.1903
75.	Auber	*La Muette de Portici*	23.04.1903
76.	Wagner	*Die Walküre*	24.04.1903
77.	Strauss	*Feuersnot*	25.04.1903*
78.	Mascagni	*Cavalleria rusticana*	25.04.1903*
79.	Wagner	*Der fliegende Holländer*	03.05.1903
80.	Beethoven	*Fidelio*	04.05.1903
81.	Saint-Saëns	*Samson et Dalila*	07.05.1903
82.	Smetana	*The Bartered Bride*	09.05.1903
83.	Strauss	*Feuersnot*	12.05.1903
84.	Mozart	*Così fan tutte*	13.05.1903
85.	Wagner	*Die Walküre*	14.05.1903
86.	Schlar	*Döberitz*	27.05.1903
87.	Scholz	*Anno 1757*	27.05.1903

1903–1904 Season

| 1. | Mozart | *Don Giovanni* | 22.09.1903 |
| 2. | Wagner | *Der fliegende Holländer* | 27.09.1903 |

3.	Beethoven	*Fidelio*	01.10.1903
4.	Wagner	*Die Meistersinger von Nürnberg*	03.10.1903†
5.	Wagner	*Die Meistersinger von Nürnberg*	05.10.1903
6.	Wagner	*Die Meistersinger von Nürnberg*	11.10.1903
7.	Mozart	*Don Giovanni*	13.10.1903
8.	Strauss	*Feuersnot*	15.10.1903*
9.	Mascagni	*Cavalleria rusticana*	15.10.1903*
10.	Wagner	*Die Meistersinger von Nürnberg*	18.10.1903
11.	Wagner	*Die Meistersinger von Nürnberg*	21.10.1903
12.	Wagner	*Die Meistersinger von Nürnberg*	29.10.1903
13.	Strauss	*Feuersnot*	30.10.1903*
14.	Mascagni	*Cavalleria rusticana*	30.10.1903*
15.	Mozart	*Die Entführung aus dem Serail*	05.11.1903
16.	Meyerbeer	*Robert le Diable*	11.11.1903
17.	Mozart	*Don Giovanni*	12.11.1903
18.	Wagner	*Die Meistersinger von Nürnberg*	15.11.1903
19.	Wagner	*Die Meistersinger von Nürnberg*	19.11.1903
20.	Strauss	*Feuersnot*	24.11.1903
21.	Wagner	*Tannhäuser*	29.11.1903
22.	Saint-Saëns	*Samson et Dalila*	13.12.1903
23.	Wagner	*Die Meistersinger von Nürnberg*	15.12.1903
24.	Beethoven	*Fidelio*	16.12.1903
25.	Mozart	*Don Giovanni*	21.12.1903
26.	Meyerbeer	*Robert le Diable*	22.12.1903
27.	Wagner	*Die Meistersinger von Nürnberg*	26.12.1903
28.	Wagner	*Tannhäuser*	30.12.1903
29.	Wagner	*Die Meistersinger von Nürnberg*	04.01.1904
30.	Weber	*Der Freischütz*	14.01.1904
31.	Wagner	*Die Meistersinger von Nürnberg*	18.01.1904
32.	Saint-Saëns	*Samson et Dalila*	24.01.1904
33.	Verdi	*Aïda*	29.01.1904
34.	Strauss	*Feuersnot*	03.02.1904
35.	Wagner	*Lohengrin*	04.02.1904
36.	Beethoven	*Fidelio*	06.02.1904
37.	Auber	*La Muette de Portici*	08.02.1904
38.	Mozart	*Don Giovanni*	09.02.1904

1904–1905 Season

1.	Wagner	*Die Meistersinger von Nürnberg*	15.10.1904
2.	Meyerbeer	*Robert le Diable*	20.10.1904
3.	Wagner	*Der fliegende Holländer*	21.10.1904
4.	Mozart	*Don Giovanni*	27.10.1904
5.	Weber	*Der Freischütz*	02.11.1904†
6.	Wagner	*Die Meistersinger von Nürnberg*	08.11.1904
7.	Nicolai	*Die lustige Weiber von Windsor*	14.11.1904†
8.	Nicolai	*Die lustige Weiber von Windsor*	27.11.1904
9.	Nicolai	*Die lustige Weiber von Windsor*	30.11.1904
10.	Nicolai	*Die lustige Weiber von Windsor*	03.12.1904
11.	Weber	*Der Freischütz*	04.12.1904
12.	Wagner	*Der fliegende Holländer*	06.12.1904
13.	Saint-Saëns	*Samson et Dalila*	14.12.1904
14.	Wagner	*Die Walküre*	23.12.1904
15.	Nicolai	*Die lustige Weiber von Windor*	26.12.1904

16.	Wagner	*Die Meistersinger von Nürnberg*	28.12.1904
17.	Auber	*Le cheval de bronze* (arr. Humperdinck)	01.01.1905
18.	Nicolai	*Die lustige Weiber von Windsor*	05.01.1905
19.	Auber	*Le cheval de bronze* (arr. Humperdinck)	09.01.1905
20.	Mozart	*Don Giovanni*	10.01.1905
21.	Wagner	*Das Rheingold*	13.01.1905
22.	Wagner	*Die Walküre*	14.01.1905
23.	Wagner	*Siegfried*	16.01.1905
24.	Wagner	*Götterdämmerung*	19.01.1905
25.	Humperdinck	*Hänsel und Gretel*	01.02.1905
26.	Wagner	*Die Meistersinger von Nürnberg*	06.02.1905
27.	Mozart	*Le nozze di Figaro*	12.02.1905
28.	Sommer	*Rübezahl und der Sackpfeifer von Neisse*	15.02.1905†
29.	Sommer	*Rübezahl und der Sackpfeifer von Neisse*	17.02.1905
30.	Beethoven	*Fidelio*	19.02.1905
31.	Sommer	*Rübezahl und der Sackpfeifer von Neisse*	25.02.1905
32.	Auber	*Le cheval de bronze* (arr. Humperdinck)	03.03.1905
33.	Wagner	*Die Meistersinger von Nürnberg*	05.03.1905
34.	Mozart	*Così fan tutte*	07.03.1905†
35.	Mozart	*Così fan tutte*	14.03.1905
36.	Sommer	*Rübezahl und der Sackpfeifer von Neisse*	15.03.1905
37.	Wagner	*Das Rheingold*	18.03.1905
38.	Wagner	*Siegfried*	21.03.1905
39.	Wagner	*Götterdämmerung*	24.03.1905
40.	Wagner	*Der fliegende Holländer*	03.04.1905
41.	Mozart	*Don Giovanni*	09.04.1905
42.	Humperdinck	*Die Heirat wider Willen*	14.04.1905§
43.	Humperdinck	*Die Heirat wider Willen*	15.04.1905
44.	Wagner	*Götterdämmerung*	19.04.1905
45.	Humperdinck	*Die Heirat wider Willen*	24.04.1905
46.	Humperdinck	*Die Heirat wider Willen*	27.04.1905
47.	Humperdinck	*Die Heirat wider Willen*	30.04.1905
48.	Weber	*Der Freischütz*	04.05.1905
49.	Wagner	*Der fliegende Holländer*	05.05.1905
50.	Humperdinck	*Die Heirat wider Willen*	07.05.1905
51.	Beethoven	*Fidelio*	09.05.1905
52.	Humperdinck	*Die Heirat wider Willen*	13.05.1905
53.	Wagner	*Die Meistersinger von Nürnberg*	15.05.1905
54.	Humperdinck	*Die Heirat wider Willen*	16.05.1905
55.	Humperdinck	*Die Heirat wider Willen*	25.05.1905
56.	Nicolai	*Die lustige Weiber von Windsor*	06.06.1905
57.	Wagner	*Die Meistersinger von Nürnberg*	11.06.1905
58.	Weber	*Der Freischütz*	18.06.1905
59.	Wagner	*Tristan und Isolde*	23.06.1905[43]
60.	Strauss	*Feuersnot*	27.06.1905*[44]
61.	Cornelius	*Der Barbier von Bagdad*	27.06.1905*[45]

1905–1906 Season

1.	Cornelius	*Der Barbier von Bagdad*	07.10.1905
2.	Humperdinck	*Die Heirat wider Willen*	12.10.1905
3.	Cornelius	*Der Barbier von Bagdad*	21.10.1905
4.	Mozart	*Don Giovanni*	24.10.1905
5.	Nicolai	*Die lustige Weiber von Windsor*	26.10.1905

6.	Auber	*Le domino noir*	28.10.1905†
7.	Auber	*Le domino noir*	29.10.1905
8.	Auber	*Le domino noir*	30.10.1905
9.	Wagner	*Der fliegende Holländer*	06.11.1905
10.	Meyerbeer	*Robert le Diable*	09.11.1905
11.	Auber	*Le domino noir*	10.11.1905
12.	Wagner	*Die Meistersinger von Nürnberg*	13.11.1905
13.	Humperdinck	*Die Heirat wider Willen*	15.11.1905
14.	Beethoven	*Leonore*	20.11.1905
15.	Beethoven	*Leonore*	01.12.1905
16.	Auber	*Le domino noir*	03.12.1905
17.	Nicolai	*Die lustige Weiber von Windsor*	12.12.1905
18.	Auber	*Le domino noir*	14.12.1905
19.	Auber	*Le domino noir*	26.12.1905
20.	Weber	*Der Freischütz*	29.12.1905
21.	Auber	*Le domino noir*	01.01.1906
22.	Mozart	*Così fan tutte*	04.01.1906
23.	Wagner	*Die Meistersinger von Nürnberg*	08.01.1906
24.	Wagner	*Tristan und Isolde*	11.01.1906
25.	Mozart	*Don Giovanni*	13.01.1906
26.	Mozart	*Die Entführung aus dem Serail*	17.01.1906
27.	Mozart	*Le nozze di Figaro*	20.01.1906
28.	Mozart	*Don Giovanni*	23.01.1906
29.	Auber	*Le domino noir*	24.01.1906
30.	Mozart	*Così fan tutte*	25.01.1906
31.	Humperdinck	*Die Heirat wider Willen*	02.02.1906
32.	Mozart	*Le nozze di Figaro*	04.02.1906
33.	Nicolai	*Die lustige Weiber von Windsor*	10.02.1906
34.	Wagner	*Die Meistersinger von Nürnberg*	12.02.1906
35.	Beethoven	*Fidelio*	16.02.1906
36.	Rossini	*Il barbiere di Siviglia*	21.02.1906
37.	Beethoven	*Fidelio*	23.02.1906
38.	Mozart	*Le nozze di Figaro*	25.02.1906
39.	Wagner	*Die Meistersinger von Nürnberg*	04.03.1906
40.	Rossini	*Il barbiere di Siviglia*	11.03.1906
41.	Wagner	*Siegfried*	15.03.1906
42.	Schillings	*Der Pfeifertag*	18.03.1906†
43.	Mozart	*Le nozze di Figaro*	27.03.1906
44.	Wagner	*Der fliegende Holländer*	28.03.1906
45.	Nicolai	*Die lustige Weiber von Windsor*	29.03.1906
46.	Mozart	*Don Giovanni*	03.04.1906
47.	Beethoven	*Fidelio*	05.04.1906
48.	Auber	*La Muette de Portici*	09.04.1906
49.	Mozart	*Le nozze di Figaro*	16.04.1906
50.	Schillings	*Der Pfeifertag*	19.04.1906
51.	Nicolai	*Die lustige Weiber von Windsor*	20.04.1906
52.	Beethoven	*Fidelio*	21.04.1906
53.	Weber	*Der Freischütz*	22.04.1906
54.	Wagner	*Die Meistersinger von Nürnberg*	28.04.1906

1906–1907 Season

1.	Auber	*Le domino noir*	02.10.1906
2.	Mozart	*Le nozze di Figaro*	06.10.1906

3.	Saint-Saëns	*Samson et Dalila*	07.10.1906
4.	Wagner	*Der fliegende Holländer*	08.10.1906
5.	Wagner	*Die Walküre*	12.10.1906
6.	Beethoven	*Fidelio*	15.10.1906
7.	Mozart	*Le nozze di Figaro*	21.10.1906
8.	Mozart	*Don Giovanni*	24.10.1906
9.	Mozart	*Don Giovanni*	27.10.1906
10.	Wagner	*Das Rheingold*	30.10.1906
11.	Wagner	*Die Walküre*	01.11.1906
12.	Wagner	*Siegfried*	03.11.1906
13.	Wagner	*Götterdämmerung*	05.11.1906†
14.	Mozart	*Don Giovanni*	12.11.1906
15.	Wagner	*Die Meistersinger von Nürnberg*	16.11.1906
16.	Mozart	*Così fan tutte*	24.11.1906
17.	Wagner	*Der fliegende Holländer*	26.11.1906
18.	Mozart	*Così fan tutte*	28.11.1906
19.	Wagner	*Die Walküre*	30.11.1906
20.	Strauss	*Salome*	05.11.1906
21.	Strauss	*Salome*	10.11.1906
22.	Wagner	*Der fliegende Holländer*	11.11.1906
23.	Strauss	*Salome*	12.11.1906
24.	Wagner	*Das Rheingold*	02.01.1907
25.	Wagner	*Die Walküre*	03.01.1907
26.	Wagner	*Siegfried*	05.01.1907
27.	Wagner	*Götterdämmerung*	08.01.1907
28.	Strauss	*Salome*	12.01.1907
29.	Cornelius	*Der Barbier der Bagdad*	15.01.1907
30.	Rossini	*Il barbiere di Siviglia*	19.01.1907
31.	Strauss	*Salome*	21.01.1907
32.	Strauss	*Salome*	25.01.1907
33.	Wagner	*Die Meistersinger von Nürnberg*	28.01.1907
34.	Strauss	*Salome*	29.01.1907
35.	Mozart	*Le nozze di Figaro*	01.02.1907
36.	Strauss	*Salome*	02.02.1907
37.	Wagner	*Der fliegende Holländer*	04.02.1907
38.	Strauss	*Salome*	07.02.1907
39.	Wagner	*Siegfried*	10.02.1907
40.	Verdi	*Falstaff*	12.02.1907†
41.	Verdi	*Falstaff*	16.02.1907
42.	Verdi	*Falstaff*	19.02.1907
43.	Wagner	*Siegfried*	22.02.1907
44.	Strauss	*Salome*	25.02.1907
45.	Wagner	*Die Meistersinger von Nürnberg*	04.03.1907
46.	Ritter	*Der faule Hans*	08.03.1907†
47.	Strauss	*Salome*	10.03.1907
48.	Strauss	*Salome*	11.03.1907
49.	Strauss	*Salome*	16.03.1907
50.	Mozart	*Le nozze di Figaro*	18.03.1907
51.	Strauss	*Salome*	19.03.1907
52.	Mozart	*Die Entführung aus dem Serail*	04.04.1907
53.	Mozart	*Don Giovanni*	06.04.1907
54.	Mozart	*Le nozze di Figaro*	07.04.1907
55.	Mozart	*Così fan tutte*	08.04.1907
56.	Strauss	*Salome*	12.04.1907

57. Strauss	*Salome*	15.04.1907
58. Strauss	*Salome*	18.04.1907
59. Wagner	*Das Rheingold*	19.04.1907
60. Wagner	*Die Walküre*	20.04.1907
61. Wagner	*Siegfried*	22.04.1907
62. Wagner	*Götterdämmerung*	24.04.1907
63. Strauss	*Salome*	26.04.1907
64. Wagner	*Die Meistersinger von Nürnberg*	28.04.1907
65. Strauss	*Salome*	30.04.1907

1907–1908 Season

1. Wagner	*Das Rheingold*	03.09.1907
2. Wagner	*Der Walküre*	04.09.1907
3. Wagner	*Siegfried*	05.09.1907
4. Wagner	*Götterdämmerung*	08.09.1907
5. Strauss	*Salome*	14.09.1907
6. Wagner	*Der fliegende Holländer*	16.09.1907
7. Strauss	*Salome*	20.09.1907
8. Strauss	*Salome*	24.09.1907
9. Mozart	*Die Entführung aus dem Serail*	28.09.1907†
10. Strauss	*Salome*	05.10.1907
11. Wagner	*Die Meistersinger von Nürnberg*	06.10.1907
12. Strauss	*Salome*	08.10.1907
13. Mozart	*Die Entführung aus dem Serail*	09.10.1907
14. Strauss	*Salome*	12.10.1907
15. Beethoven	*Fidelio*	14.10.1907
16. Weber	*Der Freischütz*	17.10.1907
17. Strauss	*Salome*	21.10.1907
18. Weber	*Der Freischütz*	05.11.1907
19. Strauss	*Salome*	09.11.1907
20. Wagner	*Das Rheingold*	22.11.1907
21. Wagner	*Die Walküre*	24.11.1907
22. Wagner	*Die Meistersinger von Nürnberg*	02.12.1907
23. Beethoven	*Fidelio*	07.12.1907
24. Strauss	*Salome*	09.12.1907
25. Cornelius	*Der Barbier von Bagdad*	11.11.1907†
26. Cornelius	*Der Barbier von Bagdad*	13.11.1907
27. Strauss	*Salome*	18.11.1907
28. Cornelius	*Der Barbier von Bagdad*	22.11.1907
29. Wagner	*Die Meistersinger von Nürnberg*	29.11.1907
30. Cornelius	*Der Barbier von Bagdad*	02.01.1908
31. Strauss	*Salome*	03.01.1908
32. Wagner	*Das Rheingold*	07.01.1908
33. Wagner	*Die Walküre*	09.01.1908
34. Nicolai	*Die lustige Weiber von Windsor*	12.01.1908
35. Strauss	*Salome*	13.01.1908
36. Mozart	*Die Entführung aus dem Serail*	15.01.1908
37. Wagner	*Der fliegende Holländer*	19.01.1908
38. Wagner	*Die Meistersinger von Nürnberg*	22.01.1908
39. Strauss	*Salome*	24.01.1908
40. Wagner	*Götterdämmerung*	26.02.1908
41. Strauss	*Salome*	01.03.1908
42. Wagner	*Die Walküre*	02.03.1908

43. Wagner	*Die Meistersinger von Nürnberg*	12.03.1908
44. Wagner	*Der fliegende Holländer*	15.03.1908
45. Nicolai	*Die lustige Weiber von Windsor*	16.03.1908
46. Wagner	*Siegfried*	18.03.1908
47. Strauss	*Salome*	29.03.1908
48. Strauss	*Salome*	06.04.1908
49. Mozart	*Così fan tutte*	09.04.1908
50. Wagner	*Die Walküre*	14.04.1908
51. Mozart	*Così fan tutte*	22.04.1908

1908–1909 Season

1. Strauss	*Salome*	30.09.1908
2. Weber	*Der Freischütz*	16.10.1908
3. Mozart	*Die Zauberflöte*	19.10.1908
4. Wagner	*Tristan und Isolde*	31.10.1908
5. Strauss	*Salome*	04.11.1908
6. Strauss	*Salome*	01.12.1908
7. Wagner	*Die Meistersinger von Nürnberg*	08.02.1909
8. Wagner	*Der fliegende Holländer*	14.02.1909

1909–1910 Season

1. Strauss	*Salome*	02.10.1909
2. Wagner	*Der fliegende Holländer*	03.10.1909
3. Nicolai	*Die lustige Weiber von Windsor*	07.10.1909
4. Strauss	*Elektra*	13.10.1909
5. Strauss	*Elektra*	24.10.1909
6. Wagner	*Der fliegende Holländer*	25.10.1909
7. Wagner	*Die Meistersinger von Nürnberg*	01.11.1909
8. Wagner	*Die Meistersinger von Nürnberg*	20.11.1909
9. Mozart	*Così fan tutte*	26.11.1909
10. Strauss	*Elektra*	27.11.1909
11. Auber	*Le domino noir*	28.11.1909
12. Nicolai	*Die lustige Weiber von Windsor*	30.11.1909
13. Wagner	*Der fliegende Holländer*	04.12.1909
14. Strauss	*Salome*	10.12.1909
15. Wagner	*Die Meistersinger von Nürnberg*	12.12.1909
16. Strauss	*Elektra*	06.01.1909
17. Wagner	*Die Meistersinger von Nürnberg*	07.01.1909
18. Mozart	*Le nozze di Figaro*	19.01.1910
19. Wagner	*Die Meistersinger von Nürnberg*	24.01.1910
20. Weber	*Der Freischütz*	29.01.1910
21. Strauss	*Salome*	02.02.1910
22. Wagner	*Die Meistersinger von Nürnberg*	20.02.1910
23. Strauss	*Elektra*	21.02.1910
24. Wagner	*Tristan und Isolde*	26.02.1910
25. Strauss	*Salome*	28.02.1910
26. Wagner	*Die Meistersinger von Nürnberg*	04.03.1910
27. Weber	*Der Freischütz*	07.03.1910
28. Nicolai	*Die lustige Weiber von Windsor*	28.03.1910
29. Wagner	*Die Meistersinger von Nürnberg*	03.04.1910
30. Strauss	*Elektra*	04.04.1910

1910–1911 Season

1.	Strauss	*Elektra*	02.10.1910
2.	Mozart	*Le nozze di Figaro*	12.10.1910
3.	Strauss	*Salome*	17.10.1910
4.	Mozart	*Le nozze di Figaro*	25.10.1910
5.	Strauss	*Elektra*	10.12.1910
6.	Strauss	*Salome*	27.03.1911
7.	Strauss	*Elektra*	30.03.1911

1911–1912 Season

1.	Strauss	*Elektra*	08.11.1911
2.	Strauss	*Salome*	11.11.1911
3.	Strauss	*Salome*	27.02.1912
4.	Strauss	*Elektra*	21.03.1912
5.	Cornelius	*Der Barbier von Bagdad*	29.05.1912

1912–1913 Season

1.	Strauss	*Salome*	17.10.1912
2.	Mozart	*Le nozze di Figaro*	22.11.1912
3.	Strauss	*Salome*	28.11.1912
4.	Mozart	*Le nozze di Figaro*	09.12.1912
5.	Strauss	*Der Rosenkavalier*	23.12.1912
6.	Strauss	*Der Rosenkavalier*	28.12.1912
7.	Gluck	*Iphigénie en Aulide*	01.01.1913
8.	Cornelius	*Der Barbier von Bagdad*	07.01.1913
9.	Strauss	*Der Rosenkavalier*	13.01.1913
10.	Beethoven	*Fidelio*	24.01.1913
11.	Beethoven	*Fidelio*	17.02.1913
12.	Strauss	*Salome*	21.02.1913
13.	Strauss	*Der Rosenkavalier*	23.02.1913
14.	Strauss	*Der Rosenkavalier*	04.03.1913
15.	Wagner	*Die Meistersinger von Nürnberg*	06.04.1913
16.	Mozart	*Die Zauberflöte*	08.03.1913
17.	Strauss	*Elektra*	11.03.1913
18.	Wagner	*Der fliegende Holländer*	16.03.1913
19.	Beethoven	*Fidelio*	19.03.1913
20.	Strauss	*Der Rosenkavalier*	24.03.1913
21.	Strauss	*Ariadne auf Naxos* (1912 version)	02.06.1913
22.	Gluck	*Orfeo ed Euridice*	03.06.1913
23.	Mozart	*Die Zauberflöte*	04.06.1913
24.	Beethoven	*Fidelio*	05.06.1913
25.	Strauss	*Der Rosenkavalier*	07.06.1913
26.	Strauss	*Ariadne auf Naxos* (1912 version)	08.06.1913
27.	Strauss	*Der Rosenkavalier*	14.06.1913
28.	Strauss	*Ariadne auf Naxos* (1912 version)	15.06.1913

1913–1914 Season

1.	Mozart	*Le nozze di Figaro*	01.11.1913
2.	Strauss	*Der Rosenkavalier*	03.11.1913

3. Strauss	*Salome*	08.12.1913
4. Strauss	*Elektra*	10.12.1913
5. Strauss	*Der Rosenkavalier*	12.12.1913
6. Strauss	*Ariadne auf Naxos* (1912 version)	14.12.1913
7. Mozart	*Le nozze di Figaro*	18.12.1913
8. Strauss	*Salome*	02.01.1914
9. Strauss	*Ariadne auf Naxos* (1912 version)	01.02.1914
10. Strauss	*Der Rosenkavalier*	07.02.1914
11. Strauss	*Elektra*	11.02.1914
12. Strauss	*Salome*	02.03.1914
13. Strauss	*Der Rosenkavalier*	06.03.1914
14. Strauss	*Ariadne auf Naxos* (1912 version)	11.03.1914
15. Strauss	*Der Rosenkavalier*	24.03.1914
16. Mozart	*Le nozze di Figaro*	26.03.1914
17. Strauss	*Salome*	31.03.1914

1914–1915 Season

1. Mozart	*Le nozze di Figaro*	07.11.1914
2. Strauss	*Tod und Verklärung* and *Salome*	26.11.1914
3. Strauss	*Tod und Verklärung* and *Salome*	22.12.1914
4. Mozart	*Le nozze di Figaro*	28.12.1914
5. Strauss	*Der Rosenkavalier*	30.12.1914
6. Beethoven	*Fidelio*	12.01.1915
7. Strauss	*Don Juan* and *Elektra*	18.01.1915
8. Strauss	*Ein Heldenleben* and *Salome*	20.01.1915
9. Strauss	*Der Rosenkavalier*	22.01.1915
10. Strauss	*Ariadne auf Naxos* (1912 version)	24.01.1915
11. Wagner	*Die Meistersinger von Nürnberg*	27.01.1915
12. Wagner	*Lohengrin*	31.01.1915†
13. Mozart	*Le nozze di Figaro*	02.02.1915
14. Wagner	*Der fliegende Holländer*	07.02.1915
15. Wagner	*Lohengrin*	10.02.1915
16. Beethoven	*Fidelio*	12.02.1915
17. Strauss	*Der Rosenkavalier*	14.02.1915
18. Wagner	*Die Walküre*	16.02.1915
19. Wagner	*Lohengrin*	21.02.1915
20. Cornelius	*Der Barbier von Bagdad*	22.02.1915
21. Weber	*Der Freischütz*	25.02.1915
22. Mozart	*Le nozze di Figaro*	27.02.1915
23. Cornelius	*Der Barbier von Bagdad*	02.03.1915
24. Strauss	*Tod und Verklärung* and *Salome*	04.03.1915
25. Strauss	*Ariadne auf Naxos* (1912 version)	11.03.1915
26. Wagner	*Lohengrin*	14.03.1915
27. Strauss	*Der Rosenkavalier*	15.03.1915
28. Cornelius	*Der Barbier von Bagdad*	20.03.1915
29. Strauss	*Don Juan* and *Elektra*	23.03.1915
30. Wagner	*Lohengrin*	09.05.1915
31. Strauss	*Don Juan* and *Elektra*	10.05.1915

1915–1916 Season

1. Schillings	*Mona Lisa*	15.10.1915†
2. Schillings	*Mona Lisa*	17.10.1915

3.	Strauss	*Der Rosenkavalier*	29.10.1915
4.	Strauss	*Ariadne auf Naxos* (1912 version)	31.10.1915
5.	Strauss	*Ein Heldenleben* and *Salome*	02.11.1915
6.	Wagner	*Der fliegende Holländer*	09.01.1916
7.	Wagner	*Lohengrin*	16.01.1916
8.	Wagner	*Der fliegende Holländer*	18.01.1916
9.	Strauss	*Ariadne auf Naxos* (1912 version)	20.01.1916
10.	Wagner	*Die Meistersinger von Nürnberg*	25.01.1916
11.	Strauss	*Ein Heldenleben* and *Salome*	30.01.1916
12.	Schillings	*Mona Lisa*	31.01.1916
13.	Mozart	*Le nozze di Figaro*	01.02.1916
14.	Schillings	*Mona Lisa*	14.02.1916
15.	Strauss	*Der Rosenkavalier*	15.02.1916
16.	Wagner	*Der fliegende Holländer*	18.02.1916
17.	Schillings	*Mona Lisa*	04.03.1916
18.	Strauss	*Elektra*	08.03.1916
19.	Strauss	*Don Juan* and *Elektra*	10.03.1916
20.	Strauss	*Der Rosenkavalier*	13.03.1916
21.	Strauss	*Tod und Verklärung* and *Salome*	15.03.1916
22.	Strauss	*Ariadne auf Naxos* (1912 version)	19.03.1916
23.	Mozart	*Le nozze di Figaro*	21.03.1916
24.	Mozart	*Le nozze di Figaro*	04.04.1916
25.	Johann Strauss II	*Die Fledermaus*	08.04.1916
26.	Schillings	*Mona Lisa*	10.04.1916
27.	Strauss	*Der Rosenkavalier*	11.04.1916
28.	Weber	*Der Freischütz*	14.04.1916
29.	Beethoven	*Fidelio*	18.04.1916

1916–1917 Season

1.	Mozart	*Le nozze di Figaro*	17.10.1916
2.	Wagner	*Lohengrin*	22.10.1916
3.	Wagner	*Die Meistersinger von Nürnberg*	25.10.1916
4.	Strauss	*Ein Heldenleben* and *Salome*	26.10.1916
5.	Wagner	*Der fliegende Holländer*	28.10.1916
6.	Beethoven	*Fidelio*	26.11.1916
7.	Wagner	*Der fliegende Holländer*	01.12.1916
8.	Mozart	*Le nozze di Figaro*	04.12.1916
9.	Verdi	*Aïda*	05.12.1916
10.	Strauss	*Der Rosenkavalier*	07.12.1916
11.	Strauss	*Tod und Verklärung* and *Salome*	11.12.1916
12.	Bizet	*Carmen*	12.12.1916
13.	Schillings	*Mona Lisa*	14.12.1916
14.	Mozart	*Le nozze di Figaro*	15.02.1917
15.	Strauss	*Ariadne auf Naxos* (1916 version)	17.02.1917
16.	Mozart	*Le nozze di Figaro*	06.03.1917
17.	Bizet	*Carmen*	11.03.1917
18.	Beethoven	*Fidelio*	14.03.1917
19.	Strauss	*Ariadne auf Naxos* (1916 version)	15.03.1917
20.	Strauss	*Der Rosenkavalier*	18.03.1917
21.	Mozart	*Le nozze di Figaro*	19.03.1917
22.	Strauss	*Ein Heldenleben* and *Salome*	23.03.1917
23.	Wagner	*Parsifal*	29.03.1917
24.	Wagner	*Parsifal*	31.03.1917

25.	Wagner	*Parsifal*	02.04.1917
26.	Strauss	*Feuersnot*	03.04.1917
27.	Wagner	*Parsifal*	04.04.1917

1917–1918 Season

1.	Beethoven	*Fidelio*	12.09.1917
2.	Wagner	*Der fliegende Hollander*	16.10.1917
3.	Strauss	*Tod und Verklärung* and *Salome*	17.10.1917
4.	Beethoven	*Fidelio*	23.11.1917
5.	Wagner	*Der fliegende Holländer*	25.11.1917
6.	Strauss	*Der Rosenkavalier*	27.11.1917
7.	Mozart	*Le nozze di Figaro*	04.12.1917
8.	Mozart	*Die Entführung aus dem Serail*	05.12.1917†
9.	Rossini	*Il barbiere di Siviglia*	11.12.1917
10.	Verdi	*Aïda*	13.12.1917
11.	Wagner	*Der fliegende Holländer*	19.12.1917
12.	Strauss	*Tod und Verklärung* and *Salome*	20.12.1917
13.	Schillings	*Mona Lisa*	31.01.1918
14.	Strauss	*Der Rosenkavalier*	03.03.1918
15.	Mozart	*Le nozze di Figaro*	05.03.1918
16.	Strauss	*Salome*	08.03.1918†
17.	Strauss	*Salome*	12.03.1918
18.	Wagner	*Tristan und Isolde*	26.03.1918
19.	Mozart	*Le nozze di Figaro*	01.04.1918
20.	Strauss	*Salome*	02.04.1918
21.	Rossini	*Il barbiere di Siviglia*	03.04.1918

1918–1919 Season

1.	Strauss	*Salome*	19.10.1918
2.	Strauss	*Der Rosenkavalier*	05.11.1918
3.	Strauss	*Salome*	07.11.1918[46]
4.	Beethoven	*Fidelio*	29.11.1918
5.	Weber	*Der Freischütz*	02.03.1919
6.	Weber	*Der Freischütz*	05.03.1919
7.	Schillings	*Mona Lisa*	09.03.1919
8.	Rossini	*Il barbiere di Siviglia*	13.03.1919
9.	Strauss	*Elektra*	25.03.1919
10.	Strauss	*Ariadne auf Naxos* (1916 version)	28.03.1919
11.	Strauss	*Der Rosenkavalier*	31.03.1919
12.	Strauss	*Ariadne auf Naxos* (1916 version)	03.04.1919
13.	Wagner	*Lohengrin*	08.04.1919
14.	Strauss	*Salome*	16.04.1919
15.	Verdi	*Aïda*	21.04.1919
16.	Rossini	*Il barbiere di Siviglia*	24.04.1919
17.	Mozart	*Don Giovanni*	25.04.1919†
18.	Mozart	*Don Giovanni*	27.04.1919
19.	Strauss	*Der Rosenkavalier*	28.04.1919
20.	Mozart	*Don Giovanni*	30.04.1919
21.	Wagner	*Der fliegende Holländer*	05.05.1919
22.	Mozart	*Le nozze di Figaro*	08.05.1919
23.	Strauss	*Der Rosenkavalier*	24.10.1919

24. Strauss	*Salome*	27.10.1919
25. Strauss	*Elektra*	12.11.1919
26. Strauss	*Der Rosenkavaler*	13.11.1919
27. Strauss	*Ariadne auf Nuxos* (1916 version)	16.11.1919
28. Strauss	*Der Rosenkavalier*	25.11.1919
29. Strauss	*Elektra*	26.11.1919
30. Strauss	*Ariadne auf Naxos* (1916 version)	29.11.1919
31. Strauss	*Salome*	01.12.1919[47]

PART I: BERLIN TONKÜNSTLER-ORCHESTER, 1901–1903[48]

1901–1902 Season

1. 21.10.1901: Liszt: *Ce qu'on entend sur la montagne*; Sgambati: Piano Concerto in G minor (Emil von Sauer,[49] piano);[50] Bruckner: Symphony No. 3.
2. 18.11.1901:[51] D'Indy: *La forêt enchantée*; Tchaikovsky: *Voyevoda*; Hausegger: *Dionysische Fantasie*; Loeffler: *Divertimento* (Karl Halir, violin); Liszt: *Tasso*.
3. 16.12.1901: Liszt: *Les Préludes*; Mahler: Symphony No. 4 (Thila Plaichinger, soprano; Gustav Mahler, conductor); Rösch: Three Lieder with Orchestra (Thila Plaichinger, soprano): Strauss: *Feuersnot* Love Scene.
4. 21.01.1902: Liszt: *Orpheus*; Rabl: *Sturmlieder*;[52] Mascagni: *A Giacomo Leopardi* (Emmy Destinn,[53] soprano); Elgar: *Cockaigne* Overture; Thuille: *Gugeline* Act 3 (Emmy Destinn, soprano; Ernst Kraus,[54] tenor, Kurt Sommer,[55] tenor).
5. 10.02.1902:[56] Blech: *Barcarolle*; Ertel: Love Scene from 'Harald' Symphony;[57] Neitzel: Piano Concerto (Otto Neitzel, piano);[58] Georg Schumann: *Variationen und Doppelfuge über ein lustige Thema*; Liszt: *Prometheus*.
6. 18.02.1902 (Posen):[59] Liszt: *Les Préludes*; Strauss: *Feuersnot* Love Scene; Beethoven: Violin Concerto (violinist not named); Strauss: *Don Juan*; Wagner: *Die Meistersinger von Nürnberg* Prelude.
7. 19.02.1902 (Halle):[60] Bruckner: Symphony No. 3;[61] Strauss: *Don Juan* and *Feuersnot* Love Scene; Liszt: *Les Préludes*.
8. 26.02.1902 (Hanover):[62] Bruckner: Symphony No. 3; Strauss: *Don Juan* and *Feuersnot* Love Scene; Liszt: *Les Préludes*.
9. 10.03.1902: Bruneau: *Messidor* Entr'acte; Pfitzner: *Oluf*; Strauss: *Pilgers Morgenlied* (Karl Scheidemantel,[63] baritone); Schillings: 'Meergruss', three Lieder from *Vier Lieder aus der Wanderzeit* (Karl Scheidemantel, baritone); Ritter: *Kaiser Rudolfs Ritt zum Grabe*; Liszt: *Mazeppa*.
10. 18.03.1902 (Stettin):[64] Bruckner: Symphony No. 3;[65] Strauss: *Don Juan* and *Feuersnot* Love Scene; Liszt: *Les Préludes*.
11. 24.03.1902: Bruckner: Symphony No. 3; Strauss: *Don Juan*; Spohr: Violin Concerto Op. 38 No. 7 (Willy Burmester, violin); Bach: Chaconne in D minor (Willy Burmester, violin); Rezniček *Till Eulenspiegel* Overture.

1902–1903 Season

1. 06.10.1902: Bruckner: Symphony No. 1; Strauss: 'Friedenserzählung' from *Guntram* (Ejnar Forchhammer,[66] tenor); Schillings: *Ein Zweigespräch*; Ritter: Monologue from *Der faule Hans*; Liszt: *Festklänge*.
2. 03.11.1902: Liszt: *Héroïde funèbre*; Sauer: Piano Concerto No. 2 (Emil von Sauer, piano); Strauss: *Aus Italien*.
3. 24.11.1902: Bischoff: *Pan*;[67] Tchaikovsky: Violin Concerto (Willy Burmester, violin); Liszt: *Hungaria*; Chabrier: *Joyeuese Marche*.
4. 28.11.1902 (Halle):[68] Wagner: *Rienzi* Overture; Tchaikovsky: *Voyevoda*; Bruneau: *Messidor* Entr'acte; Liszt: *Hungaria*; Strauss: *Aus Italien*.

5. 29.11.1902 (Hanover):[69] Wagner: *Rienzi* Overture; Tchaikovsky: *Voyevoda*; Bruneau: *Messidor* Entr'acte; Liszt: *Hungaria*; Strauss: *Aus Italien*.

6. 30.11.1902 (Braunschweig):[70] Beethoven: *Egmont* Overture; Liszt: *Les Préludes*; Bruneau: *Messidor* Entr'acte; Wagner: *Tristan und Isolde* Prelude; Strauss: *Aus Italien*.

7. 07.01.1903 (Stettin):[71] Haydn: Symphony No. 100; Beethoven: Symphony No. 3; Wagner: *Tristan und Isolde* Prelude; Strauss: *Tod und Verklärung*.

8. 19.01.1903: Liszt: *Hamlet*; Stanford: *Irish Rhapsody*; Brecher: *Aus unserer Zeit*;[72] Wolf: 'Anakreons Grab' (Hans Schütz,[73] baritone); Strauss: 'Hymnus' (Hans Schütz, baritone); Pringsheim: 'Weil auf mir'[74] (Hans Schütz, baritone): Strauss: *Tod und Verklärung*.

9. 09.02.1903 (Leipzig):[75] Wagner: *Tristan und Isolde* and *Die Meistersinger von Nürnberg* Preludes; Bruneau: *Messidor* Entr'acte; Beethoven: *Ah! Perfido* (Tilly Koenen,[76] soprano); Strauss: unspecified Lieder (Tilly Koenen, soprano) and *Aus Italien*.

10. 10.02.1903 (Halle):[77] Wagner: *Tannhäuser* Overture, *Tristan und Isolde* Prelude and *Die Meistersinger von Nürnberg* Prelude; Liszt: *Tasso*; Beethoven: *Egmont* Overture; Strauss: *Tod und Verklärung*.

11. 16.02.1903:[78] Smetana: *Tábor*; Huber: *Heroische Symphonie*;[79] Tchaikovsky: Piano Concerto No. 2 (Sophie Menter, piano); Liszt: *Hunnenschlacht*.

12. 25.02.1903 (Stettin):[80] programme unknown.[81]

13. 28.02.1903 (Tour: Dresden, Evangelischen Gemeindehaus):[82] Strauss: *Aus Italien*; Liszt: *Tasso*; Tchaikovsky: *Voyevoda*; Bruneau: *Messidor* Entr'acte; Strauss: *Tod und Verklärung*.

14. 01.03.1903 (Tour: Teplitz matinee at 11 a.m.): Beethoven: Symphony No. 7; Strauss: *Feuersnot* Love Scene; Wagner: *Tristan und Isolde* Prelude; Strauss: *Don Juan*

15. 01.03.1903 (Tour: Aussig evening concert at 8 p.m.): Beethoven: *Egmont* Overture; Liszt: *Tasso*; Bruneau: *Messidor* Entr'acte; Wagner: *Die Meistersinger von Nürnberg* Prelude; Strauss: *Aus Italien*.

16. 03.03.1903 (Tour: Prague at 7.30 p.m., Rudolfinum): Bruckner: Symphony No. 3; Smetana: *Tábor*; Strauss: *Feuersnot* Love Scene; Wagner: *Tristan und Isolde* Prelude; Strauss: *Don Juan*.

17. 04.03.1903 (Tour: Vienna at 7.30 p.m., Grossen Musikvereinsaal): Strauss: *Aus Italien*; Wagner: *Tristan und Isolde* and *Die Meistersinger von Nürnberg* Preludes; Strauss: *Tod und Verklärung*.

18. 05.03.1903 (Tour: Graz at 7 p.m., Erzherzog-Johann-Industriehalle): Wagner: *Tristan und Isolde* Prelude; Liszt: *Tasso*; Bruckner: Symphony No. 3; Strauss: *Don Juan*.

19. 06.03.1903 (Tour: Graz):[83] Strauss: *Aus Italien*; Wagner: *Die Meistersinger von Nürnberg* Prelude; Bruneau: *Messidor* Entr'acte; Strauss: *Feuersnot* Love Scene and *Tod und Verklärung*.

20. 07.03.1903 (Tour: Klagenfurt at 7.30 p.m., Grossen Musikvereinsaal): Wagner: *Tristan und Isolde* Prelude; Strauss: *Feuersnot* Love Scene and *Don Juan*; Bruckner: Symphony No. 3.

21. 08.03.1903 (Tour: Laibach matinee at 11.30 a.m., Tonhalle der Philharmonischen Gesellschaft): Beethoven: *Egmont* Overture; Bruneau: *Messidor* Entr'acte; Wagner: *Die Meistersinger von Nürnberg* Prelude; Strauss: *Aus Italien*.

22. 08.03.1903 (Tour: Zagreb evening concert at 8 p.m., Saal des Sokolgebäudes): Bruckner: Symphony No. 3; Wagner: *Tristan und Isolde* Prelude; Tchaikovsky: *Voyevoda*; Bruneau: *Messidor* Entr'acte; Strauss: *Aus Italien*.

23. 09.03.1903 (Tour: Trieste, Teatro Politeama): Beethoven: Symphony No. 1; Liszt: *Tasso*; Bruneau: *Messidor* Entr'acte; Strauss: *Aus Italien*.

24. 10.03.1903 (Tour: Venice at 9 p.m., Teatro Fenice): Bruckner: Symphony No. 3; Beethoven: *Egmont* Overture; Strauss: *Feuersnot* Love Scene and *Tod Verklärung*.

25. 11.03.1903 (Tour: Venice at 9 p.m. [Teatro Fenice][84]): Beethoven: Symphony No. 1; Wagner: *Tristan und Isolde* and *Die Meistersinger von Nürnberg* Preludes; Bruneau: *Messidor* Entr'acte; Strauss: *Aus Italien*.

26. 12.03.1903 (Tour: Bologna at 9 p.m., Teatro Communale): Beethoven: *Egmont* Overture; Wagner: *Tristan und Isolde* and *Die Meistersinger von Nürnberg* Preludes; Strauss: *Don Juan* and *Aus Italien*.

27. 13.03.1903 (Tour: Milan at 9 p.m., Regio Conservatorio di Musica): Strauss: *Aus Italien* and *Feuersnot* Love Scene; Beethoven: Symphony No. 7; Wagner: *Die Meistersinger von Nürnberg* Prelude.
28. 14.03.1903 (Tour: Milan[85]): Beethoven: *Egmont* Overture; Strauss: *Don Juan*; Bruneau: *Messidor* Entr'acte; Wagner: *Tristan und Isolde* Prelude; Liszt: *Tasso*; Strauss: *Tod und Verklärung*.
29. 15.03.1903 (Tour: Turin at 3 p.m., Teatro Vittorio): Strauss: *Aus Italien*; Wagner: *Die Meistersinger von Nürnberg* Prelude; Bruneau: *Messidor* Entr'acte; Strauss: *Tod und Verklärung*.
30. 16.03.1903 (Tour: Nice at 2.30 p.m., Théâtre de la Jetée): Beethoven: *Egmont* Overture; Bruneau *Messidor* Entr'acte; Wagner: *Die Meistersinger von Nürnberg* and *Tristan und Isolde* Preludes; Strauss: *Aus Italien*.
31. 17.03.1903 (Tour: Cannes at 8.30 p.m.): Beethoven: Symphony No. 7; Liszt: *Tasso*; Strauss: *Feuersnot* Love Scene and *Tod und Verklärung*.
32. 18.03.1903 (Tour: Marseille at 8.30 p.m., Théâtre des Nations): Beethoven: *Egmont* Overture; Bruneau: *Messidor* Entr'acte; Wagner: *Die Meistersinger von Nürnberg* and *Tristan und Isolde* Preludes; Strauss: *Aus Italien*.
33. 19.03.1903 (Tour: Geneva at 8.30 p.m., Victoria Hall): Strauss: *Aus Italien* and *Feuersnot* Love Scene;[86] Tchaikovsky: *Voyevoda*; Bruneau: *Messidor* Entr'acte; Strauss: *Don Juan*.
34. 20.03.1903 (Tour: Zurich at 8 p.m., Tonhalle): Beethoven: Symphony No. 7; Strauss: *Feuersnot* Love Scene;[87] Wagner: *Tristan und Isolde* Prelude; Strauss: *Aus Italien*.
35. 21.03.1903 (Tour: Zurich[88]): Bruckner: Symphony No. 3; Beethoven: *Egmont* Overture; Strauss: *Don Juan* and *Tod und Verklärung*.
36. 22.03.1903 (Tour: Mühlhausen at 8 p.m., Stadttheater): Strauss: *Aus Italien*; Beethoven: *Egmont* Overture; Wagner: *Die Meistersinger von Nürnberg* Prelude; Strauss: *Tod und Verklärung*.
37. 23.03.1903 (Tour: Freiburg im Breisgau at 8 p.m., Colosseum): Beethoven: *Egmont* Overture; Strauss: *Feuersnot* Love Scene; Wagner: *Tristan und Isolde* and *Die Meistersinger von Nürnberg* Preludes; Strauss: *Aus Italien*.
38. 07.04.1903:[89] Schilling-Ziemssen: *Feierlicher Marsch*;[90] Rüfer: Violin Concerto (Alfred Wittenberg,[91] violin); Blech: *Waldwanderung*; Strauss: 'Das Tal';§ (Paul Knüpfer,[92] bass); Schirach: 'Lethe' (Paul Knüpfer, bass);[93] Liszt: *Die Ideale*.

PART J: BERLIN HOF- AND STAATSKAPELLE, 1908–1920

1908–1909 Season[94]

1. 02.10.1908: Haydn: Symphony in E flat major;[95] Mozart: Symphony No. 29; Beethoven: Symphony No. 3.
2. 17.10.1908: Bach: Brandenburg Concerto No.1; Beethoven: Symphony No. 2; Liszt: *Orpheus*; Strauss: *Till Eulenspiegel*.
3. 06.11.1908: Haydn: Symphony No. 104; Berlioz: *Le Roi Lear* Overture; Wagner: *Siegfried Idyll*; Beethoven: Symphony No. 8.
4. 04.12.1908: Weber: *Euryanthe* Overture; Brahms: Haydn Variations; Beethoven: Symphony No. 5.
5. 18.12.1908: Beethoven: *König Stephan* Overture, *Die Ruinen von Athen* Overture, Turkish March and Festival March, Violin Concerto (Bernhard Dessau,[96] violin), Symphony No. 4.
6. 15.01.1909: Mahler: Symphony No. 4 (Maria Ekeblad,[97] soprano); Beethoven: Symphony No. 7; Wagner: *Die Meistersinger von Nürnberg* Prelude.
7. 12.02.1909: Beethoven: Symphony No. 6; Schumann: *Manfred* Overture; Strauss: *Sinfonia domestica*.

1909–1910 Season[98]

1. 05.10.1909: Haydn: Symphony No. 101; Weber: *Turandot* Overture;‡ Mozart: Symphony No. 40; Beethoven: Symphony No. 5.
2. 18.10.1909: Berlioz: *Romeo et Juliette* (excerpts); Wagner: *Tannhäuser* Overture; Liszt: *Eine Faust-Sinfonie* (Walter Kirchhoff,[99] tenor; men of the Berlin Hofoper Chorus).
3. 05.11.1909: Gernsheim: Symphony No. 3 ('Mirjam');‡[100] Bach: Brandenburg Concerto No. 2; Beethoven: Symphony No. 7.
4. 03.12.1909: Mahler: Symphony No. 1;‡ Spohr: *Notturno* for Wind Instruments.‡ Beethoven: *Grosse Fuge, Leonore* No. 3 Overture.
5. 17.12.1909: Weber: *Oberon* Overture; Hochberg: Symphony No. 3;§[101] Beethoven: Symphony No. 3.
6. 21.01.1910: Haydn: Symphony No. 100; Ritter: *Olafs Hochzeitsreigen*;‡ Schillings: 'Erntefest' from *Moloch*;‡, Brahms: Symphony No. 3; Berlioz: *Benvenuto Cellini* Overture.
7. 22.02.1910: Beethoven: *Egmont* Overture; Strauss: *Don Quixote*; Schubert: Symphony in C major ('Great').
8. 03.03.1910: Cherubini: *Les deux journées* Overture; Beethoven: Symphony No. 8; Tchaikovsky: Symphony No. 6.
9. 22.03.1910: Bruckner: Symphony No. 4; Strauss: *Don Juan*; Mozart: Symphony No. 41.
10. 24 and 26.03.1910: Schumann: Symphony No. 2; Beethoven: Symphony No. 9 (Frieda Hempel,[102] soprano; Marie Goetze,[103] mezzo-soprano; Walter Kirchhoff, tenor; Baptist Hoffmann,[104] bass; Hofoper Chorus).
11. 26.03.1910 (Matinee Sonderkonzert): Beethoven: *Coriolan* and *Leonore* No. 3 Overtures, Symphony No. 9 (Frieda Hempel, soprano; Marie Goetze, mezzo-soprano; Walter Kirchhoff, tenor; Baptist Hoffmann, bass; Hofoper Chorus).

1910–1911 Season[105]

1. 03.10.1910: Mozart: Symphony No. 39; Haydn: Symphony No. 88;[106] Beethoven: Symphony No. 3.
2. 18.10.1910: Saint-Saëns: Symphony No. 2; Beethoven: Symphony No. 6; Strauss: *Ein Heldonleben*
3. 31.10.1910: Berlioz: *Le Carnaval romain* Overture, Debussy: *Nocturnes* (Women of the Hofoper Chorus); Strauss: *Till Eulenspiegel*; Beethoven: Symphony No. 5.
4. 09.12.1910: Mendelssohn: *Hebrides* Overture; Beethoven: Symphony No. 4; Liszt: *Two Episodes from Lenau's Faust*; Strauss: *Also sprach Zarathustra*.
5. 20.12.1910: Strauss: *Macbeth*;‡ Berlioz: *Symphonie fantastique*; Beethoven: Symphony No. 8.
6. 20.01.1911: Haydn: Symphony No. 98; Pönitz: *Vineta*;‡[107] Strauss: *Don Quixote*; Beethoven: Symphony No. 1.
7. 09.03.1911: Weber: *Euryanthe* Overture; Schumann: Symphony No. 1; Mozart: 'Haffner' Serenade; Beethoven: *Leonore* No. 2 Overture.
8. 22.03.1911: Bach: Brandenburg Concerto No. 4; Strauss: *Don Juan*; Boehe: *Die Klage der Nausikaa*;§[108] Beethoven: Symphony No. 4.
9. 29.03.1911: Beethoven: Symphony No. 2; Strauss: *Tod und Verklärung*; Brahms: Symphony No. 4.
10. 13 and 15.04.1911: Schubert: Symphony in B minor ('Unfinished'); Beethoven: Symphony No. 9 (Andrejeva von Skilondz,[109] soprano; Marie Goetze, mezzo-soprano; Rudolf Berger, tenor;[110] Putnam Griswold,[111] bass; the Chorus of the Hofoper and Choir of the Royal Choir School).
11. 15.04.1911 (Matinee Sonderkonzert): Beethoven: *Leonore* No. 3 Overture, Violin Concerto (Bronislaw Hubermann,[112] violin), Symphony No. 3.

1911–1912 Season[113]

1. 18.10.1911: Haydn: Symphony No. 103 ('Drum Roll'); Mozart: Piano Concerto No. 23 (Georg Schumann, piano); Beethoven: Symphony No. 6.
2. 30.10.1911: Liszt: *Dante Symphony* (Marie Goetze, mezzo-soprano); Wagner: *Tristan und Isolde* Prelude; Beethoven: Symphony No. 4.
3. 10.11.1911: Beethoven: *Die Weihe des Hauses* Overture; Bach: Brandenburg Concerto No. 4; Weber: *Oberon* Overture; Schillings: *Ingwelde* Prelude to Act 2;‡ Strauss: *Sinfonia domestica*.
4. 11.12.1911: Mozart: Symphony No. 40; Mahler: Symphony No. 3 (Marie Goetze, mezzo-soprano; women of the Chorus of the Hofoper; boys from the Royal Cathedral Choir).‡
5. 15.02.1912: Hausegger: *Natursinfonie*§ (Chorus of the Hofoper, men of the Royal and Cathedral Choirs, women of the Royal Choir School); Beethoven: Symphony No. 8; Wagner: *Kaisermarsch* (Hofoper Chorus, men of the Royal and Cathedral Choirs and the women of the Royal Choir School).
6. 28.02.1912: Rüfer: Symphony No. 1;§[114] Beethoven: *Leonore* No. 3 Overture; Schubert: Symphony in C major ('Great')
7. 09.03.1912: Bruckner: Symphony No. 9;‡ D'Indy: *Istar*;‡ Beethoven: Symphony No. 5.
8. 22.03.1912: Berlioz: *Harold in Italy* (August Gentz,[115] viola); Taubert: Suite for String Orchestra;§[116] Beethoven: Symphony No. 7.
9. 4 and 6.04.1912: Mendelssohn: *Ein Sommernachtstraum* (excerpts); Beethoven: Symphony No. 9 (Andrejeva von Skilondz, soprano; Marie Goetze, mezzo-soprano; Rudolf Berger, tenor; Johannes Bischoff,[117] bass; Hofoper Chorus Choir of the Royal Choir School).

1912–1913 Season[118]

1. 18.10.1912: Haydn: Symphony No. 85; Mozart: Piano Concerto No. 26 (Waldemar Lütschg,[119] piano); Beethoven: Symphony No. 6; Weber: *Der Freischütz* Overture.
2. 08.11.1912: Scheinpflug: *Ouvertüre zu einem Lustspiel*;‡[120] Blech: *Waldwanderung*;‡ Tchaikovsky: *Romeo and Juliet*; Brahms: Symphony No. 2; Beethoven: *Leonore* No. 3 Overture.
3. 26.11.1912: Bruckner: Symphony No. 7; Mozart: *Fünf deutsche Tänze*; Beethoven: Symphony No. 7.
4. 06.12.1912: Gluck: *Iphigénie en Aulide* Overture ed. Wagner; Bach: Brandenburg Concerto No. 3;‡ Weber: *Euryanthe* Overture; Strauss: *Don Quixote*; Liszt: *Les Préludes* .
5. 20.12.1912: Beethoven: *Egmont* Overture, Violin Concerto (Leopold Premyslaw,[121] violin), Symphony No. 3.
6. 14.02.1913: Pfitzner: *Das Christelfein* Overture;‡ Reznicek: *Präludium und Fuge*;‡ Boehe: *Die Insel der Circe*;‡ Schillings: *Der Pfeifertag* Prelude to Act 3;‡ Spohr: Concerto for String Quartet and Orchestra (Robert Zeiler, violin; Leopold Premyslaw, violin; August Gentz, viola; Fritz Dechert, cello);[122] Beethoven: Symphony No. 5.
7. 28.02.1913: Cherubini: *Anacréon* Overture; Mozart: Symphony No. 41; Berlioz: *Roméo et Juliette* (three movements); Wagner: *Die Meistersinger von Nürnberg* Prelude.
8. 09.03.1913: Kaun: Symphony No. 3;‡ Berlioz: *Le Carnaval romain* Overture; Haydn: Symphony No. 95; Smetana: *The Bartered Bride* Overture.
9. 20 and 22.03.1913: Schubert: Symphony in B minor ('Unfinished')'; Beethoven: Symphony No. 9 (Andrejeva von Skilondz, soprano; Marie Goetze, mezzo-soprano; Rudolf Berger, tenor; Baptist Hoffmann, bass; Hofoper Chorus).
10. 28.03.1913: Wagner: *Huldigungsmarsch, Eine Faust-Ouvertüre, Lohengrin* Prelude, *Tannhäuser* Overture; Strauss: *Ein Heldenleben*.

1913–1914 Season[123]

1. 07.11.1913: Mahler: *Das Lied von der Erde* (Sarah-Jane Charles-Cahier,[124] alto; Hermann Jadlowker,[125] tenor);‡ Beethoven: Symphony No. 2.
2. 26.11.1913: Schumann: *Genoveva* Overture; Volkmann: Serenade (Fritz Dechert, cello); Brahms: *Tragic Overture*; Berlioz: *Béatrice et Bénédict* Overture; Strauss: *Also sprach Zarathustra*.
3. 04.12.1913: Cherubini: *Les Abencérages* Overture; Bach: Brandenburg Concerto No. 5 (Max Reger, keyboard; Robert Zeiler, violin; Emil Prill,[126] flute); Reger: 'Hiller' Variations;[127] Mozart: Symphony No. 35 ('Haffner').
4. 19.12.1913: Beethoven: *Die Geschöpfe des Prometheus* incidental music, *Leonore* No. 2 Overture, Symphony No. 3.
5. 06.02.1914: Bischoff: Symphony No. 1;‡[128] Beethoven: *Zur Namensfeier* Overture, Symphony No. 6.
6. 22.02.1914: Handel: Concerto grosso Op. 3 No.1; Gernsheim: *Ouvertüre zu einem Drama*;‡ Bruneau: *Messidor* Entr'acte;‡[129] Grainger: *Mock Morris*;‡[130] Beethoven: Symphony No. 5.
7. 09.03.1914: Scontrino: 'Romantic' Symphony;§[131] Strauss: *Don Juan*; Mozart: Symphony No. 40; Weber: *Oberon* Overture.
8. 22.03.1914: Haydn: Symphony No. 7 ('Le Midi'); Beethoven: Symphony No. 7; Georg Schumann: 'Bach' Variations;§ Liszt: *Tasso*.
9. 28 and 29.03.1914: Berlioz: *Le Roi Lear* Overture; Hausegger: *Wieland der Schmied*;[132] Beethoven: Symphony No. 9 (Andrejeva von Skilondz, soprano; Emmi Leisner,[133] mezzo-soprano; Hermann Jadlowker, tenor; Johannes Bischoff, bass; Holoper Chorus and Choir of the Royal Choir School).
10. 29.03.1914: (Matinee Sonderkonzert): Beethoven: Symphony No. 8, *Leonore* No. 3 Overture, Symphony No. 3.

1914–1915 Season[134]

1. 18.10.1914: Weber: *Der Freischütz* Overture; Haydn: Symphony No. 100; Beethoven: Symphony No. 3; Wagner: *Kaisermarsch*.
2. 06.11.1914: Mozart: Symphony No. 39; Beethoven: Symphony No. 2; Strauss: *Ein Heldenleben*.
3. 25.11.1914: Mahler: Symphony No. 2 (Käthe Herwig,[135] soprano; Emmi Leisner, mezzo-soprano; Hofoper Chorus); Beethoven: *Meeresstille und glückliche Fahrt* and *Choral Fantasia* (Ferrucio Busoni, piano, Hofoper Chorus).
4. 21.12.1914: Beethoven: *Die Weihe des Hauses* and *Coriolan* Overtures, Piano Concerto No. 5 (Waldemar Lütschg, piano), Symphony No. 6.
5. 15.01.1915: Beethoven: Symphony No. 4; Liszt: *Die Ideale*; Schubert: Symphony in C major ('Great').
6. 05.02.1915: Schumann: Symphony No. 1; Reger: 'Mozart' Variations (Max Reger, conductor);‡ Beethoven: Symphony No. 8; Reger: *Eine Vaterländische Ouvertüre* (Max Reger, conductor).‡
7. 26.02.1915: Korngold: *Sinfonietta*;‡ Liszt: *Mazeppa*; Beethoven: *Egmont* Overture and Symphony No. 5.
8. 09.03.1915: Beethoven: Symphony No. 7; Wagner: *Siegfried Idyll*; Strauss: *Sinfonia domestica*.
9. 22.03.1915: Haydn: Symphony No. 8 ('Le Soir'); Koch: *Halali*;§[136] Brahms: Haydn Variations, Symphony No. 1.
10. 01 and 03.04.1915: Beethoven: Symphonies Nos 1 and 9 (Claire Dux,[137] soprano; Marie Goetze, mezzo-soprano; Peter Unkel,[138] tenor; Johannes Bischoff, bass; Hofoper Chorus, Royal Choir School).

11. 03.04.1915 (Matinee Sonderkonzert): Schubert: Symphony in B minor ('Unfinished'); Beethoven: *Coriolan* Overture; Two marches from *Die Ruinen von Athen*, Symphony No. 3.

1915–1916 Season[139]

1. 18.10.1915: Haydn: Symphony in E flat;[140] Mozart: Symphony No. 41; Weber: *Beherrscher der Geister* and *Abu Hassan* Overtures, *Konzertstück* (Frieda Kwast-Hodapp,[141] piano) and *Oberon* Overture.
2. 03.11.1915: Bruckner: Symphony No. 9; Beethoven: Symphony No. 7; Liszt: *Les Préludes*.
3. 07.01.1916: Beethoven: *Leonore* No. 1 Overture, Symphonies Nos 1 and 3.
4. 21.01.1916: Hausegger: *Barbarossa*;§ Spohr: *Notturno* for Winds; Beethoven: Symphony No. 8.
5. 04.02.1916: Haydn: Symphony No. 26; Strauss: *Also sprach Zarathustra*; Beethoven: Symphony No. 2, *Leonore* No. 3 Overture.
6. 22.02.1916: Raff: Symphony No. 3 ('Im Walde'); Liszt: *Orpheus*; Beethoven: *König Stephan* Overture, *Wiener Tänze* and Symphony No. 5.
7. 09.03.1916: Berlioz: *Le Roi Lear* Overture; Mozart: Symphony No. 39; Mandl: *Ouvertüre zu einem Gascogner Ritterspiel*;§[142] Beethoven: Symphony No. 6.
8. 22.03.1916: Schumann: *Manfred* Overture; Mendelssohn: Overture, Nocturne and Scherzo from *Ein Sommernachtstraum*; Mozart: Sinfonia concertante K364 (Bernhard Dessau, violin; August Gentz, viola); Beethoven: Symphony No. 4.
9. 07.04.1916: Gluck: *Iphigénie en Aulide* Overture; Wagner: *Eine Faust-Ouvertüre*, *Tristan und Isolde* and Die *Meistersinger von Nürnberg* Preludes; Strauss: *Sinfonia domestica*.
10. 22.04.1916: Georg Schumann: *Im Ringen nach dem Ideal*;§ Beethoven: Symphony No. 9 (Ethel Hansa,[143] soprano; Frieda Langendorff,[144] mezzo-soprano; Alexander Kirchner,[145] tenor; Johannes Bischoff, bass; Hofoper Chorus and Royal Choir School).
11. 22.04.1916 (Matinee Sonderkonzert): Beethoven: Symphony No. 5; Strauss: *Eine Alpensinfonie*.

1916–1917 Season[146]

1. 18.11.1916: Beethoven: Symphony No. 1; Mozart: Piano Concerto No. 22 (Georg Schumann, piano); Haydn: Symphony No. 88; Weber: *Oberon* Overture.
2. 31.11.1916: Beethoven: Symphony No. 4 and *Egmont* Overture; Goldmark: *Ländliche Hochzeit*; Wagner: *Tannhäuser* Overture.
3. 28.11.1916: Mendelssohn: Symphony No. 3; Reger: *Sinfonischer Prolog zu einer Tragödie*;‡ Beethoven: Symphony No. 6 and *Leonore* No. 3 Overture.
4. 08.12.1916: Handel: Concerto grosso Op. 6 No. 7;‡ Mozart': Symphony No. 38; George Szell: *Variationen über ein eigenes Thema*;§ Schubert: Symphony in C major ('Great').
5. 19.12.1916: Beethoven: *Coriolan* Overture, Violin Concerto (Leopold Premyslaw,[147] violin), Symphony No. 3.
6. 16.02.1917: Weber: *Euryanthe* Overture; Beethoven: Symphony No. 8; Liszt: *Ce qu'on entend sur la montagne*, *Mephisto Waltz* and *Tasso*.
7. 09.03.1917: Brahms: Symphony No. 2; Strauss: *Till Eulenspiegel*; Beethoven: Symphony No. 7.
8. 22.03.1917: Müller-Hartmann: *Sinfonische Ouvertüre*;§[148] Mozart: Symphony No. 41; Strauss: *Eine Alpensinfonie*.
9. 05 and 07.04.1917: Berlioz: *Roméo et Juliette* (three movements); Beethoven: Symphony No. 9 (Ethel Hansa, soprano; Marie Goetze, mezzo-soprano; Waldemar Henke,[149] tenor; Johannes Bischoff, bass; Hofoper Chorus and Choir of the Royal Choir School).
10. 07.04.1917 (Matinee Sonderkonzert): Wagner: *Eine Faust-Ouvertüre*; Beethoven: Symphony No. 3; Strauss: *Tod und Verklärung*.

1917–1918 Season[150]

1. 18.10.1917: Büttner: Symphony No. 3;‡[151] Mozart: *Die Zauberflöte* Overture; Haydn: Piano Concerto in D major Hob. XVIII:2 (Frieda Kwast-Hodapp, piano); Beethoven: Symphony No. 8.
2. 06.11.1917: Berlioz: *Benvenuto Cellini* Overture; Weingartner: Symphony No. 4;§ Beethoven: Symphony No. 2.
3. 30.11.1917: Mozart: Symphony No. 40; Strässer: *Drei Frühlingsbilder*;§[152] Dvořák: *Scherzo capriccioso*; Beethoven: Symphony No. 5.
4. 12.12.1917: Beethoven: Symphony No. 4; Strauss: *Don Juan*; Berlioz: *Symphonie fantastique*.
5. 21.12.1917: Brahms: *Academic Festival Overture*, Violin concerto (Leopold Premyslaw, violin); Beethoven: Symphony No. 3.
6. 01.02.1918: Baussnern: Symphony No. 4;§[153] Scharwenka: Piano Concerto No. 1 (Franz Xaver Scharwenka,[154] piano); Beethoven: Symphony No. 7.
7. 02.03.1918: Schubert: Symphony in B minor ('Unfinished'); Liszt: *Mazeppa*; Strauss: *Sinfonia domestica*.
8. 03.03.1918 (Matinee Sonderkonzert): Beethoven: *Coriolan* Overture, Piano Concerto No. 4 (Artur Schnabel, piano); Strauss: *Eine Alpensinfonie*.
9. 09.03.1918: Mendelssohn: Symphony No. 4; Weber: *Der Freischütz* Overture; Künnecke: *Coer As* Overture;‡[155] Haydn: Symphony in B flat.[156]
10. 22.03.1918: Mahler: Symphony No. 1; Beethoven: Symphony No. 6, *Leonore* No. 3 Overture.
11. 28 and 30.03.1918: Mozart: Symphony No. 29; Beethoven: Symphony No. 9 (Ethel Hansa, soprano; Marie Goetze, mezzo-soprano; Waldemar Henke, tenor; Karl Armster,[157] bass; Hofoper Chorus and Choir of the Royal Choir School).

1918–1919 Season[158]

1. 18.10.1918: Mozart: *Idomeneo* Overture; Haydn: Symphony No. 94; Wetzler: *Wie es Euch gefällt* Overture;‡[159] Beethoven: Symphony No. 5.
2. 29.10.1918: Beethoven: Symphony No. 6; Mozart: Symphony No. 40; Weber: *Oberon* Overture.
3. 08.11.1918: Beethoven: *Egmont* Overture; Dopper: Symphony No. 6 ('Amsterdam');§[160] Schubert: Symphony in C major ('Great').
4. 29.11.1918: Schumann: Symphony No. 3; Andreae: *Kleine Suite*;‡[161] Beethoven: Symphony No. 7.
5. 06.12.1918: Taubert: Symphony in G minor;§ Beethoven: Two marches from *Die Ruinen von Athen*, Symphony No. 3.
6. 04.03.1919: Mozart: Symphony No. 39; Strauss: *Don Quixote*; Beethoven: Symphony No. 4.
7. 04.04.1919; Atterberg: Symphony No. 2;‡[162] Mozart: *Gran Partita*; Beethoven: *Leonore* No. 2 Overture.
8. 17 and 19.04.1919: Bach: Brandenburg Concerto No. 6; Beethoven: Symphony No. 9 (Ethel Hansa, soprano; Marie Goetze, mezzo-soprano; Josef Mann,[163] tenor; Karl Armster,[164] bass; Staatsoper Chorus).
9. 19.04.1919 (Matinee Sonderkonzert): Beethoven: *Coriolan* Overture, Violin Concerto (Leopold Premyslaw, violin), Symphony No. 5.
10. 29.04.1919: Schubert: Symphony in B minor ('Unfinished'); Trapp: *Sinfonia giocosa*;‡[165] Strauss: *Also sprach Zarathustra*.

1919–1920 Season[166]

1. 28.10.1919: Haydn: Symphony in E flat;[167] Mozart: Symphony No. 41; Beethoven: Symphony No. 6.

2. 14.11.1919: Beethoven: Symphony No. 8; Bruckner: Symphony No. 5.
3. 28.11.1919: Beethoven: Symphony No. 7; Liszt: *Eine Faust-Sinfonie* (Robert Hutt,[168] tenor, men of the Staatsoper Chorus).
4. 20.02.1920: Beethoven: Symphony No. 5; Strauss: *Sinfonia domestica*.
5. 02.03.1920: Spohr: *Jessonda* Overture; Beethoven: Symphony No. 2; Berlioz: *Symphonie fantastique*.

PART K: VIENNA STAATSOPER, 1919–1924

1919–1920 Season

Composer	Work	Date
1. Beethoven	*Fidelio*	08.12.1919
2. Mozart	*Die Zauberflöte*	11.12.1919
3. Strauss	*Elektra*	15.12.1919
4. Wagner	*Lohengrin*	01.01.1920†
5. Wagner	*Lohengrin*	03.01.1920
6. Mozart	*Die Zauberflöte*	04.01.1920
7. Wagner	*Lohengrin*	08.01.1920
8. Wagner	*Tristan und Isolde*	11.01.1920
9. Strauss	*Ariadne auf Naxos* (1916 Version)	15.01.1920
10. Wagner	*Lohengrin*	08.02.1920
11. Strauss	*Ariadne auf Naxos* (1916 Version)	10.02.1920
12. Strauss	*Salome*	12.02.1920
13. Strauss	*Der Rosenkavalier*	11.03.1920
14. Wagner	*Das Rheingold*	13.03.1920
15. Wagner	*Die Walküre*	14.03.1920
16. Strauss	*Salome*	16.03.1920
17. Beethoven	*Fidelio*	17.03.1920
18. Wagner	*Tristan und Isolde*	19.03.1920
19. Weber	*Der Freischütz*	21.03.1920
20. Wagner	*Siegfried*	25.03.1920[169]
21. Wagner	*Götterdämmerung*	28.03.1920[170]
22. Weber	*Der Freischütz*	03.04.1920
23. Mozart	*Die Zauberflöte*	06.04.1920
24. Wagner	*Lohengrin*	27.04.1920
25. Strauss	*Die Frau ohne Schatten*	04.05.1920
26. Mozart	*Die Zauberflöte*	05.05.1920
27. Strauss	*Der Rosenkavalier*	12.05.1920
28. Bizet	*Carmen*	18.05.1920
29. Wagner	*Tristan und Isolde*	23.05.1920
30. Mozart	*Così fan tutte*	26.05.1920†[171]
31. Bizet	*Carmen*	27.05.1920
32. Strauss	*Salome*	29.05.1920
33. Mozart	*Così fan tutte*	30.05.1920[172]
34. Strauss	*Ariadne auf Naxos* (1916 Version)	31.05.1920
35. Bizet	*Carmen*	02.06.1920[173]

1920–1921 Season

1. Beethoven	*Fidelio*	12.12.1920
2. Strauss	*Der Rosenkavalier*	17.12.1920
3. Weber	*Der Freischütz*	19.12.1920

4.	Strauss	*Salome*	23.12.1920
5.	Johann Strauss II	*Die Fledermaus*	26.12.1920
6.	Wagner	*Lohengrin*	30.12.1920
7.	Beethoven	*Fidelio*	01.01.1921
8.	Strauss	*Elektra*	04.01.1921
9.	Strauss	*Ariadne auf Naxos* (1916 version)	12.01.1921
10.	Mozart	*Die Zauberflöte*	14.01.1921
11.	Mozart	*Così fan tutte*	20.01.1921
12.	Strauss	*Salome*	22.01.1921
13.	Mozart	*Così fan tutte*	09.02.1921
14.	Strauss	*Salome*	14.02.1921
15.	Mozart	*Die Zauberflöte*	16.02.1921
16.	Wagner	*Lohengrin*	17.02.1921
17.	Strauss	*Ariadne auf Naxos* (1916 version)	24.02.1921
18.	Wagner	*Lohengrin*	03.03.1921
19.	Weber	*Der Freischütz*	06.03.1921
20.	Strauss	*Der Rosenkavalier*	09.03.1921
21.	Strauss	*Elektra*	11.03.1921
22.	Bizet	*Carmen*	03.04.1921
23.	Weber	*Der Freischütz*	05.04.1921
24.	Strauss	*Salome*	10.04.1921
25.	Wagner	*Tristan und Isolde*	11.04.1921
26.	Beethoven	*Fidelio*	14.04.1921
27.	Wagner	*Das Rheingold*	16.04.1921
28.	Wagner	*Die Walküre*	17.04.1921
29.	Strauss	*Ariadne auf Naxos* (1916 version)	19.04.1921
30.	Wagner	*Siegfried*	21.04.1921
31.	Wagner	*Götterdämmerung*	24.04.1921
32.	Mozart	*Così fan tutte*	26.04.1921
33.	Strauss	*Die Frau ohne Schatten*	29.04.1921
34.	Beethoven	*Fidelio*	03.05.1921
35.	Mozart	*Die Zauberflöte*	06.05.1921
36.	Strauss	*Elektra*	10.05.1921
37.	Strauss	*Die Frau ohne Schatten*	13.05.1921
38.	Mozart	*Don Giovanni*	20.05.1921†
39.	Mozart	*Don Giovanni*	22.05.1921
40.	Strauss	*Salome*	23.05.1921
41.	Mozart	*Don Giovanni*	24.05.1921

1921–1922 Season

1.	Strauss	*Salome*	27.01.1922
2.	Strauss	*Die Frau ohne Schatten*	30.01.1922
3.	Weber	*Die Freischütz*	31.01.1922
4.	Mozart	*Le nozze di Figaro*	02.02.1922[174]
5.	Beethoven	*Fidelio*	04.02.1922
6.	Strauss	*Der Rosenkavalier*	05.02.1922
7.	Mozart	*Le nozze di Figaro*	10.02.1922
8.	Strauss	*Salome*	13.02.1922
9.	Strauss	*Elektra*	16.02.1922
10.	Mozart	*Le nozze di Figaro*	17.02.1922
11.	Wagner	*Der fliegende Holländer*	18.02.1922†
12.	Wagner	*Der fliegende Holländer*	21.02.1922
13.	Wagner	*Der fliegende Holländer*	23.02.1922

14.	Mozart	*Le nozze di Figaro*	25.02.1922
15.	Wagner	*Der fliegende Holländer*	28.02.1922
16.	Mozart	*Le nozze di Figaro*	04.03.1922
17.	Mozart	*Le nozze di Figaro*	11.03.1922
18.	Beethoven	*Fidelio*	16.03.1922
19.	Strauss	*Feuersnot*	18.03.1922†*
20.	Strauss	*Josephslegende*	18.03.1922*‡
21.	Strauss	*Feuersnot*	20.03.1922*
22.	Strauss	*Josephslegende*	20.03.1922*
23.	Wagner	*Der fliegende Holländer*	25.03.1922
24.	Strauss	*Feuersnot*	26.03.1922*
25.	Strauss	*Josephslegende*	26.03.1922*
26.	Strauss	*Feuersnot*	30.03.1922*
27.	Strauss	*Josephslegende*	30.03.1922*
28.	Wagner	*Tristan und Isolde*	02.04.1922
29.	Strauss	*Feuersnot*	03.04.1922*
30.	Strauss	*Josephslegende*	03.04.1922*
31.	Strauss	*Der Rosenkavalier*	05.04.1922
32.	Wagner	*Der fliegende Holländer*	06.04.1922
33.	Strauss	*Feuersnot*	11.04.1922*
34.	Strauss	*Josephslegende*	11.04.1922*
35.	Cornelius	*Der Barbier von Bagdad*	21.04.1922*
36.	Strauss	*Josephslegende*	21.04.1922*
37.	Wagner	*Tristan und Isolde*	23.04.1922
38.	Strauss	*Feuersnot*	25.04.1922*
39.	Strauss	*Josephslegende*	25.04.1922*
40.	Strauss	*Ariadne auf Naxos* (1916 version)	27.04.1922
41.	Wagner	*Die Walküre*	30.04.1922
42.	Mozart	*Die Zauberflöte*	02.05.1922
43.	Strauss	*Salome*	05.05.1922
44.	Cornelius	*Der Barbier von Bagdad*	06.05.1922*
45.	Strauss	*Josephslegende*	06.05.1922*
46.	Strauss	*Die Frau ohne Schatten*	12.05.1922
47.	Strauss	*Salome*	11.06.1922
48.	Mozart	*Don Giovanni*	14.08.1922≏[175]
49.	Mozart	*Così fan tutte*	15.08.1922≏
50.	Mozart	*Don Giovanni*	18.08.1922≏
51.	Mozart	*Così fan tutte*	19.08.1922≏
52.	Mozart	*Don Giovanni*	22.08.1922≏
53.	Mozart	*Don Giovanni*	23.08.1922≏

1922–1923 Season

1.	Wagner	*Der fliegende Holländer*	01.12.1922
2.	Mozart	*Così fan tutte*	05.12.1922
3.	Strauss	*Elektra*	07.12.1922
4.	Rimsky-Korsakov	*Scheherazade*	13.12.1922*
5.	Strauss	*Josephslegende*	13.12.1922*
6.	Beethoven	*Fidelio*	17.12.1922
7.	Humperdinck	*Hänsel und Gretel*	23.12.1922†
8.	Humperdinck	*Hänsel und Gretel*	27.12.1922
9.	Strauss	*Die Frau ohne Schatten*	28.12.1922
10.	Cornelius	*Der Barbier von Bagdad*	30.12.1922*
11.	Strauss	*Josephslegende*	30.12.1922*

12.	Rimsky-Korsakov	*Scheherazade*	05.01.1923*
13.	Strauss	*Josephslegende*	05.01.1923*
14.	Humperdinck	*Hänsel und Gretel*	06.01.1923
15.	Strauss	*Salome*	12.01.1923
16.	Boieldieu	*Jean de Paris*	13.01.1923[176]
17.	Boieldieu	*Jean de Paris*	14.01.1923
18.	Wagner	*Der fliegende Holländer*	22.01.1923
19.	Rimsky-Korsakov	*Scheherazade*	24.01.1923*
20.	Strauss	*Josephslegende*	24.01.1923*
21.	Strauss	*Die Frau ohne Schatten*	27.01.1923
22.	Strauss	*Der Rosenkavalier*	04.02.1923
23.	Wagner	*Tristan und Isolde*	13.02.1923
24.	Strauss	*Salome*	19.02.1923
25.	Wagner	*Tannhäuser*	21.02.1923†
26.	Strauss	'Couperin' Suite (Ballet)	22.02.1923
27.	Strauss	*Ariadne auf Naxos* (1916 version)	23.02.1923
28.	Humperdinck	*Hänsel und Gretel*	26.02.1923
29.	Mozart	*Così fan tutte*	01.03.1923
30.	Strauss	*Josephslegende*	05.03.1923*
31.	Humperdinck	*Hänsel und Gretel*	05.03.1923*
32.	Strauss	*Ariadne auf Naxos* (1916 version)	08.03.1923
33.	Schillings	*Mona Lisa*	14.03.1923†
34.	Strauss	*Der Rosenkavalier*	17.03.1923
35.	Wagner	*Tannhäuser*	20.03.1923
36.	Strauss	*Der Rosenkavalier*	02.04.1923
37.	Rimsky-Korsakov	*Scheherazade*	05.04.1923*
38.	Strauss	*Josephslegende*	05.04.1923*
39.	Strauss	*Ariadne auf Naxos* (1916 version)	09.04.1923
40.	Strauss	*Die Frau ohne Schatten*	12.04.1923
41.	Strauss	*Salome*	26.06.1923φ[177]
42.	Strauss	*Salome*	28.06.1923φ
43.	Strauss	*Salome*	30.06.1923φ
44.	Strauss	*Salome*	04.07.1923φ
45.	Strauss	*Elektra*	06.07.1923†φ
46.	Strauss	*Salome*	08.07.1923φ[178]
47.	Strauss	*Elektra*	08.07.1923φ
48.	Strauss	*Elektra*	09.08.1923φ
49.	Strauss	*Salome*	20.08.1923φ[179]

1923–1924 Season

1.	Strauss	*Elektra*	06.12.1923
2.	Wagner	*Lohengrin*	09.12.1923
3.	Beethoven	*Fidelio*	11.12.1923
4.	Wagner	*Die Walküre*	16.12.1923
5.	Mozart	*Così fan tutte*	20.12.1923[180]
6.	Strauss	*Ariadne auf Naxos* (1916 version)	22.12.1923
7.	Strauss	*Die Frau ohne Schatten*	28.12.1923
8.	Wagner	*Lohengrin*	01.01.1924
9.	Wagner	*Tristan und Isolde*	05.01.1924
10.	Mozart	*Bastien und Bastienne*	12.01.1924ψ[181]
11.	Pergolesi	*La serva padrona*	12.01.1924ψ
12.	Weber	*Abu Hassan*	12.01.1924ψ
13.	Mozart	*Bastien und Bastienne*	13.01.1924ψ

14. Pergolesi	*La serva padrona*	13.01.1924ψ
15. Weber	*Abu Hassan*	13.01.1924ψ
16. Wagner	*Die fliegende Holländer*	12.02.1924
17. Nicolai	*Die lustige Weiber von Windsor*	14.02.1924
18. Mozart	*Die Zauberflöte*	15.02.1924
19. Mozart	*Bastien und Bastienne*	17.02.1924ψ
20. Pergolesi	*La serva padrona*	17.02.1924ψ
21. Weber	*Abu Hassan*	17.02.1924ψ
22. Cornelius	*Der Barbier von Bagdad*	19.02.1924*
23. Strauss	*Josephslegende*	19.02.1924*
24. Mozart	*Così fan tutte*	23.02.1924
25. Mozart	*Bastien und Bastienne*	24.02.1924ψ
26. Pergolesi	*La serva padrona*	24.02.1924ψ
27. Weber	*Abu Hassan*	24.02.1924ψ
28. Strauss	*Ariadne auf Naxos* (1916 version)	26.02.1924
29. Mozart	*Bastien und Bastienne*	27.02.1924ψ
30. Pergolesi	*La serva padrona*	27.02.1924ψ
31. Weber	*Abu Hassan*	27.02.1924ψ
32. Strauss	*Der Rosenkavalier*	29.02.1924
33. Strauss	*Elektra*	04.03.1924
34. Wagner	*Tristan und Isolde*	09.03.1924
35. Mozart	*Così fan tutte*	12.03.1924
36. Strauss	*Salome*	14.03.1924
37. Mozart	*Così fan tutte*	16.03.1924
38. Strauss	*Der Rosenkavalier*	18.03.1924
39. Strauss	*Die Frau ohne Schatten*	17.04.1924
40. Strauss	*Der Rosenkavalier*	21.04.1924
41. Mozart	*Die Zauberflöte*	24.04.1924
42. Strauss	*Elektra*	06.05.1924
43. Strauss	*Schlagobers*	09.05.1924§
44. Strauss	*Schlagobers*	12.05.1924
45. Strauss	*Die Frau ohne Schatten*	13.05.1924
46. Strauss	*Salome*	15.09.1924
47. Beethoven/Strauss	*Die Ruinen von Athen*	20.09.1924§*
48. Gluck	*Don Juan*	20.09.1924*
49. Strauss	*Ariadne auf Naxos* (1916 version)	24.09.1924
50. Beethoven/Strauss	*Die Ruinen von Athen*	25.09.1924*
51. Gluck	*Don Juan*	25.09.1924*
52. Mozart	*Così fan tutte*	28.09.1924
53. Strauss	*Der Bürger als Edelman*	01.10.1924†

Strauss posing as a conductor. Postcard, Berlin, 1910.

Extracts from *Ueber die Neueinstudierung und Neuinszenierung des Mozart'schen Don Giovanni (Don Juan) auf dem kgl. Residenztheater zu München* by Ernst von Possart

Over the years, the *drama giocoso* or *opera buffa* [*Don Giovanni*] turned into an *opera seria* later, a romantic opera and, finally, a grand opera with choruses. During this century, a complete change in the interpretation of da Ponte's and Mozart's original took place. It was the production by Schroeder and Friedrich Rochlitz, in 1801, which was the most popular edition, following the German version by Spiess, performed under Schikaneder's direction. The Royal Opera in Berlin has used this version until today and this edition accounts for most performances of *Don Giovanni*. On 29 October 1887, it was used for the celebration of the opera's 500th performance. However, this version contains fundamental and deliberate modifications.

The distortions to the original text in the first 60 years after Mozart's death, defy description.

———— ◆ ————

Bernhard Gugler has produced a score of Mozart's *Don Giovanni*, which exactly corresponds to the original. Apart from a few discrepancies, it contains da Ponte's original text. Owing to the initiative of Dr Leopold von Sonnleithner in Vienna, we have the opera's libretto in its original version, based on the first performance in Prague. Strangely enough, this was not released in print until 1867 and, the only traceable copy of the Prague libretto is owned by the Graf York von Wartenburg in Klein-Dels near Ohlau. It contains several additions, especially in regard to the action, which the score does not feature, but also presents what Mozart, following his own ideas, added to da Ponte's text, almost as an improvisation. Regarding the music accompanying the supper at the end of Act 2, there are reminders of three operas often performed at that time, of which Mozart names the first two: *Cosa rara* by Martini, and *I litiganti* by Sarti (*Fra i due litiganti il terzo gode*). At the third inserted passage, Figaro's aria 'Non più andrai', Mozart has added to the score, in his own hand, the following comic remark for Leporello: 'questo poi la conosco pur tróppo'. This passage is not in da Ponte's libretto.

I have to mention a further addition that Mozart has made to these three musical parts and which refers to their scenic arrangement.

F. P. Lyser says, in the *Neuen Zeitschrift für Musik* (vol. 21, p. 174), that, at their meeting in Dresden in 1834, Mozart's son, Wolfgang, had shown him, amongst other possessions of his father, a fragment of a German translation of *Don Giovanni*, produced and written by Mozart himself. Lyser was given permission to copy a few of the most interesting passages. In vol. 22 of the same magazine, p. 133, Lyser published this translation of two scenes. A comment regarding the Act 2 Finale says: 'The musicians play piece No. 1 (*Cosa rara*). Leporello lets the girls come in. They dance, differently for each new piece. They also scatter flowers in front of Don Giovanni'. Mozart has charmingly honoured Prague's orchestra, who played his *Le nozze di Figaro* and *Don Giovanni*, when he translates Don Giovanni's sentence: 'Chè ti par del bel concerto?' [What do you think of the beautiful playing?] and Leporello's answer: 'Oh they are just responding to your instructions', as follows, Don Giovanni: 'These people play beautifully'. Leporello: 'They are musicians from Prague'. Further down, it says: 'When Elvira enters, Leporello waves to the other girls and they leave. The music stops'.

Although the original manuscript was not passed on with Mozart's posthumous works to the Mozarteum in Salzburg, as Lyser had thought, and nothing has been heard about it, the fragment's authenticity cannot be doubted, given several other reasons established by Lyser.

I could, therefore, not resist using the remark about the dancers in the realisation of the last act, as it so effectively illustrates Don Giovanni's luxurious lifestyle shortly before his death, even though I thought I could do without Mozart's too liberal translation of the above-mentioned passages.

If we compare Sonnleithner's published, original manuscript, and the original musical score from 1787, with, what is nowadays common in the performances of *Don Juan*, we can draw the conclusion that, through deliberate additions on the one hand, and unjustified omissions on the other, the intentions of the poet and composer have been clearly put into a wrong perspective. It is almost unbelievable how people could have let the thoroughly logical and clear plot of the original be modified and distorted, in such an irresponsible way, throughout the century.

———— ◆ ————

The orchestra conducted by Mozart, at the first performance in Prague, comprised 26 musicians: 4 first violins, 4 second violins, 2 violas, 1 cello, 2 double basses, 2 flutes, 2 oboes, 2 clarinets, 2 bassoons, 2 horns, 2 trumpets and timpani. Today, the orchestra for *Don Juan,* at nearly all opera houses, is increased by an extra 25 string players. Regarding the chorus, the only ones which existed were: the chorus of peasants, for the appearance of Zerlina, and the chorus of invisible demons, in the Act 2 Finale. Today, the chorus of servants, and the so-called 'Freiheitschor', are added, as well as one for the remainder of the Act 1 Finale.

In Act 1, Scene IV, there is an original recitative between Don Juan and Leporello. This is omitted from current versions. The recitative between Don Juan, Leporello and Elvira, which comes before the aria No. 11 (Leporello's Catalogue Aria), is very much shortened. In current versions, Elvira's recitative in Scene VI is dropped, and the subsequently composed aria, 'Mich verläßt der Undankbare' is usually sung at this point. Nowadays, Elvira's aria, Scene X, No. 8, is missed out and only the first two lines of the previous recitative are played. In the original, there is a recitative for Ottavio in Scene XIV, 'Come mai creder', which is omitted in present versions, and the aria, No. 10b, 'Dalla sua pace' (not mentioned in the original) is played instead. In Act 2, the original recitative in Scene VII, between Leporello and Elvira, is not played, so, immediately after the change of scene, the sextet begins. The recitative in Scene IX, between Zerlina, Elvira, Ottavio and Masetto, and Leporello's aria, No. 7, 'Ah pietà Signori miei' are also omitted. In Scene X, the recitative between Elvira, Masetto and Zerlina, is nowadays played in a distorted way and, finally, the last scene (the sextet), after Don Juan's departure, is almost always completely dropped.

One can only ask, what remains of the opera's original conception and its well-ordered structure?

Somebody even believed that he had to improve Mozart's instrumentation. Up to today, the Commendatore is accompanied by an entourage of trombones in almost all performances.

A legend has developed, that Mozart had intended, and achieved, a special effect, by not using the pompous instruments except for the Act 2 Finale, thus giving a solemn and eerie tone. Thirty years ago, Bernhard Gugler had irrefutably pointed out, in an essay published in the *Allgemeine Musikzeitung* (1867), that the way in which these trombones are presented, so clearly contradicts the orchestration that it was impossible for Mozart to have introduced them himself. Neither the fact that, in Mozart's original score, there are no trombone parts (apart from those on the stage accompanying the Commendatore's words in the grave-yard scene) nor Gugler's evidence that they do not stress the chilling impression of the supper scene – but weaken it – could induce conductors (apart from a few exceptions) to abandon the nonsensical traditions of the past century.

———— ◆ ————

When we consider the size of the orchestra, we ask ourselves, was it necessary to double the number of musicians from 26? It has often been said that, in Prague, Mozart did not have the means to set up an orchestra of the size common today at almost all opera houses. This assumption does not hold. When Mozart arrived in Prague, for a visit, in January 1787, to convince himself personally of the general popularity and the great esteem in which his *Figaro* was held, he received the most enthusiastic welcome and people competed to please him. One of Prague's wealthiest noblemen, Graf Johann Thun, who had a splendid and well trained private orchestra himself, accommodated the Maestro in his sumptuous palace.

The Grafen Pachta, Canal and Clam, as well as the Duschecks, who were influential in musical circles and loyal to Mozart, offered their services. Duscheck, himself a brilliant pianist and composer, used to host weekly concerts by artists and art lovers. His wife, who was admired not only for being a piano virtuoso but also a singer, implored the Maestro to leave the hotel, 'Zu den drei Loewen', which was assigned to him in the contract, and to stay in the Villa Bertramka, which belonged to the Duschecks. It was here that the opera was finished.

Had Mozart had the opportunity to double the size of the orchestra at his disposal, it would not have been difficult to achieve this, with the help of such influential and wealthy patrons. . . . Mozart's *Don Giovanni* and *Figaro* are both intended for a smaller and more intimate audience, and for a theatre which allows the singers to be heard with ease. The orchestra should not overshadow the human voice, by exposing the singers to any strains which could affect the beauty of their tone. It should also allow the singers, by their own means, to emphasize their natural ability and acquired techniques.

[Previously] brass instruments were restricted to emphasizing the tonic and dominant in the so-called *tutti* passages and were, therefore, only useful as brilliant, noisy instruments in the main key. By providing them with valves, the chromatic scale could suddenly be played. This now made it possible to use them, not only as melodic instruments, but also, as equals with the other instrumental groups. As a consequence of this development, it was necessary to considerably strengthen the other instrumental groups (the strings and the woodwind) if they were not to be oppressed by the overwhelming sound of the brass instruments. The size of Mozart's orchestra was only intended for double woodwinds and 26 strings at most, and Wagner was forced to demand three to four times as many woodwinds, and 64 strings, for his later compositions.

In concert orchestras, the number of strings was also considerably increased and, because of the sound of this large body of strings, to which listeners became accustomed, earlier compositions by Mozart and Haydn were now performed by bigger orchestras. This, however, led to the irritating fact that the few woodwinds could not be heard. If one wanted to explain the orchestral effect intended by Mozart (which mainly consisted of an equal relationship between each of the instrumental groups) one had to refer back to the orchestra's structure at that time, where even a weak flute could defend itself against a string quartet.

We now come to the increasing use of the chorus in passages that Mozart originally wrote for soloists. A chorus, as such, was not originally intended. In the opera, it mainly appears in order to strengthen the action on stage and only makes two brief appearances: joining the refrain of Masetto's and Zerlina's duet; and in the Act 2 Finale, where it sings:

'Alles ist gering gegen deine Sünden. Komm, es gibt noch schlimmere Leiden'. The passage at the beginning of the Act 1 Finale, the servants' chorus at the appearance of Don Giovanni: 'Auf munter, erwachet, wir wollen lustig sein', was originally intended to be a quartet, not a chorus, and was performed like this in Prague.

———— ♦ ————

Many educated listeners have disputed the value of the Act 2 Finale. It was felt that the Commendatore's last appearance and Don Giovanni's ruin, causing deep emotion in the audience ('hier rauschen die Pforten der Ewigkeit in den Angeln,' wrote Bulthaupt), was weakened by the final sextet.

Mozart and da Ponte knew why they assembled the main characters again at the end of the drama: they did not want to leave their fate unknown and the audience should leave the theatre with a harmonious impression. Moreover, the end of the Commendatore's scene is musically not the end of the finale, but a partial end, after which further music and, finally, a conclusive ending, in the main key, is to be expected.

If we try to discover the real reasons which led to such distortions of the original, first and foremost, we will find them in external circumstances. *Don Giovanni* was planned and written for a small, intimate, opera house. Mozart and his contemporaries did not have spacious conditions. The enormous auditoriums, of the old Romans and Greeks and, of which Schiller sang: 'Wer kennt die Völker, zählt die Namen, die gastlich hier zusammen kamen?', did not exist in Mozart's and da Ponte's time. Auditoriums so big that the human voice could only be heard through a loudspeaker, and the human figure only able to act impressively when wearing especially constructed high-heeled shoes: even if we wanted, we could never have had them! The person on stage should have an effect on the person in the auditorium! Where does the artist's hard work come in, if the emotions on his face cannot be recognized, and the subtle differences in intonation not heard and appreciated? Auditoriums, as they are built nowadays, – the Imperial Opera in Moscow, the theatre in Chicago, – so big that they could accommodate the Scala of Milan and our Royal and National Theatre, are circus arenas where mass military music concerts, fairs and splendid ballets can be held. A stylish performance of Mozart's compositions, however, is impossible. *Don Giovanni* could not exist in these circumstances. After being transferred into those modern theatres with their lack of intimacy, one very quickly begins to stretch out the corpse, which was too delicate for these widths, as if it were on a Procrustean bed; the size of the orchestra was doubled and therefore the singing voices on stage were buried. When the singers complained they could not be heard and could not act effectively in such vast auditoria, with such powerful orchestras, one was forced to strengthen the solo parts with a chorus. Too much emphasis was then put on passages where the 7 main characters should have acted alone and, by this, the Maestro's most beautiful intentions were distorted. The undying masterpiece, the opera of operas, survived in spite of such major modifications. What was given to the German nation was not the legacy of their favourite Wolfgang Amadeus, and the *Stone Guest* of Herr Rochlitz and others, remains a shadow of Mozart's and da Ponte's marvellous *Don Giovanni*.

———— ♦ ————

What should we do if we want to give back, to the German audience, the wonderful *drama giocoso* in its original form? We have to meet the conditions under which it originally existed: an intimate opera house, which allows the audience to follow the performers' singing and acting; a small orchestra as required by the Maestro, which supports the singers' art and does not oppress it; excellent performers, with regard to execution and perform-ance; an exact, unchanged reproduction of the musical score and libretto and, finally, a setting with decorations and costumes, appropriate for the period of the drama.

As a solution to this problem, we, in Munich, have a theatre which could not be better suited for performing Mozart's operas. Our Residenztheater, this most wonderful opera house in Europe, where Mozart himself directed *Idomeneo*, is ideal for re-presenting the Prague première. The musicians in Munich's orchestra, as well as the opera's excellent singers, who have enjoyed high critical acclaim, from the national and international press, for the new production of *Le nozze di Figaro*, and have become familiar with Mozart's style after forty performances in one year, are our guarantee that the original score of *Don Giovanni* will also gain recognition.

With regard to the libretto, Professor Malymotta, who has complete command of German grammar and has proven himself as a teacher of the Italian language, translated Sonnleithner's original Italian libretto of the opera, as it was first performed in Prague, into prose. This is already a success. We then compared Grandaur's libretto, the best part of which corresponds to the original, and which has been used frequently in Munich, with Malymotta's translation, and eliminated all passages of Grandaur's work which differed, even in the slightest, from the original version. The next difficulty was to put these prose passages into a rhythm and rhyme corresponding to Mozart's music, as is required by the original score. This time-consuming task, requires, not only a thorough understanding of the value of the words translated but, also, a solid knowledge and appreciation of musical phrasing, and a respectful handling of each note, as the vowels of each syllable have to be taken into careful consideration. It was *Generalmusikdirektor* Levi who undertook this task, during the last 6 months of his indisposition, with such an eagerness and conscientiousness that can only result from great enthusiasm for the work. We owe the successful solution to this difficult problem to his brilliant handling of the responsible task. The critics will be easily convinced of the new libretto's quality by looking at an edition by the publishing house, A. Druckmann, Munich, which presents both the original Italian and Munich revision. These publishers had already printed an illustrated libretto of *Figaro* and, by this, enabled other opera houses to copy the Munich performance. Here, I would like to add, that I have retained Mozart's chosen name 'Don Giovanni' in all passages where the name is sung by other characters, in preference to the Spanish 'Don Juan'. I am well aware that, if one wants to translate the original Italian into German, one should adjust the characters' names, either to the country in which it takes place, or to the language in which we perform it, i.e. either Spanish or German. Neither the 3 syllables of 'Herr Johann' nor 'Don Juan' correspond to Mozart's scansion for 'Don Giovanni', containing four syllables. There are six passages where the name is sung. In the Commendatore's address in Act 2, it is so pompous in its rhythm, that the sound effect of this 'Don Giovanni' could never be achieved with a translation into 'Don Juan' with its 3 syllables I thought I had to renounce all further doubts of the benefit of this sound effect which, by the way, eliminates the problem of various pronunciations of 'Don Juan', with its aspirated 'J', being so inconvenient for singing. The preliminary conditions relating not only to space but also to the orchestra, the musical score, the manuscript and the singing, which are necessary to genuinely perform the original version, are now fulfilled. We now have to turn to the second task, that is the outward appearance of the opera, the scenery and the costumes, in order to meet the poet's and the composer's original intentions.

Therefore, we have to answer the following questions: in which era does *Don Giovanni* take place? Has da Ponte taken the subject from history, from myth, or from his own imagination? What does da Ponte's Don Giovanni, have in common with history's Don Juan, and the myth? Who is Don Juan? . . . Consequently, one could transfer the setting and the costumes into the year 1780, the time of Mozart, without ruining the subject.

——— ◆ ———

How can one perform the scene changes quickly without having six inconvenient drop-scenes, or destroying the illusion through an open change of scene, where houses and trees fly through the air, and disguised helpers jump onto the stage, to move the furniture and implements around. Each of these scene changes have to be carried out in front of the audience without darkening the stage, and must not take longer than half a minute. When the last chord of the scene fades away, and the conductor raises his baton in order to intonate the introductory recitative of the next scene, the new scenery, with all its parts, must be in place. People have unsuccessfully tried to find a solution to this task for a century. Our modern poets and composers make it easy for stage managers and scene-shifters: they no longer create dramas which require changes of scenes during an act. They have learned from experience. Instead, they are constructed so that the setting remains the same throughout an act. However complicated the scenery then might be, we are left with a pause between the acts of 5 to 10 minutes. In that time many changes can be made on stage.

Lautenschläger's most recent achievement in the field of theatre design, the 'revolving stage', was an important improvement in this direction.

Imagine the entire stage being empty, all the wings removed. The floor contains a revolving disc forming a big circle-from the prompter's box to the back of the stage and reaches both the right and left sides. On the front half of this disc stands the first scene of the play. This scenery faces the audience. On the rear half of the disc, still invisible to the audience and back to back with the first scene, stands the complete second scene. When the first scene has been performed, the disc is turned around by an electric motor and the rear, second scene, takes the place of the first. Now, the old scene is at the back and invisible to the audience. It is removed and while the second scene is being performed at the front, a third, new scene is built on the empty space. Scene 2 ends, the disc revolves again and the third scene appears in front. One can now use the revolving disc in whatever way the needs of the piece require. A quarter or a fifth of the circle can be used for a short scene in order to have more space for the following one. Lautenschläger's revolving stage has not only practical but also artistic advantages. The city of Munich will be especially thankful. One is no longer tied to the square-shaped wings and, with it, the straightforward settings. Unique, interesting effects will take place.

The monotony of rectangular rooms and halls will end, the street settings, cut off at the back, will be replaced by picturesque and ingenious views and, where, on old stages, only painted screens were possible, which could be quickly pulled up or let down, the use of fixed, different pieces of scenery increase the natural effect. Lautenschläger's revolving stage has proved to be adequate to perform the four changes of scene in each act of *Don Giovanni*, in front of the audience, a task not solved until now.

———— ◆ ————

When, some of our loyal theatre-goers find the words of one of their familiar and favourite operas has changed, they will probably say to their neighbours: 'I preferred it when they sang "Treibt der Champagner das Blut erst in Kreise" and "Herr Gouverneur zu Pferde, ich beuge mich zur Ende.' – my grandfather always sang it like that, why should I hear it differently? This is no longer my *Don Juan* or yours." – Certainly, it is not your or his *Don Juan* but it is Mozart's *Don Giovanni*. To let him come alive in his original form and completeness is an aim which is worth the greatest endeavours!

[Translated by the present author]

Structural Synopsis and Performance Analysis of Strauss's Performing Version of Mozart's *Idomeneo*

STRUCTURAL SYNOPSIS

ACT I
Overture   unchanged
Scene 1
Recitative   'Wann enden meine Leiden' (Ilia)
                 68 bars in *NMA*[1] reduced to 51 bars by Strauss. Material
                 based on the original Act 1, Scene I [*NMA*
                 p. 20] but reworked by Strauss.
Aria   'Vater und Brüder, wohl denk' ich der Pflichten' (Ilia)
                 originally, Act 1, Scene I, No. 1, 'Padre, germani, addio!'
                 [*NMA* p. 26]. Strauss cuts bars 41 to 56 and bars 81 to 92
                 [*NMA*].
Scene 2
Recitative   'Frohe Botschaft bring ich, Ilia' (Idamantes, Ilia)
                 Strauss replaces 70 bars of recitativo secco [*NMA* pp. 33–7]
                 with 15 bars of material based on themes from *Scena Ultima*
                 [*NMA* p. 477].
Rondo   'Endlich dürfen Worte sagen' (Idamantes)
                 originally Rondo from K490, Act 2, Scene I,
                 No. 10b, 'Non temer, amato bene' [*NMA* p. 196]
                 and intended as part of an alternative to
                 Act 2, Scene I, No. 10a. Strauss cuts bars 114
                 to 151 [*NMA*].
Recitative   'Nicht reize der Götter Zorn' (Idamantes, Ilia)
                 new material by Strauss
Scene 3
Chorus   'Uns leuchtet Friede'
                 originally Act 1, Scene III, No. 3, 'Godiam la pace, trionfi
                 Amore' [*NMA* p. 54]: virtually unchanged.
Scene 4
Recitative   'Höre mich, Fürst!' (Ismene, Idamantes, Chorus)
                 originally recitativo secco followed by recitativo
                 accompagnato; total length: 40 bars [*NMA* pp. 64–6].

Strauss expands scene to 48 bars with material loosely based on pp. 65–6 [*NMA*]. Arbace excluded; chorus added.

Scene 5

Recitative

'So starbst du, Idomeneo?' (Ismene)
virtually unchanged from the original, Act 1, Scene VI, 'Estinto è Idomeneo?' [*NMA* p. 67]. Strauss orchestrates – strings – the material played on the cembalo in *NMA*.

Aria

'In meinem tiefen Schmerze' (Ismene)
originally Act 1, Scene VI, No. 4, 'Tutte nel cor vi sento' [*NMA* p. 70]. Strauss cuts bars 61 to 73 and bars 109 to 124 [*NMA*].

Scene 6

Chorus

'Da seht! Götter, o helft!'
orchestrationally the same as original, Act 1, Scene VII, No. 5, 'Pietà! Numi, pietà!' [*NMA* p. 83]. Strauss redistributes and strengthens the choral material.

Scene 7

Recitative

'Gerettet! Dank dir, Gott!' (Idomeneo)
material based on Act 1, Scene VIII [*NMA* p. 93] and loose rhythmic links with Act 1, Scene IX [*NMA* pp. 95–6].

Aria

'Schon war ich ein Opfer wütender Stürme' (Idomeneo)
originally Act 1, Scene IX, No. 6, 'Vedrommi intorno l'ombra dolente' [*NMA* p. 97]. Strauss cuts bars 37 to 51; 'Allegro di molto', bars 72 to 94, and bars 109 to 113 [*NMA*].

Scene 8

Recitative

'Gottheit, wie grausam!' (Idomeneo, Idamantes)
based on the accompagnato section of Act 1, Scene X [*NMA* p. 109] which, in itself, has links with the overture and earlier material.

Scene 9

Recitative

'Was bedeutet dies Wort?' (Idamantes)
unchanged from recitative Act 1, Scene X, 'Ah qual gelido orror' [*NMA* p. 112].

Aria

'Wohl ist er gerettet vom Tode' (Idamantes)
originally Act 1, Scene X, No. 7, 'Il padre adorato' [*NMA* p. 114]. Strauss cuts bars 5 to 46 [*NMA*].

Scene 10

Marcia

Strauss retains unchanged from the original, Act 1, Scene X, No. 8 [*NMA* p. 123]; however, he abandons the second repeat.

Chorus

'Poseidon verehret! Und bringet ihm Opfer'
originally Act 1, Scene X, No. 9, 'Nettuno s'onori, quel nome risuoni' [*NMA* p. 134]. Strauss cuts bars 79 to 158 [*NMA*].

ACT II

Introduction

orchestral introduction based on the orchestral introduction to Act 2, Scene III/IV, No. 12a/b, 'Fuor del mar' [*NMA* p. 228 and p. 252]. First twelve bars unchanged. Bars 13 and 14 [*Version Strauss*] added by Strauss in the style of the preceding twelve bars.

Scene 1

Recitative

'Nun weißt du das Geheimnis!' (Idomeneo, Arbaces)
linked dramatically with the recitative, Act 2, Scene I, 'Tutto m'è noto' [*NMA* p. 173]. Musical links with earlier motivic

material; links with recitative, Act 1, Scene VIII [*Version Strauss*]; and further reference to aria, Act 2, Scene III/IV, No. 12a/b, 'Fuor del mar' [*NMA* p. 228 and p. 252].

Scene 2
Aria

'Gott! Du strafst mit harten Händen!' (Idomeneo) originally Act 2, Scene III/IV, No. 12b, 'Fuor del mar' (both alternatives printed in Strauss's score. 12a printed in full after what was 12b but as an *ossia*, with suggested cuts [*vi–de*]). Strauss cuts to the beginning of the vocal entry, bar 16 [*NMA* p. 254]; bars 38 to 44 [*NMA*]; bars 107 to 125 [*NMA*]; bars 139 to 141; and alters the accompaniment between bars 141 to 145 [*NMA*].

Scene 3
Recitative

'Die Freude spielt in deinem Aug' (Idomeneo, Ismene) material drawn from recitative Act 2, Scene IV, 'Chi mai del mio provò' [*NMA* p. 270].

Trio

'Muß ich von dir mich trennen' (Ismene, Idamantes, Idomeneo) originally Act 2, Scene VI, No. 16, 'Pria di partir, oh Dio!' [*NMA* p. 296]: virtually unchanged.

Recitative

'Darf ich dir, Vater' (Idamantes, Idomeneo) new material by Strauss, with a notable horn solo.

Scene 4
Recitative

'Dir, König, neigt sich die Verwaiste' (Ilia, Idomeneo) new material by Strauss

Aria

'Wie lang schon bewein ich in einsamen Stunden' (Ilia) originally Act 2, Scene II, No. 11, 'Se il padre perdei' [*NMA* p. 215]. Strauss cuts bars 53 to 55 and bars 106 to 108 [*NMA*].

Scene 5
Recitative

'Wie unerwartet' (Idomeneo) material reworked from recitative, Act 2, Scene III, 'Qual mi conturba i sensi' [*NMA* p. 225]. Strauss reduces from 27 bars to 18 bars, along with minor tonal and rhythmic alterations.

Scene 6
Chorus

'Wasser und Wind versöhnend leuchtet die Abendsonne!' originally Act 2, Scene V, No. 15, 'Placido è il mar, andiamo' [*NMA* p. 283]. Strauss adds an eight bar introduction based on the opening eight bars of the chorus. Cuts bars 23 to the end of the chorus [*NMA*]. Strauss joins to the next scene.

Scene 7
Aria

'Sanfte Winde, folgt dem Teuren' (Ilia) originally Act 3, Scene I, No. 19, 'Zeffiretti lusinghieri' [*NMA* p. 352]. Connected with the previous scene. Strauss cuts to vocal entry, bar 18 [*NMA*].

Recitative

'Ist dieser Donner deine Antwort' (Ilia) material adapted from Act 2, Scene VI, 'Più Allegro' [*NMA* p. 319].

Scene 8
Chorus

'Das Meer ist in Aufruhr! Der Sturm peitscht die Fluten!' originally Act 2, Scene VI, No. 17, 'Qual nuovo terrore!' [*NMA* p. 321]: unchanged.

Recitative	'Weh, neues Unheil entsteigt dem Meere!' (Ein Mann aus dem Volke) 12 bars based on the *Interludio*, composed by Strauss, between Act 2, Scenes VIII and IX, replacing 39 bar recitativo accompagnato, Act 2, Scene VI, 'Eccoti in me, barbaro Nume!' [*NMA* p. 332].
Chorus	'Aus Tiefen des Meeres' originally Act 2, Scene VI, No. 18, 'Corriamo, fuggiamo' [*NMA* p. 336]: unchanged.
Interludio	new material composed by Strauss. Contains a quote, figure 112, from Act 3, *Scena Ultima*, No. 30a [*Anhang* 12, *NMA* p. 605]. This aria, 'Torna la pace', is omitted by Strauss.
Scene 9 *Recitative*	'Würgend verbreitet Tod das Untier' (Ilia, Idamantes) material adapted from recitative Act 3, Scene II, 'Principessa, a' tuoi sguardi' [*NMA* p. 363]. Also quotes earlier motifs and makes reference to Rondo, Act 1, Scene II [*Version Strauss*], 'Endlich dürfen Worte sagen'.
Duet	'Es fehlen mir die Worte' (Ilia, Idamantes) originally Act 3, Scene II, No. 20b, 'Spiegarti non poss'io' [*NMA* p. 376]: virtually unchanged.
Scene 10 *Recitative*	'Idamantes! Mein König!' (Ismene, Ilia, Idamantes and Idomeneo) material based on earlier motifs and the *Scena Ultima* [*NMA* p. 477]. Last five bars identical to last five bars of p. 385 [*NMA*], which precede the Quartet.
Quartet	'Nein, du sollst bleiben' (Ilia, Ismene, Idamantes and Idomeneo) originally Act 3, Scene III, No. 21, 'Andrò ramingo e solo' [*NMA* p. 386].[2] Virtually unchanged except for the inclusion of an optional cut bars 103 to 112 [*NMA*]. In the British Library score, he reinforces this cut in blue pencil.
Scene 11 *Recitative*	'Du armes Kind!' (Ilia, Ismene and Idomeneo) new material by Strauss
Recitative	'Was hörte ich?' (Ismene) from Allegro (seventh bar of figure 137) to figure 139 based upon Act 3, Scene X [*NMA* p. 474], bars 5 to 24. From figure 139 to end of recitative, based on the last three bars of recitative, Act 3, Scene X [*Anhang* 11, *NMA* p. 579].
Aria	'Orestes und Ajas, ich ruf' Eure Namen!' (Ismene) originally Act 3, Scene X, No. 29a, 'D'Oreste, d'Aiace' [*Anhang* 11, *NMA* p. 580]. Strauss adds extra wind material (which double the violas), found in black ink, to the British Library score. These insertions are reproduced in the 1941 score. This recitative and aria, arranged as described above, is not found in the *Anhang* to the *Gesammtausgabe* score but as part of the opera itself. Strauss cuts bars 53 to 60 and bars 86 to 111 [*NMA*].

ACT III
Scene 1
Temple Scene   'König, wir müssen dich fragen' (Idomeneo, Oberpriester
                                  and Chorus)
                                  new material by Strauss, with reference to the *Scena Ultima*
                                  [*NMA* p. 477] in the bar preceding figure 4. Adagio, p. 259
                                  [*Version Strauss*], taken from chorus, Act 3, Scene VI,
                                  No. 24, 'Oh, voto tremendo!' [*NMA* p. 437]. Strauss cuts
                                  bars 1 to 37, as indicated in *NMA*, but alters wind, brass and
                                  timpani parts from those contained in bars 37 to 40
                                  inclusive [*NMA*], to the orchestration of bars 1 to 4 inclusive
                                  [*NMA*].

Scene 2
Sacred Dance
                                  originally Act 3, Scene VII, No. 25, 'Marcia' [*NMA*
                                  p. 451]: unaltered.

Scene 3
Scene   'Vor dir, o Gott gebeugt' (Idomeneo and chorus of priests)
                                  originally Act 3, Scene VII, No. 26, 'Accogli, oh re del mar'
                                  [*NMA* p. 452]: unaltered.
Chorus   'Heil dir, Idamantes'
                                  originally Act 3, Scene VII, 'Stupenda vittoria!' [*NMA*
                                  p.459]: unaltered.

Scene 4
Recitative   'Gerettet ist die Stadt!', (Idamantes, Idomeneo)
                                  material based on aria, Act 3, Scene IX, No. 27a, 'No, la
                                  morte' [*Anhang* 7, *NMA* p. 548]; the quartet, Act 3, Scene
                                  III, No. 21 [*NMA* p. 386]; and recitative, Act 3, Scene IX,
                                  No. 27 [*NMA* p. 461].

Scene 5
Recitative   'Halt ein, Fürst, ich sei das Opfer' (Ilia, Idamantes and
                                  Idomeneo)
                                  material based on recitative, Act 3, Scene X, 'Orsù mi svena'
                                  [*Anhang* 8, *NMA* p. 561].

Off-stage Voice   'Die Treue siegte'
                                  originally Act 3, Scene X, No. 28a/b/c/d. Strauss alters
                                  original material but, of the four alternatives offered by
                                  Mozart, the former's choice is closest in length and content
                                  to Act 3, Scene X, No. 28d, 'Ha vinto Amore' [*Anhang* 10,
                                  NMA p. 568].

Ensemble   'Erlösung! Gnade verkündend endet ein Wunder' (Ilia,
                                  Idamantes, Idomeneo, Oberpriester and chorus)
                                  new material by Strauss with reference to Act 3, *Scena
                                  Ultima* [*NMA* p. 477].

Chorus   (*Schlussgesang mit Tanz*): 'Eros führt mächtige Waffen'
                                  originally Act 3, *Scena Ultima*, No. 31, 'Scenda Amor'
                                  [*NMA* p. 483]. Strauss omits middle dance section,
                                  bars 76 to 105 [*NMA*] and the Coda, bar 75a [*NMA* p.494].
                                  In the British Library score, Strauss brackets and reinforces,
                                  in blue pencil, bars 71 to 74 inclusive [*NMA*]; in the 1941
                                  score, he indicates that these bars may be repeated *ad
                                  libitum*.

Performance Analysis of Hermann May's 1941 Recorded Fragments[3]

Excerpt 1: Interludio

In the 'Interludio' there are three basic speeds ($\downarrow$=54, $\downarrow$=66 and $\downarrow$=66), the first of which ($\downarrow$=54) is heard throughout the tutti passages, the second ($\downarrow$=66) in the passages with the solo oboe[4] and the third ($\downarrow$=66) from bars 31 to 42 inclusive. The 'Interludio' is written in a loose ternary structure in which the chromatically enriched first section (A) (bars 1 to 30) is followed by a diatonic middle passage (B) (bars 31 to 42) based on music from Act 3 'Scena Ultima' and No. 30a 'Torna la pace' (*Anhang* 12, *NMA* p. 605) that in turn is followed by a third section (A1) (bars 43 to 63) developed from material first heard at the beginning. Strauss contrasts the external and middle parts of the ternary structure by using different tempi that share the same metre: $\downarrow$=54 (A and A1) and $\downarrow$=66 (B). He then links the tempo of the passages with the solo oboe, derived from the winding figure taken from the end of the Overture (bars 158–161) and developed in the recognition scene, to that of the middle section, based on an aria sung by Idomeneo. As the music chosen for each of these sections represents the extremes of emotion experienced by the Cretan King, Strauss both relates and contrasts these feelings by means of tempo and metre ($\downarrow$=66 and $\downarrow$=66), a subtlety that might have been lost on contemporary audiences, as the aria, 'Torna la pace', was not otherwise used by Strauss.

Excerpt 2: Act II, Scene 4 ('Wie lang' schon bewein' ich in einsamen Stunden')

The recording of this excerpt begins at bar 2 (beat 2[5]) and finishes at bar 90 (first half). As in the 'Interludio', Strauss defines the architectonics of the binary structure by manipulating two main speeds ($\downarrow$=80 and $\downarrow$=72). The first tempo dominates bars 2 to 39 (beat 1) but changes from a quaver to a crotchet pulse in bars 27 and 28 and bars 30 and 31. The speed reduces to $\downarrow$=72 from bar 39 beat 2 but returns gradually to the original tempo over an eight-bar period between bars 46 and 55, the recapitulation of the opening material. From the evidence heard in the recording, the hand-annotated metronome mark in the 1941 score ($\downarrow$=126) can be dismissed as a mistake but the legato slurs (violins I) joining bars 4 (beat 4) to 5 (first semiquaver) and bars 18 (beat 4) to 19 (first semiquaver), found in the British Library score, but missing in the 1941 score, should be retained.

Excerpt 3: Quartett, Act II, Scene 10, 'Nein, du sollst bleiben'

The excerpt begins at bar 44 and clarifies the conflict between Strauss's time signature ($\mathbb{¢}$) and the metronome mark ($\downarrow$=138) inserted by another hand in the 1941 score. The speed of the excerpt is $\downarrow$=66 and is beaten in two ($\mathbb{¢}$), which is clear from Strauss's treatment of the pause in bar 67 and his approach to the rubato. The fermata is held for three beats and is prepared by a fluctuation that can best be described as 'quasi rubato', creating only the slightest impression of a rallentando. When the passage is checked against a metronome, his adjustment is so small that it falls within the parameters of the original speed, a shift typical of Strauss who wrote that 'any modification of tempo made necessary by the character of a phrase should be carried out imperceptibly so that the unity of tempo remains intact'.[6] Conversely, when the music and the libretto demand a greater sense of freedom, Strauss adjusts the tempo accordingly. Between bar 70 with the quaver upbeat and bar 82 inclusive, for example, he applies a more complex form of rubato that is intended to reflect the angst of Ilia and Idamantes who are singing of a bleak future. From bar 70 to bar 73 inclusive, he makes a slight rallentando followed by an accelerando between bars 74 and 82 that leads the listener effortlessly to the tempo primo at bar 83. He then draws attention to the pair's turbulent emotions by shaping the phrase with slight accents on the downbeats at bars 76 and 78, which, of course, do much to complement the violins' restless syncopation from bars 72 to 81 inclusive.

Excerpt 4: Act III, Scene 5, 'Erlösung!' to the end of the 'Schlussgesang mit Tanz'[7]

The excerpt begins one bar before 'Erlösung!' with breaks between bars 43 and 48 and bars 49 (second half) and 68 (first half) of the 'Schlussgesang mit Tanz'.[8] Bars 1 to 3 are treated as a separate, declamatory unit, while the passage between bars 4 to 74 inclusive of 'Erlösung!' is a juxtaposition of two tempo zones, ♪=76 and ♪=84. Bar 1 takes the form of an implied fermata that reinforces both the cadential nature of these bars and their dramatic importance.[9] Between bars 4 and 17 inclusive, he maintains a consistent ♪=76, a speed dictated in part by his orchestration, which consolidates many of the motifs heard earlier in the opera. From Idamante's entry at bar 18, he increases the speed to ♪=84 before pressing it forward to bar 37 by sitting on the front edge of the tempo. In keeping with his practice of reinforcing the architectonics of the music by a selective use of tempi, he returns to ♪=76 when the material first heard in bars 4 to 7 is recapitulated at bar 38. Between bars 75 and 78 (first half), 'poco meno Adagio', he changes the beat from eight to four and adopts a new tempo, ♩=52. From bar 78 (second half), he observes the printed accelerando culminating in ♩=104 at the beginning of the 'Schlussgesang mit Tanz', a tempo retained to the end of the opera and related directly to that heard between bars 75 and 78 ('Erlösung!').

May's recording of the final scene again confirms some of the annotations that are found in both the British Library and 1941 scores that otherwise might have remained ambiguous. At the beginning of the 'Schlussgesang mit Tanz', Strauss changes the superscription from Allegro vivace to Allegro but with the qualification, 'nicht zu schnell', an amendment that is in keeping with his speed on the recording, ♩=104. In the British Library score, he brackets bar 71 to bar 74 of the 'Schlussgesang mit Tanz' in blue pencil, indicating that these bars are to be repeated but writes 'ad lib.[itum]' above the passage in the 1941 score. In the recording, the repeat is observed, again reinforcing the importance of cross-referencing recorded sound with marked score when analyzing performance style.

Strauss's Published Commercial and Non-commercial Recordings (1905–1947)

Year	Work	Medium/Artist/ Orchestra/Opera House	Company
1905	Excerpts from *Salome*; excerpts from *Feuersnot*; 'Love Scene' from *Ein Heldenleben*	Piano rolls	Welte, Germany
1914	Excerpts from *Ariadne auf Naxos* (1912 version); excerpts from *Josephslegende*; 'Love Scene' from *Ein Heldenleben*	Piano rolls	Hupfeld, Germany
1916	*Don Juan; Till Eulenspiegel*; Suite from *Der Bürger als Edelmann*	Berlin Hofkapelle	Deutsche Grammophon, Germany
1921	Lieder	Accompanied Robert Hutt and Heinrich Schlusnus	Deutsche Grammophon, Germany
1921	Tanz from *Salome*; the Menuett and Intermezzo from *Der Bürger als Edelmann*	Anonymous orchestra (probably recorded in New York)	Brunswick, USA
1921	Accompaniments to 'Zueignung', 'Allerseelen' and 'Traum durch die Dämmerung'	Piano rolls	Ampico, USA
1922	*Don Juan*; waltzes from *Der Rosenkavalier*; 'Tanz' from *Salome*	London Symphony Orchestra	Columbia, UK
1926	Beethoven: Symphony No. 7; Mozart: Symphonies Nos. 39 and 41; *Ein Heldenleben; Tod und Verklärung*; two orchestral interludes from *Intermezzo*; waltzes from *Der Rosenkavalier*	Berlin Staatskapelle	Deutsche Grammophon, Germany
1926	Music from the film adaptation of *Der Rosenkavalier*	Augmented Tivoli Orchestra	HMV, UK
1927	Mozart: Symphony No. 40; two orchestral interludes from *Intermezzo*; waltzes from *Der Rosenkavalier*	Berlin Staatskapelle	Deutsche Grammophon, Germany

Year	Work	Medium/Artist/ Orchestra/Opera House	Company
1928	Mozart: Symphony No. 40, Overture to *Die Zauberflöte*; Beethoven: Symphony No. 5	Berlin Staatskapelle	Deutsche Grammophon, Germany
1928	Gluck: (arr. Wagner) Overture to *Iphigénie in Aulis*; Weber: Overture to *Euryanthe*; Cornelius: Overture to *Der Barbier von Bagdad*; Wagner: Overture to *Der fliegende Holländer*, Prelude to Act I of *Tristan und Isolde*; 'Tanz' from *Salome*	Berlin Philharmonic	Deutsche Grammophon, Germany
1929	*Don Juan* and *Till Eulenspiegel*	Berlin Staatskapelle	Polydor, Germany
1930	Suite from *Der Bürger als Edelmann*	Berlin Staatskapelle	Polydor, Germany
1933	*Don Quixote*	Berlin Staatskapelle	Polydor, Germany
1936–1937	*Eine Alpensinfonie* (experimental recording for Reichssenders München), *Don Juan, Tod und Verklärung*	Orchester des Reichssender München	Reichssender München
1936	*Don Quixote, Till Eulenspiegel* (to Figure 24, bar 4 only)	Sächsische Staatskapelle Dresden (Queen's Hall, London)	Probably BBC
1936	*Macbeth*	Orchester des Deutschlandsender	Deutschlandsender Berlin
1940–1941	*Don Quixote*; *Ein Heldenleben*; *Eine Alpensinfonie*; *Japanische Festmusik*; waltzes from *Der Rosenkavalier*	Bayerisches Staatsorchester	Deutsche Grammophon and Electrola (*Eine Alpensinfonie* only), Germany
1941	Mozart-Strauss, *Idomeneo*	Vienna Staatsoper	Private recording
1942	Excerpts from *Salome*	Vienna Staatsoper	Private recording
1942–1943	Lieder	Accompanied Anton Dermota, Hilde Konetzni, Alfred Poell, Maria Reining and Lea Piltti	Reichssender Wien
1942	*Also Sprach Zarathustra, Till Eulenspiegel*	Vienna Philharmonic	Probably Reichssender Wien
1944	*Don Juan*; *Till Eulenspiegel*; *Also Sprach Zarathustra*; Suite from *Der Bürger als Edelmann*; *Tod und Verklärung*; *Sinfonia domestica*; Wagner: Prelude to *Die Meistersinger von Nürnberg*	Vienna Philharmonic	Reichssender Wien
1947	*Don Juan, Burleske* (Alfred Blumen, piano), *Sinfonia domestica, Till Eulenspiegel*	Philharmonia Orchestra and BBC Symphony Orchestra	BBC

APPENDIX 5

Score Examples
Marked by Richard Strauss

Score Example 1 (Mozart's *Don Giovanni*: Act 1 Finale, Scene 20, bar 406)

Score Example 2 (Mozart's Symphony No. 41, Movt. 3, Trio)

W. A. M. 551.

W. A. M. 551.

Menuetto da capo

Score Example 3 (Mozart's Symphony No. 41, Movt. 1, bars 52 to 83 inclusive)

W.A.M.551.

Score Example 4 (Mozart's Symphony No. 41, Movt. 2, bars 13 to 33 inclusive)

W.A.M. 551.

Score Example 5 (Mozart's Symphony No. 41, Movt. 4, bars 146 to 227 inclusive)

W. A. M. 551.

W. A. M. 551.

W. A. M. 551.

W. A. M. 551.

Score Example 6 (Mozart's Symphony No. 41, Movt. 4, bars 355 to end)

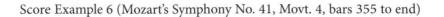

W.A.M. 551.

W.A.M.551.

Score Example 7 (Beethoven's Symphony No. 5, Movt. 1, bars 22 to 33 inclusive, ed. Chrysander)

3

Score Example 8 (Beethoven's Symphony No. 5, Movt. 1, bars 56 to 68 inclusive, ed. Chrysander)

Score Example 9 (Mozart's Symphony No. 29, Movt 1, bars 1 to 23 inclusive)

Score Example 10 (Mozart's Symphony No. 40, Movt. 1, bars 1 to 15 inclusive)

Score Example 11 (Beethoven's Symphony No. 5, Movt. 1, bars 188 to 199, ed. Chrysander)

Score Example 12 (Beethoven's Symphony No. 5, Movt. 4, bars 47 to 51 inclusive, ed. Chrysander)

125

Score Example 13 (Beethoven's Symphony No. 5, Movt. 4, bars 342 to 347 inclusive, ed. Chrysander)

Score Example 14 (Beethoven's Symphony No. 5, Movt. 4, bars 1 to 12 inclusive, ed. Chrysander)

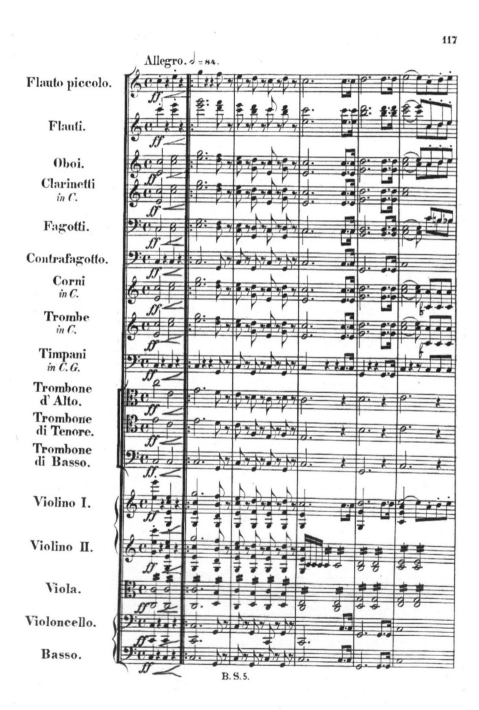

B. S. 5.

Score Example 15 (Beethoven's Symphony No. 5, Movt. 1, bars 303 to 314 inclusive, ed. Chrysander)

Score Example 16 (Beethoven's Symphony No. 5, Movt. 2, bars 183 to 191 inclusive, ed. Chrysander)

76

B. S. 5.

Score Example 17 (Beethoven's Symphony No. 5, Movt. 2, bars 245 & 246, ed. Chrysander)

83

B. S. 5.

Score Example 18 (Beethoven's Symphony No. 5, Movt. 4, bars 385 to 399 inclusive, ed. Chrysander)

175

B.S. 5.

Notes

Chapter 1 A Munich Childhood: Education and Early Impressions

1. Hans (Guido) Freiherr von Bülow (1830–1894): German conductor, pianist and composer.
2. In 1778, Karl Theodor succeeded Maximilian III Joseph, Elector of Bavaria, and brought from Mannheim to Munich his famous orchestra. The virtuosity of the Mannheim Orchestra is legendary and Mozart worked with this ensemble, most notably during the composition of *Idomeneo*, an opera that Strauss conducted in his own performing version. See Chapter 7.
3. Franz Strauss's first wife, Elise Maria Seiff, whom he married on 28 May 1851, and their two children died during a cholera epidemic.
4. Strauss's sister, Berta Johanna, b. Munich, 9 July 1867; d. 23 March 1966.
5. W. Schuh, *Richard Strauss: A Chronicle of the Early Years, 1864–1898*, trans. M. Whittall (Cambridge, 1982), p. 11.
6. Ibid.
7. R. Strauss, *Recollections and Reflections*, ed. W. Schuh, trans. L.J. Lawrence, (London, 1953), first published as *Betrachtungen und Erinnerungen*, ed. W. Schuh, Atlantis Verlag (Zürich, 1949), p. 131.
8. Franz Strauss died at Munich on 31 May 1905.
9. Franz Michael Walter (1802–1874), Franz Joseph Michael Walter (1806–1874) and Johann Georg Walter (1813–1898): German musicians.
10. F. Trenner, 'Die Vorfahren von Richard Strauss', *Bayerland* 56 (1954), pp. 23–48.
11. Wagner's *Das Rheingold, Die Walküre, Tristan und Isolde* and *Die Meistersinger von Nürnberg* were given their premières at the Munich Hofoper on 22 September 1869, 26 June 1870, 10 June 1865 and 21 June 1868 respectively.
12. Strauss, *Recollections and Reflections*, p. 127.
13. Ibid.
14. Ibid.
15. Ibid., p. 128.
16. Ibid., pp. 128–9.
17. Ibid., p. 132.
18. L. Botstein, 'The Enigmas of Richard Strauss: A Revisionist View', *Richard Strauss and His World*, ed. B. Gilliam (Princeton, 1992), p. 10.
19. August Tombo (1842–1878): German harpist and pianist.
20. Schuh, *Richard Strauss: A Chronicle of the Early Years*, p. 14
21. Benno Walter (1847–1901): German violinist. Walter joined the Munich Hofkapelle in 1863 and he was later promoted to Leader in 1875. He performed throughout the German-speaking countries and the United States of America as a soloist and as a chamber musician, notably with Benno Walter Quartet, whose other members were Michael Steiger, Anton Thoms and Hans Wihan. He also gave the first performance of Strauss's Violin Concerto, Op. 8, in Vienna on 5 December 1882, accompanied by the

composer at the piano. The cellist of the Benno Walter Quartet, the Bohemian Hans Wihan (1855–1920), was married to Dora Wihan-Weis (1860–1938), whom Strauss met first in 1883 and with whom he seems to have had an affair before marrying Pauline de Ahna.

22. The Wilde Gung'l was formed in 1864 and it performs today. Franz Strauss became its conductor on 1 October 1875. Its name was derived from the Hungarian violinist and conductor, Joseph Gung'l (1809–1889), a performer of popular dance music. It was decided to add 'Wilde' to title to differentiate it from the original ensemble established by Gung'l. The Munich orchestra owns the manuscripts of some of Strauss's early compositions, including the Festival March Op. 1, the Serenade in G major O.Op. 32, the orchestral version of Gavotte No. 4 from Five Small Piano Pieces O.Op. 59, the Symphony in D minor O.Op. 69 and the Festival March in C major O.Op. 87.

23. Friedrich Niest (1816–1892): German pianist and pedagogue.

24. Sophie Menter (1846–1918): German pianist and composer.

25. Franz Trenner, *Richard Strauss Chronik zu Leben und Werk*, ed. Florian Trenner, (Vienna, 2003), p. 16.

26. Ludwig Thuille (1861–1907): Austrian composer. Thuille was the joint author, with Rudolf Louis, of *Harmonielehre* (1907) and was Professor of Theory and Composition at the Königliche Musikschule, Munich, from 1890 until his death. Strauss conducted the following works by him: Symphony in F major (23 February 1886, Meiningen); *Theuerdank* (12 March 1897, 23 March 1897, 27 March 1897 and 27 April 1897, Munich), and Act III of *Gugeline* (21 January 1902, Berliner Tonkünstler-Orchesters, Berlin).

27. Strauss, *Recollections and Reflections*, p. 134.

28. As found in Schuh, *Richard Strauss: A Chronicle of the Early Years*, pp. 22–3.

29. Friedrich Wilhelm Meyer (1818–1893): German composer and conductor.

30. Franz Lachner (1803–1890): German composer and conductor.

31. Strauss's letter to his parents from Florence, dated 10 June 1893. Translated by the present author.

32. Trenner gives the name of the cramming school as the Widmann'sche Lehranstalt (Trenner, *Richard Strauss Chronik*, p. 10) whereas Schuh gives the name as the Widmer'sches Institut (Schuh, *Richard Strauss: a Chronicle of the Early Years*, p. 21).

33. As found in Schuh, *Richard Strauss: a Chronicle of the Early Years*, p. 18.

34. The Serenade was premièred by Franz Wüllner under the auspice of the Dresden Tonkünstlerverein on 27 November 1882 and the Suite was given its first performance by Strauss at the Munich's Odeonsaal on 18 November 1884.

35. Franz Wüllner (1832–1902): German composer and conductor.

36. For the world première of Strauss's Symphony No. 2, see Chapter 2.

37. The cellist at the first performance of *Don Quixote* was Friedrich Grützmacher.

38. Trenner, *Richard Strauss Chronik*, p. 163.

39. The Odeon in Munich was built as a concert and ballroom under the supervision of the architect, Leo von Klenze, between 1826 and 1828. It was destroyed during World War Two.

40. Hermann Levi (1839–1900): German conductor.

41. *Münchner Neueste Nachrichten*, 3 April 1881.

42. The exact date of the Horn Concerto's première is unknown.

43. The last work by the teenage Strauss to be given in Munich was his Concert Overture in C minor, which was performed by Levi at one of the Hofkapelle's Subscription Concerts on 28 November 1883 and was dedicated to the conductor as a mark of gratitude.

44. Interview with Franz Trenner, 13 May 1992.

45. In an undated letter to Thuille, Strauss expresses his father's strength of feeling about the Classical masters: '*Papa advises you to give up playing Chopin and to concentrate ONLY on classical music.*' F. Trenner, 'Selections from the Strauss–Thuille

Correspondence: A Glimpse of Strauss during His Formative Years', trans. Susan Gillespie, Gilliam, ed., *Richard Strauss and His World*, p. 216.

46. Strauss's use of the term, 'our Mozart edition', is a reference, not to an edition compiled by the Strauss family but, one assumes from the date of the letter, to the *Œuvres complettes* of Breitkopf & Härtel. Trenner notes: 'Franz Strauss was one of the few private subscribers to the first edition of Mozart's collected works.' Trenner, 'Selections from the Strauss–Thuille Correspondence', ibid., p. 236, note 124.

47. Schuh, *Richard Strauss: A Chronicle of the Early Years, 1864–1898*, trans. M. Whittall, p. 31.

48. Trenner, 'Selections from the Strauss-Thuille Correspondence', p. 200.

49. Ibid., p. 218.

50. Ibid., p. 205.

51. Ibid., p. 208.

52. Strauss, *Recollections and Reflections*, p. 89.

53. On 8 December 1883, Strauss's Sonata for Violoncello and Piano was given its first performance at Nuremberg by the Czech cellist Hans Wihan and the pianist Hildegard von Königsthal.

54. The Paris-born pianist, Elizabeth von Herzogenberg (née Stockhausen) (1847–1892), and her husband, Heinrich (1843–1900), were in the circle of Brahms.

55. Strauss's letter to his father, dated 7 December 1883.

56. Carl Reinecke (1824–1910): German composer and conductor.

57. Strauss's *Feuersnot, Salome, Elektra, Der Rosenkavalier, Intermezzo, Die ägyptische Helena* (first version), *Arabella, Die schweigsame Frau* and *Daphne* were given their premières in Dresden in 1901, 1905, 1909, 1911, 1924, 1928, 1933, 1935 and 1938 respectively.

58. Strauss visited Dresden between 9 and 19 December 1883.

59. Ernst von Schuch (1846–1914): Schuch was born at Graz in Austria and was first employed as a conductor at the Dresdner Hofoper in 1872. He rose to the rank of Generalmusikdirektor at that theatre in 1889 and conducted the premières of *Feuersnot, Salome, Elektra, Der Rosenkavalier* there in 1901, 1905, 1909 and 1911 respectively.

60. Ferdinand Böckmann (1843–1913): German cellist. Strauss dedicated his Romance in F major for Violoncello and Orchestra or Piano to Böckmann. The Romance was completed in Munich on 27 June 1883, some six months before their performance of the Sonata.

61. Robert Hausmann (1852–1909): German cellist; Gustav Leinhos (1836–1906): German horn player.

62. On 21 March 1884, Radecke conducted Weber's 'Jubel' Overture, Beethoven's Piano Concerto No. 4 (Heinrich Barth, piano), Strauss's Concert Overture in C minor and Mendelssohn's Symphony No. 3 ('Scottish'). Georg Quander in *Klangbilder: Portrait der Staatskapelle Berlin* (Frankfurt and Berlin, 1995) (p. 184) gives the date of the concert as 27 March 1884.

63. Strauss's letter to his parents, dated 22 March 1884.

CHAPTER 2 A RISING STAR: MEININGEN (1885–1886) AND FIRST MUNICH PERIOD (1886–1889)

1. F. Weingartner, *Über das Dirigieren* (1895), trans. E. Newman as *On Conducting* (London, 1906), p. 12.

2. Cosima Wagner (née Liszt) (1837–1930) was Franz Liszt's daughter. She married Bülow on 18 August 1857.

3. The first night of *Tristan und Isolde* was scheduled for 15 May 1865, but because of the indisposition of the Danish soprano, Malvina Schnorr von Carolsfeld (1825–1904), the first Isolde, the première was delayed until 10 June 1865. H. Zehetmair and J. Schläder eds., *Nationaltheater: Die Bayerische Staatsoper* (Munich, 1992), p. 65.

4. Letter from Bülow to Lassen, dated 31 July 1865. As found in K. Birkin, 'Une organisation musicale de plus rares', *Richard Strauss-Blätter* (Vienna, June 2002), Heft 47, p. 17.
5. The Alte Residenztheater or Cuvilliés Theater was built in 1753 but bombed during World War Two. It was reconstructed in 1958.
6. Strauss, *Recollections and Reflections*, p. 128.
7. Bülow conducted four performances of *Tristan und Isolde* at Munich between 10 June and 1 July 1865.
8. The world première of Liszt's *Die Legende von der heiligen Elisabeth* was given at Budapest on 15 August 1865.
9. Bülow's letter to Klindworth, dated 29 July 1869. H. von Bülow, ed. Richard Count du Moulin Eckart and S. Goddard, trans. H. Walter, *Letters of Hans von Bülow to Richard Wagner and Others* (New York, 1979), p. 10
10. Ibid.
11. Carl Bechstein (1826–1900): German piano manufacturer.
12. Bülow, *Letters of Hans von Bülow to Richard Wagner and Others*, p. 95.
13. Herzog Georg II von Sachsen-Meiningen (1826–1914).
14. Helene (Ellen) Franz (1839–1923): German actress.
15. H. Müller and V. Kern, eds., *Die Meininger kommen!* (Meiningen, 1999), p. 89.
16. Bülow had been Hofkapellmeister in Hanover from 1877 to 1879.
17. For his arrangement of Op. 133, Bülow added double basses to the scoring.
18. Frithjof Haas in *Hans von Bülow: Leben und Wirken* (Wilhelmshaven, 2002) and the records of the Staatliche Museen Meiningen only record thirty-two concerts for the tour of 31 October to 5 December 1884. They fail to mention the matinee concert that preceded the evening concert at the Odeon, Munich, on 18 November 1884. Wolf-Dieter Gewande in *Hans von Bülow* and Franz Trenner (ed. Florian Trenner) in *Richard Strauss Chronik*, however, mention the matinée.
19. The repertoire performed by the Meininger Hofkapelle on their autumn and winter tour of 1884 included Beethoven's Symphonies Nos. 1 (nine times), 3, 4 (three times), 5 (eleven times) and 8 (five times), Piano Concerto No. 4 (Hans von Bülow, piano/conductor) (six times), Overtures to *Coriolan* (six times), *Egmont* (seven times), *Leonore* Nos. 1 (three times) and 3 (six times) and *Die Geschöpfe des Prometheus*, 'König Stephan' and 'Zur Namensfeier' Overtures, Rondino for Winds (six times) and *Grosse Fuge* (five times), Berlioz's 'Le Corsaire' (ten times) and 'Le Roi Lear' (three times) Overtures, Brahms's Symphony No. 3 (nine times, two of which with Brahms conducting), 'Haydn' Variations (six times), 'Tragic' (three times) and 'Academic Festival' Overtures, Piano Concerto No. 1 (Hans von Bülow, piano/conductor) (three times), Piano Concerto No. 1 (Adagio and Rondo only) (Hans von Bülow, piano/conductor) (twice), Piano Concerto No. 2 (Hans von Bülow, piano/conductor) (three times), Piano Concerto No. 2 (Johannes Brahms, piano) (three times), Piano Concerto No. 2 (Movements 1 and 2 only) (Hans von Bülow, piano/conductor), Chopin's Nocturne Op. 37 No. 2 (Hans von Bülow, piano) and Scherzo in C sharp minor (Hans von Bülow, piano), Dvořák's 'My Home' Overture, Raff's 'Ein' feste Burg' Overture (six times), 'Hungarian' Suite (five times), Two Movements from 'Hungarian' Suite, Piano Concerto in C minor (Hans von Bülow, piano/conductor), Suite in F minor and Symphony No. 4, Rheinberger's 'Wallenstein' Symphonic Poem, Schubert's Grosse Fantasie (arr. Liszt) (Hans von Bülow, piano/conductor) (eight times), Spohr's Symphony No. 3, Strauss's Serenade Op. 7 (three times) and Suite Op. 4, Wagner's 'Faust' Overture (five times) and Weber's Overtures to *Der Freischütz* (ten times), *Euryanthe* (five times) and *Oberon* (eight times).
20. Eugen Spitzweg (1840–1914): German publisher. Spitzweg's company, Aibl Verlag, was Strauss's main publisher until *Don Quixote*.
21. Strauss's letter to Bülow, dated 3 December 1883. As found in H. von Bülow and R. Strauss, *Hans von Bülow and Richard Strauss: Correspondence*, ed. Schuh, W. and Trenner, F., trans. Gishford, A., Boosey & Hawkes (London, 1955), pp. 5–6.

22. Strauss's letter to Bülow, dated 9 August 1884. Ibid., p. 7.
23. Strauss, *Recollections and Reflections*, p. 119.
24. Theodore Thomas (1835–1905): German-born American conductor.
25. Strauss completed his Piano Quartet in C minor at Munich on 1 January 1885 and the songs 'Die Nacht', 'Zueignung', 'Nichts', 'Die Georgine' and 'Geduld' at Steinach and Munich on 11, 13, 15, 18, and 29 August respectively.
26. Hans von Bülow's letter to Richard Strauss, dated 3 June 1885. Bülow and Strauss, *Hans von Bülow and Richard Strauss: Correspondence*, pp. 11–12
27. Other regular conductors of the Berlin Philharmonic during the 1885–1886 season were Joseph Joachim, Franz Wüllner, Karl Klindworth and Georg Rauchenecker.
28. Mahler's letter to Bülow, 25 January 1884, as found in K. and H. Blaukopf, *Mahler: his Life, Work and World*, p. 57. At the time of the letter, Mahler was engaged as a junior conductor at Kassel. Bülow and the Meininger Hofkapelle gave two concerts there on 24 and 25 January 1884. At the first, Bülow performed Beethoven's Overtures to *Egmont*, *Leonore* (No.1) and 'König Stephan' Overture, Symphonies Nos. 1 and 8, the Rondino for Wind Instruments in E flat major and the *Grosse Fuge*. On 25 January, he conducted Spohr's 'Faust' Overture, Symphony No. 3 and the Adagio from Clarinet Concerto No. 2 (Richard Mühlfeld, clarinet), Brahms's 'Haydn' Variations, Beethoven's Symphony No. 4 and Weber's Overture to *Der Freischütz*.
29. B. Walter, trans. J. A. Galston, *Theme and Variations: an Autobiography* (London, 1947), pp. 85–6.
30. Princess Marie Elizabeth von Sachsen-Meiningen (1853–1923): Princess Marie Elizabeth was the daughter of Georg II by his first wife, Princess Charlotte of Prussia, and a piano student of both Hans von Bülow and Richard Strauss.
31. As a chamber musician, Strauss worked closely with other members of the music staff at Meiningen. For details, see Appendix 1.
32. On 11 October 1885, Strauss heard Bülow conduct a programme that included Beethoven's Overture to *Egmont*, Symphony No. 1 the Adagio and Rondo from Piano Concerto No. 5 (Anna Haasters, piano), piano solos by Chopin, Hiller and Liszt (Anna Haasters, piano) and Schubert's Symphony No. 8 in C major ('Great'). Records of the Staatliche Museen Meiningen.
33. Strauss, 'On Conducting Classical Masterpieces', *Recollections and Reflections*, p. 118.
34. Alexander Ritter (1833–1896): Estonian-born German composer and violinist.
35. Strauss, *Recollections and Reflections*, pp. 138–9.
36. Strauss wrote his own cadenzas for the Mozart concerto at Munich in 1885 but they are now lost.
37. See Appendix 1 for details of the programme.
38. Strauss, *Recollections and Reflections*, p. 123.
39. At Meiningen, Strauss heard Brahms conduct the Violin Concerto (Adolf Brodsky, violin), 'Haydn' Variations, 'Academic Festival' Overture and Symphony No. 4. Records of the Staatliche Museen Meiningen.
40. Strauss, *Recollections and Reflections*, p. 123
41. Ibid., p. 124.
42. Ibid., p. 123.
43. H. von Bülow, ed. M. von Bülow, *Briefe und Schriften in achten Bänden*, Band VII (Leipzig, 1896–1908), p. 350. Translated by the present author.
44. Strauss, *Recollections and Reflections*, p. 136.
45. Strauss conducted the Hofkapelle for the first time at Meiningen on 9 October 1885, when he rehearsed Tchaikovsky's Violin Concerto.
46. Strauss removed the trombones from both the *Lacrimosa* and *Quam olim Abrahae* in the Requiem. Strauss's letter to his father, dated 7 November 1885.
47. See Appendix 1 for details of the programme. The concert also included the Clarinet Concerto by Wilhelm Reif (1833–1890), a German composer, conductor and clarinet-tist. He was Musikdirektor at Meiningen, where he conducted incidental music in the

theatre. On 5 January 1886, Strauss attended, and was impressed by, his performance of Weber's *Preciosa*.

48. Trenner writes in *Richard Strauss Chronik* (p. 47) that Strauss was the soloist in the Rubinstein and Liszt and that Bülow was the conductor at the concert on 29 January 1886. This is not substantiated by the records of the Staatliche Museen Meiningen.

49. Strauss's letter to his father, dated 31 January 1886. Translated by the present author,

50. Ibid.

51. See Appendix 1 for details.

52. *Berliner Tageblatt* (XV. Jg., Nr. 100, Abendausgabe), as found in Trenner, *Richard Strauss Chronik*, p. 48. Translated by the present author.

53. Strauss's letters to his father, dated 24 February and 6 April 1886.

54. See Chapter 8.

55. 'Die Verschwiegenen' and 'Die Zeitlose' were completed on 11 and 12 November 1885 respectively.

56. *Bardengesang* is scored for male voices and orchestra.

57. Schuh, *Richard Strauss: A Chronicle of the Early Years*, p. 107.

58. Ibid.

59. Franz Strauss's letter to his son, dated 26 October 1885. Translated by the present author.

60. Strauss, 'On Conducting', *Recollections and Reflections*, p. 44.

61. Ibid.

62. Strauss, 'Ten Golden Rules for the Album of a Young Conductor', *Recollections and Reflections*, p. 38.

63. Wolfgang Sawallisch (b. 1923): German conductor.

64. Interview with Wolfgang Sawallisch, Henry Wood Hall (London), 12 December 1991.

65. Hans Swarowsky (1899–1975): Hungarian-born Austrian conductor and teacher.

66. H. Swarowsky 'Random Jottings on Strauss as Conductor and Interpreter', *Richard Strauss-Blätter 1*, pp. 3–9.

67. Strauss's letter to his parents, dated 19 April 1886.

68. Strauss's letter to his parents, dated 22 April 1886.

69. Luigi Denza (1846–1922): Italian composer.

70. Karl Freiherr von Perfall (1824–1907): German composer and arts administrator.

71. Strauss's letter to Hans von Bülow, dated 16 December [1885], Bülow and Strauss, *Hans von Bülow and Richard Strauss: Correspondence*, p. 22.

72. The Werra is the river that flows through Meiningen.

73. The Isar is the river that flows through Munich.

74. Bülow and Strauss, *Hans von Bülow and Richard Strauss: Correspondence*, p. 24.

75. Strauss wrote to the Intendant on 27 December that his decision was influenced by the planned reduction in strength of the Meininger Hofkapelle. Trenner, *Richard Strauss Chronik*, p. 45.

76. Although Strauss was contracted from 1 August 1886, his début at the Hofoper did not occur until 1 October, when he conducted Boieldieu's *Johann von Paris (Jean de Paris)*.

77. See Appendix 1 for details.

78. See Appendix 1 for details.

79. See Appendix 1 for details.

80. *Die Feen* was composed by Wagner between 1833 and 1834.

81. Franz Fischer (1849–1918): German conductor. After a brief period as Hofkapellmeister at Mannheim (1877–1879), Fischer joined the staff of the Munich Hofoper, where he worked until his retirement in 1912.

82. Strauss, *Recollections and Reflections*, p. 130.

83. Ibid., p. 131.

84. Bülow and Strauss, *Hans von Bülow and Richard Strauss: Correspondence*, p. 24.

85. Although employed as full-time conductor between August 1886 and September 1889, Strauss managed to compose during that period *Aus Italien*, *Macbeth* (first and second

versions), the Violin Sonata, *Don Juan*, the incidental music to *Romeo und Julia*, *Festmarsch* in D major (second version), 'Winternacht', 'Lob des Leidens', 'Aus den Liedern der Trauer', 'Ständchen', 'Barcarolle', 'Nur Mut!', 'Wie sollen wir geheim sic halten', 'Schön sind, doch kalt die Himmelsterne', 'Mein Herz is stumm', 'Breit' über mein Haupt', 'Wozu noch, Mädchen, soll es frommen', 'Kornblumen', 'Mohnblumen', 'All' mein Gedanken', 'Du meines Herzens Krönelein', 'Ach weh mir unglückhaften Mann' and 'Ach Lieb, ich muss nun scheiden'.

86. Bülow and Strauss, *Hans von Bülow and Richard Strauss: Correspondence*, p. 141.

Chapter 3 *Enfant terrible*: Weimar (1889–1894) and *Don Juan*

1. Strauss's salary at Weimar was 2,100 Marks
2. Hans Bronsart von Schellendorf (1830–1915): German pianist, conductor, composer and administrator. Bronsart gave the première of Liszt's Piano Concerto No. 2, of which he is the dedicatee. After leaving Hanover, Bronsart was Intendant at Weimar between 1888 and 1895.
3. Eduard Lassen (1830–1904): Danish conductor and composer.
4. Much valuable information about Strauss's Weimar period was provided by the distinguished Strauss scholar Dr Kenneth Birkin.
5. The statistic of sixteen Abonnement concerts does not include the concerts that Strauss directed for the Liszt Stiftung nor those that he gave on behalf of the Hofkapelle's fund for widows and orphans.
6. See Chapter 2.
7. See Appendix 1 for details.
8. Bernhard Stavenhagen (1862–1914): German pianist and composer; Margarete Stern (1857–1899): German pianist; Karl Halir (1859–1909): Bohemian violinist.
9. See Appendix 1 for details of Strauss's other Mozart performances at Weimar.
10. See Appendix 1 for details.
11. See Appendix 1 for details of Strauss's performances of Wagner's works at Weimar.
12. See Appendix 1 for details of Strauss's three Liszt programmes at Weimar.
13. See Appendix 1 for details.
14. Heinrich Zeller (1856–1934): German tenor.
15. See Appendix 1 for details.
16. Whilst it has been claimed that *Don Juan* was composed between 1887 and 1888, Strauss stated that he 'invented' the initial themes during a visit to the monastery of S. Antonio (Padua) in 1888.
17. Strauss, 'Gibt es für die Musik eine Fortschrittspartei?', *Betrachtungen und Erinnerungen*, pp. 13–14. Translated by the present author.
18. T.W. Adorno, 'Richard Strauss at Sixty', trans. S. Gillespie, as found in *Richard Strauss and His World*, ed. Gilliam, p. 410.
19. Here, Strauss was referring to the Czech-born Viennese critic, Eduard Hanslick (1825–1904).
20. Bülow and Strauss, *Hans von Bülow and Richard Strauss: Correspondence*, pp. 82–3.
21. Strauss, 'Recollections of My Youth and Years of Apprenticeship', *Recollections and Reflections*, p. 139.
22. Alfred Kalisch (1863–1933): German-born English music critic.
23. A. Kalisch, 'Richard Strauss: The Man', as found in E. Newman, *Richard Strauss* (London, 1908), pp. 9–21.
24. C. Ehrlich, *First Philharmonic: a History of The Royal Philharmonic Society* (Oxford, 1995), p. 247.
25. Strauss's letter to his parents, dated 8 November [1889]. Translated by the present author.
26. Ibid.
27. Ibid.

28. The 1916 recording of *Don Juan* has to be excluded from any comparative analysis, as Strauss only recorded the third and fourth sides of the original four-record set; the first two sides were conducted by his assistant, George Szell. The 1947 recording is also incomplete. See also Chapter 9.

29. Strauss, 'Erinnerungen an die ersten Aufführungen meiner Opern', *Betrachtungen und Erinnerungen*, pp. 191–2.

30. O. Klemperer, ed. P. Heyworth, *Conversations with Klemperer* (London, 1985), p. 34.

31. P. Heyworth, *Otto Klemperer His Life and Times, Vol. 1: 1885–1933* (Cambridge, 1996), p. 48.

32. Bruno Walter (b. Bruno Schlesinger) (1876–1962): German conductor and pianist.

33. B. Walter, *Of Music and Music-Making*, trans. P. Hamburger (New York: Norton, 1961), pp. 136–140.

34. Otto Klemperer (1885–1973): German conductor and composer.

35. O. Klemperer, *Minor Recollections* (London: Dobson, 1964), p. 26.

36. Wilhelm Furtwängler (1886–1954): German conductor, pianist and composer.

37. W. Furtwängler, *Notebooks 1924–1954*, trans. S. Whiteside, ed. M. Tanner (London 1995), pp. 46–7.

38. Comments on the printed score of *Don Juan*, including metronome marks, refer to that by Edition Peters, Leipzig (Nr. 4191b).

39. Although this hypothesis is likely, the present writer recognises the possibility that this photograph might have been posed.

40. Rule 6 states: 'When you think that the brass are not playing loud enough, bring them down by two notches.' See Chapter 2.

41. George Szell (György Széll) (1897–1970): Hungarian-born American conductor. Szell's recording of *Don Juan* was released by Sony Classical SBK 48272.

42. N. Del Mar, *Richard Strauss A Critical Commentary on His Life and Works* Vol. I (London, 1986), p. 71.

43. Klemperer, ed. Heyworth, *Conversations with Klemperer*, p. 111.

44. For those commentators who believe that this tone poem is in rondo form, the passage between bar 160 and 196 inclusive is central to their argument.

45. In slow movements, Strauss increased the tempo at the bridge passage, returning to the tempo primo at the second subject, creating the illusion of a reduced tempo at the subsidiary theme.

46. The printed instructions are as follows: bar 90, *molto espress.* (clarinet I and horn I); bar 235, *sehr getragen und ausdrucksvoll* (oboe I); and bar 314, *molto espr. e marc.* (horns).

47. See Chapter 9.

48. The first subject and the material from bar 313 are accepted generally as being representative of Don Juan.

49. Strauss, 'Is There an Avant-garde in Music?', *Recollections and Reflections*, pp. 12–17.

50. At Weimar, Strauss performed 'Ständchen' (Heinrich Zeller, tenor) on 28 October 1889, 'Seitdem dein Aug' in meines schaute' and 'Nichts' (Heinrich Zeller, tenor) on 13 October 1890 and four Leider from *Lotosblätter* Op. 19 (Heinrich Giessen, tenor) on 6 November 1893.

51. See Appendix 1 for details.

52. Strauss's letter to Bülow, dated 30 January 1892. Bülow and Strauss, *Hans von Bülow and Richard Strauss: Correspondence*, p. 94.

53. Bülow's letter to Strauss, dated 1 February 1892. Ibid., p. 96.

54. Operas that were conducted by Strauss as part of a double-bill have been counted separately.

55. See Appendix 1 for details.

56. See Appendix 1 for details.

57. See Appendix 1 for details.

58. Apart from the 1892–1893 season, when he was away for much of that period.

59. See Appendix 1 for details.

60. During his period of convalescence, Strauss visited Egypt, Sicily and Corfu.
61. See Appendix 1 for details.
62. Originally, the world première of *Hänsel und Gretel* was to be given by Hermann Levi at the Munich Hofoper. As one of the singers for that production was indisposed, the first Munich performance had to be postponed until 30 December 1893.
63. Strauss, 'Reminiscences of the First Performance of my Operas', *Recollections and Reflections*, p. 147.
64. Franz Strauss's letter to Richard Strauss, dated 16 March 1893.
65. Bülow and Strauss, *Hans von Bülow and Richard Strauss: Correspondence*, p. 99.

CHAPTER 4 A MOZART MISSIONARY: SECOND MUNICH PERIOD (1894–1898) AND MOZART STYLE

1. At Munich, Richard was Pauline's vocal coach and Emilie Herzog was her singing teacher.
2. Friedrich Rösch (1862–1925): German lawyer and composer. Strauss dedicated *Tod und Verklärung* to Rösch.
3. Pauline continued to perform regularly until the birth of their son, Franz (1897–1980), but then gradually withdrew from public life in the first decade of the twentieth century.
4. The summer of 1894 was a particularly busy time for Strauss both professionally and personally. Along with his work at Bayreuth (see Chapter 8), he was also engaged as a guest conductor by the Munich Hofoper to conduct performances of *Tristan und Isolde* on 29 June and 22 August and *Die Meistersinger von Nürnberg* on 2 September.
5. See Appendix 1 for details. The statistic of 272 performances includes Strauss's performances of Beethoven's *Leonore* Overture No. 2 and Act 2 of *Fidelio* on 20 April 1898 to mark the silver wedding anniversary of Prince Leopold of Bavaria. Strauss also conducted the first part of a performance at the Hofoper on 31 January 1897 to mark the centenary of Schubert's birth but that performance is not included in the tally.
6. Strauss, 'Erinnerungen an die ersten Aufführungen meiner Opern', *Betrachtungen und Erinnerungen*, p. 178.
7. K. Wilhelm, *Richard Strauss: An Intimate Portrait*, trans. M. Whittall (London, 1989), p. 56.
8. Strauss, 'Reminiscences of the First Performance of my Operas', *Recollections and Reflections*, p. 148. Nevertheless, Strauss was very productive as a composer of orchestral music and song during his second Munich period and wrote amongst other works the tone poems *Till Eulenspiegel, Also sprach Zarathustra, Don Quixote*, the melodrama *Enoch Arden* and the groups of songs Op. 29, Op. 31, Op. 32. Op. 33, Op. 34, Op. 36, Op. 37 and Op. 39.
9. Ernst von Possart (1841–1921): German actor and theatre manager. Possart was manager of the Munich Theatre from 1875 and Intendant of the Royal Theatres from 1895 to 1905. For him, Strauss composed the melodramas *Enoch Arden* and *Das Schloss am Meere*, which they premièred at Munich and Berlin on 24 March 1897 and 23 March 1899 respectively.
10. See Appendix 1 for details.
11. See Appendix 1 for details.
12. See Appendix 1 for details.
13. See Appendix 1 for details.
14. Arthur Nikisch (1855–1922): Hungarian conductor
15. See Appendix 1 for details.
16. The composers included Schillings, Rubinstein, Rheinberger, Gilson, Bussmeyer and Strauss. See Appendix 1 for details.
17. The composers included Schillings, Ritter, Brahms and Strauss. See Appendix 1 for details.
18. Symphony No. 9 was performed outside of the Abonnement series and was given at a concert at which Strauss replaced an indisposed Franz Fischer. See Appendix 1 for details.

19. Strauss conducted the première of the new production of *Don Giovanni* on 29 May 1896. He had conducted two performances of an earlier production on 12 and 26 December 1895. See Appendix 1 for details.

20. At the Paris Opéra, *Don Giovanni* was given on 26 October 1896 and *Die Entführung aus dem Serail* on 4 December 1903. C. Dupêchez, *Histoire de L'Opéra de Paris* (Paris, 1984), pp. 331–406.

21. At Cologne, *Don Giovanni* was given in the 1905–1906 season, *Le nozze di Figaro* in the 1904–1905, 1907–1908, 1908–1909 and 1911–1912 seasons and *Die Zauberflöte* in the 1905–1906 season. G. Hagen, *Die Cölner Opera seit Ihrem einzug in das Opernhaus 1902/03–1911/12* (Cöln am Rhein, date unknown), pp.17 and 48. The archive of Oper der Stadt Köln was destroyed during the 1939–1945 war. Letter to the author from the archivist of Oper der Stadt Köln, dated 30 November 1993.

22. Of the ninety-six performances, sixty-seven were of *Don Giovanni*, twenty-five were of *Le nozze di Figaro*, one was of *Die Zauberflöte*, and three were of *Bastien und Bastienne*, H. Rosenthal, *Two Centuries of Opera at Covent Garden* (London, 1958) pp. 716–762.

23. During the course of his career, Strauss conducted 328 performances of Mozart's operas.

24. *Bastien und Bastienne* was heard at Weimar in a double bill with Humperdinck's *Hänsel und Gretel*. The production of *Bastien und Bastienne* at the Royal Opera House, Covent Garden, London in 1907, was also coupled with *Hänsel und Gretel*. These performances were a direct result of the Weimar productions, which Strauss conducted (H Rosenthal, *Two Centuries of Opera at Covent Garden*, pp. 322 and 364). Later, in 1924, Strauss gave five performances of *Bastien und Bastienne* at the Vienna Staatsoper. See Appendix 1 for details.

25. *Così fan tutte* received its British première at the Haymarket Theatre, London, in 1811, and it was revived by Sir Thomas Beecham at His Majesty's Theatre, London, in 1911.

26. Sir Georg Solti (1912–1997): Hungarian-born British conductor.

27. G. Kobbe, *Kobbe's Complete Opera Book* (London, 1987), pp. 79 and 103.

28. The basis for these reforms was set out in Possart's article, *Ueber die Neueinstudierung und Neuinszenierung des Mozart'schen Don Giovanni (Don Juan) auf dem kgl. Residenztheater zu München* (Munich, 1896). A translation of part of this article can be found in Appendix 2.

29. By performing the Prague version of *Don Giovanni*, Strauss and Possart reinstated the epilogue, which had fallen from favour during the nineteenth century.

30. Strauss, 'Die Münchener Oper', *Betrachtungen und Erinnerungen*, p. 97. Translated by the present author.

31. Strauss's response to the announcement by the Senior Burgomaster of Munich of the establishment of a Richard Strauss scholarship at the University of Munich in 1949. F. Trenner, 'Richard Strauss and Munich', *Tempo*, Summer 1964, p. 12.

32. The earlier score of *Don Giovanni* (edited by B. Gugler, the first edition to be based on the autograph, published by F. E. C. Leuckart of Leipzig in 1869) is now held at the Bayerische Staatsbibliothek in Munich. Owned by the Munich Hofoper, it was used by a number of conductors and is marked heavily by them. It is difficult, therefore, to disentangle Strauss's markings from those of his colleagues.

33. Breitkopf & Härtel's *Wolfgang Amadeus Mozart's Werke. Kritisch durchgesehene Gesammtausgabe* was issued between January 1877 and December 1883 in twenty-four series. The edition was conceived by Ludwig Ritter von Köchel, the editor of the *Köchel Verzeichnis*. The editors included Brahms, Joachim, Reinecke and Wüllner.

34. Alfred Einstein (1880–1952): German-born American musicologist and critic.

35. W. A. Mozart, *Don Giovanni*, ed. A. Einstein, Ernst Eulenburg (London, 1930), p. xxvi.

36. Strauss, references to the autograph are to be found in the two Finales; Act 2, Scene VII, No. 6, the Sextet, 'Sola, sola in bujo loco'; the recitative, Act 2, Scene X^e, 'In qual eccessi, o Numi'; the recitative, Act 2, Scene XI, 'Ah ah ah ah, questa è buona!', and the placement of the personal pronoun, 'mia', in bar 11 of the recitative and aria, Act 2, No. 10, 'Crudele!' Numbering in this footnote refers to the Eulenburg edition of *Don Giovanni*.

37. Scene and bar numbers correspond to Einstein's Eulenburg edition of *Don Giovanni*.
38. Here, Strauss adds an upbeat quaver *d′*, followed by a dotted crotchet-quaver *g*, succeeded by an octave leap on *a* at the third and fourth beats and resolved by a *d* at the first beat of the new bar. The dotted crotchet-quaver figure is clearly a mistake by Strauss and it should read dotted quaver-semi-quaver. See Appendix 5, Score Example 1.
39. E. von Possart, *Ueber die Neueinstudierung und Neuinszenierung des Mozart'schen Don Giovanni* (Munich, 1896).
40. F. P. Lyser, 'Mozart's eigene Berdeutschung des Textes "Don Giovanni", nebst zwei Proben daraus', *Neue Zeitschrift für Musik*, No. 32, 19 April 1845, pp. 173–5, and 'Zweier Meister Söhne (Schlub)', *Neue Zeitschrift für Musik*, No. 44, 28 November 1844 [*sic*], pp. 133–4.
41. Above bars 2–4 of Act 2, Scene Xe, No. 8c, Strauss also writes 'nur diese im Autograph erhalten' ('only this is found in the autograph').
42. This numbering (No. 24) relates to the *Gesammtausgabe* score.
43. Mozart, ed. Einstein, *Don Giovanni*, p. xx.
44. The Donaueschingen copy, made by Anton Grams, under the supervision of Mozart, is of some importance, as it resolves the question of the trombones in Act 2; the instruments can be found in this copy. Einstein notes that his attention was drawn to the Donaueschingen copy by the English scholar, Edward J. Dent but fails to say when. Ibid., p. xxviii.
45. Ibid., p. xx.
46. Ibid., p. xiii.
47. See H.C. Robbins Landon, *Haydn in England 1791–1795* (London, 1976–80), p. 526. Rosen states: 'the sense of form in the finales is very similar to that in the symphonies and chamber music.' C. Rosen, *The Classical Style: Haydn, Mozart, Beethoven* (London, 1976), p. 304.
48. E. J. Dent, *Mozart's Operas: A Critical Study* (Oxford, 1991), p. 174.
49. Strauss, 'On Mozart's *Così fan tutte*', in *Recollections and Reflections*, pp. 72–4.
50. Mozart notes, in the autograph of *Così fan tutte*, housed in Berlin, that the aria may be cut. Strauss was either unaware of this instruction, or, perhaps, felt due to the nineteenth century's propensity for dismembering this work, that it should be included.
51. Strauss, 'On Mozart's *Così fan tutte*', *Recollections and Reflections*, pp. 72–4.
52. Edward J. Dent (1876–1957): British scholar, journalist and translator.
53. Dent, *Mozart's Operas*, p. 190.
54. R. Osborne, *Conversations with Karajan*, p. 43.
55. Donald F. Tovey (1875–1940): British music analyst, writer, pianist and composer.
56. D. F. Tovey, *Essays in Musical Analysis* (vol. VI) (Oxford, 1957), p. 30.
57. Strauss's extant marked score of *Così fan tutte* is in the Richard Strauss-Archiv, Garmisch-Partenkirchen.
58. In his annotated score of *Così fan tutte*, Strauss marks 'vi–de' above the stave in No. 6, bars 46 to 75; from the end of No. 6 to the end of No. 7; No. 11, bars 15 (second half) to 55 (second half); No. 14, bars 101 (second beat) to 109 (second beat); No 18, bars 23 to 54; No. 24, bars 23 to 33 and bars 57 to 92 (Strauss also marks alternative endings at bars 80 and 92); No. 25, bars 80 to 94; No. 26, bars 108 (second half) to 136 (second half); No. 28, bars 32 to 63 and bars 79 to 91, and No. 29, bars 39 to 57 and bars 105 (second half) to 115 (second half). If Strauss had sanctioned the above cuts, substantial gaps in the score would have resulted. As these cuts would have been contrary to Strauss's writings and detrimental to his reforms, it is probable that they were for reference only.
59. Franz Trenner (1915–1992): German musicologist.
60. Interview with the author, Munich, 13 May 1992.
61. Strauss, 'On Mozart's *Così fan tutte*', *Recollections and Reflections*, pp. 72–4.
62. Hugo von Hofmannsthal (1874–1929): Austrian poet, dramatist and librettist.

63. Strauss's letter to Hofmannsthal, dated 20 July 1909. R. Strauss and H. von Hofmannsthal, ed. F. and A. Strauss, arr. W. Schuh, trans. H. Hammelmann and E. Osers *The Correspondence Between Richard Strauss and Hugo von Hofmannsthal*, (Cambridge, 1980), p. 43.

64. Interview with the author. London, 12 December 1991. Trenner also pointed out, however, that when a fortepiano was unavailable, Strauss chose a harpsichord as an alternative instrument.

65. W. Sawallisch, *Im Interesse der Deutlichkeit: Mein Leben mit der Musik* (Hamburg, 1988), pp. 29–30.

66. For information about Strauss's recordings, see Chapter 9.

67. Between 18 October 1885 and 6 August 1943, Strauss gave more than 470 professional performances of Mozart's music.

68. Sir Adrian Boult (1889–1983): British conductor.

69. M. Kennedy, *Adrian Boult* (London, 1987), p. 58.

70. In his commercial recording of Symphony No. 39, for example, the Introduction's opening speed ($\flat$=96) is linked to that of the first movement's second subject ($\flat$=48) and to the overall tempo of the last movement ($\flat$=144), while the speed of the Introduction at bar 21 ($\flat$=104) is related to both the first movement's first subject ($\flat$=52) and the tempo of the second movement's bridge passage ($\flat$=104). See Chapter 9.

71. H.C. Robbins Landon, *Haydn in England 1791–1795* (London, 1976–1980), p. 526.

72. Recorded in 1926 with the Berlin Staatskapelle. Koch Legacy 3-7076-2 H1. See Chapter 9.

73. Nikolaus Harrnoncourt (b. 1929): Austrian conductor and cellist.

74. N. Harnoncourt, *The Musical Dialogue*, trans. M. O'Neill (London, 1989), p. 95.

75. Live recordings of Mozart's last three symphonies, recorded in the Musikvereinsaal, Vienna, on the 200th anniversary of Mozart's death, 5 December 1991. The orchestra was the Chamber Orchestra of Europe. Teldec 9031-74858-2.

76. N. Zaslaw, *Mozart's Symphonies* (Oxford, 1989), p. 500.

77. Harnoncourt, *The Musical Dialogue*, pp. 104–5.

78. Recorded with the Berlin Staatskapelle. Koch Legacy 3-7076-2 H1. See Chapter 9.

79. Recorded with the Berlin Staatskapelle. Koch Legacy 3-7119-2 H1. See Chapter 9.

80. See Appendix 5, Score Example 2.

81. *Musical Opinion and Music Trade Review*, August 1914, p. 905, 'Capriccio'.

82. *The Musical Times*, 1 August 1914, p. 541.

83. Strauss writes 'When performing Mozart there should be a difference between (particularly quick) movements – in these the *cantabile* second subject should be taken a little more slowly [*ruhiger*] (*Figaro* overture, first movement of the G minor symphony) – and (mostly slow) movements …'. Strauss, 'Dirigentenerfahrungen mit klassischen Meisterwerken', *Betrachtungen und Erinnerungen*, p. 55. Translated by the present author.

84. R. Wagner, trans. F. Dannreuther, *On Conducting* (London, 1919), pp. 42–3. [R. Wagner, *Über das Dirigieren* (Leipzig, 1869)]

85. Ibid, pp. 52–3.

86. Ibid., pp. 60–2.

87. See Appendix 5, Score Example 3.

88. See Appendix 5, Score Example 4.

89. See Appendix 5, Score Example 4.

90. Strauss, 'Dirigentenerfahrungen mit klassischen Meisterwerken', p. 56. Translated by the present author.

91. See Appendix 5, Score Example 5.

92. See Appendix 5, Score Example 5.

93. See Appendix 5, Score Example 6.

94. L. Salter, *Gramophone*, December 1991, p. 158.

95. Fritz Busch (1890–1951): German conductor; Sir John Pritchard (1918–1989): British conductor.
96. See R. Holden, *Richard Strauss: the Origin, Dissemination and Reception of his Mozart Renaissance*, Ph.D. dissertation, University of London, 1995.

CHAPTER 5 *CAUSE CÉLÈBRE*: ERSTER KÖNIGLICHER KAPELLMEISTER AT BERLIN (1898–1908) AND *SALOME*

1. *Ein Heldenleben* has two endings, the first of which was completed on 1 December 1898 and the second ending (the one usually played) on 18 December 1898.
2. Germany's copyright law dated from 1870.
3. Hans Zincke (1837–1922): German composer and scientist.
4. The new copyright laws in Germany came into force in 1901.
5. Bülow's letter to his daughter, Daniela, dated 17 August 1887. H. von Bülow, *Letters of Hans von Bülow to Richard Wagner and Others*, ed. S. Goddard, trans. H. Walter (New York, 1979).
6. Rosa Sucher (1849–1927): German soprano. Rosa Sucher (née Hasselbeck) married Josef in 1876.
7. Karl Muck conducted *Parsifal* at the Bayreuth Festival in 1901, 1902, 1906, 1908, 1909, 1911, 1912, 1914, 1924, 1925, 1927, 1928 and 1930.
8. Königsberg (now Kaliningrad) is today part of Russia and Danzig (now Gdansk) is part of Poland.
9. The Vienna Hofoper became the Vienna Staatsoper after the fall of the monarchy in 1919.
10. See Chapter 2.
11. C. Flesch, trans and ed. H. Keller, *The Memoirs of Carl Flesch* (London, 1957), p. 151.
12. Sir Henry J. Wood (1869–1944): English conductor, organist and singing teacher.
13. H. J. Wood, *My Life of Music* (London, 1938), pp. 151–2.
14. Strauss's letter to his father, dated 22 November 1898.
15. See Appendix 1 for details.
16. See Appendix 1 for details.
17. See Appendix 1 for details.
18. See Appendix 1.
19. Strauss had yet to conduct *Parsifal* because of the 'Bayreuth copyright'.
20. Strauss spent the summer of 1899 composing at his in-law's home at Marquartstein. Amongst the works composed were 'Soldatenlied' O.Op. 93, Fünf Lieder Op. 41, Zwei Männerchöre Op. 42, Drei Gesänge älterer deutscher Dichter Op. 43, the first of the Zwei grössere Gesänge Op. 44 ('Notturno') and Drei Männerchöre Op. 45.
21. For details of Strauss's Mozart performances at the Hofoper during the 1899–1900 season, see Appendix 1.
22. On 8 July 1900 at Elberfeld, Strauss conducted Liszt's 'Dante' Symphony and his own *Meinem Kinde*, *Muttertändelei*, *Wiegenlied* (Pauline de Ahna-Strauss, soprano) and *Ein Heldenleben*.
23. Strauss performed Berlioz's Overture to *Benvenuto Cellini* and an unidentified aria (Hans Giessen, tenor) at Weimar on 6 November 1893 and the Overture at Munich on 29 November 1895
24. Strauss's letter to his father, dated 14 October 1900.
25. The new productions conducted by Strauss during the 1900–1901 season were Berlioz's *Benvenuto Cellini*, Cornelius's *Der Barbier von Bagdad*, Verdi's *Falstaff* and Saint-Saëns's *Samson et Dalila*. The new production of *Falstaff* was heard first on 9 February 1901 and was given in memory of Verdi, who had died two weeks earlier on 27 January. See Appendix 1 for details.
26. Ernst Freiherr von Wolzogen (1855–1934): German critic and writer.
27. Hans Heinrich XIV, Bolko Graf von Hochberg (1843–1926): Germany politician, theatre administrator and composer.

28. Strauss, *Recollections and Reflections*, p. 149.
29. H. Blaukopf, ed., E. Jephcott, trans,. *Gustav Mahler/Richard Strauss, Correspondence 1888–1911*, (London, 1984), p. 52.
30. Here, Mahler is referring to a passage near the end of the Opera.
31. Blaukopf, *Gustav Mahler/Richard Strauss, Correspondence*, p. 53.
32. Ibid., p. 61.
33. Anton Brioschi (1855–1920): Austrian artist and scenic designer.
34. Here, Strauss means Heinrich Lefler (1863–1919): Austrian painter, decorative artist and printmaker.
35. Blaukopf, *Gustav Mahler/Richard Strauss, Correspondence*, p. 66.
36. Strauss completed 'Junggesellenschwur' from Op. 49 on 11 May 1900 at Berlin and the remainder of the songs from that group 'Waldseligkeit', 'In goldener Fülle', 'Wiegenliedchen', 'Das Lied des Steinklopfers', 'Sie wissen's nicht', 'Wer lieben will, muss leiden' and 'Ach was Kummer, Qual und Schmerzen' there on 21, 13, 20, 24, 14, 23 and 23 September 1901 respectively. 'Das Tal' from Op. 51 was completed at Berlin on 11 December 1902 and its companion piece, 'Der Einsame', was finished there on 18 February 1906. The orchestral version of 'Waldseligkeit' was completed at Garmisch on 24 June 1918.
37. With the Berlin Philharmonic, Strauss conducted a concert for the Berlin and Berlin-Potsdam Wagner Vereine on 2 November 1896 in the Philharmonic (Liszt's *Mazeppa*, Wolf's Prelude and Entr'acte from *Der Corregidor*, Strauss's *Gesang der Apollopriesterin und Verführung* [Rosa Sucher, soprano] and *Till Eulenspiegel* and Wagner's *Eine Faust-Ouvertüre* and Prelude and Liebestod from *Tristan und Isolde*), a concert at Hamburg on tour on 4 November 1897 (Mozart's Symphony No. 41, Wagner's Prelude and Liebestod from *Tristan und Isolde*, Liszt's 'Mephisto' Waltz and Strauss's *Don Juan*), a concert for the Berlin Wagner-Verein on 5 December 1898 in the Philharmonie (Wagner's Prelude to *Die Meistersinger von Nürnberg*, Othegraven's *Unheilbar*, Strauss's 'Hymnus' [Karl Scheidemantel, baritone], 'Pilgers Morgenlied' [Karl Scheidemantel, baritone] and *Don Quixote* [Anton Hekking, cello and Fridolin Klingler, viola] and Wagner's Act 3 from *Tannhäuser* [Ida Hiedler, soprano, Ludwig Müller, tenor, Karl Scheidemantel, baritone, the Sängerbund des Lehrervereins and the Boys' Choir of the Königstädtischen Gymnasium]), three concerts for the Berlin and Berlin-Potsdam Wagner-Vereine on 4 December 1899 in the Philharmonie (Wagner's *Eine Faust-Ouvertüre*, Strauss's 'Rosenband', 'Liebeshymnus', 'Morgen' and 'Cäcilie' [Pauline Strauss-Ahna, soprano] and *Also sprach Zarathustra*, Schillings's Prelude to Act 3 from *Der Pfeifertag*, Wagner's 'Gralserzählung' from *Lohengrin* and Prelude and Finale from *Parsifal* and Sommer's 'Gnomenreigen' and 'Siegeszug der Feen' from *Das Schloss der Herzen*), 19 February 1900 in the Philharmonie (Ritter's *Sursum corda*, Berlioz's *Le Cinq Mai*, excerpts from Wagner's *Parsifal* and *Götterdämmerung* and Beethoven's Symphony No. 9 [Emma Rückbeil-Hiller, soprano, Luise Geller-Wolter, mezzo-soprano, Wilhelm Grüning, tenor, Baptist Hoffmann, bass and the Lehrer- und Lehrerinnen-Gesangvereine]) and 9 April 1900 (Berlioz's 'Rob Roy' Overture, three Lieder from Mahler's *Des Knaben Wunderhorn* [Emilie Herzog, soprano], Berlioz's *Le Cinq Mai*, Wagner's *Kaisermarsch* and Beethoven's Symphony No. 9 [Emilie Herzog, soprano, Jenny Alexander, mezzo-soprano, Wilhelm Grüning, tenor, Baptist Hoffmann, bass and the Lehrer- und Lehrerinnen-Gesangvereine]), a concert for the Verein zur Förderung der Kunst on 19 March 1900 in the Philharmonie (Strauss's *Tod und Verklärung* and *Ein Heldenleben* [with Hans Pfitzner conducting excerpts from his own *Die Rose vom Liebesgarten*]) and a concert for the Berlin and Berlin-Potsdam Wagner-Vereine on 3 December 1900 in the Philharmonie (Wagner's Overture and Monologue from *Der fliegende Holländer* [Baptist Hoffmann, bass], Liszt's *Orpheus* and Strauss's 'Notturno', 'Nächtlicher Gesang' [Baptist Hofmann, bass], 'Meinem Kinde', 'Muttertändelei', 'Wiegenlied' [Pauline Strauss-de Ahna, soprano] [with Siegmund von Hausegger conducting his own *Barbarossa*]). With the Berlin Hofkapelle, Strauss conducted *Ein Heldenleben* on 22 March 1899 (Weingartner

conducted Mendelssohn-Bartholdy's *Ein Sommernachtstraum*, Weber's Overture to *Der Freischütz* and Mozart's Symphony No. 41), Beethoven's Symphony No. 3 ('Eroica') on 6 March 1899 (Karl Muck conducted Perosi's *The Raising of Lazarus*, Weber's Overture to *Der Freischütz* and Wagner's *Kaisermarsch*) and *Tod und Verklärung* on 4 January 1901 (Weingartner conducted Berger's Symphony No. 2, Mendelssohn-Bartholdy's 'Hebrides' Overture and Beethoven's Symphony No. 5).

38. Blaukopf, *Gustav Mahler/Richard Strauss, Correspondence*, p. 75.
39. For a detailed account of the Berlin Tonkünstler-Orchestra, see K. Birkin, ' ". . .wollen sehen, ob's gelingt" Richard Strauss and the Berlin Tonkünstler-Orchester', *Richard Strauss-Blätter* (Vienna, December 2001), Heft 46, pp. 3–60. Karl Gleitz (1862–1920): German composer and conductor.
40. Karl Kampf, *Allgemeine Deutsche Musik-Zeitung*, 23 November 1900, p.706. Walter's programme with the Berlin Tonkünstler-Orchestra comprised the March from Pfitzner's *Die Rose vom Liebesgarten*, Berlioz's *Symphonie fantastique*, Wagner's Overture to *Der fliegende Holländer* and Beethoven's Violin Concerto (Willy Burmester, violin).
41. Blaukopf, *Gustav Mahler/Richard Strauss, Correspondence*, p. 75.
42. Ibid., p. 55.
43. Ibid., p. 59.
44. The soprano for Strauss's performance of Symphony No. 4 was the Austrian singer and actress, Thila Plaichinger (1868–1939). Plaichinger later sang the title role in the first Berlin performance of Strauss's *Elektra* under Leo Blech on 15 February 1909.
45. For the Posen concert on 18 February 1902, Strauss records in his engagement books a fee of 700 Marks, while for the concerts in Halle and Stettin on 19 February and 18 March 1902 respectively he records a fee of 300 Marks.
46. The only concert that contained no music by Liszt during the 1901–1902 season was that given at the Kroll Opera on 24 March 1902. See Appendix 1 for details.
47. See Appendix 1 for details.
48. See R. Holden, *The Virtuoso Conductors: the Central European Tradition from Wagner to Karajan* (New Haven and London, 2005).
49. Willy Levin (1860–1926): German businessman.
50. Statistically, the 1902–1903 season resembled earlier years. Strauss conducted eighty-seven performances of twenty-nine works by sixteen composers. See Appendix 1 for details.
51. Strauss's letter to his father from Hamburg, dated 12 January 1903. Translated by the present author.
52. Ibid.
53. After the 1903–1904 season, Strauss conducted only one further performance of *Feuersnot* during his tenure, on 3 April 1917.
54. See Appendix 1 for details.
55. See Chapter 8.
56. Carl Burrian (1870–1924): Czech tenor. Burrian sang the rôle of Herodias at the première of *Salome*.
57. Marie Wittich (1868–1931): German soprano.
58. Strauss, *Recollections and Reflections*, pp. 150–1.
59. Georg Hülsen-Haeseler (1858–1922): German theatre administrator.
60. Strauss, *Recollections and Reflections*, p. 152.
61. Gustav Piffl (1864–1932): Archbishop of the Archdiocese of Vienna.
62. A. Rubinstein, *My Young Years* (London, 1973), p. 221
63. Olive Fremstad (1871–1951): Swedish-born American mezzo-soprano.
64. Rubinstein, *My Young Years*, pp. 221–2.
65. Romain Rolland (1866–1944): French writer.
66. Rolland's letter to Strauss from Paris, dated 1 December 1906. R. Myers, ed., *Richard Strauss & Romain Rolland: Correspondence and Diary Fragments* (London, 1968), p. 79.
67. Strauss conducted a second performance of *Feuersnot* at Munich on 28 December 1905.

68. Strauss conducted *Salome* at Graz on 16 and 18 May 1906, Prague on 22 May 1906, Cologne on 2 July 1906, Turin on 22, 23, 26, 27, 28, 29 and 30 December 2006, Paris on 8, 11, 14, 17, 21, 24 May 1907, Amsterdam on 16 November 1907, Rotterdam on 20 November 1907, Arnhem on 21 November 1907, Naples on 1, 3, 5, 10 February 1908 and Warsaw on 20 February 1908.

69. Strauss, *Recollections and Reflections*, p. 153

70. Romain Rolland's letter to Richard Strauss from Paris, dated 14 May 1907. Myers, ed., *Richard Strauss & Romain Rolland: Correspondence and Diary Fragments*, p. 82.

71. During the 1906–1907 season at the Berlin Hofoper, Strauss conducted sixty-five performances, of which nineteen were of *Salome*, and, during the 1907–1908 season, he gave sixty-one performances, of which sixteen were of *Salome*.

72. On their 1908 tour, Strauss and the Berlin Philharmonic performed in Hanover on 23 April, Düsseldorf on 24 April, Paris on 26 and 27 April, Bordeaux on 28 April, Madrid on 30 April and 1 and 2 May, Lisbon on 4, 5, 6 and 7 May, Porto on 8 and 9 May, Bilbao on 11 and 12 May, San Sebastian on 13 May, Barcelona on 15, 16 and 17 May, Marseille on 19 May, Lyon on 20 May, Geneva on 21 May, Lausanne on 22 May, Neuchâtel on 23 May, Bern on 24 May, Basel on 25 May, Freiburg on 26 May, Karlsruhe on 27 May, Saarbrücken on 28 May and Wiesbaden on 29 May. The touring repertoire comprised Beethoven's Symphonies Nos. 3 ('Eroica'), 5, 7 and 8, Berlioz's 'Le Roi Lear' Overture and Overture to *Benvenuto Cellini*, Liszt's 'Hungarian' Rhapsody No. 1 and *Les Préludes*, Mozart's Symphony No. 41 ('Jupiter'), Strauss's *Tod und Verklärung, Till Eulenspiegel* and *Don Juan*, Wagner's Prelude to *Die Meistersinger von Nürnberg*, Overture, Venusberg Music and Bacchanal from *Tannhäuser*, Prelude to *Lohengrin*, Prelude and Liebestod from *Tristan und Isolde*, Overture to *Der fliegende Holländer* and 'Karfreitagszauber' from *Parsifal* and Weber's Overture to *Oberon*.

73. Strauss, *Recollections and Reflections*, p. 152.

CHAPTER 6 AT THE SUMMIT: GENERALMUSIKDIREKTOR AT BERLIN (1908–1920) AND BEETHOVEN STYLE

1. The Berlin Philharmonic was founded 1882 by 54 musicians as the Frühere Bilsesche Kapelle ('Bilse's Former Orchestra') and was reorganized financially in 1887 by the Berlin agent, Hermann Wolff.

2. With the fall of the German Monarchy in 1918, the Berlin Hofkapelle became the Berlin Staatskapelle.

3. Wilhelm Taubert (1811–1891) led the Berlin Hofkapelle's Subscription Concerts from 1842 to 1883, Robert Radecke (1830–1911) from 1883 to 1886, Ludwig Deppe (1828–1890) from 1887 to 1888 and Heinrich Kahl (1839–1892) together with Josef Sucher from 1888 to 1891.

4. Weingartner made his début at the Berlin Hofoper with Wagner's *Lohengrin* on 22 May 1891.

5. F. Weingartner, trans. M. Wolff, *Buffets and Rewards*, (London, 1937), p. 191.

6. Ibid.

7. With Karl Muck, Strauss was named Generalmusikdirektor in Berlin on 26 August 1908.

8. See Appendix 1 for details.

9. See Appendix 1 details.

10. Blaukopf, *Gustav Mahler/Richard Strauss, Correspondence*, p. 100.

11. As found in Wilhelm, *Richard Strauss: An Intimate Portrait*, p. 56.

12. See Appendix 1 for details.

13. See Appendix 1 for details.

14. As found in Wilhelm, *Richard Strauss: An Intimate Portrait*, p. 82.

15. On 1 December 1872, the Vienna Philharmonic under Otto Dessoff (1835–1892) performed Weber's Overture to *Oberon*, Mozart's Piano Concerto No. 25 (Josef Labor, piano), Lachner's Andantino and Gavotte from Suite No. 6 and Beethoven's Symphony

No. 4 and, on 26 November 1882, Wilhelm Jahn (1835–1900) led the Orchestra in a programme that included Beethoven's Overture to *Coriolan*, Mozart's Piano Concerto No. 20 (Vladimir von Pachmann, piano) and Schumann's Symphony No. 1 ('Spring').

16. Artur Schnabel (1882–1951): Austrian pianist, composer and teacher.
17. Albert Gutmann (1852–1915): Austrian publisher and music retailer.
18. A. Schnabel, *My Life and Music* (New York, 1988), p. 9.
19. See Appendix 1 for details.
20. 2 April was the birthday of Herzog Georg II von Sachsen-Meiningen, the patron of the Meininger Hofkapelle.
21. Strauss's two sets of marked scores of Beethoven's symphonies are still owned by the Strauss family and are housed at the Richard Strauss-Archiv in Garmisch-Partenkirchen. Both scores of Symphony No. 5 are heavily marked and both contain rehearsal letters inserted by Strauss. It is difficult to determine accurately, therefore, which score he used for the recording. Access to these scores was kindly granted by the composer's grandson, the late Richard Strauss, and his wife, Gabriele Strauss.
22. Friedrich Chrysander (1826–1901): German music historian, editor and critic.
23. Front endpapers, Strauss's marked score (Chrysander edition) of Beethoven's Symphony No. 1.
24. 'Dieser Satz muss durchgängig stürmischen, in höchster Erregung dahinbrausenden Charakter haben, darum verwerfe ich auch jede Verbreiterung der Anfangstakte. Alle Achtelfiguren mit Akzent auf dem ersten (resp. 2.ten) Achtel spielen. Am Anfang empfiehlt sich, keinen Auftakt zu geben, sondern nur rapid das erste Viertel anzuschlagen, sonst kann es passieren, dass man hört: 𝄞 ♪ ♪♪♪♪ | ♩.
25. See Appendix 5, Score Example 7. (In his Eulenburg score, Strauss writes 'Die beiden letzten Achtel dürfen nicht "verschluckt" werden!').
26. See Appendix 5, Score Example 8.
27. Sir John Barbirolli (1899–1970): British conductor and cellist; Clemens Krauss (1893–1954): Austrian conductor.
28. See Appendix 5, Score Examples 9 and 10.
29. See Appendix 5, Example 11.
30. See Appendix 5, Score Example 12.
31. See Appendix 5, Score Example 13.
32. Strauss, *Recollections and Reflections*, p. 38.
33. 'Die vorgenommenen Abmilderungen des Blechs scheinen in diesem Satze mir unbedingt nötig!' See Appendix 5, Score Example 14.
34. Strauss seems to have changed his mind about this, as the earlier Chrysander score includes Wagner's suggested alteration to the trumpet part.
35. 'Alles Wesentliche über diese Symphonie ist von Rich. Wagner. Bezüglich der Wagnerschen Orchesterretouchen möchte ich persönlich von den Trompetenveränderungen des Anfangs des letzten Satzes abraten. Original ist charakteristischer und klingt weniger "modern"! Ganz zu verwerfen sind die von Gustav Mahler (wenn auch in guter Absicht!) vorgenommenen Vergröberungen!'.
36. See Appendix 5, Score Example 15.
37. See Appendix 5, Score Examples 16 and 17.
38. See Appendix 5, Score Example 18.
39. R. Wagner, trans. E. Dannreuther, *On Conducting* (London, 1919), p. 11.
40. Frieda Hempel (1885–1955): German soprano.
41. Unidentified review dated 6 December 1917 by a librarian. Review kindly supplied by the Berlin Staatsoper. Translated by the present author.
42. The constituent assembly of the new republic met at Weimar in February 1919 and Friedrich Ebert was elected President.
43. Unidentified review dated 25 April 1919 by a librarian. Review kindly supplied by the Berlin Staatsoper. Translated by the present author.

44. Unidentified and undated review kindly supplied by the Berlin Staatsoper. Translated by the present author.
45. A. Einstein, 'Strauss and Hofmannsthal', *Essays on Music*, (London, 1958), p. 252. By 'the piano concerto', Einstein presumably means either the *Parergon zur Symphonia domestica* (1925) or the *Panathenäenzug* for piano and orchestra (1926–1927).
46. Strauss, *Recollections and Reflections*, p. 155.
47. Cleofonte Campanini (1860–1919): Italian conductor and violinist.
48. *Elektra* was given in Munich under Felix Mottl on 14 February 1909, Berlin under Leo Blech on 15 February, Hamburg under Gustav Brecher on 22 February, Vienna under Hugo Reichenberger on 24 March and Milan under Eduardo Vitale on 6 April.
49. On 18 January 1915, Strauss coupled *Don Juan* with *Elektra*.
50. See Appendix 1 for details.
51. *Der Rosenkavalier* was given in Mainz and Zurich on 15 February 1911, in Hamburg on 22 February, in Milan on 1 March and in Prague on 4 March.
52. On 23 December 1912, Strauss conducted *Der Rosenkavalier* for the first time at the Berlin Hofoper.
53. After conducting the 1916 version of *Ariadne auf Naxos* for the first time at the Berlin Hofoper on 17 February 1917, he gave no further performances of the 1912 version at that house.
54. Letter from Hofmannsthal to Strauss, dated 1 August 1918. Strauss and Hofmannsthal, *The Correspondence between Richard Strauss and Hugo von Hofmannsthal*, pp. 307–9.
55. Ibid.
56. Letter from Strauss to Hofmannsthal, dated 5 August 1918. Ibid., pp. 309–311.
57. Ibid.
58. Ibid.
59. Georg Dröscher (1854–1944): German opera producer.

CHAPTER 7 A POISONED CHALICE: VIENNA STAATSOPER AND THE PERFORMING VERSION OF MOZART'S *IDOMENEO*

1. The Austrian republic was proclaimed on 12 November 1918.
2. Strauss, *Recollections and Reflections*, p. 166.
3. Lotte Lehmann (1888–1976): German soprano. Lehmann sang the roles of the Composer for the première of the 1916 version of *Ariadne auf Naxos*, the Dyer's Wife in *Die Frau ohne Schatten* in 1919 and Christine in *Intermezzo* in 1924.
4. Hans Gregor (1866–1945): German opera director and administrator; he led the Vienna Hofoper between 1910 and 1918.
5. L. Lehmann, trans. M. Ludwig, *Wings of Song: an Autobiography* (London, 1938), p. 149.
6. See Chapter 6.
7. See Appendix 1 for details.
8. During Strauss's Vienna tenure, he composed only a handful of significant works, including *Drei Hymnen von Friedrich Hölderlin* Op. 71 (written between 2 January and 6 April 1921 in Vienna), *Schlagobers* Op. 70 (completed on 16 September 1922 in Garmisch), *Tanzsuite aus Klavierstücken von Francois Couperin* O.Op 107 (completed in Vienna on 6 January 1923), *Intermezzo* Op. 72 (completed at Buenos Aires on 21 August 1923) and his performing version of Beethoven's *Die Ruinen von Athen* (completed at Garmisch in 1924).
9. Alfred Roller (1864–1935): Austrian designer. Roller worked at the Vienna Hofoper with Gustav Mahler and later at the Staatsoper. He designed the premières of Strauss's *Der Rosenkavalier* (Dresden, 1911) and *Die Frau ohne Schatten* (Vienna, 1919) and Strauss's performing versions of Beethoven's *Die Ruinen von Athen* (Vienna, 1924) and Mozart's *Idomeneo* (Vienna, 1931).
10. Guido Adler (1855–1941), musicologist and Professor at the Universities of Prague and Vienna, wrote in 1914: '*Così fan tutte, Die Zauberflöte, Die Entführung aus dem Serail,*

Le Nozze di Figaro, Don Giovanni – each in succession was rejuvenated, and above all it was these performances in Vienna which brought about the Mozart renaissance.' G. Adler, 'Gustav Mahler', *Gustav Mahler and Guido Adler: Records of a Friendship*, E. R. Reilly, p. 27 (Cambridge, 1982).

11. I. Barea, *Vienna*, p. 361 (London, 1992).

12. In the Overture to *Così fan tutte*, Mahler cut bars 79–175 and altered the orchestra's dynamics and articulation. This approach was carried through into the subsequent arias and ensembles. In the Trio, Act 1, No. 2, 'È la fede delle femmine', he altered the string artic- ulation in bars 14–18 from *arco* to *pizzicato*; while, in the *forte* episode, bars 19–26, he strengthened the first flute and bassoon with the second flute and bassoon. Mahler continued to change the orchestration and articulation in this fashion throughout the opera. He inserted music, both from Mozart's other works and from material already heard earlier in the opera. At the beginning of Act 2, he added a short introduction: the Finale of the Divertimento K287/271H. Later, following the recitative, 'Vittoria padroncini', and before the Finale, Act 2, No. 31, he inserted fourteen bars from the Andante of the over- ture. Many of the secco rectitaives were heavily cut. The recitative following the Chorus, Act 1, No. 8, 'Bella vita militar', was cut until 'Abbracciami, idol mio!' with ten of its twelve bars being removed. Similarly, the arias and ensembles were subjected to cuts. In the Quintet, Act 1, No. 6, 'Sento, o Dio', for example, he cut bars 40–69, eliminating more than a quarter of the whole number; while, in the Finale, Act 2, No. 31, he cut bars 36–57, 85–143, 149–153, 372 (second half) to 387 (second half), 483 (second half) to 489 (second half), 570–574 and 603–647. See B. Paumgartner, *Gustav Mahlers Bearbeitung von Mozarts 'Così fan tutte' für seine Aufführungen an der Wiener Hofoper*, Bärenreiter (Kassel, 1968).

13. Anton Wilhelm Florentin von Zuccalmaglio (1803–1869): German poet, composer and impresario.

14. G. Gruber, *Mozart & Posterity*, trans. R.S. Furness, pp. 130–1 (London, 1991).

15. G. Kobbé, *Kobbé's Complete Opera Book*, ed. The Earl of Harewood, p. 74 (London, 1992). Both the Karlsruhe and Dresden productions used Ernst Lewicki's two-act version. J. Rushton, 'Idomeneo *after* Mozart', *W.A. Mozart: Idomeneo* (Cambridge, 1993), p. 86.

16. Ibid.

17. Rushton describes Wolf-Ferrari's edition: 'Ermanno Wolf-Ferrari . . . recomposed and orchestrated the recitative in collaboration with the theatre dramaturg Ernst Leopold Stahl; the performances were conducted by Hans Knappertsbusch. Despite his Italian origins, Wolf-Ferrari conformed to post-Wagnerian tastes by savage cutting of arias, sparing mainly Ilia's. His recitatives are a weird pot-pourri of Mozart's orchestral motives, taken from scenes otherwise omitted (notably Nos. 22 and 27) and combined with material of his own including, of course, new voice-parts, the result being occa- sionally reminiscent of Weber.' Ibid. Strauss knew this version, which he described as 'Wolf-Ferrari's totally insufficient adaptation'.

18. Lothar Wallerstein (1882–1949): German conductor and producer. Wallerstein collab- orated with Strauss on productions in both Vienna and Milan.

19. N. Del Mar, *Richard Strauss: A Critical Commentary on His Life and Works*, (vol. II), p. 375 (London, 1969).

20. Shelfmark K5C19. This score will be referred to throughout as the British Library score.

21. The 1941 score is available on hire only. This score will be referred to throughout as the 1941 score. See Appendix 3.

22. The photocopy facsimile of the autograph as used by the present author was kindly provided by Strauss's grandson, the late Richard Strauss.

23. The page that follows p. 63 is numbered p. 63a.

24. The use of Breitkopf & Härtel's plates is confirmed on p. 307 (bottom right-hand corner) of both published scores (1931 and 1941): 'Druck von Breitkopf & Härtel, Leipzig'.

25. Strauss, when referring to the *Gesammtausgabe* score in the autograph, incorrectly gives the page number of Idomeneo's Act 2 aria, 'Fuor del mar', as p. 144, and the duet in the Anhang, 'Spiegarti non poss'io', as p. 351. They should read p. 143 and p. 350 respectively.

26. That said, Dr. Viktor Kreiner, President of Heinrichshofen's Verlag, writes 'we regret to inform you that all the correspondence with Dr. Richard Strauss and the sources concerned were destroyed at the end of the Second World War'. Letter to the author, 14 February 1996.
27. Letter from Hans Schneider, proprietor of Musikantiquariat Hans Schneider (Tutzing and Munich), to A.H. King, of the British Museum, dated 13 October 1958 (attached to the front endpapers of the British Library score, Shelfmark K5C19. Translated by the present author.
28. Information kindly provided by Dr. David Patmore, Sheffield.
29. On p. 36 of the autograph, Strauss writes 'Part.[itur] S.[eite] 223 Adler' and on p. 65 'Part.[itur] S.[eite] 324 Adler'.The pages referred to (S.[eite] 223 and S.[eite] 324) correspond to the *Gesammtausgabe* score of *Idomeneo*.
30. See Appendix 3.
31. Rudolf Krzyzanowski (1859–1911): Krzyzanowski was a pupil of Bruckner and a friend of Mahler.
32. See Strauss's 'Vorwort' to *Intermezzo*.
33. Gluck notes in his Preface to *Alceste* that: '[one should] not leave that sharp contrast between the aria and the recitative in the dialogue, so as not to break a period unreasonably nor wantonly disturb the force and heat of the action.' C.W. Gluck, Preface to the first edition of *Alceste* (trans. E. Blom), A. Einstein, *Gluck*, Dent, 1964, pp. 98–100, as found in, G. Pestelli, trans. E. Cross, *The Age of Mozart and Beethoven* (Cambridge, 1984), pp. 274–5.
34. E. Krause, *Richard Strauss: the Man and his Work* (Boston, 1969), pp. 148–9.
35. Del Mar, *Richard Strauss* (vol. II), p. 376.
36. In Act 1, Scene II (*Idomeneo: Vollständige Neubearbeitung von Lothar Wallerstein und Richard Strauss*, Heinrichshofen's Verlag Magdeburg, 1931, henceforth *Version Strauss*), he replaces 70 bars of *recitativo secco* (see *Idomeneo*, ed. Daniel Heartz, *Neue Mozart Ausgabe*, Serie II Bühnenwerke/Werkgruppe 5/Band 11: *Idomeneo*/Teilband 1 & 2, Barenreiter, 1972, henceforth *NMA*.) with 15 bars of material based on a theme from the 'Scena Ultima' (*NMA* p. 477). The motif found in the cellos and bass was heard first in the bar after figure 18 (*Version Strauss*) and taken from a part of Mozart's original that was not otherwise used by Strauss. Its function is not simply to depict Ilia's and Idamante's presence on stage but to develop and to underpin their relationship during the course of the opera. The motif can then be heard in an augmented form in the recitative, Act 2, Scene X (*Version Strauss*), which precedes the Quartet, 'Nein, du sollst bleiben', fleetingly in the Temple Scene and as one of the dominant themes in Strauss's extension to the 'Scena Ultima'. Similarly, in Act 1, Scene VIII (*Version Strauss*), the recognition scene, based on the accompanied recitative in Act 1, Scene X (*NMA* p.109), Strauss develops the motivic links with the overture and earlier thematic material, before introducing a motif based on bars 158 to 161 of the overture (oboes and first violins) at figure 55. As Del Mar notes, the winding figure is used 'to depict the suffering of Idomeneo on account of the dreaded secret of Idamante's identity as Poseidon's intended sacrificial victim.' The psychological implication of Idomeneo's actions is developed by Strauss both in Act 2, Scene I and in the bars that directly precede and succeed Idomeneo's comment to Arbaces [*sic*], 'Nun weisst du das Geheimnis!', where he again uses the motif to indicate Idomeneo's anguish.
37. In Strauss's extant, marked scores of Mozart's operas, housed at the Richard Strauss-Archiv, no cuts can be found in any of the secco recitatives
38. See Appendix 3.
39. Interview with the author, Munich, 13 May 1992.
40. S. Sadie ed., *The New Grove Dictionary of Music and Musicians* (London, 1980), Vol. 14, p. 288.
41. With the exceptions of twenty-five bars in Ismene's aria, Act 2, Scene XI (*Version Strauss*), 'Orestes und Ajas', where he lightly doubles the violas in the woodwind, and, earlier, where he strengthens the chorus material, Act 1, Scene VI (*Version Strauss*), 'Da seht! Götter, o

helft!' Strauss avoided the temptation to reorchestrate Mozart's existing material. These insertions are found in both the British Library and the 1941 scores but are not part of the autograph material, as provided by Strauss's grandson, the late Richard Strauss.

42. Krause, *Richard Strauss: the Man and his Work*, pp. 386–7.
43. At the Munich première, the role of Idamante was sung by the castrato, Vincenzo dal Prato.
44. The 1941 revival was part of the celebration commemorating the 150th anniversary of Mozart's death.
45. In Vienna, the role of Idamante was sung by Baron Pulini.
46. Elisabeth Schumann (1888–1952) was one of the leading sopranos of her day. She sang with Strauss, as part of his tour of the USA, in 1921. Schumann was also heard under Strauss's direction during his second Swiss tour in 1917: she sang the roles of Zerlina and Papagena at the Stadttheater, Zurich, on 17 and 20 May respectively. See Chapter 9.
47. The Hungarian singer, Maria Németh (1897–1967), was one of the leading dramatic sopranos of her generation. She was regularly heard in Vienna, London, Berlin, Paris and Milan, in roles such as the Queen of the Night, Turandot and Brünnhilde.
48. Gruber, *Mozart and Posterity*, p. 199.
49. L. von Köchel, *Chronologisch-thematisches Verzeichnis sämtlicher Tonwerke Wolfgang Amadé Mozarts*, 3rd edn., revised by A. Einstein (Leipzig, 1937), p. 445, translation as found in C. Walton, 'The performing version by Richard Strauss and Lothar Wallerstein', Rushton, *W.A. Mozart: Idomeneo*, p. 89.
50. Review by 'Hamel' held at the Richard Strauss-Institut, precise source unknown. Translated by the present author.
51. *Dresdner Nachrichten*, 15 November 1932. Translated by the present author.
52. Strauss completed the first version of *Die ägyptische Helena* at Garmisch on 8 October 1927, which received its first performance at the Dresden Staatsoper under Fritz Busch on 6 June 1928. Strauss completed a revised version of the opera on 15 January 1933, which received its première at the Salzburg Festival under Clemens Krauss on 14 August 1933.
53. Unidentified review, dated 18 April 1931. Review by courtesy of the Landeshauptstadt Magdeburg. Translated by the present author.
54. *Musical Opinion*, June 1931, p. 799.
55. The conductor for the German première was Walter Beck.
56. Unidentified review, dated 25 April 1931, kindly provided by the Landeshauptstadt Magdeburg. Translated by the present author.
57. *Magdeburgischen Zeitung*, 26 April 1931. Translated by the present author.
58. Letter from Richard Strauss to Bruno von Niessen, dated 27 February 1932. F. Grasberger ed., *Der Strom der Töne trug mich fort. Die Welt um Richard Strauss in Briefen*, pp. 338–9 (Tutzing, 1967). Translation by M. Kennedy, sleeve note for W.A. Mozart, Symphonies K550, K551 and the Overture to *Die Zauberflöte*, R. Strauss, Berlin Staatskapelle. Deutsche Grammophon, 431874-2.
59. Strauss conducted his new version at Berlin on 24 March 1933 and at Vienna with revisions on 3 December 1941.
60. Karl Böhm (1894–1981): Austrian conductor.
61. Letter from Richard Strauss to Karl Böhm, dated 27 April 1945. K. Böhm, *A Life Remembered: Memoirs*, trans. J. Kehoe, pp. 157–163 (London, 1992).
62. Fritz Busch (1951), Symposium 1274 and 1275; [Sir] John Pritchard (1956), EMI CHS 7 63685 2; Sir John Pritchard (1988), Decca 411 805-2. Luciano Pavarotti (1935–2007): Italian tenor.

Chapter 8 A German Abroad: Touring (1885–1914)

1. See Chapter 3.
2. Strauss's letter to his father, dated 9 January 1887.
3. Strauss's letter to [his father], dated 11 December 1887. Translated by the present author.

4. Strauss conducted his Symphony in F minor at the Frankfurt Museum Concerts on 7 January 1887, at Leipzig with the Gewandhaus Orchestra on 13 October 1887 and at Mannheim on 10 January 1888. Strauss's programme in Milan on 8 and 11 December 1887 consisted of Weber's Overture to *Euryanthe*, his own Symphony in F minor, Beethoven's Overture to *Leonore* No. 1 Glinka's *Kamarinskaya* and Wagner's Prelude to *Die Meistersinger von Nürnberg*. Strauss's letter to his father, dated, 3 December 1887.

5. *Aus Italien* received its première at the Odeon, Munich, conducted by Strauss on 2 March 1887.

6. Strauss performed *Aus Italien* with the Berlin Philharmonic on 23 and 25 January 1888. At the first concert, Strauss shared the podium with Bülow, while the second was part of the Orchestra's popular concerts series. At the Meiningen concert on 26 December 1888, Strauss shared the programme with Fritz Steinbach and at the Cologne concert with the Gürzenich Orchestra on 8 January 1889, with Franz Wüllner. Along with these performances, Strauss conducted the work at the Frankfurt Museum Concerts on 18 January 1888 and at the twenty-sixth Tonkünstlerversammlung des Allgemeine Deutschen Musik Veriens at Wiesbaden on 28 June 1889 in a programme that also included Brahms's Piano Concerto No. 2 (Margarete Stern, piano), Liszt's *Johanna d'Arc vor dem Scheiterhaufen*, (Marianne Brandt, soprano), Rudorff's Variations (Ernst Rudorff, conductor), Stavenhagen's *Sulieka* (Agnes Denis, soprano), Lalo's Cello Concerto (Alvin Schröder, cello), Cornelius's Trio from *Gunlöd*, and Bird's *Scène orientale* and Intermezzo for Orchestra. On 10 January 1889, Strauss performed the first version of *Macbeth* at Mannheim. Strauss also conducted the following performances during his tenure at Munich: *Wanderers Sturmlied* (world première) at Cologne with the Gürzenich Orchestra 8 March 1887, the Concert Overture with the Gewandhaus Orchestra on 24 October 1888, and Liszt's *Héroïde funèbre* and Berlioz's *L'Enfance du Christ* at the twenty-sixth Tonkünstlerversammlung des Allgemeine Deutschen Musik Veriens at Wiesbaden on 27 June 1889.

7. Strauss's letter to his father, dated 1 July 1889.

8. Felix Mottl (1856–1911): German composer and conductor.

9. Strauss's letter to his father, dated 12 July 1889.

10. Hans Richter (1843–1916): Hungarian conductor.

11. Strauss's letter to his father, dated 5 August 1889.

12. Hans von Bülow had died at Cairo on 12 February 1894.

13. Between 19 February 1890 and 19 March 1894, Strauss conducted performances of *Wanderers Sturmlied* at Berlin on 17 March 1890, Heidelberg on 22 February 1892 and Würzburg 12 and 13 March 1894; *Don Juan* at Frankfurt, Braunschweig and Cologne on 28 February 1890, 6 December 1890 and 3 February 1891 respectively; *Aus Italien* at Mainz and Karlsruhe on 18 February 1891 and 14 March 1891; *Tod und Verklärung* at Berlin on 23 and 24 February 1891, Heidelberg on 16 January 1894 and Würzburg on 12 and 13 March 1894; *Macbeth* at Berlin on 29 February 1892, and the 'Friedenserzählung' (Emil Gerhäuser, tenor) from *Guntram* at Heidelberg on 16 January 1894. Strauss conducted complete programmes at Braunschweig on 14 November 1891 (Liszt's Piano Concerto No. 1 [Bernhard Stavenhagen, piano], *Tod und Verklärung, Don Juan* and Spohr's 'Gesangsszene' [Adolph Wünsch, violin]), at Leipzig on 13 March 1891 (Schubert-Liszt 'Wanderer' Fantasy [Alexander Siloti, piano], solo piano works by Chopin and Liszt [Alexander Siloti, piano] and *Tod und Verklärung*), 29 October 1892 (*Macbeth*, an aria from Berlioz's The Trojans [Luise Reuss-Belce, soprano], Davidoff's Cello Concerto [Julius Klengel, cello], various unspecified songs [Luise Reuss-Belce, soprano], various unspecified cello works [Julius Klengel, cello] and Liszt's *Eine Faust-Sinfonie*) and 21 February 1894 (Liszt's *Héroïde Funèbre*, Bülow's *Nirwana* and Wagner's Preludes to *Tristan und Isolde* and *Die Meistersinger von Nürnberg*), at Hamburg on 22 January 1894 (Beethoven's Overture to *Coriolan*, Liszt's *Mazeppa* and *Aus Italien*) and at Berlin on 27 January 1894 (*Don Juan*, Liszt's Piano Concerto No. 1 [Moritz Rosenthal, piano], Berger's *Dramatische*

Orchesterphantasie in Ouvertürenform and Beethoven's Symphony No. 6) and 19 March 1894 (Beethoven's Symphony No. 9). Strauss also conducted Wagner's *Lohengrin* and Lortzing's *Der Wildschütz* at Leipzig on 19 and 23 February 1890 respectively, accompanied 'Ständchen' (Emilie Herzog, soprano) at Berlin on 28 January 1890, some songs and the Cello Sonata (Alvin Schröder, cello) at Leipzig on 31 March 1890 and took part in a performance of the Piano Quartet in Berlin on 26 January 1894.

14. Strauss attended or worked at the Bayreuth Festival from 1886 to 1891 inclusive.

15. R. Strauss, 'Remarks on Richard Wagner's Work and on the Bayreuth Festival Theatre', *Recollections and Reflections*, p. 70.

16. At Barcelona on 11 November 1897, Strauss conducted Beethoven's Symphony No. 3 ('Eroica'), his own *Don Juan* and Prelude to Act 1 from *Guntram*, Liszt's 'Mephisto' Waltz and Wagner's Prelude to *Die Meistersinger von Nürnberg*. On 14 November, he conducted Mozart's *Eine kleine Nachtmusik*, Beethoven's Overture to *Leonore* No. 3, Preludes to Acts 1 and 2 from *Guntram, Tod und Verklärung*, Wagner's Overture to *Tannhäuser* and the Prelude and Liebestod from *Tristan und Isolde*. At Brussels on 21 November 1897, Strauss performed *Don Juan*, 'Rosenband', 'Liebeshymnus', 'Morgen' and 'Cäcilie' (Pauline Strauss de Ahna, soprano), *Also sprach Zarathustra*, 'Allerseelen', 'Traum durch die Dämmerung' and 'Ständchen' (Pauline de Ahna, soprano; Richard Strauss, piano) and *Till Eulenspiegel*. On 22 November, he performed his 'Du meines Herzens Krönelein', 'Ach Lieb, ich muss nun scheiden', 'Meinem Kinde', 'Nachtgang', 'Heimliche Aufforderung', 'Sehnsucht', 'Himmelsboten' and 'Schlagende Herzen' (Pauline Strauss de Ahna, soprano; Richard Strauss, piano), Piano Quartet (César Thomson, violin; Leon van Hout, viola; Eduard Jacobs, cello; Richard Strauss, piano) and Violin Sonata (César Thomson, violin; Richard Strauss, piano). At Paris on 28 December 1897, Strauss shared a concert with Eduard Colonne at which he performed *Till Eulenspiegel*, 'Rosenband', 'Liebeshymnus', 'Morgen' and 'Cäcilie' (Pauline Strauss de Ahna, soprano), 'Allerseelen', 'Traum durch die Dämmerung' and 'Ständchen' (Pauline de Ahna, soprano; Richard Strauss, piano) and *Tod und Verklärung*.

17. Robert Newman (1859–1926): English bass, impresario and manager of the Queen's Hall.

18. *The Times*, 7 December 1897.

19. *The Musical Times*, 1 January 1898.

20. *The Times*, 8 December 1897.

21. August Manns (1825–1907): German-born conductor of the Crystal Palace Concerts, London.

22. *The Times*, 8 December 1897.

23. On 1 October 1898, Strauss conducted at Leipzig Rheinberger's Overture to *Der Widerspenstigen Zähmung*, a Reinecke piano concerto, Humperdinck's Overture to *Die Königskinder*, Rudorff's Variations, d'Albert's Overture to *Der Rubin* and Draeseke's *Jubelouvertüre*. The concert also contained Lieder by Scholz, Zumpe, Fuchs, Schillings, Weingartner, Wolf, Jadassohn, Sommer and Rüfer. Strauss then performed *Don Quixote* at Dresden with the Dresden Philharmonic on 11 January 1899, Beethoven's Symphony No. 7, *Also sprach Zarathustra* and Wagner's Preludes to *Lohengrin* and *Die Meistersinger von Nürnberg* with the Lamoureux Orchestra at Paris on 22 January, his Piano Quartet and 'Ich trage meine Minne', 'Heimkehr', 'Schlagende Herzen', 'Glückes genug', 'Meinem Kinde', 'Junghexenlied' and 'Befreit' (Pauline Strauss de Ahna, soprano), at Weimar on 30 January, *Die lustige Weiber von Windsor* and *Die Meistersinger von Nürnberg* at Weimar on 2 and 3 February respectively, Mozart's Symphony No. 38 ('Prague'), 'Rosenband', 'Liebeshymnus', 'Morgen', 'Cäcilie', 'Allerseelen', 'Traum durch die Dämmerung' and 'Ständchen' (Pauline Strauss-de Ahna, soprano), *Till Eulenspiegel* and *Tod und Verklärung* at Bremen on 7 February, *Also sprach Zarathustra* and *Tod und Verklärung* at Leipzig on 14 and 20 February respectively, his own Symphony in F minor, 'Meinem Kinde', 'Befreit' and 'Ständchen' (Pauline Strauss de Ahna, soprano), the Prelude to Act 2 of *Guntram* and *Wandrers Sturmlied* at

Heidelberg on 28 February, *Don Quixote*, 'Meinem Kinde', 'Befreit' and 'Schlagende Herzen' (Pauline Strauss de Ahna, soprano) and the world première of *Ein Heldenleben* at Frankfurt on 3 March, Wagner's Overture to *Tannhäuser, Also sprach Zarathustra* and *Tod und Verklärung* at Strasburg on 15 March, the melodrama *Das Schloss am Meere* (Ernst von Possart, speaker) at Dresden on 24 March, *Ein Heldenleben* and Liszt's *Orpheus* at Düsseldorf for the Niederrheinisches Musikfest on May 22, Schumann's Symphony No. 1 ('Spring'), 'Das Rosenband', 'Morgen' and 'Cäcilie' (Pauline Strauss de Ahna, soprano), Mozart's Piano Concerto No. 24 and Act 2 of Cornelius's *Barbier von Bagdad* (Pauline Strauss de Ahna, soprano) at Düsseldorf for the Niederrheinisches Musikfest on 23 May and *Tod und Verklärung* in London on 15 June.

24. To make way for Strauss's name, Gounod's was removed.
25. Strauss's letter to his father, dated 1 November 1898.
26. Strauss's letter to his father, dated 27 January 1899.
27. Wood, *My Life of Music*, pp. 98–9.
28. In 1912, the Home Secretary notified the Philharmonic Society that King George V had sanctioned the use of the 'Royal' prefix.
29. See M. B. Foster, *The History of the Philharmonic Society of London 1813–1912* (London, 1912); R. Elkin, *Royal Philharmonic: the Annals of the Royal Philharmonic Society* (London, 1946); C. Ehrlich, *First Philharmonic: a History of The Royal Philharmonic Society* (Oxford, 1995).
30. British artists that conducted concerts with the Society during the late nineteenth century included Sir William Sterndale Bennett, Sir Frederic Cowen, Sir Arthur Sullivan and Sir Alexander Mackenzie.
31. The first mention of an invitation to Strauss from the Philharmonic Society was recorded in the Directors' Minutes, dated 21 May 1897. Directors' Minute Book (1893–1898), Royal Philharmonic Society Manuscripts, Loan 48.2/11, The British Library.
32. The Philharmonic Society's first letter to Strauss, or a copy thereof, is not part of Loan 48.
33. Royal Philharmonic Society Letters, Volume 33 (Star-Sz), Royal Philharmonic Society Manuscripts, Loan 48.13/33.
34. Directors' Minutes, dated 14 October 1898. 48.2/11.
35. A copy of a letter from the Philharmonic Society to Richard Strauss, dated 23 October 1898. 48.13/33.
36. On 2 December 1897, Humperdinck directed the Overture and Introduction to Act 3 from *Königskinder*, and 'Sonntagsruhe' and 'Das Männlein im Walde' from *Hänsel und Gretel*; Sir Alexander Mackenzie conducted the remainder of the programme.
37. Directors' Minutes, dated 21 May 1897. 48.2/11.
38. Ibid.
39. Letter from Schülz-Curtius to Berger, dated 19 October 1898. Royal Philharmonic Society Letters, Volume 30 (Sal-Schul), Royal Philharmonic Society Manuscripts, Loan 48.13/30.
40. Letter from Berger to Schülz-Curtius, dated 18 and 20 November 1898. 48.13/30.
41. Letter from Schülz-Curtius to Berger, dated 23 November 1898. 48.13/30. Schülz-Curtius kept his promise. Strauss's only London engagement during the 1899–1900 season was for the Philharmonic Society.
42. Undated working translation by the Philharmonic Society of a letter from Strauss to Schülz-Curtius. 48.13/30. Hugo Becker (1864–1941): German cellist. Between 1884 and 1886, Becker was Principal Cellist of the Hofopernorchester, Frankfurt, and was engaged as a soloist with the Philharmonic Society between 1892 and 1902. Becker was also the preferred cellist of Strauss's mentor, Hans von Bülow. In a letter to his daughter, Daniela, dated 17 February 1891, Bülow wrote: 'Last night I was reminded vividly of my favourite Frankfurter 'cellist, Hugo Becker. Popper, the Viennese Jew, was whining and playing the charlatan with such appalling bad taste that I fell into the state to which you are reduced when you hear of certain lady penitent's bouquets. If you see Becker, give

him my kindest regards and tell him I am looking forward very, very much to playing the last Beethoven 'cello sonata with him at Bremen on April 7 [1891], and will he please play his part by heart too?' Richard Count du Moulin Eckart ed., trans. S. Goddard, *Letters of Hans von Bülow to Richard Wagner and Others* (New York, 1979), p. 423.

43. Letter from Berger to Schülz-Curtius, dated 18 and 20 November 1898. 48.13/30.
44. Sir Alexander Mackenzie (1847–1935): Scottish composer and conductor.
45. William Henry Squire (1871–1963): British cellist and composer. Directors' Minutes, dated 25 November 1898. 48.2/11.
46. Letter from Schülz-Curtius to Berger, dated 12 November 1898. 48.13/30.
47. Undated working translation by the Philharmonic Society of a letter from Strauss to Schülz-Curtius. 48.13/30.
48. 18 November 1898.
49. Letter from Berger to Schülz-Curtius, dated 18 and 20 November 1898. 48.13/30. Having told Strauss that the 'Soc[iety]. is not an association for speculation but devotes itself solely to the furtherance of musical art in England' (23 October 1898), the composer-conductor might have found curious Berger's comment to Schülz-Curtius that 'a third rehearsal, the expense of which would make the enterprise all but hopeless of any profit'. (18 November 1898)
50. Letter from Schülz-Curtius to Berger, dated 19 November 1898. 48.13/30.
51. After his difficulties with the Society, it might have amused Strauss to learn of the following: '24 October 1904...Dir[ectors']. Meet[ing]. 6 York St. ... Mr. Berger reported that he had written to ask Dr. Cowan whether he could undertake the production of Richard Strauss' Don Quixote with 3 rehearsals — & read his reply. It was accordingly agreed to perform the work with Casals as Solo 'Cellist. ... The perf[ormance]. of Don Quixote will be the first by an English orchestra.' Directors' Minute Book (1898–1908), Royal Philharmonic Society Manuscripts, 48.2/12. (The performance did not take place. *Don Quixote* was not heard at a Royal Philharmonic Society concert until 15 November 1928.)
52. Sir Alexander C. Mackenzie conducted the remainder of the programme. The works performed were Mackenzie's Two Orchestral Pieces from *Manfred*, Chopin's Piano Concerto No. 1 (Moritz Rosenthal, piano); *Tod und Verklärung* (Richard Strauss, conductor), Weber's 'Glöcklein im Thale' (Clementine de Vere-Sapio, soprano and Signor Sapio, piano), Gluck's 'Spiagge amate' (Clementine de Vere-Sapio, soprano and Signor Sapio, piano) and Mozart's Symphony No. 38 ('Prague').
53. Joseph Dupont (1838–1899): Belgian conductor.
54. On 5 November 1899, Strauss conducted Berlioz's 'Le Roi Lear' Overture, Beethoven's Symphony No. 7, unspecified Lieder by Schubert (Anton van Rooy, baritone) and 'Wotan's Farewell' from Wagner's *Die Walküre* (Anton van Rooy, baritone).
55. Strauss visited Paris between 26 February and 12 March 1900.
56. On 4 March 1900, Strauss conducted Berlioz's 'Le Roi Lear' Overture, Beethoven's Symphony No. 5, Shillings's Prelude to *Ingwelde* and *Ein Heldenleben*, while on 11 March, he performed Wagner's Overture to *Tannhäuser, Don Quixote* (Hugo Becker, cello), Wagner's *Eine Faust-Ouvertüre*, Tchaikovsky's 'Rococo' Variations (Hugo Becker, cello) and *Ein Heldenleben*.
57. On 8 March 1900, Strauss performed his Violin Sonata (Joseph Lederer, violin), 'Allerseelen', 'Morgen' and 'Ständchen' (Frl. Lombroso, soprano) and Piano Quartet.
58. On 4 June 1900 at Aachen, Strauss conducted Berlioz's *Roméo et Juliette* (excerpts), Cornelius's *Der Cid* (duet), *Also sprach Zarathustra* and Beethoven's Symphony No. 9 ('Choral') and, on 5 May, Schillings's *Ingwelde* (excerpts) and Wagner's *Siegfried* (Closing Scene).
59. Karl Franz Brendel (1811–1868): German critic and commentator.
60. On 7 June 1934 in Wiesbaden, the ADMV presented *Die Tageszeiten* for male choir and orchestra, *Burleske* and *Sinfonia domestica*.
61. Strauss conducted at Düsseldorf and at Bremen on 19 and 20 May respectively.
62. *Das Schloss am Meere* by Strauss and *Eleusinisches Fest* by Max von Schillings.

63. Edgar Speyer (1839–1934) was a German-born English banker, philanthropist and amateur musician. He was the son of Wilhelm Speyer (1790–1878), a German violinist, composer and critic. Edgar was a financial advisor and close friend of Strauss. After moving from Germany to London in 1859, he became a successful banker. Although business matters occupied much of his time, he maintained close links with the music profession throughout his life; he often provided funds to meet the loss incurred at the end of Proms season before World War One. A collection of letters and postcards from Strauss to Speyer, covering the years 1899 to 1922, is housed at the British Library. According to Kurt Wilhelm, Speyer advised Strauss to deposit his savings 'in the Bank of England,' as 'this was the safest place for them.' The funds were sequestrated during World War One. Wilhelm, *Richard Strauss: An Intimate Portrait*, p. 153 and Letters to E Speyer 1899–1922, Egerton MS. 3246 (ff. 3–24), British Library, London.
64. Here, Strauss is referring to Mozart's *Don Giovanni* (*Don Juan*) and not to his own tone poem. He conducted the six hundredth performance of this opera at the Berlin Hofoper on 12 June 1902.
65. Strauss's letter to his father, dated 27 May 1902. Translated by the present author.
66. Jan Kubelík (1880–1940): Czech violinist and composer.
67. Wilhelm Backhaus (1884–1969): German pianist.
68. 31 May 1902.
69. 2 June 1902.
70. Strauss and von Possart gave the first performance of *Enoch Arden* at the Mathildeneaal (Munich) on 24 March 1897. The poem was translated into German by Adolf Strodtmann (1829–1879).
71. 4 June 1902.
72. 6 June 1902.
73. Elkan Kosman (b.1872): Dutch violinist.
74. The second Boer War ended on 31 May 1902.
75. Strauss conducted in America for the first time in 1904.
76. Strauss's letter to his father, probably 3 June 1902. Translated by the present author.
77. Strauss's engagement book for 1902, p. 50.
78. The remainder of the programme with the Queen's Hall Orchestra included Beethoven's Symphony No. 5 and Tchaikovsky's Piano Concerto No. 1 in B flat minor (Teresa Carreño, piano).
79. An advertisement in *The Times* on 6 December 1902 announced 'Richard Strauss. Hugo Gorlitz [*sic*] begs to announce that he has been appointed SOLE AGENT for Richard Strauss in all English-speaking countries. All communications should be addressed to 119, New Bond-street, W.'
80. *The Times*, 6 December 1902.
81. Strauss's letter to his father, written after his return to Berlin and dated 15 December 1902. Translated by the present author.
82. For these early performances of *Ein Heldenleben*, both Strauss and Wood engaged a solo violinist. For the first London performance, the violinist was one 'Herr Zimmermann of Amsterdam', while, for the second, the soloist was Karl Halir, concertmaster in Berlin and a member of the Joachim Quartet.
83. Strauss's letter to his father from Hamburg, where he was conducting a concert for the Vereins Hamburgische Musikfreunde, dated 12 January 1903. Translated by the present author.
84. Bubi was the affectionate nickname for Strauss's son, Franz, named after his famous grandfather. Franz was born on 12 April 1897 and died on 14 February 1980.
85. Emil Tschirch (1855–1942): Actor.
86. In 1903, Strauss moved to Joachimsthaler Strasse 17, Berlin.
87. Strauss's letter to his parents, probably written on 1 June 1903. Translated by the present author.
88. Willem Mengelberg (1871–1951): Dutch conductor.

89. Percy Pitt (1870–1932): English conductor. He was the chorus-master for Strauss's performance of Schumann's *Manfred* in 1902. A collection of letters and cards from Strauss to Pitt is held at the British Library (Egerton MS. 3306, ff. 122–129). See R. Holden, 'Percy Pitt: Richard Strauss' English Correspondent', *Richard Strauss-Blätter*, Hans Schneider Verlag (Vienna, June 1998, Heft 38).

90. 'Das Rosenband', 'Morgen' and 'Cäcilie' (Pauline Strauss-de Ahna, soprano).

91. 'Traum durch die Dämmerung', 'Ständchen' and 'Ich trage meine Minne' ['Ich trage meine Minne' replaced 'Ein Obdach'] (Pauline Strauss-de Ahna, soprano).

92. 'Meinem Kinde', 'Muttertändelei' and 'Wiegenlied' (Pauline Strauss-de Ahna, soprano).

93. 'Freundliche Vision', 'Befreit' and 'Heimliche Aufforderung' (Pauline Strauss-de Ahna, soprano).

94. 'Hymnus' and 'Pilgers Morgenlied' (David Ffrangcon-Davies, baritone).

95. The pianist for *Burleske* was Wilhelm Backhaus. According to the concert billing in *The Times* on 8 June 1903, *Ein Heldenleben* was 'Repeated by special request'. From *Guntram*, Strauss conducted the Preludes to Acts I and II and the *Friedenserzählung* and *Schluss* to Act II (John Harrison, tenor).

96. Strauss's letter to his parents, dated 10 June 1903. Translated by the present author.

97. Review of a concert given by the Vienna Philharmonic, conducted by Hans Richter, on 15 January 1893. As found in E Hanslick, *Hanslick's Music Criticisms*, trans. and ed. H. Pleasants (New York, 1988), p. 293.

98. 'Musical Gossip of the Month' by Common Time, *Musical Opinion and Music Trade Review*, 1 July 1903, p. 753–4.

99. Strauss holidayed on the Isle of Wight between 12 June and 16 July 1903.

100. Philipp Wolfrum (1854–1919): German conductor.

101. Henry Thode (1857–1920); German art historian.

102. *Taillefer* was given its first performance at the Heidelberg Stadthalle on 26 October 1903.

103. Strauss's letter to his father, dated 22 June 1903. Translated by the present author.

104. Strauss directed the Scottish Orchestra in Edinburgh and Glasgow on 7 and 8 December 1903. These concerts included the first complete British performance of *Aus Italien*.

105. 10 December 1903.

106. *The Times*, 10 December 1903.

107. Hector Berlioz (1803–1869).

108. *The Times*, 11 December 1903.

109. Strauss revised Berlioz's *Instrumentationslehre* between 1903 and 1904. It was published by C. F. Peters, Leipzig, in 1905.

110. The violinist was Evalyn Amethé.

111. *The Times*, 12 December 1903.

112. The letter was begun on 17 December and completed the following day.

113. Max Mossel (1871–1927): Dutch violinist.

114. Strauss's letter to his parents, probably written on 18 December 1903. Translated by the present author.

115. The 'press agent' was, in fact, Hugo Görlitz, who had travelled to America with Strauss and his wife.

116. *Tribune*, New York, 25 February 1904.

117. Strauss's letter to his parents, dated 2 March 1904.

118. At the White House on 26 April 1904, Strauss performed some of his Lieder with his wife, Pauline, and *Enoch Arden*, presumably in English, with the actor, Dean Wrightson. On 28 April 1904, Strauss and his wife set sail from Hoboken, New Jersey, for Cuxhaven.

119. The New York Philharmonic Orchestra's other guest conductors that season were Victor Herbert, Henry J. Wood, Gustave F. Kogel, Edouard Colonne, Felix Weingartner and Wasili Sajanoff.

120. Review kindly provided by the archive of the New York Philharmonic Orchestra.

121. At London on 16 December 1904, Strauss performed the Violin Sonata (Max Mossel, violin), some Lieder and the Piano Quartet. At Edinburgh on 17 December, he

performed the Cello Sonata (Ossian Fohström, cello), Lieder and the Violin Sonata (Johann Kruse, violin). At London on 18 December, he performed the Violin Sonata, and on 19 December at the Queen's Hall with the Queen's Hall Orchestra, he conducted Schumann's Piano Concerto, Chopin's Piano Concerto No. 1, Saint-Saëns's Piano Concerto No. 4 (all with Ethel Newcomb, piano) and *Tod und Verklärung*. At Birmingham on 20 December, he conducted *Don Juan*, the Violin Concerto (Max Mossel, violin), *Tod und Verklärung* and *Ein Heldenleben*. At the Schiller Institute at Manchester on 21 December, he played the Cello Sonata (Carl Fuchs, cello) and the Piano Quartet (Adolf Brodsky, violin, Simon Speelman, viola, and Carl Fuchs, cello).

122. Strauss performed the *Sinfonia domestica* with the Concertgebouw Orchestra of Amsterdam in Arnhem and Den Haag, on 28 and 29 March 1905 respectively.

123. Strauss performed the work with the Queen's Hall Orchestra. The remainder of the programme was conducted by Henry J. Wood and included Mendelssohn's Overture to *Ein Sommernachtstraum*, Bach's Orchestral Suite in B minor, Debussy's *Prélude à l'après-midi d'un faune* and Brahms's 'Academic Festival' Overture.

124. *The Times*, 3 April 1905.

125. Quoted in D. Cox, *The Henry Wood Proms* (London, 1980), pp. 49–50.

126. Strauss's letter to his parents, dated 5 April 1905. Translated by the present author.

127. The other works on the programme were conducted by Henry J. Wood and included excerpts from Mozart's *Gran Partita*, Bach's Brandenburg Concerto No. 6, Elgar's 'Enigma' Variations and an excerpt from Beethoven's *Die Geschöpfe des Prometheus*.

128. *The Musical Times*, 1 December 1905, p. 809.

129. *The Times*, 6 November 1905.

130. Edyth Walker (1867–1950): American soprano and teacher; Anna Bahr-Mildenburg (1872–1947): Austrian soprano; Hermann (Friedrich) Weidemann (1871–1919): German baritone.

131. Ernest Newman (1868–1959): Critic and writer on music.

132. *The Nation*, 26 February 1910.

133. George Bernard Shaw (1856–1950): Irish dramatist, essayist and critic.

134. See G. B. Shaw, *The Bodley Head Bernard Shaw: Shaw's Music Vol. 3 1893–1950*, ed. D. H. Laurence (London, 1981), pp. 594–623.

135. T. Beecham, *A Mingled Chime* (London, 1987), p. 90.

136. H. Rosenthal, *Two Centuries of Opera at Covent Garden* (London, 1958), p. 347.

137. Alfred Kalisch (1863–1933): German-born English music critic.

138. *The Times*, 22 June 1914.

139. Emil Mlynarski (1870–1935): Polish conductor, composer and violinist; Charles Villiers Stanford (1852–1924): British composer, teacher and conductor; Frederic Hymen Cowen (1852–1935): Jamaican-born English pianist, conductor and composer.

140. *The Times*, 22 June 1914.

141. Elena Gerhardt (1883–1961): German mezzo-soprano. As an encore, Gerhardt and Nikisch performed *Morgen*.

142. *The Times*, 22 June 1914.

143. *Das Schloss am Meere* was composed in 1899. It was first performed by Ernst von Possart and Richard Strauss in Berlin on 23 March 1899. Lena Ashwell (1872–1957): British actress; Stanley Hawley (1867–1916): British composer and pianist.

144. The production was choreographed by Michel Folkine.

145. Harry von Kessler (1868–1937): German diplomat and director of the Cranach-Presse, Weimar.

146. Shaw, *The Bodley Head Bernard Shaw: Shaw's Music Vol. 3 1893*–1950, pp. 648–75.

147. The production was funded by Beecham's father, Sir Joseph Beecham.

148. Beecham, *A Mingled Chime*, p. 128.

149. The other honorary doctors were the Duke of Saxe-Coburg, Walter Hines Page (the United States' Ambassador to Britain), Lord Bryce (former Ambassador to the USA) and Dr. Ludwig Mitteis, Professor of Law at the University of Leipzig.
150. 28 June 1914.

CHAPTER 9 A TARNISHED ICON? TOURING AND RECORDING (1914–1947)

1. President Woodrow Wilson.
2. Strauss's letter to Hofmannsthal, dated 8 October 1914. Strauss and Hofmannsthal, *The Correspondence between Richard Strauss and Hugo von Hofmannsthal*, p. 211.
3. Apart from two concerts in Munich on 18 and 23 September and a series of engagements at Frankfurt between 13 and 18 November, Strauss spent the autumn and winter of 1914 either at Berlin or at his home in the German Alps.
4. In 1915 and 1916, Strauss conducted in Berlin, Dresden, Leipzig, The Hague, Amsterdam, Vienna, Budapest, Prague, Chemnitz, Wiesbaden, Stuttgart, Frankfurt, Breslau, Hamburg and Halle.
5. 'Pianola' was the trade name for instruments manufactured by the Aeolian Company of New York.
6. 'Love Scene' from *Ein Heldenleben* is the passage consisting Figs. 32 to 41 of the Leuckart Verlag full score.
7. Strauss was in the studio on 5, 6, 13, 15 and 20 December 1916.
8. *Don Juan*: Deutsche Grammophon matrix 1057–60 LC; single sides nos. 040872–5; first issue 69525–6; second issue 65856–7. *Der Bürger als Edelmann*: Grammophon matrix 1047 LC, 1048 1/2 LC, 1049 LC, 1050 LC, 1053 1/2 LC, 1054 1/2 LC; single side nos. 040866–71, B20267; first issue 69522–4, 69658; second issue 65853–5, 66289. The Overture to *Ariadne auf Naxos*: Deutsche Grammophon matrix 1051 1/2 LC; single side no. 040869; first issue 69523; second issue 65854. *Till Eulenspiegel*: Deutsche Grammophon matrix 1061 LC, 1062 1/2 LC, 1063 LC, 1064 LC; single side nos. 040876–9; first issue 69527–8; second issue 65858–9. Waltzes from *Der Rosenkavalier*: Deutsche Grammophon matrix 1065–6 LC; single side nos. 040880–1; first issue 69529; second issue 65860.
9. During World War One, the Royal Opera House, Covent Garden, was used as a warehouse, and during World War Two as a dance hall.
10. J. Saul, 'A Personal Account of George Szell', *Le Grand Baton* Vol. 9 Nos. 1 and 2 (USA, 1972), p. 86.
11. *The Gramophone* became the *Gramophone* from the June 1969 issue.
12. R. Wimbush, 'Here and There', *The Gramophone*, May 1968, p. 585.
13. Written in response to a request for verification by Yale Collection of Historical Sound Recordings. P. Morse, 'Richard Strauss' Recordings: A Complete Discography', *Journal of the Association for Recorded Sound Collections*, (vol IX, no. 1) (USA, 1977), p. 12.
14. Strauss's 1917 Scandinavian tour included engagements at Copenhagen, Christiana, Stockholm and Gothenburg.
15. Strauss visited Switzerland between 20 January and 2 February and, again, between 14 and 29 May 1917. The repertoire for the first trip was performed by the combined Hofkapellen of Mannheim and Meiningen and the Tonhalle Orchestra and included *Elektra, Ariadne auf Naxos* (1916 version), *Also sprach Zarathustra, Burleske*, (Vera Schapira, piano), *Don Quixote, Till Eulenspiegel*, the 'Tanz' from *Salome* and *Ein Heldenleben*. The repertoire for the second trip was played by the combined Hofkapellen of Meiningen and Dessau and it included some of Strauss's Lieder and *Elektra* and Mozart's *Don Giovanni* and *Die Zauberflöte*. Information kindly provided by the archive of the Zurich Opera.
16. *Zürcher Post*, 19 May 1917.
17. See Chapter 8, Note 63.
18. See Chapter 7.

19. The archivist of the Chicago Symphony Orchestra gives the date of the concert as 18 December 1921.
20. Frederick Stock (1872–1942): German composer and conductor.
21. Unidentified review kindly provided by the archive of the Chicago Symphony Orchestra.
22. 'Tanz' from *Salome*: Brunswick 50002 (matrix X7001 and X7004). 'Menuett' from *Der Bürger als Edelman*: Brunswick 50017 (matrix 7005). Intermezzo from *Der Bürger als Edelman*: Brunswick 50017 (matrix 7007-2).
23. In 1921, Strauss also recorded some Lieder with Robert Hutt and Heinrich Schlusnus in Berlin for Deutsche Grammophon.
24. For Columbia, he recorded *Don Juan*, waltzes from *Der Rosenkavalier* and the 'Tanz' from *Salome* with the London Symphony Orchestra at the company's London studios on 18 January 1922.
25. The programme for 17 January included 'Die heiligen drei Könige', 'Cäcilie', 'Ständchen' and 'Morgen' sung by Ethel Frank. Strauss also conducted a concert with the Hallé Orchestra in Manchester on 21 January and a second concert in London 23 January.
26. *The Times*, 18 January 1922.
27. *The Times*, 14 January 1922.
28. Robert Wiene (1881–1938): German film director and producer.
29. Karl Alwin (1891–1946): German composer and conductor.
30. Otto Singer (1863–1931): German conductor.
31. On 13 April 1926, Strauss and the Augmented Tivoli Orchestra recorded excerpts of the film music score for HMV at the Queen's Hall.
32. The Tivoli was built in the Strand in 1890 and was one of London's most famous music-halls. It closed in 1914 and a cinema with the same name was built on the site in 1923. The cinema was demolished in 1957.
33. *The Times*, 13 April 1926.
34. Thomas Arne (1710–78): English composer.
35. *The Times*, 13 April 1926.
36. *Musical Opinion*, May 1926, p. 808.
37. Leopold Stokowski (1882–1977): British composer and conductor.
38. Deutsche Grammophon Matrix 360bg–369bg; single side nos. B20657–20666; Polydor 69840–4; Brunswick 25000–4.
39. Strauss does not observe the repeat at the end of the exposition.
40. Walter Wohllebe's earlier recording of Beethoven's Symphony No. 7 for Polydor also had a cut (Polydor set 69659–69662).
41. Compton Mackenzie (1883–1972): Scottish writer and critic. Mackenzie founded *The Gramophone* in 1923.
42. *The Gramophone*, September 1926, p. 164.
43. H. C. Schonberg, *The Great Conductors* (London, 1977), p. 241. Schonberg's book was first published in 1968.
44. *The Gramophone*, August 1926, p. 122. The review is signed 'K.K.'. According to Anthony Pollard of the *Gramophone*, this was probably written by Compton Mackenzie.
45. In *Abenteuer der Silvester-Nacht* (*Adventures of New Year's Eve*) Hoffman wrote 'Berger was at the piano again and he played the andante from Mozart's sublime E flat major symphony, and on the swan's wings of song my radiant love soared high'.
46. Strauss's Hamburg programme on 3 March 1926 included *Don Juan, Der Bürger als Edelmann* and *Ein Heldenleben*.
47. *The Gramophone*, August 1926, p. 122.
48. Morse, 'Richard Strauss' Recordings: A Complete Discography', p. 25.
49. At Berlin, Strauss was in the studio on 28 March and 2 April 1927 and on 1 October and 6, 10 and 17 December 1928.
50. Strauss conducted two concerts with the Hallé Orchestra on 6 and 13 November.
51. The *Festliches Präludium für grosses Orchester und Orgel* was composed for the opening of Vienna's Konzerthaus on 19 October 1913.

52. *The Times*, 10 November 1926.
53. *The Musical Times*, 1 December 1926, p. 1122.
54. *The Times*, 10 November 1926.
55. *Musical Opinion*, December 1926, p. 257.
56. In Milan in March 1928, Strauss performed *Salome, Der Rosenkavalier, Josephslegende* and *Le nozze di Figaro*. In Rome on 24 November 1929, Strauss conducted *Don Juan, Der Bürger als Edelman* and the *Sinfonia domestica*.
57. W. R. Anderson, *The Gramophone*, November 1932, p. 211.
58. Schonberg, *The Great Conductors*, p. 241.
59. Salter, *Gramophone*, December 1991, p. 158.
60. Morse, 'Richard Strauss' Recordings: A Complete Discography', p. 16.
61. C. Matthews, sleeve notes for *Eine Alpensinfonie* Op.64, Richard Strauss, Bavarian Staatskapelle. EMI CDC 7546102.
62. With the Berlin Philharmonic in 1928, Strauss recorded Gluck's Overture to *Iphigenie in Aulis* (arr. Wagner), Weber's Overture to *Euryanthe*, Cornelius's Overture to *Der Barbier von Bagdad*, Wagner's Overture to *Der fliegende Holländer* and Prelude to Act I of *Tristan und Isolde*, and the 'Tanz' from *Salome*.
63. W. R. Anderson, *The Gramophone*, June 1930, p. 23.
64. Moerike's recording (Parlophone E10222–6) was part of the first complete recorded cycle of the Beethoven symphonies, which he shared with Frieder Weissmann.
65. Strauss conducted *Salome* on 3 June, *Elektra* on 7 June, *Der Rosenkavalier* on 1 and 12 June, *Die Frau ohne Schatten* on 9 June, *Intermezzo* on 4 and 6 June, *Die ägyptische Helena* on 11 June and the recordings of *Don Juan* and *Till Eulenspiegel* and the première of *Gesänge des Orients* with Koloman von Pataky (1896–1964).
66. Deutsche Grammophon matrix 779 1/2 Bi I, 780 1/2 Bi I, 781 Bi I, 782 Bi I; single side nos. B 21177–80; Polydor 66887–8; US Brunswick 90044–5; CD reissue Pearl GEMM CD 9366.
67. Deutsche Grammophon matrix 791–4 Bi I; single side nos. B21191–4; Polydor 66902–3; US Brunswick 90046–7; CD reissue Pearl GEMM CD 9366.
68. *The Gramophone*, January 1933, p. 320.
69. The date given for the recording in the review is 13 September 1939. That date seems unlikely, however, as Strauss was in Switzerland at the time; 5 June 1929 remains, then, the most likely date for this recording.
70. *The Gramophone*, January 1961, p. 401.
71. Deutsche Grammophon matrix 219–24 bm; single side nos. B 20733–8; Polydor 69849–51; US Brunswick 25026–8.
72. Deutsche Grammophon matrix 360–4 bg, 6 bm and 366–9 bg; single side nos. B 20657–66; Polydor 69840–4; US Brunswick 25000–4.
73. In 1930, Strauss was in the studio on 20, 25 and 28 June. The sessions were held in Berlin.
74. Sir Adrian Boult recalled: 'The years 1931 to 1939 saw a meteoric development in broadcasting. . . . The housing of the [BBC Symphony] orchestra had caused some headaches. The Concert Hall in Broadcasting House was designed for the pre-1930 studio orchestra of thirty-five, and of course, Savoy Hill could provide nothing adequate. We began in a huge disused wine warehouse immediately east of Waterloo Bridge. . . . Richard Strauss and Bruno Walter both conducted there.' Adrian Boult, *My Own Trumpet* (London, 1974), p. 107.
75. Margarete Teschemacher (1903–1959): German soprano.
76. The first performance of *Drei Hymnen von Friedrich Hölderlin* was given in Berlin on 4 November 1921. In the pre-season promotional material, *Ein Heldenleben* had been advertised as the main work in the programme.
77. Percy Scholes (1877–1958): English organist, critic and musicologist.
78. Percy Scholes, 'Strauss: Master of Musical Description', *Radio Times*, 16 October 1931, pp. 177 and 214.
79. Ibid., p. 210.

80. Ibid., p. 190.
81. *Musical Opinion*, November 1931, pp. 141–2.
82. *The Times*, 22 October 1931.
83. *The Observer*, 1 February 1931.
84. Other founders of the Salzburg Festival were Hugo von Hofmannsthal, Max Reinhardt and Bernhard Paumgartner.
85. On 21 August 1932, Strauss and the Vienna Philharmonic performed *Also sprach Zarathustra* and *Eine Alpensinfonie* and, on 28 August, Mozart's Symphony No. 39, Beethoven's Symphony No. 6 and Weber's Overture to *Euryanthe*. Beethoven's *Fidelio* was given on 24 and 31 August. H. Jaklitsch, *Die Salzburger Festspiele Band III: Verzeichnis der Werke und der Künstler 1920–1990*, (Salzburg, 1991), pp. 23–24
86. On 6 August 1943, Strauss and the Vienna Philharmonic performed an all-Mozart programme that included Symphony No. 40, Piano Concerto No. 26 ('Coronation') (Conrad Hansen, piano) and Symphony No. 39. Ibid., p. 54.
87. On 1 August 1944, an edict was announced closing all theatres and festivals in the Third Reich. This meant that only the general rehearsal of *Der Liebe der Danae* could take place at the Salzburg Festival that year. The opera's official première took place at Salzburg on 14 August 1952, some three years after Strauss's death.
88. Information kindly provided by the archive of the Magyar Állami Operaház, Budapest.
89. B. Walter, trans. J. A., Galston, *Theme and Variations: an Autobiography*, (London, 1947) p. 329.
90. Strauss conducted Wagner's *Parsifal* at Bayreuth on 22 and 31 July and 2, 10 and 19 August 1933 and again on 22 July and 1 and 3 August 1934.
91. Viorica Ursuleac (1894–1985): Romanian soprano. Ursuleac was married to Strauss's close associate, Clemens Krauss, under whose baton she sang the eponymous heroines for the world premières of *Arabella*, *Die ägyptische Helena* (Vienna version) and *Die Liebe der Danae* on 1 July, 1933, 14 August 1933 and 16 August 1944 respectively and Maria and the Countess at the first performances of *Friedenstag* and *Capriccio* on 24 July 1938 and 28 October 1942 respectively.
92. Here, the critic is referring to *The Adventures of Don Quixote* (1933), which was directed by Georg Wilhelm Pabst, starred Feodor Chaliapin and George Robey and had music by Jacques Ibert.
93. Enrico Mainardi (1897–1976): Italian cellist.
94. *The Gramophone*, June 1934, pp. 10–11.
95. Stefan Zweig (1881–1942): Austrian novelist, biographer and playwright.
96. Strauss's letter to Zweig, dated 17 June 1935. R. Strauss and S. Zweig, trans. M. Knight, *A Confidential Matter: The Letters of Richard Strauss and Stefan Zweig, 1931–1935* (London, 1977), pp. 99–100. The letter was found in the Gestapo's files in 1948. After the rise of Nazism, Zweig spent his remaining years in Britain, the United States and Brazil, where he and his second wife, Lotte, committed suicide on 22 February 1942.
97. *The Times*, 9 November 1936.
98. Karl Böhm conducted *Der Rosenkavalier, Tristan und Isolde, Don Giovanni, Le nozze di Figaro*, and a concert with the orchestra (12 November).
99. *The Times*, 7 November 1936.
100. *The Times*, 9 November 1936.
101. Havergal Brian (1876–1972): British composer.
102. H. Brian, 'The Richard Strauss Festival', *Musical Opinion*, December 1936, p. 208.
103. Ibid.
104. The programme for the RPS concert, on 5 November 1936, was Bliss's *Music for Strings*, Brahms's Violin Concerto (Joseph Szigeti, violin) and Strauss's *Also Sprach Zarathustra*. The London Philharmonic Orchestra was conducted by Dr. Adrian Boult and the Gold Medal was presented by Sir Hugh Allen (1869–1946). *The Musical Times* of December 1936 (p. 1081) contains a transcript of Allen's speech and Strauss's reply. (*The Musical Times* gives the date of the concert incorrectly as 19 November.)

105. The Queen's Hall concert on 7 November 1936 also contained Mozart's Symphony No. 40.
106. At about the same time, Strauss was filmed by Tobis-Filmgesellschaft conducting excerpts from *Eine Alpensinfonie* at the Deutsches Museum in Munich.
107. Strauss recorded the *Japanische Festmusik* 12 November 1940.
108. Strauss conducted *Salome* at the Vienna Staatsoper on 15 February, 5 March, 23 March and 6 May 1942. See Chapter 7 and Appendix 3 for information concerning Strauss's performing version of *Idomeneo*.
109. Christian Zimmerli undertook the digital remastering, audio restoration and editing of Koch's CD. Sleeve notes, Koch Schwann 3–1453–2 Y4, p.9.
110. Zimmerli, Ibid., pp. 10–11.
111. During the 1944 session with the Vienna Philharmonic, Strauss also recorded the *Couperin Suite* and the *Festliches Präludium*. These recordings have never been published and it is possible that they are no longer extant.
112. 'Der persönliche Verkehr unserer führenden Männer mit Dr. Strauss soll unterbleiben. Der Aufführung seiner Werke sollen jedoch, wie der Führer heute auf Rückfrage des Reichsministers Dr. Goebbels entschied, keine Schwierigkeiten bereitet werden'. A communiqué issued by Der Leiter der Partei-Kanzlei (Party Headquarters) of the Nationalsozialistische Deutsche Arbeiterpartei on 24 January 1944.
113. Ernst Roth (1896–1971): Czech-born music publisher.
114. On 5 October, the programme included the Suite from *Le Bourgeois Gentilhomme*, the Closing Scene from *Feuersnot*, the *Symphonische Fantasie aus Die Frau ohne Schatten* (Norman Del Mar, conductor) and *Don Quixote* (Paul Tortelier, cello). On 12 October, programme included *Macbeth*, an entr'acte from *Intermezzo, Ein Heldenleben* and the Closing Scene from *Ariadne auf Naxos* (Maria Cebotari, soprano).
115. Excerpts of Strauss's concerts in London in 1947 have been released recently on Testament (SBT21441).
116. E. Roth, *The Business of Music: Reflections of a Music Publisher* (London, 1969), p. 194.
117. *The Times*, 21 October 1947.
118. The singers included Erna Schlüter, Elisabeth Höngen, Ljuba Welitsch and Paul Schöffler and the orchestra was the Royal Philharmonic. The performance broadcast on 26 October has been released commercially by Arkadia (ARK9).
119. *Guardian*, 30 October 1947.

CONCLUSION

1. G. Solti, *Solti on Solti* (London, 1998), p. 80.
2. Ibid., pp. 80–1.
3. Ibid., pp. 81–2.
4. Ibid., p. 82.
5. As Strauss only conducted the final bars of Act 2 from *Der Rosenkavalier* on 10 June 1949, his performance of *Till Eulenspiegel* at the Royal Albert Hall, London, on 29 October 1947 must be considered his last professional engagement.

APPENDIX 1 STRAUSS'S PERFORMANCES AS A TENURED CONDUCTOR

1. The information found in this Appendix is based on the records in the Staatliche Museen Meiningen, the Deutschen Nationaltheaters und der Staatskapelle Weimar, the Berlin Staatsoper, the Vienna Staatsoper, Strauss's letters and engagement books, performance materials held at the Richard Strauss-Archiv and the Richard Strauss-Insitut, Garmisch-Partenkirchen, and information kindly provided by Dr Kenneth Birkin and the late Dr Franz Trenner.
2. § indicates a world première.
3. Therese Malten (1855–1930): German soprano.

4. ‡ indicates a local first performance.
5. † indicates a new production.
6. * indicates performed as part of a double-bill.
7. On 26 January 1892, Strauss preceded *Der Freischütz* with Wagner's *Kaisermarsch* to mark the birthday of Wilhelm II the following day.
8. Strauss's performance of *Lohengrin* on 11 March 1892 was given in Eisenach.
9. Strauss conducted four Subscription Concerts with the Weimar Hofkapelle during the 1889–1890 season.
10. *Suleika* was conducted by the composer.
11. Hans Giessen [Karl Buff] (1862–1907): German tenor.
12. Strauss conducted four Subscription Concerts with the Weimar Hofkapelle during the 1890–1891 season.
13. Josef Weiss (b. 1864): Polish composer and pianist.
14. Strauss conducted four Subscription Concerts and one Pension Fund Concert with the Weimar Hofkapelle during the 1891–2 season.
15. Muriel Elliot (dates unknown): British pianist.
16. Jenny Alt (b. 1860): Austrian soprano.
17. Luise Tibelti (b. 1867): German contralto.
18. Strauss conducted four Subscription Concerts and one Pension Fund Concert with the Weimar Hofkapelle during the 1893–4 season.
19. Eugen Donderer (dates unknown): German violinist.
20. Antonio Buzzini (1818–1897): Italian violinist and composer.
21. Adolf Jensen (1837–1879): German composer and pianist.
22. Part E also includes the performances that Strauss conducted at his summer Mozart and Wagner festivals, which often continued into the following autumn.
23. On 6 November 1895, Strauss conducted *Le nozze di Figaro* at the Residenztheater.
24. From 29 May 1896 Strauss transferred the majority of his Mozart performances to the Residenztheater.
25. For the performance marking the centenary of Schubert's birth on 31 January 1897, Strauss conducted the first part of the programme only.
26. (Joseph) Miroslav Weber (1854–1906): Czech violinist and composer.
27. Fannie Bloomfield-Zeisler (1866–1927): German-born American pianist.
28. Katharina Bettaque (1862–1927): German soprano.
29. Josef Becht (1859–1926): German organist.
30. Paul Gilson (1865–1942): Belgian composer.
31. Emanuela Frank (1870–1940): German soprano.
32. Betty Schwabe (b. 1876): German violinist.
33. Hans Bussmeyer (1853–1930): German composer and pianist.
34. Raoul Walter (1865–1917): Austrian tenor.
35. Otto Neitzel (1852–1920): German composer and pianist.
36. Hugo Heerman (1844–1935): German violinist.
37. Pablo de Sarasate (1844–1908): Spanish violinist and composer.
38. Willy Burmester (1869–1933): German violinist.
39. Selma Nicklas-Kempner (1850–1928); German soprano.
40. Wilhelm Stenhammar (1871–1927): Swedish composer and pianist.
41. Émile Sauret (1852–1920): French violinist.
42. Leopold Auer (1845–1930): Hungarian violinist.
43. This performance was given by the Berlin company at an opera festival in Cologne.
44. This performance was given by the Berlin company at an opera festival in Cologne.
45. This performance was given by the Berlin company at an opera festival in Cologne.
46. Strauss's performance of *Salome* on 7 November 1918 was his last for the Berlin Hofoper. With the fall of the monarchy in November 1918, the theatre became known as the Berlin Staatsoper. On 11 November 1918, Richard Strauss and the producer, Dr Georg Dröscher, undertook interim administrative responsibility for the Berlin

Staatsoper. In December 1918, Dröscher assumed sole administrative responsibility for the Staatsoper and with the appointment of Max von Schillings as Intendant the following year, Strauss was no longer artistically responsible for the theatre.

47. Although conducting in Berlin, Strauss began his duties as joint Director of the Vienna Staatsoper, with Franz Schalk as the other Director, on 1 December 1919. Strauss's first performance as joint Director of the Vienna Staatsoper was on 8 December 1919, when he conducted Beethoven's *Fidelio*.

48. With the exceptions of the cities named, all other concerts took place in Berlin at the Kroll Opera House.

49. Emil von Sauer (1862–1942): German pianist.

50. Giovanni Sgambati (1841–1914): Italian composer.

51. Strauss records a fee of 500 Marks for this concert.

52. Walter Rabl (1873–1940): Austrian composer, conductor and teacher.

53. Emmy Destinn (1878–1930): Czech soprano.

54. Ernst Kraus (1863–1941): German tenor.

55. Kurt Sommer (1868–1921): German tenor.

56. Strauss records a fee of 500 Marks for this performance.

57. Jean Paul Ertel (1865–1933): German composer.

58. No pianist is named by Strauss.

59. Strauss records a fee of 700 Marks for this performance.

60. Strauss records a fee of 300 Marks for this performance.

61. Strauss records simply 'D moll Sinfonie Bruckners'.

62. Strauss records a fee of 300 Marks for this performance and simply 'Bruckners D moll'.

63. Karl Scheidemantel (1859–1923): German baritone.

64. Strauss records a fee of 300 Marks for this performance but no programme details.

65. Strauss records simply 'D moll Sinfonie Bruckners'.

66. Ejnar Forchhammer (1868–1928): Danish tenor.

67. Hermann Bischoff (1868–1936): German composer.

68. Strauss records a fee of 500 Marks for this performance.

69. Strauss records a fee of 500 Marks for this performance.

70. Strauss records a fee of 500 Marks for this performance.

71. Strauss records a fee of 500 Marks for this performance.

72. Gustav Brecher (1879–1940): German composer.

73. Hans Schütz (1862–1917): German baritone.

74. Klaus Pringsheim (1883–1972): German composer.

75. Strauss records a fee of 1000 Marks for this performance, the name of the soloist but omits from the programme *Ah! Perfido* and his Lieder.

76. Tilly Koenen (1873–1941): Indonesian-born Dutch soprano.

77. Strauss records a fee of 500 Marks for this performance.

78. Strauss records a fee of 500 Marks for this performance.

79. Hans Huber (1852–1921): Swiss composer.

80. Strauss records a fee of 500 Marks for this performance.

81. Strauss writes simply to his parents on 24 February 1903 that 'tomorrow concert in Stettin, Saturday the actual tour begins in Dresden'.

82. With the exception of the Dresden concert, where he records a fee of 500 Marks for the performance, Strauss notes a fee of 650 Marks for each of the other performances given on the 1903 tour.

83. No venue is given by Strauss in his engagement books for the second Graz performance.

84. No venue is given for the second Venice concert by Strauss in his engagement books.

85. No venue is given for the second Milan concert by Strauss in his engagement books.

86. In Strauss's engagement book for 1903 p. 22, he gives '[Liszt's] Mazeppa' instead of the 'Love Scene' from *Feuersnot*.

87. Ibid.

88. No venue is given for the second Zurich concert by Strauss in his engagement books.

89. Strauss records a fee of 500 Marks for this performance but no venue.
90. Hans Schilling-Ziemssen (1869–1950): German composer and conductor.
91. Alfred Wittenberg (1880–1952): German violinist.
92. Paul Knüpfer (1865–1920): German bass.
93. Friedrich von Schirach (1870–1924): American-born German composer.
94. The Berlin Hofkapelle's 1908–1909 season comprised eleven Subscription Concerts and one Special Concert. Leo Blech conducted the Subscription Concert on 9 March 1909, Robert Laugs conducted the Subscription Concerts on 22 March and 8 & 10 April 1909 and Edmund von Strauss and Hugo Rüdel conducted the Sonderkonzert on 18 November 1908.
95. The records of the Berlin Staatsoper give only the key and not the number of the Symphony.
96. Bernhard Dessau (1861–1923): German violinist. Dessau was the Leader of the Berlin Hofkapelle at the time of the 1908 concert.
97. Maria Ekeblad (b. 1875): Swedish soprano.
98. The Berlin Hofkapelle's 1909–1910 season comprised eleven Subscription Concerts and two Special Concerts. With the exception of the Special Concert conducted by Leo Blech on 17 November 1909, all the concerts were conducted by Strauss.
99. Walter Kirchhoff (1879–1951): German tenor.
100. Friedrich Gernsheim (1839–1916): German composer.
101. Hans Heinrich Bolko Graf von Hochberg (1843–1926): German composer and administrator. At the time of the concert, Hochberg was Generalintendant of the Royal Theatres in Berlin.
102. Frieda Hempel (1885–1955): German soprano.
103. Marie Goetze (1865–1922): German soprano.
104. Baptist Hoffmann (1864–1937): German bass.
105. The Berlin Hofkapelle's 1910–1911 season comprised eleven Subscription Concerts and two Special Concerts. With the exception of one Special Concert conducted by Leo Blech and Hugo Rüdel on 16 November 1910, all the concerts were conducted by Richard Strauss.
106. The records of the Berlin Staatsoper state 'Symphonie G-dur (No. 13) Haydn'.
107. Franz Pönitz (1850–1913): German composer.
108. Ernst Boehe (1880–1938): German composer.
109. Andrejeva von Skilondz (1882–1969): Russian soprano.
110. Rudolf Berger (1874–1915): Czech tenor.
111. Putnam Griswold (1875–1914): American bass.
112. Bronislaw Hubermann (1882–1947): Polish violinist.
113. The Berlin Hofkapelle's 1911–1912 season comprised eleven Subscription Concerts and one Special Concert. With the exceptions of the Special Concert and one Subscription Concert conducted by Leo Blech on 22 November and 18 December 1911 respectively, all the concerts were conducted by Richard Strauss.
114. Philippe Rüfer (1844–1919): Belgian composer.
115. See Note No. 122.
116. Ernst Eduard Taubert (1838–1934): Polish (Pomeranian) composer.
117. Johannes Bischoff (1874–1935): German bass/baritone.
118. The Berlin Hofkapelle's 1912–1913 season comprised eleven Subscription Concerts and one Special Concert. With the exception of one Subscription Concert conducted by Leo Blech on 20 November 1912, all the concerts were conducted by Richard Strauss.
119. Waldemar Lütschg (1877–1948): Russian pianist.
120. Paul Scheinpflug (1875–1937): German composer and conductor.
121. See Note No. 122.
122. Robert Zeiler, Leopold Premyslaw, August Gentz and Fritz Dechert were all members of the Berlin Hofkapelle during Strauss's tenure.
123. The Berlin Hofkapelle's 1913–1914 season comprised eleven Subscription Concerts and two Special Concerts. With the exceptions of a Subscription Concert conducted

by Leo Blech on 18 October 1913, a second on 4 December 1912 at which Strauss shared the direction with Max Reger and a Sonderkonzert conducted by Leo Blech on 26 October 1913, all the concerts were conducted by Richard Strauss.

124. Sarah-Jane Charles-Cahier (1870–1951): American contralto.
125. Hermann Jadlowker (1877–1953): Latvian tenor.
126. Emil Prill (1867–1940): German flautist and member of the Berlin Hofkapelle during Strauss's tenure with orchestra.
127. Max Reger conducted the 'Hiller' Variations on 4 December 1913.
128. Hermann Bischoff (1868–1936): German composer.
129. Alfred Bruneau (1857–1934): French composer.
130. Percy Grainger (1882–1961): Australian composer and pianist.
131. Antonio Scrontino (1850–1922): Italian composer.
132. Siegmund von Hausegger (1872–1948): Austrian composer and conductor.
133. Emmi Leisner (1885–1958): German mezzo-soprano.
134. The Berlin Hofkapelle's 1914–1915 season comprised eleven Subscription Concerts and one Special Concert. Strauss conducted at all twelve concerts but shared the podium with Max Reger on 5 February 1915.
135. Käthe Herwig (1891–1953): German soprano.
136. Friedrich Koch (1862–1927): German composer.
137. Claire Dux (1885–1967): German soprano.
138. Peter Unkel (1880–1942): German tenor.
139. The Berlin Hofkapelle's 1915–1916 season comprised ten Subscription Concerts and two Special Concerts. With the exception of the Special Concert on 17 November 1915, which was conducted by Hugo Rüdel, all the concerts were conducted by Strauss.
140. The records of the Berlin Staatsoper give only the key and not the number of the symphony.
141. Frieda Kwast-Hodapp (1880–1949): German pianist. According to the records of the Berlin Staatsoper, Kwast-Hodapp was 'Hessische Kammervirtuosin'.
142. Richard Mandl (1859–1918): Austrian composer.
143. Ethel Hansa (dates unknown): German soprano.
144. Frieda Langendorff (1868–1947): German mezzo-soprano.
145. Alexander Kirchner (1876–1948): Austrian tenor.
146. The Berlin Hofkapelle's 1916–1917 season comprised eleven Subscription Concerts and two Special Concerts. With the exceptions of a Subscription Concert conducted by Leo Blech on 31 January 1917 and a Special Concert on 22 November 1916 under Hugo Rüdel, all the concerts were given by Richard Strauss.
147. Leopold Premyslaw (dates unknown): Polish violinist. See Note 122.
148. Robert Müller-Hartmann (1884–1950): German composer. The records of the Berlin Staatsoper state that Müller-Hartmann's *Sinfonische Ouvertüre* was played from the manuscript ('Manuskript zum 1. Mal').
149. Waldemar Henke (1876–1945): German tenor.
150. The Berlin Hofkapelle's 1917–1918 season comprised eleven Subscription Concerts and two Special Concerts. With the exceptions of a Subscription Concert on 1 February 1918 at which Waldemar von Baussnern conducted his own work and a Special Concert on 21 November 1917 conducted by Hugo Rüdel, all the performances were given by Richard Strauss.
151. Paul Büttner (1870–1943): German composer.
152. Ewald Strässer (1867–1933): German composer.
153. Waldemar von Baussnern (1866–1931): German composer.
154. Franz Xaver Scharwenka (1850–1924): German composer, pianist and teacher.
155. Eduard Künnecke (1885–1953): German composer.
156. Number not specified in the records of the Berlin Staatsoper.
157. Karl Armster (1883–1943): German bass.
158. The Berlin Hof/Staatskapelle's 1918–1919 season comprised eleven Subscription Concerts and one Special Concert. With the exception of the Subscription Concert on

21 March 1919, which was conducted by Leo Blech, all the performances were given by Richard Strauss.

159. Hermann Hans Wetzler (1870–1943): German composer.
160. Cornelis Dopper (1870–1939): Dutch composer and conductor.
161. Volkmar Andreae (1879–1962): Swiss composer and conductor.
162. Kurt Atterberg (1887–1974): Swedish composer.
163. Josef Mann (1883–1921): German tenor.
164. Karl Armster (1883–1943): German bass.
165. Max Trapp (1887–1971): German composer and teacher.
166. The Berlin Staatskapelle's 1919–1920 season comprised ten Subscription Concerts and two Special Concerts. Richard Strauss conducted five Subscription Concerts, Leo Blech (9 and 31 January 1920) and Wilhelm Furtwängler (3 April and 4 May 1920) two each and Max von Schillings (10 December 1920) one. Schillings and Furtwängler conducted one Sonderkonzert each on 19 November 1919 and 2 April 1920 respectively.
167. The records of the Berlin Staatsoper state only '1. Sinfonie Es-dur Haydn'.
168. Robert Hutt (1878–1942): German tenor.
169. In Strauss's engagement book, the date given for *Siegfried* is 18 March.
170. In Strauss's engagement book, the date given for *Götterdämmerung* is 21 March.
171. For the new production of *Così fan tutte* first seen on 26 May 1920, Strauss acted as producer, conductor and continuo player.
172. On 30 May 1920, Strauss also conducted a matinee concert with the Vienna Philharmonic that included Mahler's Symphony No. 1 and his own *Also sprach Zarathustra*.
173. In Strauss's engagement book, he records that *Elektra*, not *Carmen*, was performed on 2 June 1920.
174. Strauss's performances of *Le nozze di Figaro* on 2, 10, 17, 25 February and 4, 11 March 1922 were given in the Hofburg's Redoutensaal.
175. — indicates a performance by the Vienna Staatsoper at the Salzburg Festival.
176. Strauss's performances of *Jean de Paris* on 13 & 14 January 1923 were given in the Hofburg's Redoutensaal.
177. φ indicates a performance given on tour in South America with the Vienna Staatsoper at the Teatro Colón.
178. On 8 July 1923, Strauss conducted *Salome* in the afternoon and *Elektra* in the evening.
179. On 20 August 1923, Strauss preceded *Salome* with *Don Juan*.
180. Strauss's performances of *Così fan tutte* on 20 November 1923, 23 February 1924, 12 & 16 March 1924 and 28 September 1924 were given in the Hofburg's Redoutensaal.
181. ψ indicates a triple-bill.

APPENDIX 3 Structural Synopsis and Performance Analysis of Strauss's Performing Version of Mozart's *Idomeneo*

1. In this synopsis, *NMA* refers to the score of *Idomeneo* published in the *Neue Mozart Ausgabe*, ed. Daniel Heartz (Kassel: Bärenreiter, 1972).
2. Strauss follows the vocal parts, as used at the Munich première. See 'Vorwort', *NMA*, pp. xvii–xix.
3. See Chapter 9.
4. The tutti passages include bars 1 to 8, 11 to 18, 21 to 22, 25 to 26, 43 and 63. The solo oboe passages include bars 9 to 10, 19 to 20, 23 to 24 and 27 to 30.
5. When beaten in four.
6. Strauss, *Recollections and Reflections*, p. 45.
7. The use of the term, *Schlussgesang mit Tanz*, is curious, as Strauss omits the central, dance-like section, as found in Mozart's original.
8. The bars in *Erlösung!* and the *Schlussgesang mit Tanz* are numbered separately.
9. At bar 1, the chorus and principals sing *Erlösung!* or 'salvation'

Bibliography

Altena, J., Reveyoso, S. and Ryding, E., *Recorded Performances of Bruno Walter (1876–1962)*, on-line publication <www.geocities.com/walteriana76/BWrecordsB.htm>

Baker-Carr, J., *Evening at Symphony: A Portrait of the Boston Symphony Orchestra* (Boston: Houghton Mifflin Company, 1977)

Bamberger, C., ed., *The Conductor's Art* (New York: Columbia University Press, 1965)

Barea, I., *Vienna* (London: Pimlico, 1992)

Barenboim, D., *A Life in Music* (London: Weidenfeld & Nicolson, 1991)

Bauer, W. A., and Deutsch, O. E., eds., *Mozart. Briefe und Aufzeichnungen. Gesamtausgabe*, volume II (Kassel, 1962–3)

Bauer-Lechner, N., *Erinnerungen an Gustav Mahler* (Leipzig: E. P. Tal Verlag, 1923)

Bauer-Lechner, N., ed. P. Franklin, trans. D. Newlin, *Recollections of Gustav Mahler* (London: Faber Music, 1980)

Beecham, T., *A Mingled Chime* (London: Columbus Books, 1987)

Berlioz, H., trans. J. Broadhouse, *The Conductor: The Theory of His Art*

Bernstein, L., *The Unanswered Question* (Cambridge, MA: Harvard University Press, 1976)

Birkin, K., 'Richard Strauss in Weimar' Part 1, *Richard Strauss-Blätter* (Vienna: Hans Schneider Verlag, June 1995, Heft 33), pp. 3–36

Birkin, K., 'Richard Strauss in Weimar' Part 2, *Richard Strauss-Blätter* (Vienna: Hans Schneider Verlag, December 1995, Heft 34), pp. 3–56

Birkin, K., ' "... wollen sehen, ob's gelingt" Richard Strauss and the Berlin Tonkünstler-Orchester', *Richard Strauss-Blätter* (Vienna: Hans Schneider Verlag, December 2001, Heft 46), pp. 3–60

Black, A. and C., *Who Was Who, 1971–1980* (London: Adam and Charles Black, 1981)

Blackwood, A., *Sir Thomas Beecham: The Man and the Music* (London: Ebury Press, 1994)

Blaukopf, K., trans. I. Goodwin, *Mahler* (London: The Arts Book Club, 1973)

Blaukopf, H., ed., trans. E. Jephcott, *Gustav Mahler/Richard Strauss, Correspondence 1888–1911* (London: Faber & Faber, 1984)

Blaukopf, K. and H., trans. P. Baker and others, *Mahler: His Life, Work and World* (London: Thames & Hudson, 2000)

Blom, E., ed., *Grove's Dictionary of Music and Musicians*, Fifth Edition, volume VII (London: Macmillan & Co, 1975)

Böhm, K., trans. J. Kehoe, *A Life Remembered: Memoirs* (London and New York: Marion Boyars, 1992)

Böhm, K., *Begegnung mit Richard Strauss* (Vienna: Doblinger, 1964)

Böhm, K., *Ich erinnere mich ganz genau* (Vienna: Fritz Molden Verlag, 1970)

Boult, A., *Boult on Music* (London: Toccata Press, 1983)

Boult, A., *My Own Trumpet* (London: Hamish Hamilton, 1973)

Brockhaus Riemann Musiklexikon (Mainz: Schott, 1979)

Brown, C., 'Bowing Styles, Vibrato and Portamento in Nineteenth-Century Violin Playing', *Journal of the Royal Musical Association*, vol. 113 (1988)

Bülow, H. von, ed., Richard Count du Moulin Eckart and S. Goddard, trans. H. Walter, *Letters of Hans von Bülow to Richard Wagner and Others* (New York: Da Capo Press, 1979)

Bülow, H. von, ed. M. von Bülow, *Briefe, Band 1 1841–1853* (Leipzig, 1899)

Busch, F., *Aus dem Leben, eines Musikers,* (Frankfurt: Fischer, 1949)

Busch, G. and Mayer, T., *Fritz Busch: Der Dirigent* (Frankfurt: Fischer, 1990)

Busch, G., *Fritz Busch: Dirigent* (Frankfurt: Fischer, 1985)

Cardus, N., ed. D. Wright, *Cardus on Music* (London: Hamish Hamilton, 1988)

Chasins, A., *Leopold Stokowski: A Profile* (London: Robert Hale, 1979)

Chesterman, R., *Conversations with Conductors* (London: Robson Books, 1976)

Chevalley, H., ed., *Arthur Nikisch: Leben und Wirken* (Berlin: Bote & Bock, 1922)

Clément, F. and Larousse, P., *Dictionnaire des Opéras (Dictionnaire Lyrique)* (Paris: Librairie Larousse, 1905)

Clough, F. F. and Cuming, G. J., 'Diskography', *Gramophone Record Review* (August and September 1959), pp. 718–719, 824

Colles, H. C., ed., *Grove's Dictionary of Music and Musicians,* Third Edition, vol IV (London: Macmillan & Co, 1928)

Cox, D., *The Henry Wood Proms* (London: British Broadcasting Corporation, 1980)

Daniel, O., *Stokowski: A Counterpoint of View* (New York: Dodd, Mead & Company, 1982)

Del Mar, N., *Richard Strauss: A Critical Commentary on His Life and Works, 3 vols* (London: Faber & Faber, 1986)

Dent, E. J., *Mozart's Operas: A Critical Study* (London: Chatto and Windus, 1913)

Dent, E. J., *Mozart's Opera: A Critical Study,* 2nd edn (Oxford: Clarendon Press, 1947)

De Wolfe Howe, M. A., *The Boston Symphony Orchestra: An Historical Sketch* (Boston: The Atlantic Monthly Press, 1914)

Doráti, A., *Notes of Seven Decades* (London: Hodder & Stoughton, 1979)

Dupêchez, C., *Histoire de L'Opéra de Paris* (Paris: Librairie Académique Perrin, 1984)

Dyment, C., 'Felix Weingartner', *Musica,* no. 17 (Milan, April 1980), pp. 142–52

Eaton, Q., *The Boston Opera Company* (New York: Appleton–Century, 1965)

Ehrlich, C., *First Philharmonic: A History of The Royal Philharmonic Society* (Oxford: University Press, 1995)

Elkin, R., *Queen's Hall 1893–1941* (London: Rider, 1942)

Elkin, R., *Royal Philharmonic: the Annals of the Royal Philharmonic Society* (London: Rider, 1946)

Fifield, C., *True Artist and True Friend: a Biography of Hans Richter* (Oxford: Clarendon Press, 1993)

Flesch, C. and Keller, H., *The Memoirs of Carl Flesch* (London: Salisbury Square, 1957)

Forner, J., ed., *Die Gewandhaus-Konzerte zu Leipzig* (Leipzig: VEB Deutscher Verlag für Musik Leipzig, 1981)

Foster, M. B., *The History of the Philharmonic Society of London, 1813–1912* (London: The Bodley Head Press, 1912)

Franklin, P., *The Life of Mahler* (Cambridge: Cambridge University Press, 2001)

Furtwängler, W., trans. and ed. R. Taylor, *Furtwängler on Music: Essays and Addresses* (Aldershot: Scolar Press, 1991)

Furtwängler, W., trans. S. Whiteside and ed. M. Tanner, *Notebooks, 1924–54* (London: Quartet Books, 1995)

Gaisberg, F. W., *Music on Record* (London: Robert Hale, 1946)

Galkin, E. W., *A History of Orchestral Conducting in Theory and Practice* (New York: Pendragon Press, 1988)

Gay, P., *Pleasure Wars* (London: Fontana Press, 1998)

Geissmar, B., *The Baton and the Jackboot* (London: Columbus Books, 1988)

Gilliam, B., ed., *Richard Strauss and His World* (Princeton: Princeton University Press, 1992)

Gilliam, B., ed., *Richard Strauss: New Perspectives on the Composer and His Work* (Durham and London: Duke University Press, 1992)

Gillis, D., *Furtwängler and America* (Woodhaven, NY: Maryland Books, 1970)

Goossens, E., *Overture and Beginners: A Musical Autobiography* (London: Methuen, 1951)

Gould, G., *Selected Letters*, ed. J. P. L. Roberts and G. Guertin (Toronto: Oxford University Press, 1992)

Gregor, J., *Richard Strauss, der Meister der Oper* (Munich: Piper Verlag, 1939)

Gruber, G., *Mozart and Posterity*, trans. R. S. Furness (London: Quartet Books, 1991)

Haas, F., *Hans von Bülow: Leben und Wirken Wegbereiter für Wagner, Liszt und Brahms* (Wilhelmshaven: Florian Noetzel Verlag Heinrichshofen-Bücher, 2002)

Hadamowski, F., *Die Wiener Hoftheater (Staatstheater)*, vol. 2 (Vienna: Verlag Brüder Hollinek, 1975)

Haeusserman, E., *Herbert von Karajan* (Vienna: Verlag Fritz Molden, 1978)

Hagemann, C., *Bühne und Welt: Erlebnisse und Betrachtungen eines Theaterleiters* (Wiesbaden: Verlag Der Greif, Walther Gericke, 1948)

Hagen, G., *Die Cölner Oper seit Ihrem einzug in das Opernhaus, 1902/03–1911/12* (Cologne: n.d)

Hanslick, E., *Vom Musikalisch-Schönen* (Leipzig: Barth, 1854)

Hanslick, E., trans. G. Cohen, *The Beautiful in Music* (New York: Da Capo, 1974)

Hanslick, E., trans. and ed. H. Pleasants, *Hanslick's Music Criticisms* (New York: Dover, 1988)

Harnoncourt, N., trans. M. O'Neill, *The Musical Dialogue* (London: Christopher Helm, 1989)

Hartmann, R., trans. G. Davies, *Richard Strauss: The Staging of his Operas and Ballets* (Oxford: Oxford University Press, 1982)

Hennenberg, F., *The Leipzig Gewandhaus Orchestra* (Leipzig: VEB Edition Leipzig, 1962)

Herzfeld, F., *Wilhelm Furtwängler: Weg und Wesen* (Leipzig: Wilhelm Goldmann Verlag, 1942)

Heyworth, P., *Otto Klemperer: His Life and Times, Volume 1: 1885–1933* (Cambridge: Cambridge University Press, 1996)

Heyworth, P., *Otto Klemperer: His Life and Times Volume 2: 1933–1973* (Cambridge, Cambridge University Press, 1996)

Higgins, J., ed., *Glyndebourne: A Celebration* (London: Jonathan Cape, 1984)

Higgins, J., *The Making of an Opera* (London: Secker & Warburg, 1978)

Hinrichsen, H.-J., *Musikalishe Interpretation: Hans von Bülow* (Stuttgart: Franz Steiner Verlag, 1999)

Hirsch, F., *Das Grosse Wörterbuch der Musik* (Wilhelmshaven: Heinrichshofen Verlag, 1984)

Hirsch, H. J. and Saul, J., 'A George Szell Discography', *Le Grand Baton* 9: 1–2 (USA: 1972), p. 86

Hofmann, J., *Piano Playing with Piano Questions Answered* (New York: Doubleday, Page and Company, 1909)

Holden, R., Richard Strauss: the Origin, Dissemination and Reception of his Mozart Renaissance, Ph.D. dissertation, University of London, 1995.

Holden, R., 'Richard Strauss: The Mozart and Beethoven Recordings', *Richard Strauss-Blätter* (Vienna: Hans Schneider Verlag, June 1996, Heft 35)

Holden, R., 'Richard Strauss' Performing Version of Idomeneo', *Richard Strauss-Blätter* (Vienna: Hans Schneider Verlag, December 1996, Heft 36)

Holden, R., 'Richard Strauss in London', *Richard Strauss-Blätter* (Vienna: Hans Schneider Verlag, June 1997, Heft 37)

Holden, R., 'Percy Pitt: Richard Strauss' English Correspondent', *Richard Strauss-Blätter* (Vienna: Hans Schneider Verlag, June 1998, Heft 38)

Holden, R., 'Recording *Don Juan*: the Composer's Perspective', *Richard Strauss-Blätter* (Vienna: Hans Schneider Verlag, December 1998, Heft 40)

Holden, R., 'Richard Strauss and the Philharmonic Society, London', *Richard Strauss-Blätter* (Vienna: Hans Schneider Verlag, December 2000, Heft 44)

Holden, R., 'Richard Strauss: An Organised Mozartian', *Richard Strauss-Blätter* (Vienna: Hans Schneider Verlag, December 2001, Heft 46)

Holden, R., 'Richard Strauss: the *Don Juan* recordings', *Performance Practice Review*, vol. 10, no. 1 (USA: Spring 1997)

Holden, R., *Glorious John: A Collection of Sir John Barbirolli's Lectures, Articles, Speeches and Interviews* (Uttoxeter: The Barbirolli Society, 2007)

Holden, R., *The Virtuoso Conductors: The Central European Tradition from Wagner to Karajan* (New Haven and London: Yale University Press, 2005)

Horowitz, J., *Understanding Toscanini* (London: Faber & Faber, 1987)

Hoyer, H., *Chronik der Wiener Staatsoper, 1945 bis 1995* (Vienna and Munich: Verlag Anton Schroll & Co, 1995)

Hughes, S., *Glyndebourne* (London: Methuen, 1965)

Hunt, J., *More 20th Century Conductors* (London: John Hunt, 1993)

Hunt, J., *Philharmonic Autocrat* (London: John Hunt, 1993)

Hunt, J., *Leopold Stokowski Discography and Concert Register* (London: John Hunt/Leopold Stokowski Society, 1996)

Hyatt King, A., *Musical Pursuits* (London: The British Library, 1987)

Jacobs, A., *Henry J. Wood: Maker of the Proms* (London: Methuen, 1995)

Jaklitsch, H., *Die Salzburger Festspiele Band III: Verzeichnis der Werke und der Künstler, 1920-1990* (Salzburg: Residenz Verlag, 1991)

Jefferson, A., *The Life of Richard Strauss* (Newton Abbot: David & Charles, 1973)

Johnson, E., ed., *Stokowski: Essays in Analysis of his Art* (London: Triad Press, 1973)

Kapp, J., *Richard Strauss und die Berliner Oper* (Berlin-Halensee: Max Hesses Verlag, 1939)

Karajan, H. von, as told to F. Endler, trans. S. Spencer, *Herbert von Karajan: My Autobiography* (London: Sidgwick & Jackson, 1989)

Kende, G. K., 'Was Richard Strauss in Wien dirigierte', *Richard Strauss-Blätter* (Vienna: Hans Schneider Verlag, June 1988, Heft 19)

Kennedy, M., *Adrian Boult* (London: Hamish Hamilton, 1987)

Kennedy, M., *Barbirolli: Conductor Laureate* (London: MacGibbon & Kee, 1971)

Kennedy, M., *Richard Strauss* (London: Dent, 1988)

Kennedy, M., *Strauss Tone Poems* (London: BBC, 1984)

Kennedy, M., *The Hallé Tradition: A Century of Music* (Manchester: Manchester University Press 1960)

Kipnis, I., 'Molto improvvisato', *Classic Record Collector*, Winter 2000

Klemperer, O., trans. J. Maxwell Brownjohn, *Minor Recollections* (London: Dobson Books, 1964)

Klemperer, O., Heyworth, P., *Conversations with Klemperer* (London: Faber & Faber, 1985)

Klemperer, O., ed. M. Anderson, *Klemperer on Music: Shavings from a Musician's Workbench* (London: Toccata Press, 1986)

Kobbé, G., ed. G. Harewood, *Kobbé's Complete Opera Book, 10th Edition* (London: Bodley Head, 1987)

Köhler, J., trans. S. Spencer, *Richard Wagner: The Last of the Titans* (New Haven and London: Yale University Press, 2004)

Kraus, H. and Schreinzer, K., *Wiener Philharmoniker, 1842-1942* (Vienna: Universal Edition, 1942)

Kropfinger, K., trans. P. Palmer, *Wagner and Beethoven: Richard Wagner's reception of Beethoven* (Cambridge: University Press, 1991)

Kuret, P., *Mahler in Laibach: Ljubljana, 1881-2* (Vienna, Cologne and Weimar: Böhlau Verlag, 2001)

Ku čerová, D., 'Gustav Mahler v Olomouci', *Hudební věda* 4 (Prague, 1968), Eng., Ger. Résumés, pp. 649-51, 653-5

La Grange, H.-L. de, *Mahler* vol. 1 (London: Gollanz, 1974)

La Grange, H.-L. de, *Gustav Mahler*, vol. 3, *Vienna: Triumph and Disillusion (1904-1907)* (Oxford: Oxford University Press, 1999)

La Grange, H.-L. de and Weiss, G., *Ein Glück ohne Ruh': Die Briefe Gustav Mahlers an Alma* (Munich: BTB, 1997)

Landon, H. C. Robbins, (ed.), *The Mozart Compendium - A Guide to Mozart's Life and Music* (London: Thames & Hudson, 1990)

Landon, H. C. Robbins, *Haydn, Chronicle and Works*, vol. 3, *Haydn in England 1791–1795* (London: Bloomington, 1976–80)

Landon, H. C. Robbins, *Mozart: The Golden Years* (London: Thames & Hudson, 1989)

Landon, H. C. Robbins, *Mozart and the Masons* (London: Thames & Hudson, 1991)

Landon, H. C. Robbins, *Mozart and Vienna* (London: Thames & Hudson, 1991)

Landon, H. C. Robbins, *Mozart's Last Year* (London: Thames & Hudson, 1988)

Lang, K., *The Karajan Dossier*, trans. S. Spencer (London: Faber & Faber, 1992)

Lang, P. H., *Music in Western Civilization* (New York: Norton; London: Dent, 1963)

Lebrecht, N., *Mahler Remembered* (London: Faber & Faber, 1987)

Lebrecht, N., *The Maestro Myth* (London: Simon & Schuster, 1991)

Lehmann, L., *My Path through Life* (New York: Putnams, 1914)

Leinsdorf, E., *On Music* (Portland: Amadeus Press, 1997)

Louis, R., 'Bruno Walter au disque', *Diapason 415* (Supplement May 1995), pp. xiv–xviii

Lyser, F. P., 'Zweier Meister Söhne (Schlub)', *Neue Zeitschrift für Musik*, no. 44 (1844)

Lyser, F. P., 'Mozart's eigene Berdeutschung des Textes "Don Giovanni", nebst zwei Proben daraus', *Neue Zeitschrift für Musik*, no. 32 (1845)

Macclintock, C., *Readings in the History of Music in Performance* (Bloomington, IN Indiana University Press, 1979)

Mahler, G., trans. E. Wilkins, E. Kaiser and B. Hopkins, ed. K. Martner, *Selected Letters of Gustav Mahler* (London: Faber and Faber, 1979)

Mahler, A., *Gustav Mahler: Memories and Letters*, trans. B. Creighton, ed. D. Mitchell and K. Martner (London: Cardinal, 1990)

Mahler-Werfel, A., trans. and ed. A. Beaumont, *Alma Mahler-Werfel: Diaries 1898–1902* (London, Faber & Faber, 1998)

Mann, W., *Richard Strauss: A Critical Study of the Operas* (London: Cassell and Company, 1964)

Marek, G. R., *Richard Strauss: The Life of a Non-Hero* (London: Gollancz, 1967)

Marsh, R. C., *Dialogues and Discoveries: James Levine, His Life and His Music* (New York: Scribner, 1998)

Marsh, R. C., 'The Heritage of Bruno Walter', *High Fidelity* 14 (1964), pp. 44–8, 103–9

Martner, K., *Gustav Mahler im Konzertsaal: eine Dokumentation seiner Konzerttätigkeit) 1870–1911* (Kopenhagen: K-M Privatdruck, 1985)

Masini, U. pref., 'Discografia di Bruno Walter', *Musica 8* (June 1984), pp. 32–9

Meyer, G. E., *100 Jahre Münchner Philharmoniker* (Munich: Alois Knürr Verlag, 1994)

Meyers Taschen-Lexikon Musik (Mannheim: B. I. Taschen Buch Verlag, 1984)

Millington B. and Spencer S., eds., *Wagner in Performance* (New Haven and London: Yale University Press, 1992)

Moberly, R. and Raeburn, C., 'Mozart's "Figaro": The Plan of Act III', *Music & Letters*, vol. 46 (Oxford: Oxford University Press, 1965)

Morse, P., 'Richard Strauss' Recordings, A Complete Discography', *Journal of the Association for Recorded Sound Collections*, 9:1 (1977)

Moulin-Eckart, R., *Hans von Bülow* (Munich: Rösl & Cie, 1921)

Müller, H. and Gerasch V., eds., *Südthüringer Forschungen 28* (Meiningen: Staatliche Museen Meiningen, 1995)

Müller, H. and Kern V., eds., *Die Meininger kommen!* (Meiningen: Staatliche Museen Meiningen, 1999)

Myers, R., ed., *Richard Strauss and Romain Rolland: Correspondence and Diary Fragments* (London: Calder and Boyars, 1968)

Newlin, D., *Bruckner–Mahler–Schoenberg* (London: Marion Boyars, 1979)

Osborne, R., *Conversations with Karajan* (Oxford: University Press, 1989)

Osborne, R., *Herbert von Karajan: A Life in Music* (London: Chatto & Windus, 1998)

Ott, A., ed., *Die Münchner Philharmoniker, 1893–1968: Ein Kapitel Kulturgeschichte* (Munich: Peter Winkler Verlag, 1968)

Panigel, A. and H.-J., 'Félix Weingartner', *Disques* 1 (Paris: 15 January 1948)

Paumgartner, B., *Gustav Mahlers Bearbeitung von Mozarts 'Così fan tutte' für seine Aufführungen an der Wiener Hofoper* (Kassel: Bärenreiter, 1968)

Pearton, M., *The LSO at 70: A History of the Orchestra* (London: Gollancz, 1974)

Philip, R., *Early Recordings and Musical Style: Changing Tastes in Instrumental Performance, 1900–1950* (Cambridge: University Press, 1994)

Philip, R., *Performing Music in the Age of Recording* (New Haven and London: Yale University Press, 2004)

Pickett, D. A., Warren, R. rev., *A Bruno Walter Discography – Part One: Commercial Recordings: Issued Discs Only*, Bruno Walter Society, 1973

Pickett, D. A., Gustav Mahler as an Interpreter: A Study of his Textural Alterations and Performance Practice in the Symphonic Repertoire, Ph.D. Dissertation (1988), University of Surrey

Piendl, S. and Otto, T., eds., *Stenographische Umarmung* (Regensburg: ConBrio, 2002)

Pine, L. G., ed., *Who's Who in Music* (London: Shaw Publishing, 1949–50)

Pitou, S., *The Paris Opéra – An Encyclopaedia of Opera, Ballets, Composers and performers – 'Growth and Grandeur 1815–1914'*, volume M-Z (Westport: Greenwood, 1990)

Possart, E. von, *Ueber die Neueinstudierung und Neuinszenierung des Mozart'schen Don Giovanni (Don Juan) auf dem kgl. Residenztheater zu München* (Munich: A. Bruckmann's Verlag, 1896)

Praeger, F., *Wagner as I Knew Him* (New York: Longmans, 1893)

Prawy, M., *Die Wiener Oper* (Vienna: Molden, 1969)

Previn, A., ed., *Orchestra* (London: Macdonald & Janes, 1979)

Prieberg, F. K., trans. C. Dolan, *Trial of Strength: Wilhelm Furtwängler and the Third Reich* (London: Quartet Books, 1991)

Pritchard, J., 'Conducting Mozart', *Opera Annual* 2 (London: Opera, 1956)

Quander, G., *Klangbilder: Portrait der Staatskapelle Berlin* (Frankfurt: Ullstein; Berlin: Propyläen, 1995)

Rees, C. B., *100 Years of the Hallé* (London: MacGibbon & Kee, 1957)

Rehkemper, H., 'Details of Radio Recordings', *The Record Collector*

Reid, C., *John Barbirolli* (London: Hamish Hamilton, 1971)

Reilly, E. R., *Gustav Mahler and Guido Adler: Records of a Friendship* (Cambridge: Cambridge University Press, 1982)

Rigby, C., *John Barbirolli: A Biographical Sketch* (Altrincham: John Sherratt, 1948)

Robinson, P., *Karajan* (London: MacDonald & Janes, 1975)

Roman, Z., *Gustav Mahler and Hungary* (Budapest: Akadémiai Kiadó, 1991)

Roman, Z., *Gustav Mahler's American Years, 1907–1911: A Documentary History*, (Stuyvesant: Pendragon Press, 1989)

Rosen, C., *The Classical Style: Haydn, Mozart, Beethoven* (London: Faber & Faber, 1976)

Rosenthal, H., *Two Centuries of Opera at Covent Garden* (London: Putnam, 1958)

Rösler, W., Haedler, M. and von Marcard, M., *Das 'Zauberschloss' Unter den Linden: Die Berliner Staatsoper Geschichte und Geschichten von den Anfängen bis heute* (Berlin: Edition Q, 1997)

Rushton, J., ed., *W.A. Mozart: Idomeneo* (Cambridge: Cambridge University Press, 1993)

Ryding, E. and Pechefsky, R., *Bruno Walter: A World Elsewhere* (New Haven and London: Yale University Press, 2001)

Sachs, H., *Toscanini* (London: Robson Books, 1993)

Sadie, S., ed., *The New Grove Dictionary of Music and Musicians* (London: Macmillan, 1980)

Saul, J., 'A Personal Account of George Szell', *Le Grand Baton* 9:1–2 (1972)

Sawallisch, W., *Im Interesse der Deutlichkeit: Mein Leben mit der Musik* (Hamburg: Hoffmann und Campe, 1988)

Schabas, E., *Theodore Thomas, America's Conductor and Builder of Orchestras, 1835–1905* (Urbana and Chicago: University of Illinois Press, 1989)

Schaefer, H.-J., 'Gustav Mahlers Wirken in Kassel', *Musica*, 14:6 (1960), p. 350

Schlötterer-Traimer, R., *Richard Strauss und die Musikalishe Akademie in München* (Munich: Hypo–Vereinsbank Kulturgesellschaft, 1999)

Schmoll gen. Eisenwerth, R., ed., *Die Münchener Philharmoniker von der Gründung bis heute* (Munich: Wolf & Sohn, 1985)

Schnabel, A., *My Life and Music* (New York: Dover, 1988)

Schonberg, H., *The Great Conductors* (London: Gollancz, 1977)

Schönzeler, H-H., *Furtwängler* (London: Duckworth, 1990)

Schuh, W., trans. M. Whittall, *Richard Strauss: A Chronicle of the Early Years, 1864–1898* (Cambridge: Cambridge University Press, 1982)

Schwarzkopf, E., *On and Off the Record: A Memoir of Walter Legge* (London: Faber & Faber, 1982)

Schuller, G., *The Compleat Conductor* (Oxford: Oxford University Press, 1997)

Shanet, H., *Philharmonic: A History of New York's Orchestra* (New York: Doubleday, 1975)

Shirakawa, S. H., *The Devil's Music Master* (Oxford: University Press, 1992)

Shore, B., *The Orchestra Speaks* (London: Longmans Green,1938)

Shostakovitch, D., ed. S. Volkov, *Testimony: The Memoirs of Dmitri Shostakovich* (London: Faber & Faber, 1979)

Simek, U., ed., *100 Jahre Wiener Volksoper* (Vienna, Cologne and Weimar: Böhlau Verlag, 1998)

Slonimsky, N., rev., *Baker's Biographical Dictionary of Musicians,* 8th edn (New York: Schirmer Books, 1992)

Snyder, L., *Community of Sound: Boston Symphony and its World of Players* (Boston: Beacon Press, 1979)

Solti, G., *Solti on Solti* (London: Vintage, 1998)

Stewart, A., *The LSO at 90: from Queen's Hall to the Barbican Centre* (London: London Symphony Orchestra, 1994)

Stokowski, L., *Music for All of US* (New York: Simon & Schuster, 1943)

Strasser, O., trans. J. Williamson, 'Beethoven's Ninth and the Vienna Philharmonic', sleeve notes, Deutsche Grammophon CD 435 325-2

Strauss, R. and Zweig, S., trans. M. Knight, M., *A Confidential Matter: The Letters of Richard Strauss and Stefan Zweig, 1931–1935* (Berkely, CA and London: University of California Press, 1977)

Strauss, R., ed. W. Schuh, *Betrachtungen und Erinnerungen* (Zurich: Atlantis Verlag, 1949)

Strauss, R., ed. W. Schuh, W., *Briefe an die Eltern, 1882–1906* (Zurich: Atlantis Verlag, 1954)

Strauss, R., ed. G. Brosche, *Briefwechsel mit Clemens Krauss* (Vienna: Institut für Österreichische Musikdokumentation, 1997)

Strauss, R., ed. R. Tenschert, *Briefwechsel mit Josef Gregor* (Salzburg: Otto Müller Verlag, 1955)

Strauss, R., ed. W. Schuh, *Briefwechsel mit Willi Schuh* (Zurich, 1969)

Strauss, R., ed. W. Schuh and F. Trenner, trans. A. Gishford, *Hans von Bülow and Richard Strauss: Correspondence* (London: Boosey & Hawkes, 1955)

Strauss, R., ed. W. Schuh, trans. L. J. Lawrence, *Recollections and Reflections* (London: Boosey & Hawkes, 1953)

Strauss, R., ed. F. and A. Strauss, arr. W. Schuh, trans. H. Hammelmann and E. Osers, *The Correspondence between Richard Strauss and von Hofmannsthal* (Cambridge: Cambridge University Press, 1980)

Stroff, S. M. 'Albert Coates', *Le Grand Baton,* March 1980 45/17:1

Tovey, D. F., *Essays in Musical Analysis* vol. 6 (Oxford: Oxford University Press, 1957)

Trenner, F., *Richard Strauss – Werkverzeichnis* (Vienna: Doblinger, 1985)

Trenner, F., 'Richard Strauss and Munich', trans. G. Simon, *Tempo 69,* Summer 1964 (London: Boosey & Hawkes)

Trenner, F., 'Richard Strauss am Pult der Münchner Oper', *Richard Strauss-Blätter* (Vienna: Hans Schneider Verlag, June 1991, Heft 25)

Trenner, F., 'Anmerkungen zur Aufführung von Beethovens Symphonien', *Neue Zeitschrift für Musik*, June 1964 (125).

Trenner, Franz., ed. Florian Trenner, *Richard Strauss: Chronik zu Leben und Werk* (Vienna: Verlag Richard Strauss, 2000)

Trotter, W. R., *Priest of Music: The Life of Dimitri Mitropoulos* (Portland: Amadeus Press, 1995)

Tschulik, N., *Musiktheater in Österreich: Die Oper im 20. Jahrhundert* (Vienna: Österreichischer Bundesverlag, 1984)

Turnbull, R., *The Opera Gazetteer* (New York: Rizzoli, 1988)

Vaughan, R., *Herbert von Karajan – a biographical portrait* (London: Weidenfeld & Nicolson, 1990)

Vermeil, J., trans. C. Naish, *Conversations with Boulez: Thoughts on Conducting* (Portland: Amadeus Press, 1996)

Wagner, R., *My Life* (London: Constable, 1994)

Wagner, R., trans. M. Whittall, ed. A. Gray, *My Life* (Cambridge: Cambridge University Press, 1983)

Wagner, R., trans. W. Ashton Ellis, *Actors and Singers* (Lincoln and London: Bison Books, 1995)

Wagner, R., trans. W. Ashton Ellis, *Jesus of Nazareth and Other Writings* (Lincoln and London: Bison Books, 1995)

Wagner, R., trans. W. Ashton Ellis, *Pilgrimage to Beethoven and Other Essays* (Lincoln and London: Bison Books, 1994)

Wagner, R., trans. W. Ashton Ellis, *Art and Politics* (Lincoln and London: Bison Books, 1995)

Wagner, R., *Über das Dirigieren* (Leipzig: Breitkopf & Härtel, 1869)

Wagner, R., trans. E. Dannreuther, *On Conducting* (London: Reeves, 1897)

Walter, B., trans. T. Walter Lindt, *Gustav Mahler* (London: Quartet, 1990)

Walter, B., trans. P. Hamburger, *Of Music and Music-making* (London: Faber & Faber, 1961)

Walter, B., trans. J. A. Galston, *Theme and Variations: An Autobiography* (London: Hamish Hamilton, 1947)

Walton, C., 'Richard Wagner als Dirigent in Zürich', *Tribschener Blätter* 55/56, September 1998

Warfield, S., 'Friedrich Wilhelm Meyer: Some Biographical Notes on Richard Strauss's Composition Teacher', *Richard Strauss-Blatter* (Vienna: Hans Schneider Verlag, June 1997, Heft 37)

Warrack, J. and West, E., *The Oxford Dictionary of Opera* (Oxford: Oxford University Press, 1992)

Weingartner, F., trans. M. Wolff, *Buffets and Rewards: A Musician's Reminiscences*, (London: Hutchinson, 1937)

Weingartner, F., *Die Symphonie nach Beethoven* (Leipzig: Breitkopf & Härtel, 1897)

Weingartner, F., trans. A. Bles, *The Post-Beethoven Symphonists: Symphony Writers since Beethoven* (London: W. Reeves, n.d.)

Weingartner, F., *Über das Dirigieren* (Leipzig: Breitkopf & Härtel, 1895)

Weingartner, F., trans. E. Newman, *On Conducting* (New York: Dover, 1969)

Weingartner, F., *Ratschläge für Aufführung der Symphonien Beethovens* (Leipzig: Breitkopf & Härtel, 1906)

Weingartner, F., trans. J. Crosland, *On the Performance of Beethoven's Symphonies* (London: Breitkopf & Härtel, 1907)

Weingartner, F., *Ratschläge für Aufführungen Klassischer Symphonien Band III Mozart* (Leipzig: Breitkopf & Härtel, 1923)

Westernhagen, C. von, 'Wagner', *The New Grove Dictionary of Music and Musicians*, vol. 20, ed. S. Sadie (London: Macmillan, 1980)

Westernhagen, C. von, trans. M. Whittall, *Wagner: A Biography, Volume 1: 1813–64* (Cambridge: Cambridge University Press, 1978)

Wilhelm, K., trans. M. Whittall, *Richard Strauss: An Intimate Portrait* (London: Thames & Hudson, 1989)

Williamson, J., *Strauss: Also Sprach Zarathustra* (Cambridge: Cambrige University Press, 1993)

Willnauer, F., *Gustav Mahler und die Wiener Oper* (Vienna: Löcker Verlag, 1993)

Wolff, K., *Schnabel's Interpretation of Piano Music* (London: Faber Music, 1972)

Wood., Henry J., *My Life of Music* (London: Gollancz, 1938)

Wurmser, L., 'Richard Strauss as an Opera Conductor', *Music & Letters* 45 (Oxford: Oxford University Press, 1964)

Young, K., *Music's Great Days in the Spas and Watering Places* (London: Macmillan, 1968)

Zaslaw, N., *Mozart's Symphonies: Context, Performance Practice, Reception* (Oxford: Oxford University Press, 1989)

Zimdars, R. L., trans. and ed., *The Piano Master Classes of Hans von Bülow: Two Participants' Accounts* (Bloomington and Indianapolis: Indiana University Press, 1993)

Zehetmair H. and Schläder J., eds., *Nationaltheater: Die Bayerische Staatsoper* (Munich: Bruckmann, 1992)

Index

Adler, F. C., 99, 100
Adler, Guido, 98
Adorno, Theodor, 31
Ahna, Adolf de, 45
Ahna, Pauline de, *see under* Strauss,
  Pauline (née de Ahna)
Albert, Eugen d', 13, 23, 47, 68, 136; *Die
  Abreise*, 67; 74
Allen, Hugh, 155
Allgemeiner deutscher Musikverein, 118
Altman, Wilhelm, 85
Alwin, Karl, 141
Ampico, 136, 140
Anderson, W. R., 147–148
Anstalt für musikalische
  Aufführungsrechte (Institute for
  Performing Rights in Music), 64
Arne, Thomas, 141
Ashwell, Lena, 132
Atterberg, Kurt, 83
Auber, Daniel, 11, 40, 69, 88; *La Muette de
  Portici*, 11, 41, 68; *Le cheval de bronze*,
  68, 69; *Fra Diavolo*, 71
Auersperg Palace (Vienna), 98

Bach, Johann Sebastian, 18, 29, 83;
  Brandenburg Concertos Nos. 1 to 6;
  Brandenburg Concerto No. 1, 82;
  Brandenburg Concerto No. 3, 83;
  Orchestral Suite No. 1, 83; Orchestral
  Suite No. 2 (ed. Bülow), 83; Orchestral
  Suite No.3, 83; Concerto for Two Violins
  in D minor, 83
Backhaus, Wilhelm, 119
Bahr-Mildenburg, Anna, 131
Ballets Russes, 132
Barbirolli, John, 86, 87
Barea, Ilsa, 98
Bayerisches Staatsorchester, *see under*
  Munich Hofkapelle

Bayreuth Festival, 5, 12, 65, 99, 110, 111,
  112, 152
BBC Symphony Orchestra, 150–151, 158
Beaumarchais, Pierre Augustin Caron
  de, 98
Bechstein, Carl, 16
Becker, Hugo, 116–117
Beecham, Thomas, 129, 131, 132, 157, 158
Beethoven, Ludwig van, xi, 5, 7, 11, 16, 17,
  18, 19, 22, 29, 30, 31, 32, 34, 35, 36, 42,
  47, 57, 58, 82, 83, 84, 85, 86, 111, 113,
  114, 118, 122, 142–144, 152, 162;
  Symphony No. 1, 19; Symphony No. 2,
  21; Symphony No. 3 ('Eroica'), 21–22,
  29, 85; Symphony No. 5, 19, 29, 85–88,
  147–148; Symphony No. 6 ('Pastoral'),
  19, 29, 34; Symphony No. 7, 5, 19, 29,
  114, 143–144, 145; Symphony No. 8, 29;
  Symphony No. 9 ('Choral'), 13, 35, 36,
  37, 73, 84–85, 87, 111; *Grosse Fuge* (from
  String Quartet Op. 133), 17; *Leonore* No.
  3 Overture, 11, 85; Overture to *Egmont*,
  19, 57; Overture to *Coriolan*, 85; Piano
  Concerto No. 3, 122; Piano Concerto
  No. 4, 19, 129; Piano Concerto No. 5
  ('Emperor'), 19; *Fidelio*, 41, 63, 67, 152
Benno Walter Quartet, 9
Berg, Alban, 76
Berger, Francesco, 116–117
Berger, Wilhelm, 111
Berlin Hofkapelle (later Berlin
  Staatskapelle), 13, 66, 71, 72, 78, 81–85,
  88, 137–138, 144–145, 147–148, 150, 152
Berlin Hofoper (later Berlin Staatsoper),
  63, 64–71, 72, 74–6, 78, 81, 88–93,
  105, 137
Berlin Philharmonic, 18, 39–40, 46–47, 71,
  72, 78, 81, 84, 111, 147, 152
Berlin Staatskapelle, *see under* Berlin
  Hofkapelle

Berlin Staatsoper, *see under* Berlin Hofoper
Berliner Tageblatt, 22
Berlin Tonkünstler-Orchester, 71–74, 78, 82
Berlioz, Hector, 17, 39, 69, 111, 114, 118, 124, 125; *Benvenuto Cellini*, 69; Overture to *Benvenuto Cellini*, 69; 'Le Roi Lear' Overture, 81–82; *Symphonie fantastique*, 113; *Rêverie et Caprice*, 124; *Nuits d'Été*, 124; *Damnation of Faust*, 124; *Enfance du Christ*, 124; *Treatise on Instrumentation and Modern Orchestration* (ed. Richard Strauss), 124
Bischoff, Hermann (composer), 198, 203
Bischoff, Johannes (bass), 202, 203, 204
Bizet, Georges, 69, 88; *Carmen*, 69, 71, 135
Blech, Leo, 73, 81
Blumen, Alfred, 158
Bock, Hugo, 13
Böckmann, Ferdinand, 13
Böhe, Ernst, 83
Böhm, Karl, 105, 153, 155, 161
Boieldieu, François-Adrien, *La Dame blanche*, 11
Bormann, Martin, 157
Bösendorfersaal (Vienna), 10
Boston Symphony Orchestra, 65, 126, 129
Bote & Bock (publishers), 98
Botstein, Leon, 5
Boult, Adrian, 54, 158
Brahms, Johannes, 13, 17, 18, 20, 21, 22, 31, 32, 136, 149; Symphony No. 4, 20; *Schicksalslied*, 21; 'Academic Festival' Overture, 22
Breitkopf und Härtel (publishers), 49, 99, 102
Brendel, Franz, 118
Brian, Havergal, 155
Brioschi, Anton, 71
British Broadcasting Corporation (BBC), 146, 149, 150–151, 158
British Library, 98, 99, 100
Bronsart von Schellendorf, Hans, 29, 39, 41, 42
Bruckner, Anton, 65, 73, 83, 95; Symphony No. 3, 73; Symphony No. 5, 95
Brunswick 'Light-Ray' Method, 143–145
Brunswick Records, 140
Bülow, Cosima von (née Liszt), *see under* Wagner, Cosima (née Liszt)
Bülow, Hans von, xi, 3–4, 13, 15–22, 23, 25, 26, 27, 29, 31, 32, 39–40, 42, 46, 52, 58, 65, 66, 67, 69, 72, 73, 83, 84, 85, 109, 110, 111, 136; *Nirwana*, 21

Burrian, Carl, 75
Busch, Fritz, 61, 106, 161

Campanini, Cleofonte, 90–91
Cardus, Neville, 158
Carnegie Hall (New York), 126–129
Carreño, Teresa, 136
Cervantes, Miguel de, 153
Chabrier, Emmanuel, 67, 68; *Briséïs*, 67, 68
Chaliapin, Feodor, 153
Charles V, 82
Chauvet, Charles-Alexis, 114
Cherubini, Luigi, *Les deux journées*, 41
Chicago Symphony Orchestra, 140
Chopin, Frédéric, 17, 19, 122; *Berceuse*, 122; Mazurka Op. 7 No. 3, 122; Grand Valse, Op. 42, 122; Ballade Op. 47, 122
Chrysander, Friedrich, 85, 86
Cologne Stadttheater, 48
Columbia Records, 140
Concertgebouw (Amsterdam), 113
Concertgebouw Orchestra, 121, 122, 146
Cornelius, Peter, 118, 147
Cowen, Frederic, 131
Czerny, Carl, 55

Davidoff, Karl, 111
Debussy, Claude, *Nocturnes*, 114; *La Mer*, 114
Del Mar, Norman, 32, 36, 101
Dent, Edward J., 52
Denza, Luigi, 25; *Funiculí, Funiculà*, 25
Deppe, Ludwig, 81
Dessau Hofkapelle, 139
Deutsche Grammophon, 85, 137–138, 143–146, 148, 150, 152, 156
Deutsches Landestheater (Prague), 65
Diaghilev, Serge, 132
Domschule (Cathedral School) (Munich), 8
Donizetti, Gaetano, *La favorite*, 26
Draeseke, Felix, 34
Drei Masken Verlag (publishers), 49
Dresden Hofkapelle, 9, 13, 155
Dresden Hofoper, 75, 91, 103, 137, 141, 153, 154–155
Dresden Staatskapelle (Sächsische Staatskapelle), *see under* Dresdner Hofkapelle
Dresden Staatsoper (Sächsische Staatsoper), *see under* Dresdner Hofoper
Dröscher, Georg, 92
Duo-Art, 136
Dupont, Joseph, 118
Dvořák, Antonin, 17

Edison, Thomas, 135–136
Edward VII, British monarch, 76
Einstein, Alfred, 49, 50, 90, 103–104
Electrola, 156
Elgar, Edward, 122, 162; incidental music
    to *Grania and Diarmid*, 122
Ernst Eulenburg (publishers), 49, 85–87
Ertel, Jean Paul, 73
Exposition universelle (World's Fair, Paris),
    118

Fiebach, Otto, *Bei frommen Hirten*, 41
Fischer, Franz, 26–27, 29
Flotow, Friedrich von, 40
Fort Oglethorpe, Georgia (USA), 65
Frankfurt Museum Concerts, 64, 109
Frankfurt Stadttheater, 135
Franz, Ellen, 16
Franz Ferdinand of Austria, 133
Frederick the Great, King of Prussia, 81
Fremstad, Olive, 76
Friedman, Ignaz, 136
Fürstner (publishers), 78
Furtwängler, Wilhelm, 35, 36, 148, 152

Geiss, Josef, 139
Genossenschaft deutscher Tonsetzer
    (Fellowship of German Composers), 64
Georg II, Herzog (Duke) von Sachsen-
    Meiningen, 16, 22, 25
Gérard, Henri-Philippe, 114
Gerhardt, Elena, 131, 132
Gernsheim, Friedrich, 47, 83
Gesellschaft der Musikfreunde
    (Vienna), 95
Gewandhaus Orchestra, 111
Gleitz, Karl, 72
Gluck, Christoph Willibald von, 21, 92,
    100–101, 104, 147; *Iphigénie en Tauride*
    (Strauss's performing version), 100–101;
    Iphigénie en Aulide, 41; Overture to
    Iphigénie en Aulide, 21
Glyndebourne Festival Opera, 106
Goebbels, Joseph, 152, 157
Goethe, Johann Wolfgang von, 29, 119
Görlitz, Hugo, 119, 120, 121, 124
Gounod, Charles, 127; *Faust*, 127; *Roméo et
    Juliette*, 127
Grafton Galleries, 131
Gramophone, (The), 60, 138–139, 143, 147,
    149, 153
Granfeldt, Lillian von, 139
Graz Gymnasium, 66
Gregor, Hans, 96

Grieg, Edvard, 136
Gruber, Gernot, 98, 103
Gürzenich Orchestra (Cologne), 10, 73
Gürzenich Subscription Concerts
    (Cologne), 9
Gutmann, Albert J., 84

Halir, Karl, 30, 121
Halir Quartet, 109
Hallé Concerts Society, 146
Hamburg Philharmonic, 65–66
Hamburg Stadttheater, 19, 65
Hamburg Subscription Concerts, 19, 111
Handel, George Frideric, 18, 83;
    Semele, 21
Hanslick, Eduard, 31, 122
Harbni Orchestra, 9
Harnoncourt, Nikolaus, 55
Hausegger, Siegmund von, *Zinnober*, 46
Hausmann, Robert, 13
Hawley, Stanley, 132
Haydn, (Franz) Joseph, 5, 21, 82, 83;
    Symphony No. 7 ('Le midi'), 83;
    Symphony No. 104 ('London'), 83
Heidelberg, University of, 65, 123
Heidelberg Music Festival, 123
Heine, Heinrich, 119
Heinrichshofen's Verlag (publishers), 98, 99
Hempel, Frieda, 89
Herald, The, 126
Herzogenberg, Elizabeth von, 13
Herzogenberg, Heinrich von, 13
Hess, Myra, 136
Hey, Hans Erwin, 139
Heyworth, Peter, 36
Hiller, Ferdinand, 19
Hitler, Adolf, 76, 152, 157
Hochberg, Hans Heinrich, Bolko Graf von,
    70, 83
Hoffman, Josef, 136
Hofmannsthal, Hugo von, 53, 90, 91, 92,
    96, 97, 131, 132, 135, 141, 153, 157, 161
Hölderlin, Friedrich, 150
Holst, Gustav, *The Planets*, 158
Hoyer, Bruno, 10
Hülsen-Haeseler, Georg, 76, 78
Hummel, Johann Nepomuk, 55
Humperdinck, Engelbert, 69, 115, 136;
    Hänsel und Gretel, 41, 68
Hupfeld, 137

Joachim III, Prince-Elector of
    Brandenburg, 81
Joachim, Joseph, 4, 13

Joachim Quartet, 13
Joseph Aibl (publishers), 64

Kahl, Heinrich, 81
Kaim Orchestra, 72
Kalisch, Alfred, 32, 131
Kalmus, Alfred, 104
Karajan, Herbert von, 52, 161
Kaun, Hugo, 83
Kemp, Barbara, 139
Kennedy, Michael, 32
Kessler, Harry von, 132
Keudell, Walter von, 154
Kienzl, Wilhelm, 69, 76
King, A. Hyatt, 99
Klemperer, Otto, 35, 36, 61, 65
Klindworth, Karl, 13, 16
Knüpfer, Paul, 139
Kobbé, Gustav, 126
Koch Schwann, 156
Komische Oper (Vienna), 65
Koomun, Elkun, 119
Krause, Ernst, 101, 103
Krauss, Clemens, 86, 98, 152, 161
Kreutzer, Conrad, Das Nachtlager in
  Granada, 41
Kroll Opera, 72, 73
Krzyzanowski, Rudolf, 101
Kubelik, Jan, 119

Lachner, Franz, 7
Lamoureux, Charles, 114
Lamoureux Orchestra, see under Orchestre
  Lamoureux
Landon, H. C. Robbins, 51, 54–55
Langham Hotel (London), 119
Lassen, Eduard, 29, 33, 39, 42, 66
Laugs, Robert, 81
Le Borne, Aimé, 68; Mudarra, 68
Leborne, Charles-Joseph, 114
Lefler, Heinrich, 71
Lehmann, Lotte, 96
Leinhos, Gustav, 13, 18
Leipzig Conservatorium, 66
Leipzig Stadttheater, 65
Leoncavallo, Ruggiero, I Pagliacci, 74
Leuckart F. E. C. (publishers), 64
Levi, Hermann, 10, 25, 42, 47, 48, 50, 66,
  89, 110–111
Levin, Willy, 73–74
Liszt, Franz, 3, 19, 21, 29, 30, 31, 32, 33, 39,
  66, 73, 82, 111, 113, 118, 122; Eine Faust-
  Sinfonie, 6, 30; Die Legende von der
  heiligen Elisabeth, 15; Fantasie über

ungarische Volkweise, 21, 122; Die Ideale,
  30; Totentanz, 30; Ce qu'on entend sur la
  montagne, 30; Les Préludes, 30; Mazeppa,
  30; Festklänge, 30
Liszt-Stiftung (Liszt Foundation,
  Weimar), 30
London Symphony Orchestra, 140–141
Lortzing, Albert, 40; Der Wildschütz, 68;
  Der Waffenschmied, 71
Ludwig II, King of Bavaria, 3, 5, 15, 16
Ludwig-Maximilians-Universität
  (Munich), 12
Ludwigs-Gymnasium (Munich), 8, 12, 103
Lyser, F. P., 50

Mackenzie, Alexander, 116
Mackenzie, Compton, 143, 144–145
Magdeburg Stadttheater, 105
Mahler, Alma, 76
Mahler, Gustav, 18–19, 34, 35, 47, 54, 66,
  70, 71, 72, 76, 81, 82, 83, 87, 92, 97, 98,
  139, 136; Symphony No. 1 ('Titan'), 82,
  Symphony No. 2 ('Resurrection'), 82;
  Symphony No. 3, 72, 82; Symphony No.
  4, 72, 82; Symphony No. 5, 71;
  Symphony No. 8, 99; Das Lied von der
  Erde, 82
Mainardi, Enrico, 153
Manns, August, 113
Mannstädt, Franz, 13, 18, 66
Marie Elizabeth, Princess von Sachsen-
  Meiningen, 19, 21
Marschner, Heinrich, 40; Hans Heiling, 11
Marseillaise, 125
Mascagni, Pietro, Cavalleria rusticana,
  68, 74
Matthews, Colin, 147
Max, Duke of Bavaria, 4
May, Hermann, 156
Méhul, Étienne-Nicholas, 40
Meiningen, Duchess of, 135
Meininger Hofkapelle, 9, 13, 16–23, 25–26,
  69, 73, 139
Meininger Hoftheater, 16
Mendelssohn, Felix, 5, 18, 23, 114; Piano
  Trio in D minor, 12; incidental music to
  Ein Sommernachtstraum (A Midsummer
  Night's Dream), 26; Gondellied, 129
Mengelberg, Willem, 113, 121, 122, 146
Menter, Sophie, 6
Metropolitan Opera House (New York), 76,
  90, 125, 136
Metzdorff, Richard, Hagbart und Signe, 41
Meyer, Friedrich Wilhelm, 7, 8, 9

Meyerbeer, Giacomo, *Robert le Diable*, 71, 74
Mlynarski, Emil, 131
Moerike, Eduard, 148
Molière, Jean Baptiste, *Le bourgeois gentilhomme*, 91
Morse, Peter, 145, 147
Mossel, Max, 124
Mottl, Felix, 110, 111; *Fürst und Sänger*, 41
Mozart, Franz Xaver Wolfgang, 50
Mozart, Leopold, 5–6
Mozart, Wolfgang Amadeus, xi, 5–6, 10, 11, 18, 24, 29, 30, 32, 34, 35, 36, 37, 40, 45–61, 69, 74, 82, 83, 84, 89, 97–106, 113, 126–129, 139, 144–147, 150–151, 152, 154, 156; *Bastien und Bastienne*, 41, 48; *Idomeneo*, 53, 97, 98–105; *Idomeneo* (Strauss's performing version), *see under* Strauss, Richard; *Die Entführung aus dem Serail*, 41, 47, 48, 68, 89, 97; *Le nozze di Figaro*, 48, 53, 68, 89, 97, 98, 104, 132; *Don Giovanni*, 47, 48, 49–51, 68, 75, 89–90, 97, 102, 104, 119, 139; *Così fan tutte*, 26, 47, 48, 49, 51–53, 68, 89, 97, 98, 102; *Die Zauberflöte*, 6, 7, 10, 40, 45, 47, 48, 69, 97, 104, 139; Overture to *Die Zauberflöte*, 53, 147; Symphony No. 29, 54, 86; Symphony No. 39, 56, 138, 144–145, 150–151; Symphony No. 40, 54, 56, 57, 86, 132, 144, 145, 146, 147, 155; Symphony No. 41 ('Jupiter'), 11, 30, 53–61, 86, 126–129, 131, 145, 158; Piano Concerto No. 20, 84; Piano Concerto. No. 24, 20; Mass K. 257, 55; Requiem, 21, 73; *Eine kleine Nachtmusik*, 112
Muck, Karl, 64, 65, 66, 67, 91
Münchner Neueste Nachrichten, 10
Munich Hofburg, 48
Munich Hofkapelle (later Bayerisches Staatsorchester), 3, 4, 5, 6, 10, 11, 46–47, 71, 109, 156
Munich Hofoper (later Bavarian Staatsoper), 5, 7, 10, 11, 15, 25–27, 29, 42, 45, 52, 54, 63, 66, 85, 161–162
Munich Tonkünstlerverein, 10
Musical Opinion, 57, 104, 116, 123, 141–142, 146, 150, 155
Musical Times, The, 57, 112, 130, 146
Music Club of London, 131

Nation, The, 131, 132
National Gallery (London), 158
National Society of French Teachers in England, 124

Nazi Party, 118, 151–155, 157
Neitzel, Otto, 73
Németh, Maria, 103
Neumann, Angelo, 65
Newman, Ernest, 131, 132
Newman, Robert, 112, 114, 120
New York Evening World, The, 127
New York Philharmonic, 18, 126–129
New York Telegraph, The, 126
Nicolai, Otto, 69
Niest, Friedrich, 6
Nikisch, Arthur, 47, 65, 66, 71–72, 129, 131, 132
North Rhine Music Festival, 118

Observer, The, 151
Odeon (Munich), 10, 17, 109
Offenbach, Jacques, *The Tales of Hofmann*, 135
Orchester des Deutschlandsender Berlin, 155
Orchester des Reichssender München, 156
Orchestre Lamoureux, 114, 118
Oxford, University of, 132

Paris Conservatoire, 49
Paris Opéra, 48, 132
Parlophone Records, 148
Pataky, Koloman von, 148
Pavarotti, Luciano, 106
Perfall, Karl von, 25, 26–27, 29, 85
Pergolesi, Giovanni Battista, *La serva padrona*, 96
Philadelphia Orchestra, 142
Philharmonia Orchestra, 158
Philharmonic Concerts (Berlin), *see under* Berlin Philharmonic
Philharmonic Society (New York), 126–129
Philharmonic Society of London, *see under* Royal Philharmonic Society of London
Piffl, Gustav, 76
Pitt, Percy, 121
Pius X, 82
Platt, Richard, 122
Polydor Records, 138, 148
Ponte, Lorenzo da, 50
Possart, Ernst von, 46, 47, 48, 49, 50, 89, 97, 118, 119
Prinzregententheater (Munich), 162
Pritchard, John, 61, 106
Pschorr Beer Hall (Munich), 3
Pschorr, Georg, 3–4
Pschorr, Johanna, 8
Puccini, Giacomo, 76

Queen's Hall (London), 54, 57, 112–113, 120, 124, 129, 130, 131, 132, 150, 155
Queen's Hall Orchestra, 54, 119, 124, 125, 129, 130, 131, 132

Rabl, Walter, 73
Rachmaninoff, Sergei, 136
Radecke, Robert, 13, 81
Radio Times, 150
Raff, Joachim, 17, 18
Raff Conservatorium, 18
Rathenau, Walther, 154
Reichsmusikkammer, 152, 154
Reichssender Wien, 156–157
Reif, Wilhelm, 21
Reinecke, Carl, 13, 66
Reiner, Fritz, 161
Reinhardt, Max, 135
Residenztheater (Cuvilliés Theater) (Munich), 15, 48, 49, 50, 52, 53, 97
Rheinberger, Josef, 17; Overture to *Der Widerspenstigen Zähmung* 21
Richard Strauss-Archiv (Garmisch-Partenkirchen), 49, 98
Richter, Hans, 110
Rieter-Biedermann (publishers), 85
Rimsky-Korsakov, Nicolai, *Scheherazade*, 96
Ritter, Alexander, 19, 20, 26, 40, 47; *Wem die Kron?*, 40; *Der faule Hans*, 40
Ritter, Julie, 20
Ritter viola, 17
Robey, George, 153
Rolland, Romain, 76–78, 118
Roller, Alfred, 97
Roosevelt, Theodore, 125
Rösch, Friedrich, 45, 64
Rose, Frances, 131
Rosen, Charles, 51
Rosenthal, Moritz, 115
Rossini, Giacomo, 88; *Il barbiere di Siviglia*, 25, 68
Roth, Ernst, 157, 158
Royal Albert Hall (London), 141, 158, 161
Royal Opera House, Covent Garden, 48, 129, 130–131, 137, 155
Royal Philharmonic Orchestra, 158
Royal Philharmonic Society of London, 33, 114–117, 155
Rubinstein, Anton, 21, 47; Piano Concerto No. 3, 21
Rubinstein, Arthur, 76
Rüdel, Hugo, 81
Rüfer, Philippe, 83

St. James's Hall (London), 121, 124
Saint-Saëns, Camille, 47, 69; *Samson et Dalila*, 69; *Javotte*, 74; *Danse macabre*, 142
Salter, Lionel, 60, 147
Salzburg Festival, 152
Saturday Symphony Concerts (Queen's Hall, London), 120
Saul, Jack, 138
Sauret, Émile, 47
Savoy Hotel, 131, 158
Sawallisch, Wolfgang, 24, 53, 61
Schalk, Franz, 66, 92, 95, 96, 97
Scheinpflug, Paul, 83
Schiller, Friedrich, 29, 119
Schillings, Max von, 47, 72, 74, 83, 88, 118; *Der Pfeifertag*, 74
Schlosskapelle St. Veit, 45
Schnabel, Artur, 84
Schneider, Hans, 99
Schoenberg, Arnold, 76
Scholes, Percy, 150
Scholz, Bernhard, *1757*, 74
Schonberg, Harold C., 143–144, 147
Schopenhauer, Arthur, 12, 20, 82
Schubert, Franz, 5, 7, 17, 19, 20; Symphony in B minor ('Unfinished'), 21
Schuch, Ernst von, 13, 34, 70, 75, 90, 91
Schülz-Curtius, Alfred, 112, 115–117, 119
Schumann, Clara, 109
Schumann, Elisabeth, 103, 104, 139
Schumann, Robert, 5, 11, 21, 35, 82; Symphony No. 2, 85; *Manfred*, 118, 119
Scottish Orchestra, 124
Sechter, Simon, 65
Seidl, Anton, 66
Serkin, Rudolf, 136
Sgambati, Giovanni, 73
Shakespeare, William, 12, 135
Shaw, George Bernard, 131, 132
Sieger, Fritz, 77
Singer, Otto, 141
Social Democratic Party (Austria), 95
Society of Participating Artists, 99
Solti, Georg, 48, 161
Sommer, Hans, *Loreley*, 41
Sophocles, *Electra*, 103
Specht, Richard, 32
Speyer, Edgar, 119, 120, 121, 122
Spitzweg, Eugen, 17, 45, 64
Spohr, Louis, 5, 17, 111. 114
Squire, W. H., 116
Stanford, Charles Villiers, 122, 131; Irish Rhapsody No. 2, 122
Star Spangled Banner, The, 65

Stavenhagen, Bernhard, 30
Stenhammar, Wilhelm, 47
Stern, Margarete, 30
Stock, Frederick, 140
Stokowski, Leopold, 142
Strauss, Edmund von, 81
Strauss, Franz ('Bubi') (son), 121, 123
Strauss, Franz Joseph (father), 3–5, 7, 8, 9,
    10, 12, 13, 15, 17, 21, 23, 33, 42, 69, 73,
    74, 85, 109, 110, 113, 118, 119, 120, 122,
    123,124, 125, 130
Strauss, Johanna (sister), 6, 7
Strauss, Josepha (née Pschorr) (mother),
    3–4, 9, 12, 13, 33, 69, 73, 74, 113, 118,
    119, 122, 123, 124, 125, 130
Strauss II, Johann, 68
Strauss, Pauline (née de Ahna) (wife), 30,
    45, 82, 121, 122, 124, 125, 161
Strauss, Richard Georg, birth, 3–4; rela-
    tionship with father, 5–6; education, 6–8,
    12; first piano lesson, 6; lessons in coun-
    terpoint, harmony and composition with
    Friedrich Wilhelm Meyer, 7–8; hears an
    opera for the first time, 6–7; early
    responses to Wagner's music, 11–12; first
    visit to the Bayreuth Festival, 12; attends
    university, 12; as a pianist, 6, 10, 20, 109,
    110, 118, 119, 121, 124, 125, 136–137,
    140; as a violinist, 6; first visits to
    Leipzig, Berlin and Dresden, 12–13;
    meets Bülow for the first time, 17;
    attends Bülow's piano masterclasses in
    Frankfurt, 18; impact of Bülow as a
    conductor; 19, 27; thoughts on Bülow as
    a composer, 21; influence of Alexander
    Ritter, 20; conversion to Zukunftsmusik
    and the writings of Wagner and
    Schopenhauer, 20, 32; marriage to
    Pauline de Ahna, 45; conducting debut
    at Munich, 17; debut at Meiningen, 20;
    Hofmusikdirektor at Meiningen, 18–22,
    25–26; advice on composition by
    Brahms at Meiningen, 20; as a piano
    teacher at Meiningen, 19; as a choral
    conductor at Meiningen, 19, 22; rela-
    tionship with the Meininger Hofkapelle,
    22; as possible successor to Bülow at
    Meiningen, 22; resignation from
    Meiningen, 22; as Musikdirektor at the
    Munich Hofoper, 25–27; as
    Kapellmeister at the Weimar Hoftheater
    and Hofkapelle, 29–30, 33, 39, 40–42,
    46; as Kapellmeister and
    Hofkapellmeister at the Munich

Hofoper, 42, 45–49, 63; as conductor of
    the Philharmonic Concerts (Berlin),
    46–47; as Erster Königlicher
    Kapellmeister at Berlin Hofoper, 63–71,
    74–78, 88–93; as conductor of the Berlin
    Tonkünstler-Orchester, 71–74, 78, 82; as
    conductor of the Berlin Hofkapelle's
    subscription concerts, 81–85; as
    Generalmusikdirektor in Berlin, 81,
    88–93; as joint Director of the Vienna
    Hof/Staatsoper, 92–106, 109; as a Mozart
    conductor, 24, 26, 29, 30, 34, 35, 36, 37,
    40, 41, 45–61, 82, 83, 84, 86, 89–90, 92,
    97–106, 112, 113, 119, 126–129, 131,
    132, 139, 144–145, 146, 147, 150–151,
    152, 155, 156; as a Beethoven conductor,
    29, 30, 34, 35, 36, 41, 42, 47, 82, 83,
    84–88, 111, 113, 114, 118, 143–144,
    147–148, 152; as a Wagner conductor,
    26, 30, 34, 39, 40, 41, 46, 89, 92, 111,
    112, 113, 114, 118, 157; on conducting
    technique, 23–25, 150–151; on the
    'avant-garde', 30–31, 39; on form and
    content, 31–32; on cuts, 34; on textual
    fidelity, 34–35; on composers' rights,
    63–64; 'Schneider' Polka, 8; 'Panzenburg'
    Polka, 8; String Quartet, 9; Serenade for
    Thirteen Wind Instruments Op. 7, 9, 13,
    17; Sonata for Cello and Piano, 9, 13;
    Suite in B flat major for Thirteen Winds
    Op. 4, 9, 17, 131; Piano Quartet, 9, 18,
    109, 124; Violin Sonata, 119, 124, 131;
    Wandrers Sturmlied, 9, 111, 152;
    Bardengesang, 22; Taillefer, 123; Violin
    Concerto, 10, 124; Horn Concerto No. 1,
    10, 13, 18; Burleske, 22, 122, 158;
    Parergon zur Symphonia domestica, 90;
    Panathenäenzug, 90; Concert Overture
    in C minor, 13; Symphony No. 1, 10;
    Symphony No. 2, 9, 13, 18, 20, 31,
    109–110, 113, 117, 126; Aus Italien, 25,
    30, 39, 110, 111, 122; Macbeth, 30, 39,
    83, 110, 111, 121, 150, 155; Don Juan,
    29–39, 42, 53, 57, 73, 111, 117, 118, 119,
    122, 131, 132, 137, 138–139, 141, 146,
    148–149, 150, 152, 155, 156, 158; Tod
    und Verklärung, 39, 57, 91, 111, 112,
    113, 117, 118–119, 121, 122, 131, 132,
    140, 141, 145, 149, 150, 152, 155, 157;
    Till Eulenspiegel, 9, 53, 63, 112, 113, 117,
    118, 119, 121, 122, 132, 137, 141,
    148–149, 152, 155, 156, 157, 159; Also
    sprach Zarathustra, 113, 114, 120, 121,
    140, 156; Don Quixote, 9, 63, 113,

115–117, 120, 121, 130, 149, 152–153, 155, 156; *Ein Heldenleben*, 63, 64, 113, 120, 121, 122, 126, 131, 137, 145, 146, 149, 152, 156, 157; *Sinfonia domestica*, 75, 82, 123, 124, 126, 129–130, 142, 149, 150–151, 157, 158; Suite from *Der Bürger als Edelmann*, 137, 140, 149, 150, 156; *Festliches Präludium*, 146; *Eine Alpensinfonie*, 83, 90, 141, 146, 155, 156; *Der Rosenkavalier* film music, 140–142; *Japanische Festmusik*, 156; 'Zueignung', 18, 140; 'Nichts', 18; 'Die Nacht', 18; 'Die Georgine', 18; 'Geduld', 18; 'Die Verschwiegenen', 22; 'Die Zeitlose', 22; 'Allerseelen', 22, 140; 'Ständchen', 30; 'Cäcilie', 132, 150; 'Morgen', 132, 150; 'Traum durch die Dämmerung', 140; 'Wiegenlied', 132; Leider Op. 48, 69; Leider Op. 49, 69, 71; Op. 51, 71; *Drei Hymnen von Friedrich Hölderlin*, 150–151; *Gesänge des Orients*, 148; *Enoch Arden*, 118, 119; *Das Schloss am Meere*, 131–132; performing version of Gluck's *Iphigénie en Tauride* (*Iphigenie auf Tauris in drei Aufzüge für die deutsche Bühne bearbeitet*), 100–101; *Guntram*, 40, 41–42, 45, 46, 47, 69, 70, 122; *Feuersnot*, 13, 63–64, 69–71, 74, 77, 137; 'Love Scene' from *Feuersnot*, 121, 140, 142; *Salome*, 13, 23, 56, 63, 74–78, 90, 91, 137, 140, 142, 146, 147, 148, 152, 156; *Elektra*, 13, 23, 90–91, 103, 129, 130–131, 132, 148, 158; *Der Rosenkavalier*, 13, 34, 53, 90, 91, 137, 145, 146, 148, 152, 156, 158, 161, 162; *Ariadne auf Naxos*, 90, 91–92, 137, 155; *Die Frau ohne Schatten*, 96, 148; *Intermezzo*, 13, 90, 145, 146, 148; *Die ägyptische Helena*, 13, 104, 148, 152; performing version of Mozart's *Idomeneo*, 97–106, 156; *Arabella*, 13; *Die schweigsame Frau*, 13, 153–154; *Daphne*, 13; *Die Liebe de Danae*, 152; *Capriccio*, 101; *Josephslegende*, 129, 132, 137; *Schlagobers*, 90, 104, 142
Stravinsky, Igor, 162
Strohm, Reinhard, 102
Stuttgart Hofoper, 91
Sucher, Josef, 64–65, 67, 81
Sucher, Rosa, 65
Sullivan, Arthur, 136
Sun, The, 127
Swarowsky, Hans, 24
Szell, George, 36, 138–139, 161

Taubert, Wilhelm, 81
Tennyson, Alfred, 119
Teschemacher, Margarete, 150
Theatre Royal, Drury Lane, 158
Thode, Henry, 123
Thomas, Ambroise, *Mignon*, 135
Thomas, Theodore, 18, 126
Thuille, Ludwig, 6, 11, 45; Symphony in F major, 21; *Theuerdank*, 46
Times, The, 112, 119, 120, 122, 124, 129, 130, 141, 146, 150, 155, 158
Tivoli Cinema (London), 141–142
Tolbecque, Auguste, 114
Tombo, August, 6
Tonkünstlerversammlung des Allgemeine Deutschen Musik Vereins, 23, 119
Toscanini, Arturo, 152, 154
Tovey, Donald F., 52
Trenner, Franz, 52, 53, 102
Tribune, 125
Tschirch, Emil, 121, 122

Universum Film AG (UFA), 157
Ursuleac, Viorica, 152

Verdi, Giuseppe, 69, 88; *Aïda*, 25; *Un ballo in maschera*, 26; *Falstaff*, 69; *Il Trovatore*, 77
Vienna Hofoper (later Vienna Staatsoper), 48, 65, 66, 70–71, 81, 92–106, 109, 156
Vienna Philharmonic, 66, 84, 96, 106, 156, 157
Vienna Staatsoper, *see under* Vienna Hofoper
Vienna Volksoper, 66

Wagner, Cosima (née Liszt), 3, 15, 110, 111, 123
Wagner, Franziska, 20
Wagner, Richard, xi, 3–5, 7, 11, 15, 17, 20, 21, 26, 30, 31, 32, 34, 35, 39, 40, 41, 46, 57, 58, 59, 64, 65, 67, 69, 70, 73, 74, 82, 85, 87, 88, 89, 92, 101, 110, 112, 113, 114, 118, 123, 147, 149; *Siegfried Idyll*, 30, 131, 132; *Die Feen*, 26–27; *Rienzi*, 41, 46, 65, 68, 85; *Der fliegende Holländer*, 65, 89; *Tannhäuser*, 5, 40, 46, 65, 111; Overture to *Tannhäuser*, 112, 'Bacchanale' from *Tannhäuser* (Paris Version), 30; *Lohengrin*, 5, 15, 40, 65, 89, 111; Prelude to *Lohengrin*, 114; *Tristan und Isolde*, 4–5, 6, 15, 41, 46, 65, 67, 89, 110; Prelude to *Tristan und Isolde*, 112; Prelude and Liebestod from *Tristan und*

WAGNER, RICHARD (cont.)
  Isolde, 30; *Die Meistersinger von
  Nürnberg*, 4–5, 15, 41, 46, 65, 75, 89,
  110; Prelude to *Die Meistersinger von
  Nürnberg*, 112, 114, 157; *Das Rheingold*,
  4, 68; *Die Walküre*, 4, 11, 68, 89;
  Siegfried, 11, 68; *Götterdämmerung*, 68;
  Der Ring des Nibelungen, 65, 68, 89, 126;
  Parsifal, 5, 12, 65, 68, 89, 110–111, 125,
  152; 'Karfreitagzauber' *Parsifal*, 112
Walker, Edyth, 131
Wallerstein, Lothar, 98, 100, 103, 104, 105
Wall Street Crash, 136
Walter, Benno, 6, 10
Walter (born Schlesinger), Bruno, 34–35,
  72, 145, 152, 154
Walter, Franz Joseph Michael, 4
Walter, Franz Michael, 4
Walter, Johann Georg, 4
Weber, Carl Maria von, 17, 40, 68, 82, 83,
  92, 147, 152; *Abu Hassan*, 96; *Der
  Freischütz*, 6, 7, 11, 41; Overture to *Der
  Freischütz* 57; Overture to *Oberon*, 57
Weidemann, Hermann, 131
Weimar Hofkapelle, 29–30, 33, 39, 46
Weimar Hoftheater, 27, 29, 40–42, 45,
  66, 101
Weimar Republic, 89
Weingartner, Felix von, 18, 64, 66–67, 71,
  78, 81, 83, 84, 86, 143, 148; *Malawika*,
  66; *Sakuntala*, 66
Weingartner, Guido von, 66
Weingartner, Karoline von, 66
Welte-Mignon, 136–137

Welzhofer, Carl, 8
Western Electric, 146
Wetlzer Symphony Orchestra, 125, 126
White House, The, 125
Widmann'sche Lehranstalt, 8
Wiene, Robert, 141
Wiener academischen Gesangsverein
  (Vienna Academic Choir), 65
Wiener Sängerknaben (Vienna Boys
  Choir), 65
Wilde Gung'l Orchestra (Munich), 6
Wilhelm II, Emperor of Germany, 63, 64,
  67, 75, 78, 82, 135, 154
Wilson, Woodrow, 135
Wimbush, Roger, 138
Wittich, Marie, 75
Wolf-Ferrari, Ermanno, 98
Wolff, Hermann, 13, 20, 39, 46, 47
Wolfrum, Philipp, 123
Wolzogen, Ernst von, 69, 70
Wood, Henry J., 67, 112, 114, 120, 121,
  125, 129, 130
Wüllner, Franz, 9–10, 13, 64; *Stabat Mater*, 9

Zaslaw, Neal, 55
Zeller, Heinrich, 30
Zemlinsky, Alexander, 76
Zimmerli, Christian, 156
Zincke, Hans, 64
Zuccalmaglio, Anton Wilhelm Florentin
  von, 98; *Der Hof in Melun*, 98
Zürcher Post, 139
Zurich Municipal Theatre, 139
Zweig, Stephan, 153–154, 157